On the Arizona Trail

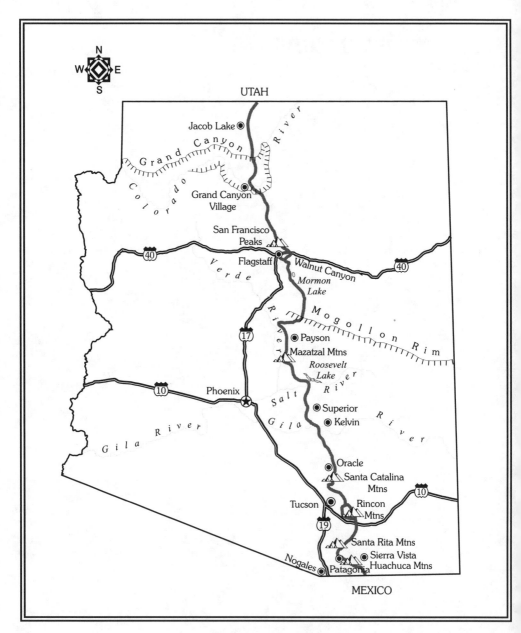

STATE OF ARIZONA

On the Arizona Trail

A Guide for Hikers, Cyclists, and Equestrians

Kelly Tighe and Susan Moran

PRUETT PUBLISHING COMPANY
BOULDER, COLORADO

© 1998 by Kelly Tighe and Susan Moran

ALL RIGHTS RESERVED. No part of this book may be reproduced without written permission from the publisher, except in the case of brief excerpts in critical reviews and articles. Address all inquiries to:

PRUETT PUBLISHING COMPANY
2928 Pearl Street, Boulder, Colorado 80301

Cover & book design: Polly Christensen, *Christensen & Son Design*
Cartography: Terragraphics
Cover photographs by Eric Wunrow: front panel,upper Sabino Basin at Mt. Lemmon; back panel, the Grand Canyon Bright Angel Trail (Plateau Point), South Rim
Interior photographs: Susan Moran and Kelly Tighe, except where noted otherwise

WARNING: The Arizona Trail passes through some extremely rugged and remote country. The extremes in temperature, presence of poisonous animals, and scarcity of water in some areas are all things to be reckoned with. Although we have made every effort to ensure the accuracy of information in this book, there may remain errors or omissions. Because the Arizona Trail is still evolving, it is possible that some routes will be changed after this guide has been published. Also, since the trail is so new, large sections have not yet been wheeled to obtain accurate mileages.

Wilderness requires that users assume responsibility for their own safety. This book is not intended to be instructional; it is, rather, a guide for those who already have the requisite training, skills, and experience to endure the rigors of backcountry travel. It is the users' responsibility to decide whether they possess the backcountry skills and physical fitness required for each trip. Judgments regarding trail and weather conditions are also the responsibility of the user. The authors, publisher, and all those associated with this publication, directly or indirectly, disclaim any liability for accidents, injuries, damages, or losses that may occur to anyone using this book.

Printed in the United States

10 9 8 7 6 5 4 3 2 1

Library of Congress Cataloging-in-Publication data

Tighe, Kelly, 1945–
    On the Arizona Trail : a guide for hikers, cyclists, and
equestrians / Kelly Tighe and Susan Moran.
        p.   cm.
    Includes bibliographical references (p. 287) and index.
    ISBN 0-87108-884-3 (pbk.)
    1. Hiking—Arizona—Guidebooks. 2. All terrain cycling—Arizona—
Guidebooks. 3. Horsemanship—Arizona—Guidebooks. 4. Trails—
Arizona—Guidebooks. 5. Arizona—Guidebooks. I. Moran, Susan,
1943–   . II. Title.
GV199.42.A7T54   1998
917.9104'53—dc21   97-42170
                                                    CIP

Contents

Foreword   xi
Acknowledgments   xiii

Introduction   1
Wildlife, Flowers, and Trees: Arizona's Biotic Communities   5
History Along the Arizona Trail   7
Traveling the Arizona Trail: What to Know Before You Go   19
How to Use this Guide   39

1   Huachuca Mountain Passage
(U.S.-Mexico Border to Parker Canyon Lake Overlook)   45

1-A. U.S.-Mexico Border to Montezuma Pass   49
1-B. Alternate Livestock and Bicycle Route from Montezuma Pass
    to the U.S.-Mexico Border   52
1-C. Montezuma Pass to Bathtub Spring   54
1-D. Bathtub Spring to Sunnyside Canyon   56
1-E. Alternate Bicycle Route Around the Miller Peak Wilderness
    from Montezuma Pass to Sunnyside Canyon   60
1-F. Sunnyside Canyon to Parker Canyon Lake (Overlook) Trailhead   62

2   Canelo Hills Passage
(Parker Canyon Lake to Patagonia)   67

2-A. Parker Canyon Lake to Canelo Pass   70
2-B. Canelo Pass to Harshaw Road to Patagonia   73

3   Santa Rita Mountain Passage
(Patagonia to Oak Tree Canyon/Empire-Cienega)   77

3-A. Temporal Gulch Trailhead to Gardner Canyon Road Trailhead   81
3-B. Alternate Bicycle Route Around the Mt. Wrightson Wilderness
    from Patagonia to Gardner Canyon Road   85
3-C. Gardner Canyon Trailhead to Kentucky Camp   86
3-D. Kentucky Camp to Oak Tree Canyon/Empire-Cienega   88

4 Empire-Cienega Passage
(Oak Tree Canyon/Empire-Cienega to Interstate 10)   91

5 Cienega Creek Passage
(Interstate 10 to Colossal Cave Mountain Park)   94

6 Rincon Valley Passage
(Colossal Cave Mountain Park to Saguaro National Park)   96

7 Happy Valley Passage
(Interstate 10 to Miller and Turkey Creek Trailheads)   98

8 Rincon Mountains Passage
(Miller and Turkey Creek Trailheads to Redington Road)   101
8-A. Turkey Creek Trailhead to Manning Camp   104
8-B. Manning Camp to Redington Pass Road   107
8-C. Alternate Bicycle Route Around the Rincon Mountain
    Wilderness: Santa Rita Mountain Passage to Redington Passage   110

9 Redington Pass Passage
(Redington Road to Molino Basin)   113
9-A. Redington Pass Road to Molino Basin   116

10 Santa Catalina Mountains Passage
(Molino Basin to Mount Lemmon)   119
10-A. Molino Basin Campground to Hutch's Pool   122
10-B. Hutch's Pool to Summerhaven   126
10-C. Alternate Bicycle Route Around the Pusch Ridge Wilderness
    from Molino Basin to Summerhaven   129

11 Mount Lemmon/Oracle Ridge Passage
(Mount Lemmon to American Flag Trailhead)   131
11-A. Summerhaven to Catalina Camp to American Flag   135

12 Oracle Passage
(American Flag Trailhead to Highway 77)   141
12-A. American Flag Trailhead to American Avenue   144

13 Black Hills (Sonoran Desert) Passage
(Highway 77 to Freeman Road)   147

14 Tortilla Mountains (Sonoran Desert) Passage
(Freeman Road to the Gila River)   149

15 White Canyon Passage
(Gila River to Telegraph Canyon Road)   151

16 Alamo Canyon Passage
(Telegraph Canyon Road to Picketpost Trailhead/Highway 60)   152

**17 Picketpost Mountain/Reavis Trail
Canyon Passage** (Picketpost Mountain Trailhead
to Rogers Trough Trailhead)   153

17-A. Picketpost Mountain Trailhead to Rogers Trough   157

18 Superstition Wilderness Passage
(Rogers Trough Trailhead to Forest Road 83 Junction
     with Cottonwood Canyon)   161

18-A. Rogers Trough to Reavis Ranch   164
18-B. Reavis Ranch to Forest Road 83 Junction with
     Cottonwood Canyon Trail #120   167
18-C. Alternate Bicycle Route Around the Superstition
     Wilderness from Picketpost Trailhead to
     Theodore Roosevelt Bridge   171

19 Roosevelt Passage
(Forest Road 83 to Theodore Roosevelt Lake)   175

19-A. Black Brush Ranch, Forest Road 83 to Roosevelt Bridge   179

20 Four Peaks Wilderness Passage
(Roosevelt Bridge to Lone Pine Saddle)   185

21 Pine Mountain/Boulder Creek Passage
(Lone Pine Saddle to Sunflower)   186

22 Saddle Mountain Passage
(Sunflower to Mount Peeley)   187

23 Mazatzal Wilderness Passage
(Mount Peeley to East Verde River)   188

24 Whiterock Mesa/Hardscrabble Mesa Passage
(East Verde River to Pine Trailhead)   189

25 Highline Passage
(Pine Trailhead to Forest Road 300)   191

25-A. Pine Trailhead to Geronimo Camp   195
25-B. Geronimo Camp to Washington Park   198
25-C. Washington Park to General Springs Cabin   200

26 Blue Ridge Passage
(Forest Road 300 to Highway 87)   203

26-A. General Springs Cabin to Rock Crossing Campground   206
26-B. Rock Crossing Campground to Blue Ridge Campground   209

27 Unnamed Passage
(Highway 87 to Lake Mary Road)   212

28 Unnamed Passage
(Lake Mary Road to Marshall Lake)   213

29 Walnut Canyon (Equestrian Bypass) Passage
(Marshall Lake to Interstate 40 [Cosnino])   215

29-A. Marshall Lake to Forest Road 303   217
29-B. Forest Road 303 to Interstate 40 (Cosnino)   221

30 Turkey Hills (Equestrian Bypass) Passage
(Interstate 40[Cosnino] to Schultz Pass)   223

31 Flagstaff Passage
(Marshall Lake to Buffalo Park)   224

32 Elden–Dry Lake Hills Passage
(Buffalo Park to Schultz Pass)   225

33 San Francisco Peaks Passage
(Schultz Pass to Cedar Ranch)   226

34 Babbitt Ranch Passage
(Cedar Ranch to Moqui Stage Station)   227

35 Moqui Stage/Coconino Rim Passage
(Moqui Stage Station to Grandview Lookout)   229

35-A. Moqui Stage Station to Russell Tank   232
35-B. Russell Tank to Grandview Lookout   234

36 Grand Canyon National Park—South Rim Passage
(Grandview Lookout to Bright Angel Trailhead)   238

37 Grand Canyon National Park—Inner Gorge Passage
(Bright Angel Trailhead to North Kaibab Trailhead)   241
37-A. Bright Angel Trailhead to Phantom Ranch   244

38 Grand Canyon National Park—North Rim Passage
(North Kaibab Trailhead to National Park/National
     Forest Boundary)   247

39 Kaibab Plateau Trail—Southern Passage
(National Park/National Forest Boundary to Telephone Hill)   249
39-A. Grand Canyon National Park Boundary to East Rim View   252
39-B. East Rim View to Telephone Hill   254

40 Kaibab Plateau Trail—Central Passage
(Telephone Hill to Orderville Trailhead)   259
40-A. Telephone Hill (FR 241) to Murray Trailhead (FR 205)   262
40-B. Murray Trailhead (FR 205) to Orderville Trailhead (U.S. 89A)   265

41 Kaibab Plateau Trail—Northern Passage
(Orderville Trailhead to Winter Road)   268

42 Buckskin Mountain Passage
(Winter Road to the Arizona-Utah State Line)   270

Appendixes

A. Nearest Services (by Passage)   272
B. Livestock: Outfitting, Transport, and Overnight
     Boarding Services   277
C. Recommended Maps   281
D. Where to Obtain Permits   284
E. Suggested Resources   285

References and Suggested Reading   287
Index   290

Foreword

WHEN I CAME TO ARIZONA in the early 1970s, it was simply to make a grubstake and get out. I had a passport and a large Kelty Expedition pack. If I made a lot of money, I intended to travel around the world. If I made a smaller amount, I would hike the Appalachian Trail. Neither happened. Work with a geophysical exploration company put me into the remote deserts, canyons, and mountains of Arizona. The job required pre-dawn starts and after-sunset quitting times. Daily wildlife, flora, and geologic surprises were unending. Within weeks I was converted to an arid-lands nomad. Arizona got me.

Since then, I haven't left Arizona for any extended length of time. Like many Arizonans, I spend most of my free time exploring the state. The extended backpacking trips I have taken in the Santa Ritas, Rincons, Superstitions, Mazatzals, along the Mogollon Rim, and in the Grand Canyon led me to believe a long-distance trail was right for Arizona. A management agency map of the state confirmed that most of a north-south Arizona Trail could be on public lands. The vision of such a trail was shared by a number of people and organizations, and the commitment of the U.S. Forest Service and Arizona State Parks, partnered with Kaibab Forest Products, got the first piece of Trail on the ground. At this time, the Arizona Trail Association is a thriving support group for the Trail.

So what is the Arizona Trail about? For several hundred years the American West has endured waves of human endeavors. Many have left permanent scars, while only faint traces remain of others. The Arizona Trail is a thread of Arizona's past. It ties us to those who came before and those yet to come. The "freeze 'ya, fry 'ya, stick 'ya, sting 'ya" experiences are the same for us as they were for Native Americans, explorers, settlers, and others. People will continue to come to Arizona.

I believe the Arizona Trail will help our growing population maintain a reverence for the history and beauty of Arizona. Kelly Tighe's and Susan Moran's book is filled with reverence and love for the state. From early on I knew their book would be more than a "go there, do this" guide. They have blended trail information with a sense of place and awe that *is* Arizona. However complete, it is still a guide. It is your "git up go" spirit that will let you discover Arizona. See 'ya on the Trail.

D. R. Shewalter, *Founder of the Arizona Trail*
Flagstaff, Arizona
December 1997

"For the Arizona Trail"

Rex Allen

& "KoKo"

Used by permission of Rex Allen

Acknowledgments

SPECIAL THANKS TO

Eric Smith, past *Arizona Trail Steward, Arizona State Parks*
Our husbands, Slim Tighe and Peter Moran
Our horses, Manchado, Street, and Sandy
Dale Shewalter, *for having the dream and seeing it through*
The Arizona Trail Association and the many agencies and volunteers who
have worked so hard to make the trail a reality.

Thanks to the following for help along the Trail: Jan and Jim Edgerton,
Pat Crowley-Mauzy, Lil LeClerc, Susan and Mike LeSueur, Phyllis Harrold,
Rosemary Minter, Georgia Keefer, Jim and Andrea Gillis, Kathy Olszewski,
Dean Prichard, Mike Tighe, George Lakich, Rachel Redel, Kate Ladson, and
Brad Kissinger.

Thanks to the following for technical information or proofing: Jim
Schmid, past Arizona Trail Steward, U.S. Forest Service. Coronado National
Forest: Cathy Kahlow, Sierra Vista RD, Mark South and Steve Goldman, No-
gales RD. Dale Mance and Bob Magon, Santa Catalina RD. Tonto National
Forest: Stuart Herkenhoff, Globe RD. Greg Hansen, Mesa RD. Brad Orr,
Tonto Basin RD. Walt Thole, Payson RD. Coconino National Forest: Don
Muise, Blue Ridge RD. John Nelson, Mormon Lake RD. Brian Poturalski,
Peaks RD. Kaibab National Forest: Ken Olson, Tusayan RD. Sue Spear and
Susan Hittson, North Kaibab RD. Teri Cleeland, Chalender RD. Coronado
National Memorial: Edward Lopez and Barbara Alberti, Saguaro National
Park: Dwayne Moates, John Williams, Paula Nasiatka. Oracle State Park:
Frank Hogg. Grand Canyon National Park: Dan Blackwell. Pruett Publish-
ing: Marykay Scott. Arizona Poison & Drug Information Center: Jude Mc-
Nally. Amerind Foundation: Alan McIntyre. Sinclair Browning, Annette and
Marty Cordano, Molly Jo Fuller, Leonard Taylor, Dean Prichard, Steve Saway,
Rod Crick, Betsy Tighe, Bill Lemos, and Sandy Upson. Mapping: Jenny and
J. Dolak of Terragraphics. Songs and Poetry: The Desert Sons, Greg Scott,
and Jim Bob Tinsley.

I want to see the world, to look around the bend.
My bags are always packed, my heart is in the wind.
But not long after I have touched a distant land,
I know that I'm a child of the desert sand.

Deep rocky canyons where the summer waters flow.
High mountain ridges white with first winter snow.
Sloping bajada covered with the cactus thorn.
The Sonoran Desert is the place where I was born.

Mysterious pueblos blended with the mesas high,
Ancient remnants waiting for my careful searching eye.
Rainbow sandstones where the Dineh, the people, dwell.
Their voices call to me, I know them well.

Es maravilloso when you see the monsoon come.
Es infierno when you feel the desert sun.
Único sitio saguaros touch the sky.
La Hediondilla aroma almost makes me cry.

—"Arizona Home," John A. Ryberg II, 1988
(Used with permission.)

For information on The Desert
Sons' tapes, CDs, or bookings see
Appendix E.

Introduction

THERE ARE FEW hiking trails on the continent that take you on a journey that is the equivalent of walking from Mexico to Canada in a day. From the Sonoran Desert and its saguaros, North America's largest and most famous cactus, the Arizona Trail climbs to cool mixed-conifer forests of the Canadian life zone, as it traverses some of Arizona's highest peaks. There are other long-distance trails in the United States, but none offer the incredible diversity of climate, geology, and plant and animal life that is found in Arizona. The Arizona Trail is a 780-mile nonmotorized pathway that stretches across the state, linking Old Mexico with the grandest canyon in the world.

The Arizona Trail begins in the heart of the "wild west." This is the land where Apache warriors Cochise and Geronimo battled with the U.S. cavalry, and where calvary troops were sent across the border to pursue the Mexican revolutionary Pancho Villa. The origin of the Arizona Trail is less than 30 miles from two historic and fascinating Arizona towns—Tombstone, home of Boot Hill, infamous outlaws, and the shootout at the O.K. Corral; and Old Bisbee, "queen of the copper camps."

From the U.S.-Mexico border, the Arizona Trail winds a north-south path across the state. The trail links old mining camps, beautiful lakes, ghost towns, Indian cliff dwellings, and charming little communities like Patagonia and Jacob Lake, with some of the most beautiful sky islands in the southwest. The Arizona Trail is unique in its vision. This is a trail for everyone: Hikers, mountain bicyclists, equestrians, llama packers, and cross-country skiers are all welcome. In areas such as wilderness or national parks, where trail uses are restricted, alternate routes are being identified.

Arizonans can be proud of this project, which has come about through the combined efforts of many different agencies and volunteers. Arizona State Parks, the U.S. Forest Service, the National Park Service, the Bureau of Land Management, Arizona State Land Department, counties, cities, and communities through which the route passes, private landowners, grants from the Arizona Heritage Fund, corporations such as BHP Copper and Kaibab Forest Products, organizations such as the Sierra Club, Pima County Sheriff's Posse, Arizona Boys' Ranch, and hundreds of other private companies, associations, and volunteers have all been working together to complete the trail by 2000.

A TRAIL IS BORN

The Arizona Trail began as the dream of Flagstaff schoolteacher Dale Shewalter. While hiking in the Santa Rita Mountains in the early 1970s, Shewalter envisioned a continuous, nonmotorized trail stretching north through Arizona from Mexico to Utah.

During the summer of 1985 Shewalter spent twenty-four days walking from Nogales to the Utah border. Dale carried a thirty-five-pound pack as he tentatively mapped an interlocking route of trail systems that traversed the state. He planned the route around rural post offices so that trail users would be able to send supplies ahead.

After completing his trek, Dale presented his concept of a border-to-border trail to Arizona State Parks and gained their support and the support of the Arizona State Committee on Trails (ASCOT). Next Dale put together a slide presentation about the Arizona Trail and showed it to communities and organizations throughout the state. Input from the public and dozens of newspaper and magazine articles revealed a great deal of interest in a border-to-border trail, so Dale involved the public in choosing the most feasible, appealing, and practical route.

After gaining the support of the U.S. Forest Service (which manages 70 percent of the trail), crews began to build links between existing trails along the Arizona Trail corridor. Dale was hired by Kaibab National Forest (but was funded by all four national forests) in 1988 to serve as the first coordinator (steward) for the trail. On July 1, 1988, the Kaibab Plateau Trail north of the Grand Canyon was dedicated. This was significant for two reasons: It was the first segment of the Arizona Trail officially opened to the public, and it represented a remarkable cooperative effort between two sometimes opposing factions, Kaibab Forest Products, a lumber company, and the Sierra Club.

Two college students from Prescott, Arizona, were inspired by Dale's vision of a long-distance trail across the state. In October of 1988 Kiyo Taylor and Kate Beardsley left Prescott on horseback to spend seven months scouting portions of the Arizona Trail route. Riding from the Whiterock Mesa/Hardscrabble Mesa Passage south to the U.S./Mexico border and back, they documented trail access points, water supplies, and potential hazards.

Dale established a small network of trail stewards from various parts of Arizona. These stewards worked closely with the various governing agencies selecting routes and requesting public input. As a result of this effort, many major segments of the trail were completed and formally dedicated. Some of the original stewards continue to work on the Arizona Trail project today.

In October 1993 three federal agencies and Arizona State Parks entered into an intergovernmental agreement (IGA) to plan for the development

Scouting the Arizona Trail corridor, 1995. Former Arizona Trail stewards Jim Schmid (standing far left) and Eric Smith (on horseback far left), and segment stewards and volunteers.

Photo by Kelly Tighe

and completion of the Arizona Trail. The IGA established a fund to hire an Arizona Trail steward to prepare a management guide and coordinate efforts between agencies. Jim Schmid, former trails coordinator for the Coronado National Forest, served on a special duty assignment as the Arizona Trail steward from October 1993 to April 1994. Eric Smith, former state trails planner for Arizona State Parks, served as the Arizona Trail steward from April 1994 through July 1996.

Dale Shewalter served as the Arizona Trail coordinator until 1991. Today, as president of the Arizona Trail Association, he is still actively involved in the planning of the trail in northern Arizona. Since 1985, hundreds of trail enthusiasts, inspired by his vision, have been working to make the Arizona Trail a reality.

VOLUNTEERS

Volunteers are crucial to the ongoing success of the Arizona Trail. A network of volunteer trail stewards has been organized to help complete trail work, and since 1991, volunteer training sessions have been held in different locations across the state. Much of the labor required to construct and maintain the Arizona Trail is accomplished through volunteers in cooperation with governing agencies. For example, the Huachuca Hiking Club has adopted over 50 miles (the first two passages) of the Arizona Trail. They organize four to six work weekends per year. The club has assisted both the U.S. Forest Service and Coronado National Memorial with trail construction and maintenance since 1989.

In December 1993 a group of interested volunteers formed The Arizona Trail Association (ATA). The ATA is a nonprofit organization that helps coordinate planning, development, management, and promotion of the Arizona Trail. Recruiting volunteers and trail stewards is one of the association's most important functions, and there are typically openings for Arizona Trail (segment) stewards.

Stewardship affords a unique opportunity for volunteers to participate in the building and the history of the Arizona Trail. Stewards are assigned to a particular segment of the trail and receive specialized training. They work closely with the governing agency and the ATA, and their duties can include research, mapping and developing passage information sheets, exploring new trail alignments, monitoring trail conditions, organizing trail construction and maintenance workshops, and recruiting volunteers. The ATA offers several membership categories and has wonderful Arizona Trail T-shirts, sweatshirts, patches, mugs, and posters for sale. If you would like

Volunteers play an essential role in the ongoing development of the Arizona Trail, from scouting trail routes to trail building, signing, and maintenance.

Photo by Susan Moran

to become a member, a volunteer, or purchase a T-shirt, contact the ATA at P.O. Box 36736, Phoenix, AZ 85067, (602) 202-4794. See the last page of this book for more information on joining the ATA.

Wildlife, Flowers, and Trees: Arizona's Biotic Communities

Way back in my early years
There were places I could go
When the long low storms came rolling in
And the winds of change did blow.

Above the rain, above the clouds
Where eagles and angels fly
They bide the test of time and space
The "Islands in the Sky."

— **"Islands in the Sky," Skelly Boyd**
(Used with permission.)

BECAUSE OF THE STATE's variable topography, a surprisingly diverse wealth of plant and animal life exists in Arizona. Some of these species, representing tropical ecosystems, are living at the northernmost limits of their range. Extremely rare plants, mammals, birds, reptiles, amphibians, and insects seen nowhere else in the United States, and in some cases in the world, are found here.

The Arizona Trail offers a remarkable journey along a chain of mountains that tower like islands above the surrounding seas of the Chihuahuan and Sonoran Deserts. The trail traversing these "Sky Islands" leads travelers through a series of biological communities stacked one upon the other, from the cactus of the subtropical desert to fir forests of the Canadian zone. As the elevation increases, the temperature drops and the precipitation increases, creating a variety of ecosystems that feature plants and animals adapted to life at different elevations. For instance, the kangaroo rat, which burrows underground and survives on desert plants and seeds, is found in the lower elevations but could not survive at the top of the mountain. In contrast, the long-eared Abert's squirrel depends on ponderosa pine trees for its livelihood and is not found on the mountain below the ponderosa forests of the Transition zone. Cactus wrens live in the lower elevations, whereas mountain chickadees and hermit thrushes frequent the higher life zones. These life zones were first described by C. H. Merriam in 1889, when he compared the vertical communities of a mountain to a trip from Mexico to Canada.

Arizona's mountain ranges are only one facet of the state's ecological diversity. Arizona is the only state that claims all four North American desert ecosystems: Sonoran, Chihuahuan, Mojave, and Great Basin, and the Arizona Trail travels through three of them.

Arizona's pride, the giant saguaro cactus of the Sonoran Desert, symbolizes the southwest. Its lovely white blossoms, which appear April through June, are Arizona's state flower. Saguaros are amazing plants. They are very slow growing, taking 50 years to reach a height of 7 feet. After 75 years a cactus may sprout its first "arm." Saguaros that live to be 150 years old can reach heights of 50 feet and weigh up to 8 tons. Despite their impressive size, saguaros are very fragile, their existence hanging by a thread. One hard freeze could kill an entire community. Vandals and cactus thieves take their toll, and livestock destroy "nurse" plants that cactus seedlings need for survival. In addition, the longnose bat, which plays an important role in pollinating the cactus, is rapidly losing its winter habitat in Mexico.

One of the loveliest of Arizona's biotic communities is found in the riparian habitats along streams and canyon bottoms. The Arizona Trail travels through many such riparian areas. These lush strips of vegetation along canyon bottoms stand in stark contrast to the surrounding upland desert. In some cases Saguaro cactus, prickly pear, cholla, and barrel cactus mingle with giant old sycamores and cottonwoods, offering an interesting mixture of two distinct plant communities. Welcome pools of water lie along riparian canyon bottoms, which offer a cool and shady oasis from the desert heat. Many wildlife species in Arizona are dependent upon riparian deciduous forests.

Through grasslands, wetlands, desert, chaparral, forests, riparian canyons, and mountain ranges, the Arizona Trail spans all of the life zones except Alpine Tundra, offering a wealth of world-class trail opportunities.

Some unusual mammals are frequently seen in southern Arizona, including coatimundi, ringtail cats, javelinas, and Coues whitetail, the second smallest deer in the United States. Mexican wolves and some rare species of bats have been reported, and jaguars, long extinct in the United States, sometimes wander into the southern Arizona mountains from Mexico. Pronghorn antelope live in Arizona's grassland savannas. Small herds of bighorn sheep live in some of Arizona's mountain ranges. The beautiful tassel-eared Kaibab squirrel is unique to northern Arizona's Kaibab Plateau. The squirrel is an example of a species that, isolated over millennia, developed its own distinctive coloring and characteristics. Arizona has many other rare and unusual small mammals. More common mammals include jackrabbits, cottontails, whitetail deer, mule deer, elk, coyotes, foxes, raccoons, mountain lions, bobcats, porcupines, and black bears.

From hummingbirds to golden eagles, over five hundred species of birds have been identified in Arizona. In fact, more species of hummingbirds have been recorded at Ramsey Canyon Preserve in the Huachuca Mountains than anywhere else in the United States. One of the rarest birds seen in Arizona is the elegant trogon. This beautiful bird is the northernmost member of a tropical family that includes the resplendent quetzal. Other unusual birds that are seen in Arizona include the tiny elf owl, vermilion flycatcher, pyrrhuloxia, phainopepla, hooded oriole, montezuma quail, painted redstart, bridled titmouse, gray hawk, black hawk, bald eagle, sandhill crane, and others, including some extremely rare hummingbirds. Wild parrots occasionally cross into Arizona from Mexico. California condors have been released in an area north of the Grand Canyon, a place where they were originally seen in the last century.

Many more species of rare and endangered plants and animals live in Arizona. These include butterflies and moths, a rare lily, an orchid, some very small, rare rattlesnakes, and a new species of frog discovered in the late 1980s that vocalizes under water.

History Along the Arizona Trail

THE HISTORY OF THE ARIZONA TRAIL is intriguing. Linking landscapes and people, the trail provides an opportunity to experience and reflect upon Arizona's dynamic natural, cultural, and historical heritage. The statewide trail begins at the U.S.-Mexico border, where the Spanish began their exploration of the American Southwest over four hundred years ago. The Arizona Trail links ruins of prehistoric cities, old mining camps, the site of the last battle fought between Apache Indians and the U.S. Cavalry, ranch lands that once belonged to vast Spanish land grants, and the largest expanse of ponderosa forest in the world.

On the Arizona Trail features excerpts from old (and some contemporary) songs and poems that describe so beautifully the landscape and history of Arizona. Native Americans, the Spanish, the cavalry, ranching and mining industries, and the Forest Service have all played leading roles in creating the heritage of Arizona.

ARIZONA'S FIRST PEOPLE

Once I moved about like the wind. Now I surrender to you. And that is all.

—*Geronimo (upon surrendering to General Crook)*

Arizona has a rich Native American history. The Lehner and Naco Mammoth Kill Sites, less than 20 miles from the beginning of the Arizona Trail, are over 12,000 years old. Archeologists have found clovis-style projectile points and the bones of mammoths that were hunted by ancient Arizonans.

Between 200 and 500 B.C. Arizona's Native Americans advanced from being wandering hunters to living a more settled existence in farming communities. Eventually three distinct cultures emerged. The Hohokam, who lived in the Phoenix area until A.D. 1450 were a sophisticated people with a culture that spanned 2,000 years. They built over 500 miles of irrigation canals, which created a major agricultural area for large numbers of villages. They produced beautifully decorated woven cotton garments, jewelry, and pottery. Since *Hohokam* is also a Pima word meaning "those who have vanished," it is thought that the present day Pima may be their descendants.

The Anasazi ("the ancient ones") lived in multilevel pueblos in the northern part of Arizona. Up to five stories high, the villages were usually located on high plateaus or mesas, or under large, overhanging cliffs. Between A.D. 1000 and A.D. 1400 thousands of pueblos were scattered over a wide area of northern Arizona, but by the late 1500s few remained. The Hopi Indians are direct descendants of the Anasazi. Old Oraibi, a Hopi village dating back to 1150, still exists and is considered the oldest continuously inhabited settlement in the United States.

The Mogollon (pronounced "Mo-ghee-on") were an ancient people who inhabited the central and eastern areas of Arizona. Living in forests and mountainous areas, they hunted and farmed and are believed to have been the first people to make pottery. From these prehistoric cultures, subcultures such as the Salado and the Sinagua developed. The Arizona Trail passes the remains of several of their ancient cities. The disappearance of these people is a mystery, with drought, disease, and incursions by enemies all being possible causes. By the late 1500s empty rooms and ruins were all that remained of the culture.

The Navajo and Apache are believed to have arrived in Arizona between A.D. 1200 and 1400, from the far north. Their language, Athabascan, is similar to languages spoken in Canada and Alaska.

Gold is what brought the Spanish to southern Arizona in 1540. Spanish priests and settlers came to the area and introduced Native Americans to many new vegetable crops, sheep, cattle, and horses. The acquisition of horses gave the Apaches mobility and power. Their endurance and skills in guerrilla warfare were formidable, and for years they succeeded in preventing Spanish settlement beyond the presidio of Tucson.

Treaties with Mexico and the discovery of gold in California in 1848 brought an influx of new Americans and the inevitable conflict of two different cultures laying claim to the same land. With the Gadsden Purchase in 1854 southern Arizona became territory of the United States, and the conflict between Native Americans and settlers intensified. Geronimo and Cochise, two of Arizona's most well-known Native Americans, were both Chiricahua Apaches. Both played leading roles in the war between the U.S. government and Native Americans fighting for their Arizona homeland. They were as popular with the journalists and novelists in the late 1800s as they are today. In 1861 Cochise was falsely accused of stealing a child and some cattle, and the incident escalated into a full-blown war between the Apaches and settlers in southern Arizona. In 1863 a series of military forts was established and more troops were brought to Arizona to protect American settlements from the Apaches.

In the northern part of the territory, Kit Carson was commissioned to invade and conquer the Navajo Indians. Carson and his troops laid waste to the Navajo and their lands, destroying farms and livestock. The Navajo people who survived were marched several hundred miles to prisoner of war camps, and the trek later became known as "the long walk." The Hualapais were defeated in 1869, and the Yavapais, in 1875. All of the Chiricahua Apaches except Cochise's band were eventually sent to prison camps in Florida. After Cochise died in the Dragoon Mountains in 1874, the remaining members of his tribe were sent to the San Carlos Apache Reservation.

One Chiricahua Apache rebel, Geronimo, escaped from San Carlos and continued to raid settlers and wage war against troops on both sides of the Mexican border. In 1886 troops from Fort Huachuca who had followed the defiant Geronimo into Mexico finally persuaded the Apaches to cross the U.S. border and surrender. With Geronimo's surrender to General Miles, the "subjugation of the hostiles" and an end to the "Apache Campaign" were announced on October 7, 1886. Geronimo and his band were sent to Florida and later moved to Oklahoma. Geronimo was never allowed to return to Arizona and died at Fort Sill, Oklahoma, in 1909. Today, over a hundred years after they were forced from their land in Arizona, Chiricahua Apaches from Oklahoma plan to build a resort near the Dragoon Mountains in Cochise County. The tribe wants to return its culture to an area that its members once roamed.

Not all Native Americans fought against the flag. Alchesay, the last of the White Mountain Apache chiefs, was recently honored by Fort Huachuca for his service in the U.S. Cavalry and his efforts to promote peace. The ceremony, held at Fort Huachuca, was attended by Alchesay's descendants and members of the White Mountain Apache Tribe. Native Americans from Arizona have fought in World War I, World War II, the Korean and Vietnam Wars, and in the Persian Gulf. It was Navajo Code Talkers who came up with signals that the Japanese could not decipher during WWII. Ira Hayes, a Pima Indian and a marine, helped to raise the flag over Iwo Jima.

Arizona is still "Indian Country." There are more Native American cultures here than anywhere else in the United States. Arizona has twenty reservations representing fourteen different tribes, and almost 25 percent of Arizona lands are owned by Native Americans. The vast Navajo Nation, which extends into New Mexico and Utah, is the largest Indian reservation in North America.

Some of Arizona's reservations hold ceremonial dances, craft fairs, rodeos, and other events to which the public is invited. Each reservation has its own rules regarding visitors. Tribal permits are required to hunt, fish, or camp on reservations. (For more information, contact the Native American Tourism Center, 4130 North Goldwater Boulevard, Scottsdale, AZ 85251, (602) 945-0771.) Native Americans in Arizona impact the state's economy and culture. Agriculture, timber, livestock management, light industry, outdoor recreation, gambling casinos, the arts, and tourism are all big businesses both on and off the reservations. The ancient Anasazi would surely be amazed by the incredible array of "pueblo-style" adobe buildings in the Southwest, from lavish guest resorts to huge condominium complexes and shopping malls, all influenced by their early architecture.

SPANISH EXPLORATION

> When the dreamers of old Coronado,
> From the hills where the heat ripples run,
> Made a dust to the far Colorado
> And wagged their steel caps in the sun,
> They prayed like the saint and the martyr
> And swore like the devils below
> For a man is both angel and Tartar
> In the land where the dry rivers flow.
>
> —"The Border," Badger Clark, 1911

The Arizona Trail begins at Coronado National Memorial on the United States–Mexico border. Spanish exploration of the American Southwest began here, less than 50 years after Columbus discovered America. The memorial was established to commemorate Francisco Vásquez de Coronado's exploration of the Southwest during his two-year search for gold and the fabled Seven Cities of Cíbola, and highlights the importance of the Hispanic-Mexican background in Southwestern history and culture.

Coronado began his journey in the spring of 1540 with over three hundred Spanish soldiers, four Franciscan priests, several hundred Indian troops, and fifteen hundred stock animals. One can almost imagine the scene! Hundreds of soldiers on horseback with their metal armor and helmets glinting in the sun. The voices and laughter, the lowing of cattle, the creaking of cart wheels, and the dust. The expedition commander and his entourage heading north from the shadows of the Huachuca Mountains into the shimmering heat of the San Pedro River Valley.

Although they did not find the cities of gold, members of Coronado's party did discover the Grand Canyon and several pueblos. Coronado made it all the way to what is now Kansas before abandoning his quest and returning to Mexico in disgrace. He died at forty-two, never knowing the ramifications of his incredible journey, which paved the way for later Spanish explorers and missionaries to colonize the Southwest.

Father Eusebio Francisco Kino, a Jesuit priest, came to the area in 1692. Father Kino's impact on the Southwest was tremendous. Founding missions in Arizona and northern Mexico, he converted thousands of Native Americans. He taught his converts agriculture—how to raise vegetable crops and livestock. He is credited with producing the first accurate maps of southern Arizona and northern Mexico. San Xavier Mission (known as "The White Dove of the Desert"), south of Tucson on the Tohono O'Odham Reservation, was founded by Father Kino in the early 1700s. The mission is considered one of the finest examples of Spanish Mission architecture in the United States. The mission has a museum, offers a daily mass, and provides a Spanish service on Sundays.

After Father Kino, Spanish settlers, miners, and ranchers soon followed, forcing Native Americans to defend their territories. The Spanish established a presidio (fort) at Tubac in 1752. In 1775 settlers built an adobe wall around Tucson to protect themselves from Apaches, and today Tucson is still referred to as "The Old Pueblo." Native American uprisings in 1802, the Mexican Revolution with Spain in 1810, and ongoing problems with the Apache, contributed to the abandonment of all settlements except those of Tucson and Tubac. When Mexico won independence from Spain in 1821, the Arizona region became a territory of Mexico. Mexican Independence Day—16 de Septiembre—is still celebrated in Tucson.

As American hunters and trappers began to drift into Arizona, the area was marked by American and Mexican conflicts in addition to ongoing territorial warfare with Native Americans. The Mexican-American War began in 1846 and ended in 1848 with the signing of the Treaty of Guadalupe Hidalgo. All of Arizona north of the Gila River became United States property. The Gadsden Purchase of 1854 joined southern Arizona and Tucson with the rest of Arizona Territory.

Arizona continues to have close ties with Mexico—they are two vast lands, separated by a wire fence. Nineteen percent of Arizona's population is of Spanish descent, and Spanish is still widely spoken in Arizona. The Arizona Trail passes mountains, canyons, and other landmarks that bear Spanish names. In Arizona, old family names, place names, architecture, food, and music still reflect the Spanish influence.

THE CAVALRY

We wint to Arizona for to fight the Injins there;
   We came near being made bald-headed,
      but they never got our hair.
We lay among the ditches in the yellow dirty mud,
   And we never saw an onion, a turnip or a spud.

—Indian War Soldiers' Song, Fort Huachuca Museum, circa 1870s

U.S. cavalry soldiers, bugle blaring, charging to the rescue of settlers or fellow soldiers trapped by "savage" Apache warriors is a scenario immortalized by the silver screen. John Ford and other motion picture directors used Old Tucson Studios to produce these action-packed classics. *Stagecoach,* starring John Wayne, was based on the Butterfield Stage Line, which traveled through Apache Pass in the Chiricahua Mountains, which are visible from the first passage of the Arizona Trail.

The war between the United States and Mexico brought the first U.S. cavalry troops to Arizona. The ensuing treaty with Mexico and the discovery of gold in California, which both occurred in 1848, brought an influx of Americans to the area, and conflicts between settlers and Native Americans escalated. The signing of the Gadsden Purchase in 1854 brought another wave of settlers and more conflict.

Fort Defiance, in the northern part of the state, was established in 1851. During the Civil War the majority of U.S. troops in Arizona were sent elsewhere, and Native Americans took the opportunity to continue raiding American settlements. Fort Bowie, abandoned in 1894, is now a national historic site. It was established in 1862 to protect the Butterfield Stage Line from Cochise's Chiricahua Apaches. Apache Pass, in southeastern Arizona, was the location of several battles between U.S. troops and Apaches.

In 1863 Arizona became a territory, and the military established forts there. More troops were brought to Arizona to protect American settlements from Native Americans. That same year, Kit Carson was commissioned to take the Navajo lands. Camp Lincoln (renamed Camp Verde) was built by volunteers who wanted a fort to defend settlers from Apache raids. Camp Verde was occupied by cavalry and infantry soldiers from 1865 to 1891. It was used as a base by Colonel Devin, who was sent in 1868 to command troops in northern and central Arizona, and later by General George Crook's troops during Indian campaigns of the 1870s. Camp Verde is now a state historic park.

Between 1871 and 1873 General Crook constructed a 200-mile trail along the Mogollon Rim to be used for moving troops and supplies between Fort Apache, Camp Verde, and Fort Whipple near the territorial capital of Prescott. The trail was used by troops patrolling the northern boundary of Apache territory until Geronimo's surrender in 1886. Portions of the General Crook Trail still exist, and the Arizona Trail crosses it near Battleground Ridge, the site of the last conflict between Apaches and the U.S. Cavalry.

Fort Lowell in Tucson was a key military post during the 1870s and 1880s. The Fort Lowell Museum displays authentic military equipment and photographs and has reconstructed some of the original buildings. Fort Huachuca, at the northern end of the Huachuca Mountains, was established as a U.S. Army outpost in 1877 to protect settlers from Apache Indians. Fort Huachuca is the nation's only remaining cavalry fort that is still an active army post and its main post has been registered as a national historic landmark.

It was troops from Fort Huachuca who gained Geronimo's surrender in 1886. The troops again patrolled an uneasy border in the early 1900s. A raid on American soil by the infamous Mexican revolutionary, Pancho Villa, resulted in Fort Huachuca troops entering Mexico again in 1916. This eleven-month pursuit of Pancho Villa, known as the "Punitive Expedition" and led by General Pershing, was the last major maneuver to be carried out by horse cavalry in the United States.

The Buffalo Soldiers, famed Black cavalry and infantry troops, played an active role in the history of Arizona Territory. The Ninth and Tenth Regiments were sent west to fight Native Americans, guard stagecoaches, or defend the U.S. border. These two cavalry regiments comprised 20 percent of America's Indian-fighting cavalry. At various times the Buffalo Soldiers were stationed at Fort Huachuca and took part in both the sixteen-month Geronimo Campaign and the Pancho Villa Punitive Expedition. The Buffalo Soldiers are featured at the Fort Huachuca Museum, and a portion of State Route 90 was recently dedicated as the Buffalo Soldier Trail.

The U.S. Army honors its heritage at Fort Huachuca with its mounted "B" Troop cavalry in frontier-era uniforms and its excellent historical museum. The Fort Huachuca Museum offers dioramas, exhibits, and authentic mementos of the Apache Wars, the Punitive Expedition, and the Buffalo Soldiers.

PROSPECTORS

Then the white man came, as the East growed old,
  And blasted his trail with the wreck of war
He riled the rivers to hunt for gold
  And found the stuff he was lookin' for

—"God's Reserves," Badger Clark, 1908

The word *prospector* brings to mind a Gabby Hayes–type character with a burro and a floppy hat. Probably the most famous of Arizona's prospectors was Jacob Waltz, mysterious owner of the Lost Dutchman Mine. The Lost Dutchman Mine, which produced high-grade gold ore, was supposedly hidden in the rugged Superstition Mountains within the shadow of Weav ers Needle, but no one except Waltz knew for sure. Those who attempted to track him back to his hidden treasure disappeared, and when Waltz died in 1891, he took the secret with him.

Arizona has a rich mining history, and ridges and canyons across the state bear the scars of extensive mining activity. The southern part of the state, especially, is riddled with thousands of long-abandoned shafts and tunnels.

The first prospectors in Arizona were Spanish explorers searching for gold and silver. The discovery of gold near Prescott prompted the designa- tion of Arizona as a territory in 1863. In the late 1800s and early 1900s boomtowns appeared and died seemingly overnight as fortune hunters flocked to areas rumored to have a strike. Along with the gold came trou- ble in the form of gamblers, rustlers, and gunslingers. Fortunes were made and lost in a day.

Many of the mines had interesting and colorful names like The Glory Hole, Lucky Cuss, Copper Queen, Toughnut, Let Her Rip, and Total Wreck. A few of the settlements, such as Bisbee, Miami, and Superior became full- blown mining towns, but for most, little remains but the memory. The southern passages of the Arizona Trail pass dozens of old mine sites.

The ghost town of Sunnyside is near the Arizona Trail in the Huachuca Mountains. Unlike most of the mining camps of the late 1800s, Sunnyside did not have bars, brawls, or hangings. It began as a religious colony under the leadership of Samuel Donnelly and has been described as a peaceful place, where the sound of piano music and hymns could be heard on Sun- days. Up to fifty families lived in this communal setting, working the Cop- per Glance Mine and later, a sawmill. Donnelly died in 1901 and the town was disbanded when the mine closed in 1934. Although several of the orig- inal buildings remain, the entire townsite is privately owned, and the owner has posted "no trespassing" signs.

The Arizona Trail passes through the main streets of two other ghost towns that are in the Coronado National Forest and that may be explored. The adobe buildings of Kentucky Camp, tucked into the foothills of the Santa Rita Mountains, make for an interesting visit in a beautiful setting. Coronado National Forest's Nogales Ranger District is doing a great job of restoring this site. Read the chapter on the Santa Rita Mountain passage for more information on Kentucky Camp's fascinating history. The gold mine camp of Catalina is along the Mount Lemmon/Oracle Ridge passage of the Arizona Trail.

Bisbee, 25 miles east of the beginning of the Arizona Trail, is a classic example of an old Arizona mining town, with mining shacks and Victorian homes clinging to the sides of the canyons. Quite the opposite of Sunnyside, this was a wild town with more than its share of saloons, gambling houses, brothels, and gunfights. The "queen of the copper camps," Bisbee was once the largest copper mining town in the world. Visitors can take tours of the vast open pit mine and of an underground mine. Decked out in hard hats with lights and yellow slickers, visitors are transported in an actual mine train for a fascinating glimpse into the lives of the men who labored underground. The Bisbee Mining and Historical Museum, across from the Copper Queen Hotel, offers dioramas and changing artifact and photographic displays.

The mining claims of Arizona's early prospectors developed into one of Arizona's leading industries, and today Arizona ranks first in the nation in copper production. The stacks of the smelters near Arizona's mining communities attest to the continuation of mining in the state.

COWBOYS

All day on the prairie in a saddle I ride,
  Not even a dog, boys, to trot by my side.
My fire I must kindle with chips gathered round
  And boil my own coffee without being ground.
I wash in a puddle and wipe on a sack,
  I carry my wardrobe right here on my back.
—"The Cowboy," author unknown, circa 1885

The paintings of Frederic Remington and Charles Russell and the stories of authors like Zane Grey romanticized the west. Silver screen stars such as Hopalong Cassidy, Gene Autry, Roy Rogers, Rex Allen, and John Wayne also glamorized cowboys, contributing to a worldwide love affair and fascination with the Old West. For many, the term *cowboy* brings to mind the image of a white-hatted hero, guns blazing, fighting outlaws, or galloping after a runaway stagecoach. Tombstone, Wyatt Earp, and the gunfight at the O.K. Corral symbolized the six-gun law of the West.

Tombstone epitomized the tough mining towns of the 1880s. Its saloons and gambling establishments attracted some of the West's most notorious and colorful figures. Billie and Ike Clanton and the McLaury brothers, known as the Cowboy Gang, rustled cattle and held up stagecoaches throughout southeastern Arizona. A longstanding feud between the Cowboy Gang and the Earp brothers resulted in the famous Tombstone shootout in 1881. The landmark Dragoon Mountains, which are visible from several passages of the Arizona Trail, mark the site of Tombstone.

The first real cowboys of Arizona were Mexican vaqueros—skilled horsemen who had perfected the art of roping cattle, using ropes of braided rawhide. Tucson celebrates La Fiesta de la Vaqueros Rodeo every February, highlighted by a three-hour, completely nonmotorized, horse-drawn parade. Prescott's Frontier Days Celebration and Rodeo held Fourth of July week, dates back to 1888. The Navajo Tribe holds a large fair and rodeo every Labor Day weekend at Window Rock. Many other rodeos held across the state showcase the skills of Arizona's cowboys.

Stock raising is Arizona's oldest industry and accounts for a quarter of the state's agricultural yield. Seventy percent of the land in Arizona, which includes national forest, is used for grazing cattle. Much of the Arizona Trail passes through land that has grazing allotments, affording the possibility of seeing a cattle drive or seeing working cowboys on horseback.

Music and Poetry of the Arizona Cowboy

Arizona's multicolored canyons, alpine mountains, and exquisite deserts are captivating. The dramatic landscapes and colorful history of the state have long been an inspiration to poets, artists, and writers as well as the regular folks who lived, worked, and traveled the state. There are some wonderful songs, handed down by verse, the original authors long forgotten, that record the old days in Arizona. Many songs and poems written in the early 1900s are still being sung and recorded today.

Badger Clark came to Arizona from South Dakota in 1906, after being diagnosed with tuberculosis. Taking a job as a cowboy on a ranch between Bisbee and Tombstone, Clark was soon putting his surroundings to verse, writing about the Sonoran Desert, the mountains, and the people in a way that made readers feel the heat, the dust, and the remoteness and beauty of the land. An environmentalist before his time, many of Clark's poems reflected his concern for the land:

I rode across a valley range
I hadn't seen for years.
The trail was all so spoilt and strange
It nearly fetched the tears.

Although Badger Clark was only in Arizona for four years, he wrote many timeless poems about the Southwestern landscape and people. In recent years some of Badger Clark's verse has been set to music.

Many of the well-known Western songs of the 1930s and 1940s originated in Arizona. "Cool Water," one of the most popular Western songs ever recorded, was written by a Tucson schoolboy as a class assignment. Bob Nolan, who went on to write many more Western songs, including "Tumbling Tumbleweeds," was one of the founding members of the Sons of the Pioneers. "Ridin' Down the Canyon" was written by Smiley Burnett, as he and Gene Autry traveled through Oak Creek Canyon. "Ghost Riders" was written by a Douglas cowboy, and "Where the Mountains Meet the Sky" was inspired by the sight of the beautiful San Francisco Peaks north of Flagstaff.

In recent years, Western poetry and music has had a resurgence in popularity, and cowboy poetry festivals and gatherings are being held throughout the West. The Western Music Association, a national organization dedicated to the enhancement of Western music, is headquartered in Tucson. Groups like Arizona's Desert Sons, Riders in the Sky, and The Sons of the San Joaquin continue to carry on the tradition of the Sons of the Pioneers.

RANGERS

Why are we fighting from dark until day,
    From summit to canyon wall?
Twice for the Service, and once for the pay—
    Most, the hot fun of it all!
    —"The Forest Ranger," Badger Clark, 1915

The U.S. Forest Service was established in 1905. Early rangers patrolled Arizona forests on foot and by horseback. A ranger's district was typically accessed by trails: up and down canyons, through ponderosa forests, and across vast grazing areas where a horse was essential. From college-educated easterners to lumberjacks to cowboys, early forest rangers in Arizona came from a variety of backgrounds. Their equipment consisted of a Forest Service badge, a compass, telescope, notebook, shovel, rake, and axe. The ranger had to provide his own horse and bedroll.

The major responsibility of rangers in the early days was fire control. "Fire guards" were hired during the driest months of the year to staff lookout towers in strategic areas and report all sightings of smoke or fire. In the early 1900s some lookouts were connected by telephone wire. In 1916, Arizona was the first region in the Forest Service to use shortwave radios. The earliest lookout stations (eventually replaced by wooden structures) were actually tall trees, fitted with platforms and ladders! The Arizona Trail passes by one of these now-fallen lookout trees in the Kaibab Plateau Southern Passage. The ladder and pieces of telephone line are still attached. When a fire call came to a ranger station, the ranger gathered his fire crew and walked or rode to the fire. Fire crews consisted of whomever could be recruited, including cowboys from local ranches, mine and lumber mill workers, and Native Americans.

The typical forest ranger was a man of many talents. In addition to fighting fires he had to supervise timber sales, oversee grazing permits, and be knowledgeable about water, watersheds, and erosion. Rangers also served as deputy game wardens and were responsible for arresting poachers. The Forest Service was sometimes involved in violent conflicts between sheepmen and cattlemen in Arizona. Although many rangers were married, housing conditions were primitive—often a one-room cabin with wood-burning cook stove, oil lamps, hand-filled water tanks, and outside toilets. The Blue Ridge Passage of the Arizona Trail begins at the site of a historic Forest Service log cabin, one of three such cabins along the Mogollon Rim.

The Arizona Trail passes through Flagstaff, a town surrounded by the largest ponderosa pine forest in the world, and the site of some of Arizona's earliest fire lookouts. Flagstaff was named for a tall ponderosa, stripped of branches and bark and hung with an American flag on Independence Day, 1876. Flagstaff's lumber industry had its beginning with a mill built in 1882 to furnish railroad ties for the Atlantic and Pacific Railroad. With the advent of the railroad, Flagstaff's lumbering industry became well established. Because of its proximity to the Grand Canyon, Sunset Crater Volcano, the San Francisco Peaks, Meteor Crater, Indian ruins, lakes, campgrounds, museums, and festivals, Flagstaff is a popular vacation destination along the Arizona Trail.

In the 1930s there was an active period of lookout tower construction, and most of the tall steel towers in use today date back to that period. South of the Grand Canyon the Arizona Trail passes Grandview Lookout Tower, built in 1936 by the Civilian Conservation Corps. In the 1950s young, well-trained college professionals, representing many different specialties, began joining the Forest Service. Paleontologists, hydrologists, range scientists, engineers, archeologists, landscape architects, botanists, biologists, and public affairs specialists began to replace the traditional forester. The U.S. Forest Service rangers of today are administrators, overseeing the vast resources of Arizona's national forests.

Seventy percent of the Arizona Trail Corridor is on four national forests: Coronado, Tonto, Coconino, and Kaibab. The Arizona Trail also passes through a state park, two national parks, and a national memorial, each with its own unique history.

Traveling the Arizona Trail: What to Know Before You Go

THE ARIZONA TRAIL is slated for completion by 2000. The 750-mile trail traverses the state from Mexico to Utah, using a network of older trails, new trails, and primitive roads. The trail offers a wilderness experience that is suited to both weekend users and long-distance travelers. Because the Arizona Trail has been developed as a multiuse trail, this guide attempts to provide information that will be useful to all trail users—hikers, equestrians, bicyclists, and llama packers.

The Arizona Trail passes through some wild country—rugged and remote. The intense heat that may be encountered in some areas, coupled with the high, sky island topography of other areas, demands that travelers (human and animal) be physically fit and acclimated to the elevations and climate. All users need to be well prepared and familiar with basic backcountry techniques. Be sure to read the Hazards and Precautions section and the Backcountry Courtesy section of this guide before planning your trip.

Unlike other long-distance trails that follow one mountain range, such as the Pacific Crest Trail or the Appalachian Trail, the corridor of the Arizona Trail was developed to emphasize the wide range of ecological diversity in the state. The corridor was also planned to incorporate already existing trails into one continuous trail. These older trails already have their own names and trail numbers. When we refer to the Arizona Trail, we are referring to a system of existing trails, linked by sections of new trail and in some cases, by roads. Trails that have been designated as part of the Arizona Trail do not lose their original identity. These trails will be identified by their original name and number and as the route of the Arizona Trail (e.g., Kaibab Plateau Trail 101/AT).

Although the vision of the Arizona Trail is for a nonmotorized long-distance trail, at some points it was necessary to link with dirt roads. Users who choose to avoid these "roaded" sections on weekends (when use is higher) will be able to enjoy a primitive experience along the Arizona Trail.

PASSAGES

Governing agencies of the Arizona Trail corridor have divided the route into forty-two passages to aid the public in using the trail. Passages are portions of the trail that can be traveled in one to three days. Passage lengths are often determined by the presence of trailheads or good access points. Some passages are easily accessed and offer great opportunities for day hikes or loop trips, whereas others are remote, offering solitude and a quality wilderness experience for long-distance travelers. Passages have descriptive names that emphasize the diverse geography through which the trail passes. *On the Arizona Trail* highlights certain passages across the state and, for practicality, divides each passage into a series of trips. It features detailed descriptions of over 300 miles of the Arizona Trail. The authors have traveled every trip presented in this book either on foot or horseback with the exception of Passage 41. The description for that passage is provided by the U.S. Forest Service. Bicycle routes were traveled and mapped by car.

Although many trail users will be long-distance, border-to-border travelers, the majority will travel the Arizona Trail by the trip or by the passage. For day hikes or extended treks, trail users can backtrack, arrange for a car shuttle, or swap keys with friends who are traveling the same trip in the opposite direction. Most of the small communities along the route of the Arizona Trail do not have public transportation available.

 ## SIGNAGE

There are many variations in signage along the Arizona Trail. Some trailheads have wonderful, large wooden or metal signs that include area and statewide maps of the trail. Markers used along the route vary from one governing agency to the next. In some passages, agencies have incorporated Arizona's Old West history by packing an iron brand up the trail, heating it in a fire, and branding existing trail signs with the Arizona Trail symbol (a rounded triangle with the state outline inside; a plaque bearing the AT logo has been mounted onto some existing signposts, but not all). In other areas, agencies have set branded 4x4 posts or brown, flexible fiberglass (Carsonite) markers bearing an "AT" decal in the ground. Long stretches of the trail statewide use rock cairns, especially in areas such as stream crossings. Some of the older trails that have been incorporated into the Arizona Trail have their own trail markers, consisting of wooden signs, blazes on trees, or colored disks or triangles.

In some passages the Arizona Trail follows a single trail for its entirety, but more often it links to several different trails or primitive roads within a passage. Although the passages highlighted in the text are considered "open to the public," some unsigned junctions, where the route of the AT leaves one trail or primitive road to follow another, still exist. In some cases, signs have been vandalized or lost. This guide helps users by identifying each time the route of the AT changes, becomes faint or indistinct, or passes a junction that may be unclear. Watch for the caution (exclamation point) symbols in the margins of the trail descriptions in this guide.

MAPS

To date, the Arizona Trail appears on few maps, but several of the preexisting trails now designated as part of the AT can be found on Forest Service and USGS maps, identified by their original name and trail number. There are plans to map these trails using Global Positioning Systems. (Please see appendix C for information on ordering maps.)

PERMITS

Permits are required for overnight stays in several sections of the Arizona Trail that travel through national parks, preserves, or state trust lands. Permits for some areas, such as the Grand Canyon, are in great demand and need to be secured well in advance. (Please see appendix D for information on securing permits.)

BICYCLES

In Arizona, bicycles are not permitted in wilderness areas. Bicycles are also prohibited on the trails in some national parks. Look for the bicycle symbol at the beginning of each trip description to determine if bicycles are permitted on that section of trail. We have suggested alternate routes for bicyclists for trips that travel through areas where bicycles are prohibited. In most cases they follow paved, and sometimes heavily traveled roads, where safety may be a concern. Cyclists may opt to custom design their own alternate routes around wilderness areas.

LIVESTOCK

Livestock are not permitted in developed campgrounds, although horses and mules are allowed in most national parks (with the appropriate permit). Pack animals (llamas, pack goats, pack dogs) are not, and hikers wishing to use them should contact governing agencies for more information. Look for the horse and/or pack animal symbol at the beginning of each trail description to determine if or what livestock is allowed on that section of trail.

Grass and water are often scarce along the Arizona Trail. In some areas grazing is prohibited. Plan to pack in your own animal feed. Contact governing agencies or local outfitters for more information on availability of water, feed, and grazing restrictions. See appendix B for information on horse and llama outfitters, boarding, and transporting livestock.

LONG DISTANCE TRAVEL

When it is completed the 780-mile Arizona Trail will afford a unique primitive experience for long-distance trail enthusiasts.

Planning

Users should obtain as much information as possible before beginning a long-distance trip. Appendix A gives a list of communities, services, and useful phone numbers along the Arizona Trail. Keep in mind that this information may change, and we recommend that you contact communities along the route for updated information prior to your trip. If you plan to travel with livestock, be sure to consult appendix B for information on boarding and transporting livestock. Plan carefully the time of year you begin your journey to avoid winter snowstorms and desert heat. Consider caching supplies in strategic locations along the route prior to your trip.

Future Versus Interim Routes

The Arizona Trail presents complications to long-distance travelers because the trail is incomplete (as of this writing). Trail users determined to do a statewide trek before the Arizona Trail is complete will have to research and plan their own routes. Sometimes governing agencies have recommendations about roads or utility corridors that allow connections to be made; however, fences without gates will still pose a problem, especially for those traveling with livestock.

Resupply/Stopover Opportunities

Few amenities exist for long-distance users at this time. Resupply points are spaced few and far between. The Arizona Trail passes through, or very close to, several small communities and two large urban areas that provide welcome stopovers. Unfortunately, for most of the route, grocery and sporting goods stores, banks, post offices, and feed stores are in towns that are far from the trail. (See appendix A for a list of communities and information on services along the Arizona Trail.)

Other Options

In areas where supplies are not available, long-distance travelers have three options:

1. Rely on friends or family members to meet you along the way with fresh supplies.
2. Mail yourself nonperishable items and dehydrated foods, so they will be waiting for you at conveniently located post offices. Send the package to "Your Name," c/o General Delivery, Town, State, Zip Code, and mark the package "Hold for Arizona Trail Hiker (or Rider)."
3. Cache food, water, and other supplies (stove fuel, batteries, animal feed, etc.) in strategic locations along the trail prior to beginning your journey and accurately map every cache location. Water containers must be a type that will not break, leak, or lose a cap, and food must be stored so that odors will not attract wildlife. Use containers that deter coyotes, rodents, and other creatures, and secure them so that they are not visible to other humans. Any containers used must be packed out so that no trace is left.

BACKCOUNTRY COURTESY

Let no one say,
And say it
To your shame,
That all was
Beauty here
Until you came.
—Anonymous

There are many rules and regulations in place for the protection of our beautiful land and the wildlife and plant life therein. In reality, the only true protection of our magnificent Arizona backcountry lies with the attitudes of the people who visit it. By following a few simple backcountry rules, you can help ensure the preservation and beauty of Arizona's wild places.

Leave No Trace

Trash

- Remember that others will follow you. Leave the area as you would like to find it. If you packed it in, pack it out.
- Do not bury trash or food. Wild animals will dig it up after you leave. If you find trash left by others, pack that out too.
- Cigarette butts, eggshells, orange peels, peanut shells, and so on will eventually biodegrade, but in a campsite or on the trail they are trash. Pack them out.

Trails

- Stay on designated trails. Do not cut switchbacks. It takes a great deal of work by underfunded agencies and volunteers to maintain these trails and reestablish areas eroded by careless trail users.

Camp

- Camp in designated or already impacted campsites when possible and don't camp in meadows. Try to camp on nonvegetated soil to avoid killing fragile plants.
- Do not build structures or dig trenches around tent sites.
- Never cut green trees or bushes.
- Naturalize the area before you leave.

Water

- Arizona Game and Fish Department regulations prohibit camping within ¼ of a mile of water sources. Water must be protected from pollution, and it may be the only close source of water for area wildlife, and in some cases, cattle. Be considerate. Camp far enough away that wild animals or cattle will not be afraid to drink.
- Keep all soap (including biodegradable varieties) out of streams and springs. Carry a pot of water back to your camp and do your washing there.

Sanitation

- Carry a small trowel to dig a hole at least 6 inches deep for burying human waste.
- Choose a location that is far from water sources, trails, and campsites, and after use, fill in the hole completely, burying waste and toilet paper. Better yet, burn or pack out paper.
- Larger groups should establish a latrine or use a portable toilet for packing out human waste.

Fire

- Smoking is not permitted when fire restrictions are in effect. Be careful when smoking and pack out your butts.
- Lightweight stoves are an alternative to campfires and have much less impact on a campsite.
- Wildfire is an extremely serious hazard. Do not build fires if it is windy, clear a circle of bare dirt around any campfire before lighting it, and never leave a campfire unattended.
- Use only dead and down wood.
- Do not try to burn nonflammable things such as tinfoil.
- Always make sure your fire is out cold—use water and stir the ashes.
- If you have used a fire ring, scatter the rocks before you leave to restore the area's natural appearance.

Historical and Archeological Sites

- The Arizona Trail passes through some historically significant and interesting places, including old mining camps, ghost towns, homesteads, and prehistoric ruins. Remember, take only photographs, leave only footprints!

The National Leave No Trace Program advocates minimal impact. For more information call 1-800-332-4100.

SHARING THE TRAIL

Those with hooves
    Remember them that hoove not.
Those with tires
    Be mindful of the tire less.
Those that's hoofin' down the trail
    Think of them that ain't.
Those that's ridin' rubber
    Watch for them that cain't.
—"Sharing the Trail," Anonymous

Hikers, bicyclists, ranchers, hunters, llama packers, equestrians, and most of all, the wildlife all have a right to be here. Most people you encounter will be on the trail for the same reasons you are. They are seeking beauty, solitude, or a wilderness experience far from the noise, pollution, and pressures of daily life.

Wildlife

When you reach the trail, you have left your home and entered the home of wild plants and animals. All wildlife is protected in Arizona. It is illegal to pursue, collect, or kill any animal (mammals, birds, fish, reptiles, or amphibians) unless you are carrying a valid license issued by the Arizona Game and Fish Department. Do not disturb wildlife or plants (this includes rattlesnakes), and do not handle baby animals. Respect wild animals and their habitats.

Right-of-Way—Know and Follow
Proper Trail Etiquette

Mountain bicyclists yield the right-of-way to equestrians and hikers, and hikers yield to equestrians. When two similar groups meet, the group traveling uphill has the right-of-way.

Equestrians may seem to receive preferential treatment, but horses and mules have the right-of-way over smaller pack animals, bicyclists, and hikers, because they have the greatest potential for creating an accident. The first instinct of a frightened equine is to leap or run away from a perceived threat, and because of their size, this can make for a dangerous situation on a narrow trail. If you meet equestrians or pack animals, move off the trail with your pack or bike, on the downside if possible, and stand quietly. Never make a sudden movement or noise or try to touch an animal as it passes you. If the animal seems nervous about passing you, ask the rider what you should do. The equine may fear anything from your bicycle to the shape of the backpack looming above your head.

Horses also have right-of-way over llamas, for the simple reason that some horses are terrified by the sight and smell of these animals.

Mountain Bicyclists

If you travel the trail by bicycle, stay on designated trails to minimize erosion and protect fragile plants and desert environments. Ride at a safe pace and approach turns carefully, anticipating that someone may be just around the bend. When you approach a hiker or a horse from the rear, let the other trail user know you are there and ask if you may pass. If you approach oncoming hikers, stop and allow them to pass, and if you approach an oncoming horse, stop and pull off to the downhill side of the trail to let the horse pass.

Bicycles are not permitted in wilderness areas or on some trails within state parks and national parks and monuments. When possible, we have suggested an alternate route.

Horses, Llamas, and Other Pack Animals

When using pack animals, be sure to stay on designated trails, because cutting switchbacks destroys fragile habitat. When you take a break, move the animals off the trail to rest and relieve themselves, thereby minimizing the amount of manure on the trail. You should approach each turn in the trail with caution, assuming someone is just around the bend. Let other trail users know if your animal is safe to pass. Although equestrians have the right-of-way over other trail users, everyone may not know this. Be courteous to others.

Forage may be scarce. To feed your animals, pack weed-seed-free pellets when possible, because whole grains may eventually sprout and compete with natural vegetation.

Livestock can damage a camping spot. Instead of tying horses and llamas directly to trees, stake or hobble them, or use a portable electric fence or a high line tied between two trees in a position so that the animal cannot chew on the trees. You can also use tree saver straps.

Avoid areas with fragile vegetation or wet ground, and rotate sites several times a day, making sure to scatter manure before you leave a site. Camp well away from the trail and other campsites and avoid camping with livestock in campsites that are frequented by backpackers and cyclists. Keep livestock away from water sources unless they are actually drinking. Allowing animals to relax for several minutes away from the water, prior to drinking, encourages them to relieve themselves away from the water.

Livestock should be healthy, wormed for parasites, have current vaccinations, and be properly shod (or, in the case of llamas, have properly trimmed toenails). You should carry a first aid kit for your animals, although they should be in condition and used to rough, steep, dry, rocky, and hot (or cold) conditions. The Arizona Trail is not the place for a "green" horse or an out-of-shape backyard pet.

Llamas and pack goats are not allowed on Saguaro National Park trails or on trails within Grand Canyon National Park.

Dogs

Dogs are not allowed on trails within national parks, and they should be leashed when in the national forest. Do not allow your dog's barking to disturb the wilderness experience of others, and do not allow them to chase wildlife or cattle. Make sure that your dog is in good physical condition and able to tolerate rocky terrain and heat, and don't forget to carry water for your pet.

Ranchers and Hunters

Much of the Arizona Trail passes through state and federal land that has been leased to area ranchers for grazing. Some of these grazing allotments have been held by the same ranching families for generations, and sections of the Arizona Trail have been made possible through their assistance and cooperation.

On some parts of the Arizona Trail the only water for miles is provided by area ranchers, many of whom have invested their own money and labor to make improvements in these areas. In some cases the wells, the windmills, and the water tanks from which area wildlife and Arizona Trail travelers drink, have been provided by the lease holders at their own expense.

Likewise, some of the beautiful old trails that are now a part of the Arizona Trail may have been built by the rancher or his ancestors. Respect the lease holder's property: Do not disturb cattle. Close gates that you find closed. If a gate has been obviously propped open, leave it as you found it. Don't leave vehicles blocking access to loading chutes and corrals. Corral gates may have been left open to provide cattle access to water. If you use corrals on forest or state land, be sure that you are not preventing access to water. Don't disturb old homestead sites.

Regardless of what your personal view on hunting may be, it is legal and very popular in Arizona. Remember, too, that proceeds from hunting and fishing licenses as well as taxes on certain sporting goods provide funds for state management and educational programs for all wildlife in Arizona. Most public lands through which the Arizona Trail passes are legally open to hunting during designated seasons. It is poor planning to arrange a riding or hiking trip in the forests during hunting season. Deer season is usually around the last week in September and the first two weeks in November. Elk, javelina, and quail seasons also bring hunters into the backcountry. Schedules of hunting times are available at most stores that sell hunting/camping supplies. For more information, call the Arizona Game and Fish Department at (602) 942-3000.

HAZARDS AND PRECAUTIONS

How happy am I when I crawl into bed!
  A rattlesnake hisses a tune at my head;
A gay little centipede, all without fear,
  Crawls over my pillow and into my ear.

—"Greer County," anonymous, circa 1900

After reading this section you may well wonder why anyone ventures into the wilds of Arizona! But knowledge is powerful; it gives us the ability to remain in control of a difficult situation. Information contained in this section will be helpful not only in planning for a safe trip but in knowing how to respond to an emergency if one should arise.

We are happy to say that after many years of hiking and riding in Arizona, we don't know anyone who has fallen victim to any of the hazards mentioned in this section with the exception of scorpion stings (which are common in southern Arizona but generally occur in people's homes rather than on a hike). According to Arizona Poison Control, there has not been a reported death from a scorpion sting in over thirty-five years. Death from snake bite is also extremely rare, and there have been none reported in Arizona in the last few years.

More important to planning a safe trip than the critters you may encounter is your physical condition and acclimation to Arizona's high elevations and heat. If you are in good physical condition, you will be far more likely to "weather the storm" successfully. Backcountry users should also know how to use maps and compasses. Plan ahead, be alert, watch and listen, and enjoy the beautiful Arizona Trail.

The Weather

Arizona Trail elevations range from 2,000 to 9,000 feet and feature a variety of climates. Extremely cold temperatures can be encountered at the higher elevations, and the deserts can be unforgiving with heat in the summer months.

Heat: Probably the greatest danger to hikers in Arizona, especially in the lower elevations, is heat. Parts of the Arizona Trail pass through the Sonoran Desert, where temperatures can go as high as 120 degrees Fahrenheit. Dehydration, heat exhaustion, heat stroke, and sunburn are very real dangers. It is best to avoid a desert journey from May through September. If you are traveling then, plan your trip for the cooler parts of the day, early morning or late afternoon. Carry a minimum of 1 gallon of fluid per person per day and make sure there will be water available for livestock, or better still, leave animals, including dogs, at home. Hydrate yourself before you start and take electrolyte-replacement fluids such as Gator Aid as you hike to replace sodium and other essential electrolytes that are lost through perspiration. Always wear sunscreen, a lightweight hat, and light-colored, long-sleeved shirt and pants. Plan your trip so that you will reach a shaded rest stop during the hottest part of the day.

Muscle cramping, nausea, dizziness, weakness, profuse sweating, or pale, clammy skin are all signs of possible heat stroke. A person exhibiting such symptoms needs to be cooled down immediately. Because you are not likely to find a cool stream in a desert setting, try to get the person to a shady spot with a breeze. Use water to wet down the head, neck, underarms, abdomen, and groin and encourage the victim to drink fluids. Wait until evening to walk out. Heat stroke is a medical emergency that can lead to brain damage and death. Be aware.

Don't forget to watch for heat-related illness in animals. If necessary, move them out of the sun, remove saddles or packs, and cool them down. Wait until evening to lead them out.

Hypothermia: Hypothermia, or generalized body chilling, can also be a very real threat, and not only on the mountaintops. A hot desert day can quickly become a wet and chilling desert night. The combination of cold and wet, especially if accompanied by wind, exhaustion, anxiety, or injury, can drop the body's core temperature to dangerous levels. Nationwide, hypothermia is said to be the primary killer of outdoor recreationists.

Snow can be found at higher elevations from October through May. Be aware of the weather and dress accordingly. Don't wear cotton, which tends to absorb moisture and takes a long time to dry. Instead, dress in layers of lightweight, synthetic fabrics such as polypropylene, which are designed to wick moisture away from your skin and can be purchased in most stores that carry backpacking supplies. You can decrease body heat loss by 50 percent if you wear a warm hat. Carry rain gear, high-energy foods, extra clothing, and waterproof matches. Chemical "instant heat" body warmers are inexpensive and available at most sporting goods stores. Drink plenty of fluids, but avoid alcohol, which dilates blood vessels and accelerates body heat loss.

Symptoms of hypothermia include uncontrolled shivering, pale, cold skin, loss of muscle coordination, impaired judgment, slurred speech, and drowsiness. Hypothermia can be a life-threatening situation, and a person exhibiting the symptoms needs immediate care. Get the victim out of the wind, and after removing wet clothing, into a (prewarmed, if possible) sleeping bag. Use a commercial heat pack or hot water bottle or climb into the sleeping bag and warm the victim with the heat of your body. Encourage the victim to ingest warm fluids and high-energy foods. Hot baths or showers can cause shock or fatal arrhythmias and are not recommended for victims of hypothermia. As soon as you get back to a vehicle, seek medical attention.

Lightning: Most of Arizona experiences what we call monsoon from late June through early September. The storms roll in daily, generally in the early to late afternoon, usually accompanied by a spectacular show of lightning, thunder, and sometimes hail. Lightning is a real danger at this time of year. Plan your trips so that you are off mountaintops and exposed ridgelines or out of flat open areas by early afternoon. If you are caught on a mountaintop trail during a lightning storm, retreat to a lower area, avoiding solitary or tall trees, lone rocks, and rock faces. Arizona mountains can be extremely rugged, so it may be better to wait the storm out and climb back up to the trail then to try to bushwhack your way down.

If a lightning storm occurs when you are in open country, head for any sort of depression and crouch down. Insulate yourself from the ground if possible (using your pack, plastic tarp, etc.) and squat down, allowing only your feet to touch the ground.

Flash Flood: Don't drop too far down to get away from that lightning, because monsoons sometimes mean flash floods. Avoid narrow canyon bottoms, stream beds, and washes during heavy rains. Be alert. Most summer storms are localized—it could be sunny where you are and raining several miles up-canyon, bringing a torrent of water in your direction.

Venomous Creatures

Oldtime Arizona cowboys had the recipe for a worry-free night in rattlesnake country. They circled their bedroll with a horsehair rope, believing that a snake would not cross the rope. If you are concerned about sharing your bed with a snake, scorpion, or other uninvited guest, using a lightweight backpacking tent or insect netting is probably a more reliable way to ensure yourself a good night's sleep.

Rattlesnakes: Rattlesnakes are found in all parts of Arizona. There are many different species, ranging from the rarely seen, small, reclusive twin-spotted rattlesnake, to the large, heavier-bodied western diamondback. The toxicity of a rattlesnake bite can vary depending on the species, the amount of venom injected, and the location of the bite.

We have seen (or heard) many rattlesnakes while hiking or riding in Arizona, but have never had a problem with them. In most cases, a snake will not bite unless it feels threatened. The best way to avoid being bitten is to keep your eyes and ears open. In very hot weather, rattlesnakes usually find shade during the day under logs, rocks, or bushes and become more active at night. In cooler weather, they are more likely to be active during the warmer hours of the day.

Rattlesnakes are earth tone colors: brown, black, tan, yellow, and gray. In other words, they are well camouflaged. Don't sit down or step over or reach under rocks, logs, or bushes without looking first. Don't walk at night without a flashlight and carry a venom extractor in your first aid kit (which should always be packed in the top of your pack) and know how to use it.

Do you know what a rattlesnake sounds like? Unless you have heard the sound before, you might not recognize it. It's actually a buzzing rather than a rattling. A smaller snake sounds almost like a locust buzzing among the leaves. If you hear a buzzing, always assume it is a rattlesnake. Stop, determine where the sound is coming from, and pick a route around it. If the terrain is such that it is impossible to go around, wait for the snake to move off the trail.

If you are bitten, do not panic. Remember that death from rattlesnake bite is very rare. Don't run—an elevated heart rate will spread the toxin more quickly. Do not attempt to kill, capture, or identify the species of rattlesnake that bit you. You only risk being bitten again, and according to Arizona Poison Control identification is not necessary because all rattlesnake bites are treated with the same antivenin. Move a safe distance away from the snake and get out your first aid kit.

According to poison control, for maximum effectiveness, the extractor MUST BE USED WITHIN THE FIRST FEW MINUTES of a person's being bitten.

Unless it is a "dry" bite (with no envenomization), which is possible, there will be pain and swelling. Cutting the site of the wound or use of tourniquets or ice are no longer recommended. A constricting band may be used between the swelling and the heart, but it should not be too tight. You must be able to slip at least two fingers under the band, and it needs to be checked frequently if the limb is swelling. Remove any rings or jewelry and elevate the affected extremity at heart level.

The action you should take next depends on a number of factors, such as location of the bite, distance to the nearest vehicle, and the number of people in your group. Anyone bitten by a rattlesnake should seek medical attention. If it is possible to carry the victim, or a horse is available, that is ideal. If not, have the victim walk out slowly, taking frequent rest stops. If it is a long way from the trailhead where your vehicle is parked to a medical facility and an extra person is available, have that person go on ahead to summon help.

If the person who has been bitten is unable to walk or the terrain is extremely difficult, it might be better to stay put and have someone go for help. The victim should be kept warm and comfortable, with the affected limb elevated, but not above heart level. Arizona Poison Control recommends that the victim drink lots of water and does not use alcohol or any aspirin-based products.

Rattlesnakes don't always rattle before they strike. It is possible to be bitten without ever seeing or hearing the snake. With any sudden, unexplained, severe pain and swelling, assume that you have been bitten by a rattlesnake and seek medical attention.

If your horse, llama, or dog is bitten, try to keep the animal calm. Shave the hair around the bite and use a snake bite extractor but do not apply a tourniquet. Lead the animal out, stopping frequently to let it rest. Avoid having the animal walk any farther than is absolutely necessary. Have someone go on ahead to meet you with a trailer if possible and seek medical attention.

Coral Snakes: Although coral snakes are rarely seen, they are a poisonous Arizona snake. Coral snakes are less than 20 inches long, with a black head that is followed by colorful bands of yellow/red/yellow/black. Several species of harmless snakes have similar coloration, so never attempt to handle (or harm) these beautifully patterned snakes. If you are bitten, seek medical attention immediately.

Gila Monsters: Up to 20 inches long, Gila monsters are the only venomous lizards in the United States, and they are also the largest. Their gaudy black and orange skin has a beaded appearance. Although the bite of a Gila monster is poisonous, these slow-moving animals are not aggressive unless they are being handled or teased, so admire them from a distance. Gila monsters are rarely seen and are protected by Arizona law, so you should count yourself lucky if you are fortunate enough to see one of these unusual lizards.

Gila monsters have a tenacious bite and are difficult to disengage once they bite. According to Arizona Poison Control, the best way to encourage a Gila monster to let go is to give it footing (in other words don't try to shake it off—it will just hang on tighter!). In thirty percent of bites the animals' broken teeth have been left in the wound. Encourage bleeding from the site and wash it with soap and water. Infection and low blood pressure are possible complications. Anyone bitten by a Gila monster should seek medical attention and get a tetanus booster.

Scorpions: Scorpions are found in most parts of Arizona, however they are more prevalent in the southern part of the state and in the lower elevations. Scorpions do not bite, but they have a stinger at the tip of their tail that can deliver a painful sting. There are many different species of scorpions that vary in size from tiny, to the giant desert hairy scorpions that you may have seen for sale as souvenirs entombed in plastic paperweights and bolo ties.

Toxicity of the sting varies depending on the species. Most common scorpions inflict a painful, but generally not dangerous, sting. In Arizona only one species, the bark scorpion, is considered dangerous. The bark scorpion is small, straw-colored, and slender, generally 1 to 1.5 inches long.

Scorpions hide during the day, coming out at night to hunt for insects. Expect to find them under bark, rocks, or pieces of old wood. As you would with rattlesnakes, watch where you put your hands. If you are collecting wood for a fire or moving rocks, look under each one to see what is clinging to the underside and don't carry a load of dead wood with bare arms. Don't leave boots or clothing lying around on the ground and unless they have been stored in a tent or sealed bag at night, shake them out well before putting them on. Shake out those horse blankets too.

There has been no documented death from a scorpion sting in almost 40 years. If you are stung, there will be pain at the site, and there may be involuntary muscle spasms in the affected limb. The toxin may cause a numbness or tingling sensation in all extremities, which could last for several days. Arizona Poison Control recommends using a cool compress and over-the-counter pain relievers for discomfort. Small children, adults with heart problems, or anyone with more acute symptoms, such as shortness of breath, visual changes, or severe muscle spasms should seek medical attention.

Centipedes: Centipedes hide in the same sorts of places that scorpions do. The giant desert centipede is an amazing creature that can reach a length of up to 12 inches. Although the centipede's bite can be very painful, it is not considered dangerous. Again, marvel at this unusual arthropod but don't handle (or harm) it. If you are bitten by a centipede, routine wound care with an antiseptic or a dilute ammonia solution is recommended.

Conenose (Kissing) Bugs: Conenose bugs are bloodsucking parasites. These brown or black insects are usually less than an inch long and have orange along the margin of their wings and small cone-shaped heads. They usually remain hidden during the day, coming out at night to take blood from a sleeping host. A conenose bite causes severe itching, pain, and swelling. Allergic reactions and infection sometimes occur. Arizona Poison Control recommends routine wound care, over-the-counter pain medication, and an antihistamine such as Benadryl to relieve swelling. Continued swelling could indicate an infection requiring medical care.

Tarantulas: Talk about defamation of character! It's a good thing tarantulas don't have lawyers. Tarantulas are still being depicted by Hollywood as evil and deadly monsters stalking hysterically screaming women. No wonder these harmless creatures are the innocent victims of uninformed people. Large, hairy, and slow moving, the tarantulas frequently seen in the summer months are generally ten- to twelve-year-old males who have left the safety of their burrows in search of a mate. Although unaggressive, they may bite in self-defense if being handled or teased. Tarantula hairs are barbed and contain a toxin that can cause painful itching and sores. Don't hurt tarantulas—they deserve our protection.

Black Widow Spiders: It is the female black widow spider that will bite, and it is very distinctive and easy to identify. The body is large and round—a shiny, black marble with legs, and there is a red "hourglass" marking on the underside. Juveniles are patterned with red, brown, and beige. Webs can be found under logs, in rock crevices, in the entrance of abandoned rodent holes, or in seldom-used outhouses (always check under the seat).

According to Arizona Poison Control, a black widow spider bite may cause immediate pain at the site of the bite and symptoms of nausea, dizziness, headache, and progressive muscle cramping within two to six hours. Over-the-counter pain medication is recommended, but if symptoms become severe, or the victim is an elderly person or a child, seek medical attention.

Arizona Brown Spiders: A brown, long-legged spider with a fiddle-shaped pattern on the upper part of its body, the brown recluse spider can be found in the same places as other spiders. Since this spider's bite does not produce immediate pain, you might not see the spider or know you were bitten.

After two to eight hours there may be pain, followed by fever, chills, weakness, vomiting, or joint pain. After several days a bull's-eye lesion may form at the site of the wound. Medical attention is recommended.

Africanized (Killer) Honey Bees: Africanized honey bees are new to the United States. African bees were brought to South America in an experiment to increase honey production in the tropics. Some of the bees escaped and began moving north from Brazil in 1957. The first Africanized bees reached Arizona in 1993, and the state is now considered "colonized."

Africanized bees look just like the common or European honey bee, and the sting is no more harmful. They have been nicknamed "killer" bees because they are far more aggressive, and will defend their territory with less provocation and in greater numbers than other bees. Human deaths have been reported from their attacks in Arizona. Here are some Africanized honey bee safety recommendations:

- Be alert. According to the Arizona Department of Agriculture Africanized Honey Bee Advisory Committee, wild honey bees nest in a wide variety of locations such as old pipes, holes, animal burrows, or cavities in trees or cactus.
- If you see or hear bees, stop and determine the location of the colony and stay away from it. If the colony is along the trail and there will be others coming behind you, try to leave them a warning.
- Wear light-colored clothing. Bees tend to go after dark, leathery, or furry objects and see the color red as black.
- Don't use scents of any sort, including strongly scented shampoos, soaps, insect repellent, sunblock, and so on. If riding, don't use fly-control products on your horse that have citronella or a lemony odor.
- If you are attacked by bees, the best action is to run as far and fast as possible, or to shelter (tent, building, vehicle) if it is available. Because the bees tend to go for the face and eyes, the advisory committee recommends pulling your shirt up to cover your face.
- If for some reason you are unable to run to safety, do not swat at the bees or flail your arms. Instead, cover yourself with a backpacking tent, sleeping bag, rain poncho, or whatever is available and wait for the bees to leave or until it is dark. If you are unable to run and there is nothing with which to cover yourself, retreat into dense, dark underbrush.
- Once you have reached safety, remove all stingers. When a bee stings, it leaves the stinger in the skin, and the venom continues to enter the wound for a short time. Do not pull stingers out with tweezers or your fingers, because this will squeeze out more venom. Instead, scrape them out using your fingernail, a knife blade, or other straight-edged object.
- If you have been stung more than fifteen times, are feeling ill, or are allergic to bee stings, seek medical attention. According to Arizona Poison Control the worst reactions, including shock caused by an allergic reaction, occur within the first hour.

- A cool compress, on ten minutes, off ten minutes, may help relieve pain and swelling, and antihistamines are helpful for symptoms of allergic reaction.
- Dogs have been treated successfully with Benadryl, and horses may be given "Bute" (phenylbutazone) to minimize inflammation, swelling, and pain. If the animal has been stung excessively, seek medical attention.

Disease

Giardia: Giardia is a protozoa that is often found in natural streams, ponds, and lakes. There is no way to tell by looking whether that beautiful, clear, mountain stream is contaminated, so you should always assume that every water source is contaminated and take precautions. Water should be boiled for at least five minutes, filtered with a portable filtration device (these may be purchased at camping supply stores), or treated chemically.

Symptoms of Giardia infection include diarrhea, cramps, nausea, weakness, and weight loss, and it could take anywhere from a few days up to two weeks for symptoms to appear. If not treated, the symptoms may disappear on their own but may then recur later on. If you become infected, seek medical attention.

Rabies: Arizona state law requires that dogs be vaccinated for rabies every three years, and it is recommended that horses in pasture receive annual vaccinations. If you see a wild animal that appears to be ill, or is behaving oddly, avoid it. Wild animals carry some very serious diseases, and if you are bitten by one, you should seek medical attention immediately.

Hanta Virus: The Hanta virus is an airborne disease carried by rodents. Although it was first identified in the Four Corners area (Utah, Colorado, New Mexico, Arizona) of the Navajo Nation, it has since been discovered in other parts of Arizona, in other states, South America, and Canada. The National Center for Infectious Diseases recommends the following precautions:

- Avoid contact with rodents and their burrows or nests.
- Do not use cabins or other enclosed shelters that are rodent infested.
- Do not pitch tents or place sleeping bags in areas that are near rodent feces, burrows, or possible shelters, such as woodpiles.
- If possible, do not sleep on the bare ground, instead use a cot or tents with floors.
- Keep food and trash in rodent-proof containers and pack out excess.
- For drinking, cooking, washing dishes, and brushing teeth, use only bottled water or water that has been disinfected.

The Hanta virus is potentially fatal. Symptoms that may appear from one to five weeks after contact are initially flu-like: fever, chills, cough, shortness of breath, headache, vomiting, and diarrhea. If you suspect you have contacted the virus, seek medical attention immediately.

Plague: A very few cases of the bubonic plague have been reported over the years in New Mexico, Colorado, California, and Arizona. Fortunately, bubonic plague is easily treated with antibiotics, particularly if it is diagnosed early. Plague is a bacterial infection carried by rodents (rats, mice, squirrels, and prairie dogs) and is transmitted from rodent to man through the bite of an infected flea. Precautions for plague are the same as those listed for Hanta virus.

Incubation period is usually two to five days. Early symptoms are flu-like: abrupt onset with chills, fever, and enlarged and painful lymph nodes. If you have been exposed to rodents and have these symptoms, seek medical attention immediately.

Other Precautions

Cactus: The Arizona Trail passes through some spectacular cactus country. These fascinating plants demand respect, a lesson learned too late by the careless. Prickly pear cactus are well named—their tiny hair-like spines are irritating and very difficult to remove. Hikers should carry tweezers and tape for removing the small spines. One type of cholla cactus has been nicknamed "jumping cactus" for good reason. If it is brushed by an unwary passerby, a whole section of the cactus may detach from the plant, latching onto the hiker with barbed spines. Trail users should carry a comb for easy removal of cholla cactus spines without having to use bare hands. Barrel cactus spines are hooked and have a toxic substance that can cause pain and swelling. They can cripple a horse if not removed immediately, so riders should carry pliers to remove spines. Some agave species also have spines that are extremely sharp and unyielding. The tips contain a toxin and can cause a puncture wound with pain and swelling. The best prevention is to watch where you are going and wear protective clothing. If riding on horseback be careful that your horse's legs don't pick up any cactus spines, and if they do, remove the spines immediately.

Abandoned Mines: Arizona is littered with long-abandoned mines, mine shafts, and tunnels. Unbelievable as it may seem, these dangerous abandoned mine shafts are frequently not fenced, covered, barricaded, or flagged in any way to prevent unwary hikers or wildlife from falling in. Old mine shafts may be camouflaged by vegetation—invisible until you are right on the brink. Shafts could be several hundred feet deep and partially filled with water. If you travel off of the trail, always look where you are stepping. Entering abandoned mine tunnels is strongly discouraged, because they may not have enough oxygen to support life, may contain poisonous or explosive gases, or may harbor rattlesnakes.

Potentially Dangerous Animals: Generally all wild animals, including bears and mountain lions, will go out of their way to avoid any contact with humans, so a confrontation with an aggressive animal is very improbable. However, in the unlikely event that you should encounter an animal in a situation where it feels threatened or is protecting its offspring, it could be aggressive.

Whether the animal is a bear or an angry cow, turning your back and running may be the worst thing you could do—the animal could interpret your body language to be saying, "chase me." Face the animal and, avoiding direct eye contact, slowly back away, keeping your voice low. According to a recently published article on animal communication, in the animal world high-pitched vocalizations indicate fear. As you back away, try to make yourself look as large as possible. You may want to hold your pack in front of you or pick up a sturdy stick. Once you are safely away, detour around the area and regain the trail. If the terrain makes a detour impossible, your alternatives are to backtrack out of the immediate area or take a break and give the animal time to move on.

Bears: A close encounter with a bear is highly unlikely, even though the trail does pass through some black bear country. Although people love to see wild bears at a distance, they don't want them in their camps. Never keep food in your tent or sleeping bag and suspend all food products, including canned goods, dog food, horse sweet feed, and garbage, from a tree, 100 yards from camp. The food should be suspended 10 feet in the air and 4 feet from the trunk of the tree. Hanging your food supplies also helps to keep skunks and rodents out of your camp.

Lost and Found

The Arizona Trail is still evolving. Trail signs, trail markers, and even some portions of the route that are described here could have changed or disappeared since this book went to print. Such changes could cause trail users to take a wrong turn somewhere along the route.

It is not a good idea to travel into primitive areas alone. People must weigh the risks versus their desire for solitude. Before a trip, hikers should leave information with relatives or friends, including an itinerary, names and telephone numbers of each member in their group, vehicle descriptions, and expected time of return. If an individual or group is seriously overdue, the county sheriff or Forest Service should be notified.

Plan your route carefully, using this guide, topographic maps, and updated information from governing agencies or the Arizona Trail Association. Always know your location on the map and the best way from that location to a vehicle or a phone. When traveling on foot, allow an hour for every 2 miles, plus an additional hour for each 1,000-foot gain in altitude. Check with authorities within each district for trail and road conditions and any recent changes in trail route or signage. Be properly equipped. Always carry an area map and compass and know how to use them. A flashlight (with extra bulb and batteries), waterproof matches, whistle and signal mirror, candle, knife, water purification tablets, protective clothing, first aid kit, and extra food and water are all items you do not want to leave behind.

The Arizona Trail typically follows natural ridgelines or drainages. If you become lost, don't panic. The best plan is to retrace your route back to where you lost the trail. If this is not possible, sit down and study your maps and surroundings. Look for a familiar landmark such as a distant peak or canyon. If you don't have a compass, remember that the sun and moon rise and set from east to west, north-facing slopes are always more heavily vegetated, and barrel cactus almost always lean toward the south.

If traveling in a group, especially with children, plan ahead to use the "hug a tree" strategy for anyone who becomes separated from the group: If an individual becomes confused by the terrain and is not sure how to find the others, they should go directly to the biggest tree they see and stay there. Chances are they will not have wandered far off the trail.

Following are emergency signals that are considered standard by most search and rescue groups, and which may be sent by a firearm, whistle, or mirror:

- Distress—three evenly spaced signals given in quick succession.
- Acknowledgment—two signals given in quick succession.
- Return to camp—four evenly spaced signals given in quick succession.

How to Use this Guide

Governing agencies have divided the Arizona Trail into forty-two passages, numbered 1–42, from south to north. Generally, passage beginnings and endings are accessible by road; however, in remote areas these may be very primitive 4WD roads.

PASSAGES

On the Arizona Trail describes each passage of the trail, starting at the U.S.–Mexico border and traveling north to Utah. The guide highlights certain passages and divides those passages into trips. Depending on the length, topography, and access points, a passage may have anywhere from one to six trips.

Other passages that are in varying stages of completion (from "officially open," to "won't be completed for several years") are presented with less detail and do not feature maps. We hope to include these passages in a later edition. We do indicate approximate mileage of these passages, where they begin and end, and current status at time of publishing. We also include governing agencies, nearest services, and other information such as features and history when it is available. Although we have included the proposed or designated route for each passage, the authors have not traveled the passages that are not presented with maps. Rather, we obtained trail routes from the Arizona Management Guide produced in 1995, with updates from governing agencies. We strongly urge readers to contact governing agencies for updated information before attempting to hike these passages.

Passages are organized as follows: a passage description, Governing Agencies, For More Information, and Nearest Services. The description explains how long the passage is, where it begins and ends, and how many trips it comprises. This information is followed by an overview of the passage: type of terrain, highlights, and interesting recreational opportunities in the area. The remaining text is devoted to history, interesting plant or animal life, and so on.

Governing Agencies

This section lists names, addresses, and phone numbers for governing agencies.

For More Information

This section identifies other resources, such as chambers of commerce, museums, or books with information specific to the passage.

Nearest Services

The nearest services section gives the distance and direction to nearest services from the beginning of each passage.

TRIPS

All trip descriptions—with the exception of Trip 1-A—are from south to north. Trips may be anywhere from 3 to 18 miles long, and all mileages given (again, with the exception of Trip 1-A) are one way. Because of the remoteness and distance of some passages, it has not been possible to end every trip at a trail-head or point that is accessible by vehicle. In some cases a trip ends at a popular destination point that has good camping opportunities, water, and is accessible by several other trails, offering the possibility for loop trips. The Huachuca Mountains, Rincon Mountains, Santa Catalina Mountains, and Superstition Passages, and Grand Canyon National Park–Inner Gorge Passage all contain trips that travel through remote areas with no vehicle access. In three or four passages the topography did not allow for a reasonable place to end a trip, and those passages are composed of only one trip each—the length of the passage.

Trips are organized as follows: a brief overview, Nature Highlight, Maps, Difficulty Rating, Length, Elevation, Recommended Season, Water Availability, Camping, Livestock, Directions to Trailhead or Trail Access Point, Other Trails in the area, and a detailed Trail Description. The overview tells you where the trip begins and ends. This information is followed by an overview of the trip: type of terrain, highlights, and interesting recreational opportunities in the area.

Nature Highlight

The nature highlight section describes natural events that we saw along the trail, but not necessarily something that the reader will see (e.g., an interesting animal or a blooming plant).

Maps

This section lists maps that may be used in conjunction with the trip description. Older portions of the trail will be found under their original name or trail number; however, newer portions of the trail are not on most maps.

Difficulty

Degree of difficulty, of course, is a matter of opinion. In general, difficulty is rated here according to steepness and length. But remember that all of our trail descriptions travel south to north, so a mostly downhill trip that the guide rates as easy to moderate would not have the same rating if it were traveled in the opposite direction. An easy, downhill grade could become a long, uphill climb.

Length

Because the Arizona Trail is so new, most passages have not been wheeled to obtain an accurate mileage measurement. We have used mileages provided by governing agencies, have taken mileages from maps, and, in some cases, have guesstimated from minutes-per-mile averages. Getting exact mileages for some trips has been difficult. We wish to thank Leonard Taylor, author of *Hiker's Guide to the Huachuca Mountains*, for providing us mileages he wheeled on the first two passages of the Arizona Trail.

Elevation

Both high and low points for individual trips are given in this section.

Recommended Season

(Please read the section on hazards and precautions.) In many central and southern passages, the trail is accessible all year, depending on the weather. A mild winter or unusually cool spring can afford ideal hiking conditions. Recommending a season as best for trail use again relies on opinion, and a recommended season is not as easy to identify in Arizona as it might be in other parts of North America. Because of the sky island topography, a trip can begin in the sweltering heat of the desert and end in a mountain snowstorm! In general it is best to avoid elevations below 4,000 feet from May through September. Summer monsoons bring severe thunderstorms to Arizona, and with them comes the danger of lightning and flash floods. Monsoon storms generally occur in the afternoons from mid-July to mid-September.

Snow may be present in higher elevations from October through May and can be quite deep on north-facing slopes. Areas that may be snowbound in the winter months include the Huachuca, Santa Rita, Rincon, and Santa Catalina Mountains of southern Arizona, the Superstition, Mazatzal, and Four Peaks Wildernesses of central Arizona, and the Mogollon Rim, San Francisco Peaks, Grand Canyon, and Kaibab Plateau of northern Arizona. On the Kaibab Plateau the snow is so deep that the North Rim of Grand Canyon National Park is closed from October 15 to May 15.

Water

(Please read the section on hazards and precautions.) Water is scarce and not dependable along some parts of the trail. You may want to consider caching water in strategic locations prior to your trip. Unless water is taken from a campground spigot, assume that it is unsafe to drink unless treated or filtered. Hikers should carry a minimum of 1 gallon of water per person, per day, or plan to treat or filter water along the route. Do not assume that all water sources listed in this book will be reliable at all times of the year. In many cases the reliability of water sources is unknown or depends upon rainfall. We have indicated dirt stock tanks for users who are traveling with livestock. Generally these tanks are very polluted and effectively filtering or treating the water for human consumption would be a challenge. As a rule, wildlife "trick tanks" are fenced and not accessible to livestock. In an emergency, hikers could cross the fence to fill a canteen, but those traveling with livestock should carry a collapsible bucket to carry water to the animal.

Camping

(Please read the section on back country courtesy.) Because of the remoteness of some of the trips, we have identified camping possibilities along the Arizona Trail. There are a few developed campgrounds along the AT, but most camping opportunities are primitive. When a campground is called developed, it means that there are developed campsites, privies, garbage bins, and sometimes, potable water. Developed campgrounds generally require a fee and have a campground host. Livestock are prohibited in developed campgrounds, and firewood is usually scarce, so if you are driving in, bring your own. Designation as primitive means there are no improvements. Just pull off the road (or trail) and camp. Firewood may also be scarce in primitive areas, so if you are driving in, bring your own firewood and water. Arizona Trail trailheads have not been developed as camping areas, but some do have parking areas and a rest room.

Livestock

The livestock section identifies parking areas large enough to turn trailers, and have hitching posts, corrals, water sources, and availability of feed. We have included precautionary notes, when applicable, for each trip. See appendix B for information on boarding stables and transportation of livestock.

Directions to Trailhead or Trail Access Point

In this section, directions are given to the beginning of each trip and include information on the type of vehicle required to get there: 4WD, high clearance, or passenger car (horse trailers are included in the passenger car category). Keep in mind that in inclement weather a passenger car access may become 4WD. For directions to the trailhead at the end of the trip, see the next linking trip. For trips that do not link to another, directions to trailheads at both ends of the trip are given.

Other Area Trails

This listing provides brief descriptions of other trails that access the Arizona Trail, to alert the reader to possible loop or exit opportunities. If you are planning to use any of these trails, contact governing agencies or refer to local guidebooks and maps for more information.

Trail Description

Large sections of the Arizona Trail are not shown on Forest Service or USGS maps, and not all junctions along the trail are signed. Trail descriptions in this guide are very detailed, calling attention to each junction and to places where the trail may be indistinct or overgrown. As the trail becomes more traveled, its route will be easier to identify. If you think you have lost the trail, backtrack to the point where you lost it. In general, the less obvious sections of trail are well marked with cairns or fiberglass markers. Spots that we found were easily lost, hidden, or hazardous are noted in trail descriptions with an extra exclamation! hazard sign in the margin. The trail is generally a footpath, but in places it follows dirt roads of varying grades: graded road (generally has some traffic), 4WD road (unlikely, but there may be a vehicle), little-used road (a faint, seldom-used two-track), and abandoned road (closed to motor vehicles). The term *route* is used interchangeably with *trail*.

1 Huachuca Mountain Passage
U.S.–Mexico Border to Parker Canyon Lake Overlook

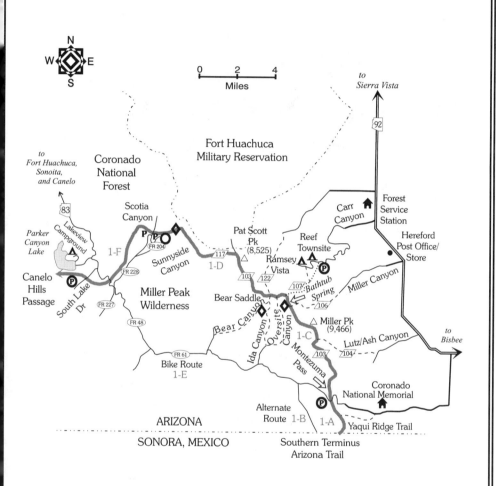

N
W • E
S

0   2   4
Miles

to Sierra Vista

92

Fort Huachuca
Military Reservation

to Fort Huachuca, Sonoita, and Canelo

Coronado
National
Forest

Carr
Canyon

Forest
Service
Station

83

Scotia
Canyon

Pat Scott
Pk
(8,525)

Reef
Townsite

Hereford
Post Office/
Store

Parker Canyon Lake

Lakeview Campground

P

FR 204

1-F

Sunnyside
Canyon

117

1-D

103   122

Ramsey
Vista

107 Bathtub
Spring

Miller Canyon

Canelo
Hills
Passage

P

FR 228

South Lake Dr

FR 227

Miller Peak
Wilderness

Bear Saddle

Bear Canyon

Ida Canyon

Oversite Canyon

106

Miller Pk
(9,466)

1-C

Lutz/Ash Canyon

to Bisbee

FR 48

FR 61

Bike Route
1-E

Montezuma
Pass

103   104

Coronado
National Memorial

ARIZONA

SONORA, MEXICO

Alternate
Route 1-B

P

1-A

Yaqui Ridge Trail

Southern Terminus
Arizona Trail

FR102 Forest Road	Boundary	Trailhead and Parking
Paved Road	River, Stream, or Wash	Trailhead, no Parking
State/Interstate	Canyon Rim	P Parking
Arizona Trail	Campground	Town or City
Trip Access Trail	Water	Point of Interest
122 Other Trail Area	Ranger Station	Mountain Peak

View of the Huachuca Mountains, the first Passage of the Arizona Trail.

> *With mountains of green all around me*
> *And mountains of white up above*
> *And mountains of blue down the sky-line,*
> *I follow the trail that I love.*

—**"The Old Prospector," Badger Clark, 1907**

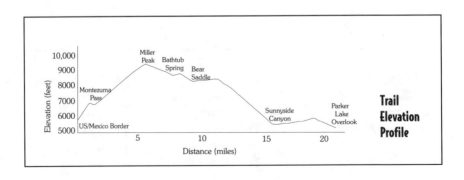

Trail Elevation Profile

FOUR HUNDRED AND FIFTY *years after Francisco Vásquez de Coronado began his exploration of the Arizona wilderness, we begin ours; traveling through what is now known as the Coronado National Forest.*

This 21-mile passage is divided into six trips: Trip 1-A travels 1.76 miles from the U.S.-Mexico border to Montezuma Pass. Since bicycles and livestock are not permitted on Trip 1-A, Trip 1-B affords an alternate route to the border. Trip 1-C travels 6 miles from Montezuma Pass to Bathtub Spring, a site within the wilderness that is not accessible by vehicle. Trip 1-D links to 1-C, traveling 8 miles from Bathtub Spring to Sunnyside Canyon. Trip 1-E is the alternate route for bicycles, which are not allowed in the wilderness area. Trip 1-F travels 5.4 miles from Sunnyside Canyon to the Parker Canyon Lake (Overlook) trailhead.

This southernmost passage of the Arizona Trail has a marvelous example of a sky island, with 9,466-foot Miller Peak representing the Canadian zone. Much of the Huachuca Mountain (pronounced Whachooka) Passage is within the 20,000-acre Miller Peak Wilderness. The abrupt rise from the arid grassland, agaves, and oaks of the Upper Sonoran life zone, to the aspen and mixed conifer of the Canadian life zone, gives this passage a tremendous variety of plant and animal life.

About 10 miles of the passage follows what has been described as a "skywalking pathway" along the highest ridges of the Huachuca Range. On a clear day you can see all the major mountain ranges of southeastern Arizona, including the Chiricahuas, the Pinalenos, Santa Ritas, Rincons, Santa Catalinas, and the Sierra Madre Mountains in Mexico. The route affords the opportunity of a side trip to the top of Miller Peak and is joined by numerous trails that offer the option of planning loop trips.

Other Huachuca Mountain Passage area opportunities include a small museum and nature walk and wildlife viewing at Coronado National Memorial, fishing and camping at Parker Canyon Lake, unexcelled bird and wildlife watching at Ramsey Canyon Preserve, and visits to the Fort Huachuca Museum or the old mining town of Bisbee.

Historically, the Huachuca Mountains are intriguing. The Coronado National Memorial and the Coronado National Forest are both named for the historic expedition led by the Spanish explorer Francisco Vásquez de Coronado. Coronado National Memorial lies on the United States-Mexico border within sight of the route taken by Coronado during his two-year search for the fabled Seven Cities of Cíbola.

The Huachucas have a colorful mining history dating back to the Spanish who mined silver for the kings of Spain. Prospectors and miners blasted and tunneled the mountain in their search for silver, copper, and gold. Pat Scott Peak, along this passage of the Arizona Trail, is named after an early prospector. In the late 1800s and early 1900s, small communities, such as Hamburg in Ramsey Canyon and Reef Townsite in Carr Canyon, evolved to support the mining and lumbering activities. Although some of these townsites were large enough to have post offices at one time, little remains of them today. The best preserved of these communities, the ghost town of Sunnyside, is privately owned and "no trespassing" signs are posted.

Fort Huachuca, at the northern end of the Huachuca Mountains, was established as a U.S. Army outpost in 1877 to protect settlers from Apache Indians. The Buffalo Soldiers, famed Black cavalry and infantry troops, played an active role in the history of Fort Huachuca. Still an active military base today, Fort Huachuca's big, white, aerostat radar system balloon is visible, floating above the highest peaks of the Huachuca Mountains, and may be seen for many miles in any direction.

GOVERNING AGENCIES

Coronado National Memorial, 4101 E. Montezuma Canyon Road, Hereford, AZ 85615. The visitor center has a small museum and picnic area, rest rooms, and water. The memorial offers a variety of trails, including a hike to Coronado Cave. No camping is allowed within the memorial. For more information call (520) 366-5515.

Coronado National Forest, Sierra Vista Ranger District, 5990 S. SR 92, Hereford, AZ 85615. (520) 378-0311.

FOR MORE INFORMATION

Ramsey Canyon Preserve, 27 Ramsey Canyon Road, Hereford, AZ 85615. Famed for its hummingbirds and other wildlife, the preserve requires all visitors to call for reservations because parking is limited. The preserve offers hiking trails, a gift shop, and rental cabins. No pets are allowed. For further information call (520) 378-2785.

Fort Huachuca Museum, Hours 9:00 A.M. to 4:00 P.M. weekdays and 1:00 P.M. to 4:00 P.M. weekends. Admission is free. For further information call (520) 533-3638.

Hiker's Guide to the Huachuca Mountains, by Leonard Taylor. Can be purchased in local bookstores.

Bisbee Chamber of Commerce, 7 Main St., P.O. Box BA, Bisbee, AZ, 85603. (520) 432-5421.

Sierra Vista Chamber of Commerce, 77 S. Calle Portal No. A140, Sierra, Vista, AZ, 85635. (520) 458-6940.

NEAREST SERVICES TO U.S.-MEXICO BORDER TRAILHEAD

Rest rooms and potable water at the memorial visitor center. Rest room and parking area at Montezuma Pass.

Coronado Memorial Road joins SR 92 approximately 16 miles south of Sierra Vista and 21 miles west of Bisbee. Sierra Vista is the larger of the two communities. The nearest market, gas, and post office are in the small community of Hereford, approximately 11 miles south of Sierra Vista on SR 92.

Trip 1-A

U.S.-Mexico Border to Montezuma Pass

There is no vehicle access to the very beginning of the Arizona Trail at the U.S.-Mexico border, so if you truly want to begin at the beginning, you must hike to the border and back from the Montezuma Pass parking area. For this reason, we describe this Trip from north to south; all other Trips in this guide are described from south to north. Because it is necessary to backtrack to the parking area before proceeding north on the Arizona Trail, this is also the only trip for which a round-trip mileage is given.

Livestock are not allowed on this trip. Bicycles are not allowed on any trails within the memorial and are restricted to developed roads (see trips 1-B and 1-E for alternate routes).

When this guide went to press, the Yaqui Ridge trail was not yet completed. The route has been designated, and approximately two-thirds of the trail is built.

Trip 1-A offers sweeping views of Sonora, Mexico, and the San Pedro River Valley, the route of the first European exploration of the American Southwest over 400 years ago. The route begins at scenic Montezuma Pass and follows Joe's Canyon Trail as it traverses the east side of Coronado Peak to a trail junction. The Arizona Trail follows the Yaqui Ridge Trail, descending a ridgeline in open country via switchbacks as it makes its steep descent toward Mexico. A seven-foot-high monument marks the international border and the beginning of the Arizona Trail.

Nature Highlight: A red-tailed hawk soars above us, occasionally swooping down for a better look.

Maps: Coronado National Forest, USGS Quad: Montezuma Pass

Difficulty: Difficult

Length: 3.52 miles round trip

Elevation: 6,675–5,930 feet

Recommended Season: All year, weather permitting

Water: (Treat all water unless noted otherwise. During dry weather, water sources are not reliable.) Montezuma Pass has potable water that is turned off in the winter.

Camping: This area is adjacent to an international border infamous for its problems with illegal immigration and drugs. However, few problems have been reported in the area of Montezuma Pass.

Unfortunately, there are no convenient camping areas adjacent to the beginning of the Arizona Trail. Camping is not allowed within Coronado National Memorial. The only developed camping areas are a long way from the trailhead: Parker Canyon Lake, 19 miles west, or campgrounds in Carr Canyon, 7 miles north on SR 92, then 7 miles up a steep, unpaved mountain road. Primitive camping is possible in the Coronado National Forest along FR 61 west of Montezuma Pass, or in the National Forest along Ash Canyon Road, 1.5 miles north of the Coronado Memorial Road on SR 92.

Livestock: Coronado National Memorial does not allow livestock on any trail except the Crest/Arizona Trail (see Trip 1-C for more information).

Directions to the Trailhead: Passenger cars can access the trailhead via Coronado Memorial Road from the east. There is a 24-foot limit on the length of vehicles driving up to Montezuma Pass on Coronado Memorial Road.

Passenger cars drive south of Sierra Vista 13 miles on State Highway 92 to Coronado Memorial Road and turn west toward Coronado National Memorial. Montezuma Pass is 8 miles from Highway 92, 6 miles of which is paved. After the road turns to a graded gravel road, it is steep and has hairpin turns. This road can be icy in the winter.

At Montezuma Pass there are signs, paved parking, and rest rooms. The Arizona Trail follows Joe's Canyon (Coronado Peak) Trail south from the parking area.

Photo by Peter Moran

The authors at the beginning of the Arizona Trail, beside International (U.S.-Mexico) Border Monument #102.

Other Area Trails:

- **Coronado Peak Trail** (route of the Arizona Trail south) leaves the south side of the parking area in front of the ramada and travels a steep 0.4 miles to the top of Coronado Peak. This scenic trail features interpretive signs with quotations from the Coronado expedition journals and conveniently placed benches for enjoying the panoramic views.
- **Joe's Canyon Trail** travels south from the parking area 0.1 mile to a junction with the Coronado Peak Trail, which goes to the right. Three-fourths of a mile farther you meet a second junction with the Yaqui Ridge Trail (the southern route of the Arizona Trail). From this junction, Joe's Canyon Trail continues east another 2.25 miles in a steep descent to the Coronado Memorial Road, across from the visitor center.

TRAIL DESCRIPTION

The Arizona Trail leaves the parking area on the east side of the ramada at Montezuma Pass. It travels south on Joe's Canyon Trail. In approximately 0.1 mile you meet a junction with the Coronado Peak Trail that heads off to the right (west). Stay on Joe's Canyon Trail, following the ridge. The area is scarred by a burn that occurred in 1988, but vegetation is regrowing. If you look on both sides of the ridge you will see Montezuma Canyon to the north and Mexico to the south. Three-fourths of a mile past the junction with the Coronado Peak Trail you meet the Yaqui Ridge Trail. Take the Yaqui Ridge Trail to the right, descending on an open ridge about 0.25 mile to the first of several switchbacks. The route descends on switchbacks for about 0.5 mile to where, at the time of this writing, the completed section of the trail ended. Views from the ridge and switchbacks include San Jose Peak and large ranches in the expansive Mexico valleys. Vegetation along the Yaqui Ridge Trail consists of desert grasses, shrubs, sotols, and a few oaks dispersed on the surrounding hillsides. The proposed route for the completed trail to the Mexico and United States border descends southwest another 0.25 mile around a hillside. The international boundary for Mexico and the United States is at 5,930 feet elevation. There is a 7-foot concrete monument (number 102 on the Mexico side) of a three-faceted boundary. This marks the boundary for Mexico, Coronado National Memorial, and Coronado National Forest. End your trip here and retrace your steps to the parking area.

Trip 1-B

Alternate Livestock and Bicycle Route from Montezuma Pass to the U.S.-Mexico Border

Coronado National Memorial does not allow bicycles or livestock on Trip 1-A, which is the very beginning of the Arizona Trail. For those who just have to touch that border fence, here is an alternate route.

A rocky, 4WD road beginning near Copper Canyon Wash, 1.3 miles west of Montezuma Pass, travels south to the U.S.-Mexico border. Passing a stock tank and some picturesque old log corrals, the route winds through oak and juniper woodland to Old Mexico.

Nature Highlight: A roadrunner watches us from the top rail of the old corral. With a flick of his tail, he is down and running into the oak chaparral.

Maps: Coronado National Forest, Nogales and Sierra Vista ranger districts.

Difficulty: Easy to moderate.

Length: From Montezuma Pass: 3.6 miles, one way. From Copper Canyon/FR 61 junction: 2.3 miles, one way.

Elevation: 6,575–5,800 feet

Season: All seasons, depending on the weather.

Water: (Treat all water unless noted otherwise. During dry weather, water sources may not be dependable.)

- **Copper Canyon:** Water is seasonal. There is a metal stock tank near corrals.

Camping: Copper Canyon: Primitive. This area is adjacent to an international border, and there are potential risks associated with camping here (see Camping section of Trip 1-A). There are some level areas and shade trees, and there is room to pull off FR 61. Camping farther down the road requires a high-clearance vehicle.

Livestock: There is room to pull off, park, and turn several trucks and trailers. It is 0.3- mile down a 4WD road to corrals and a stock tank. If you use these corrals do not block the lease holder's access. Be sure that you are not preventing cattle from accessing water. Leave gates as you found them (see also Trip 1-C).

Directions to Copper Canyon: A passenger car can drive to Copper Canyon, but a high-clearance vehicle is needed from FR 61 to the border. From Montezuma Pass, follow FR 61 as it travels west in a steep and narrow descent. There is a junction with a 4WD road 1.3 miles from the pass on the left: the alternate route to Mexico. A small sign for Copper Canyon is just beyond the junction.

ROUTE DESCRIPTION

There is room for passenger cars or several trucks with horse trailers to pull off FR 61 and park. To travel farther in on the dirt road requires high-clearance vehicles. Do not block this road. Passing over a cattle guard, the road is very rough and rocky as it drops steeply through oak and juniper trees 0.3 mile to a wire corral and metal stock tank.

The road passes through a wire gate 0.4 mile from FR 61 (please be sure to close the gate). The route turns left (east) past a beautiful old oak and juniper corral. Traveling southeast, the road winds through Upper Sonoran woodland, paralleling a major drainage on the left, as it travels a gentle downgrade. The route becomes less rocky and there are some nice camping possibilities in the final mile to the border.

The road ends at a seven-strand barbwire fence 2.3 miles from FR 61. Stick your toe under the wire, and you can say that you have been in Mexico!

One rough and very steep mile to the east is the official beginning of the Arizona Trail. International border marker #102, a cement monument to the treaty of 1848, sits atop Yaqui Ridge. The monument is situated on the Mexico side of the fence at the boundary of Coronado National Memorial and Coronado National Forest. The gate between the memorial and the forest is wired closed.

Trip 1-C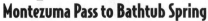
Montezuma Pass to Bathtub Spring

The end of this trip is not accessible by vehicle. A permit is required to leave a vehicle at Montezuma Pass overnight and you should make prior arrangements with Coronado National Memorial to get one. The area is not patrolled at night, though visitor center staff report few instances of vandalism or theft. Take the same precautions that you would when leaving a vehicle unattended anywhere.

Bathtub Spring is a popular destination, which can be accessed by many different trails. Trip 1-C connects to Trip 1-D for through-travelers may wish to continue to Sunnyside Canyon, another 8 miles. Those who wish to begin or end this trip via Reef Townsite Campground or Ramsey Vista Campground in Carr Canyon need to add an additional 3.5 miles of trail.

We do not recommend this section of trail in inclement weather. Since most of the route follows exposed ridgelines, lightning and snowstorms can be a real danger.

There are no Arizona Trail markers along this route. The Arizona Trail symbol has been branded into existing signs for the Crest Trail #103.

Bicycles are not allowed in the wilderness. See alternate route described in Trip 1-E.

Beginning at Montezuma Pass and ending at a spring in the Miller Peak Wilderness, this trip follows the Crest/Arizona Trail into the highest country of the Huachuca Mountains. After a steep ascent, Trip 1-C passes below the summit of Miller Peak, traveling through a majestic forest of old growth pine, aspen, and fir. The trip ends at Bathtub Spring, in a saddle tucked into the mountains between Miller and Carr Peaks.

The route offers opportunities for loop trips as it skywalks the upper reaches of the Huachucas on the backbone of an extensive network of trails. Towering cliffs, high peaks, and magnificent views stretching into Mexico and southern Arizona are highlights. This trip affords opportunities for viewing the incredible range of plant and animal species living within this sky island.

Nature Highlight: A bald eagle floating high above Miller Peak sails in slow, seemingly effortless spirals.

Maps: Coronado National Forest, Sierra Vista Ranger District.
- Hikers' Map of the Huachuca Mountains by Leonard Taylor.
- USGS Quads: Montezuma Pass, Miller Peak.

Difficulty: Difficult. A steep, long climb.

Length: 6 miles, one way.

Elevation: 6,575–9,125 feet

Recommended Season: All year, depending on the weather and snowfall in the higher elevations.

Water: (Treat all water unless noted otherwise. During dry weather, water sources may not be dependable.)

- **Montezuma Pass:** Potable water is turned off in the winter.
- **Bathtub Spring:** Water may be turned off in the winter.

Camping:

- **Montezuma Pass:** Camping is not allowed within the memorial (see Trip 1-A for detailed information on camping options).
- **Bathtub Spring:** This area is small with few level places. Remember to camp well away from water so that wildlife can access the spring. There are some comparatively level, grassy sites 0.25-mile north of the spring.

Livestock: Livestock is not allowed in the memorial except on the Crest/Arizona Trail. This strenuous trip is possible for experienced trail animals in good physical condition. There are narrow cliff-hanger sections as well as steep, rocky areas.

The memorial does not recommend trailers over 24 feet long on the section of road between the visitor center and Montezuma Pass because the road is narrow and winding. A safer option for long trailers is to access the pass from the west (Fort Huachuca or Sonoita). You must make prior arrangements with Coronado National Memorial to leave trucks and trailers overnight at the pass. Another option for long-distance travelers is to leave your rigs and have your animals transported to the trailhead (see appendix B for information on boarding and transporting livestock).

Directions to Montezuma Pass Trailhead: Passenger car. Drive south of Sierra Vista 13 miles on SR 92 to Coronado Memorial Road (FR 61). Turn right (south) on FR 61, and it is 8.2 miles to Montezuma Pass. The road is paved as it passes the national memorial visitor center on the right and a picnic area on the left. Shortly after passing the visitor center, the pavement ends. A sign warns against trucks or trailers over 24 feet in length. The route becomes a very narrow, winding mountain road with several sharp switchbacks up to the pass.

Other Area Trails:

- **Lutz Canyon Trail** travels a steep and brushy 3 miles to Ash Canyon. It is another 2.5 miles to SR 92.
- **Miller Canyon Trail #106** is a very popular day trip for hikers and equestrians. The maple and ash trees in the lower portion of this steep, 3.5-mile trail offer spectacular fall colors. The trail drops to the end of Miller Canyon Road.

TRAIL DESCRIPTION

The trailhead is on the north side of the road across from the Montezuma Pass parking lot. The Arizona Trail follows Crest Trail #103 in a steep and strenuous ascent, as it clings to the side of the mountain. Gaining a saddle, there is a fabulous first view to the west of the San Rafael Valley. To the south are vistas of Mexico. San Jose Peak is to the southeast. The green line of the distant San Pedro River and the copper mine smelter in Cananea, Mexico, are visible. The vegetation is upper Sonoran pinyon pine, oak, bear grass, and cactus.

One mile and 1,100 feet from Montezuma Pass the trail leaves the national memorial, enters Coronado National Forest, and begins a switchbacking ascent to a saddle. The trail levels, then climbs again, through scrubby, sometimes dense oak to the highest ridgeline of the range.

Four miles from Montezuma Pass, at an elevation of 8,650 feet, is the junction with Lutz Canyon Trail on the right (east). A short distance farther is a junction with the trail to Bond Spring on the left. The trail down to Bond Spring is extremely steep and overgrown. It is a struggle to reach the spring, which is disappointingly small and muddy.

This is the high country, at an elevation of over 8,500 feet. As the elevation increases, the mountainside vegetation changes from oak, to pine and fir. After the Bond Spring junction the trail becomes very rocky and steep as it switchbacks up through granite boulders. Traveling on the western side of the ridgeline, the route affords unsurpassed views of the San Raphael Valley and Mexico. To the northwest the far-away glimmer of Parker Canyon Lake, nestled in the eastern folds of the Canelo Hills, marks the distant end of the Huachuca Mountain Passage.

There is a junction with the spur trail to Miller Peak on the right, 4.5 miles from the trailhead. Many hikers yearn to be at the top of the world, and this is an opportunity to do so. A 0.5-mile climb through impressive old growth forest to the 9,466- foot peak gives you a 360-degree view of the world below. (If you look north on a clear day at the corridor of the Arizona Trail, a string of sky islands is visible. The Santa Ritas, the Rincons, and far beyond, the Santa Catalinas, rise above Sonoran "seas." The white aerostat radar balloon floating above the peaks is Fort Huachuca's "eye in the sky," today's alternative to the cavalry troops that once patrolled our border. To the east are the Mule Mountains and Bisbee, "queen of the copper camps." To the northeast the ragged Dragoon Mountains mark the location of Tombstone, Arizona, and the final resting place of Cochise.)

Continuing north on the Crest/AT, a lovely, slightly downhill walk through deep forests of towering evergreens and aspen takes us the final 1.5 miles to Bathtub Spring. In autumn the brilliant yellow leaves of the aspen create a fairyland experience. The spring brings ferns and wildflowers, giving the illusion of a rain forest.

Six miles from Montezuma Pass is Bathtub Spring and a junction with Miller Canyon Trail #106. A short distance north, the Crest/AT climbs a saddle to a junction with Carr Peak Trail #107. (To exit the AT to Carr Canyon, refer to Trip 1-D.)

Trip 1-D
Bathtub Spring to Sunnyside Canyon

 This trip begins at Bathtub Spring, and is not accessible by road. Bathtub Spring is a popular destination that can be accessed by many different trails. Those who wish to begin or end this trip at either of the campgrounds in Carr Canyon need to add an additional 3.5 miles of trail.

We do not recommend this section of trail in inclement weather. Much of the route follows exposed ridgelines, and lightning and snowstorms can be a real danger.

There are no Arizona Trail markers along this route. The Arizona Trail symbol has been branded into existing signs.

Bicycles are not allowed in the wilderness. See the alternate route for bicycles described in Trip 1-E.

Trip 1-D travels from Bathtub Spring to the Miller Peak Wilderness boundary in Sunnyside Canyon. Leaving Bathtub Spring in the shade of Canadian life zone pine, juniper, and fir, the route follows the 8,500-foot-high Crest Trail, offering scenic vistas at almost every turn.

Several side canyons and trails along the way afford the opportunity for loop trips. The canyons offer historic sites as well as sometimes rare and unusual plant and animal life. The last 2.5 miles of the trip travel down beautiful, riparian Sunnyside Canyon, past foundations and remnants of an old mine.

Nature Highlight: The trail passes a stunning Huachuca agave in full bloom. The long stalk is heavily adorned with golden bell-shaped flowers.

Maps: Coronado National Forest, Sierra Vista Ranger District.
- USGS Quads: Miller Peak, Huachuca Peak; Hiker's Map to Huachuca Mountains by Leonard Taylor.

Difficulty: Moderate, mostly downhill for through-travelers, if starting at Bathtub Spring. (If starting from Carr Canyon, there is a 3.5-mile climb.)

Length: From Bathtub Spring: 8 miles, one way. From Carr Canyon: 11.5 miles, one way.

Elevation: 8,540 feet to 5,940 feet.

Season: Year-round, depending on the weather and snowfall in the higher elevations.

Water: (Treat all water unless noted otherwise. During dry weather, water sources may not be dependable.)
- **Bathtub Spring:** Water may be turned off in the winter.
- **Reef Townsite Campground:** (3.5 miles off the route of the Arizona Trail) has potable water that is turned off in the winter.
- **Sunnyside Canyon Creek and pools:** Water may be seasonal.

Camping:
- **Bathtub Spring:** See description in Trip 1-C.
- **Reef Townsite Campground in Carr Canyon:** This is a developed, fee area campground with potable water (turned off in the winter). It is not convenient for through-travelers but can be used for day or loop trips. The campground is located in Carr Canyon, 3.5 miles down the mountain from Bathtub Spring on Trail #107, at the site of an old mining camp that was active in the late 1800s. The facility offers single-unit sites with tables and grills and an interpretive loop trail. It is 6.8 miles down Carr Canyon Road to SR 92 (see directions to trailhead).

- **Ramsey Vista Campground in Carr Canyon:** This campground, 1.5 miles west of Reef Townsite, offers developed campsites and public horse corrals, but there is no water.
- **Sunnyside Canyon:** There are primitive camping areas along the creek, the road, and in upper Sunnyside Canyon.

Livestock: Access to Bathtub Spring from Miller Canyon or Carr Canyon is possible for experienced trail animals in good physical condition. All routes have rocky, narrow areas and steep switchbacks.
- **Ramsey Vista Campground** has public corrals but no water.
- **Upper Sunnyside Canyon** offers inviting camping possibilities with seasonal pools of water along the creek and abundant grass.

Directions to Carr Canyon Trailheads: There is no vehicle access to Bathtub Spring, but it can be reached from two trailheads in Carr Canyon, which can be accessed by passenger car. Travel south from Sierra Vista on SR 92 for 7 miles to Carr Canyon Road. Turn right (west) on Carr Canyon Road. It is 6.8 miles from SR 92 to the Reef Townsite campground. The paved road soon turns to gravel as it climbs steeply with hairpin turns, blind corners, and the possibility of snow and ice in the winter. The trailhead is directly across from the campground. There is a $2.00 parking fee to use this trail, which connects with the Carr Peak Trail #107.

Approximately 1.5 miles west, Carr Canyon Road ends at a second campground, Ramsey Vista, which offers developed campsites and public horse corrals but no water. This is the trailhead for Carr Peak Trail #107.

Other Area Trails:
- **Miller Canyon Trail:** See description in Trip 1-C.
- **Carr Peak Trail #107** is thought by some to be the easiest access to Bathtub Spring. This 3.5-mile trail travels from the Crest Trail to Ramsey Vista Campground, with a right fork that travels to Reef Townsite Campground in Carr Canyon. (From Reef Townsite it is another 6.8 miles to SR 92.) This steep, scenic mountainside trail travels through an extensive burn area that now supports groves of young aspen and grassy areas dotted with wildflowers in the summer.
- **Oversite Canyon Trail** travels south a steep 3 miles to an old road, which eventually links to FR 61.
- **Bear Canyon (Ida Canyon) Trail** drops south to Bear Spring and a junction. From Bear Spring two trails, Ida Canyon Trail and Bear Canyon Trail, travel down to FR 61.
- **Ramsey Canyon Trail** travels northeast, linking to other trails on the east side of the range. The trail terminates at the Ramsey Canyon Preserve.

TRAIL DESCRIPTION

Leaving Bathtub Spring the Arizona Trail follows Crest Trail #103. The route passes the junction with Miller Canyon Trail #106, then travels north, climbing the ridge to a saddle and junction with Carr Peak Trail #107 on the right. One-quarter of a mile above the spring are some comparatively level and grassy camping possibilities. The route travels to the southwest side of the ridge, affording magnificent vistas of Lone Mountain, Mexico, and the San Rafael Valley. Traveling through a mixed forest of pine, oak, and madrone, the trail switchbacks down past several Huachuca agave.

There is a junction with Oversite Canyon Trail #112 0.8 mile from Bathtub Spring. From the junction the route treads through an array of granite outcroppings with nice views to the west of the San Rafael Valley and the Patagonia Mountains. The long, low formation that you see is Lone Mountain. From here, travel is fairly level to Bear Saddle through a delightful forest of massive pines.

One and one-half miles from the spring is Bear Saddle and a four-way junction. Bear Canyon/Ida Canyon Trail drops away to the south, eventually accessing FR 61. To the right (north) is the Wisconsin Trail, which eventually leads to the Ramsey Canyon Preserve (no livestock). Bear Canyon Trail travels 0.5-mile, with a 500-foot drop in elevation to Bear Spring. The area offers dependable water and level areas beneath huge ponderosa and alligator juniper trees.

The Crest/AT continues to the west. From Bear Saddle the route climbs steadily as it circles the south side of Granite Peak. The trail travels first on the south and then on the north side of the ridge as it climbs moderately through pine and oak forest. Each time the route crosses a saddle travelers are afforded far-reaching views of Parker Canyon Lake to the west and the San Pedro River Valley and the suburbs of Sierra Vista to the east.

The junction with Pat Scott Canyon Trail #123 offers views of Ramsey Peak and the wedding cake–layered cliffs of Ramsey Canyon. The views of the surrounding valleys and mountains are impressive. The trail circles the summit of the peak past a huge, ancient alligator juniper. (The trip to Scott Peak, a bushwhack of about 0.1 of a mile, rewards you with far-reaching vistas.)

There is a junction with Sunnyside Canyon Trail #117—which may also be signed as Copper Glance Trail—3.3 miles from Bathtub Spring. This open, level area offers an inviting rest stop, with wildflowers to enjoy in spring and summer. The Arizona Trail abandons the Crest Trail here and follows Sunnyside Canyon Trail #117 to the left. The route follows an old wire fence line, then makes a steep, switchbacking descent down a well-defined trail. The route passes a mine shaft on the left and a trail junction 1.2 miles from the Crest Trail. A sign indicates that the trail bends right (north). The steep switchbacks end, and soon after, the trail drops into upper Sunnyside Canyon.

Five and one-half miles from Bathtub Spring the trail passes an old stone well on the right and the remains of the Copper Glance mining camp. An abandoned road becomes a gently descending route through the riparian canyon. Here, walnut and sycamore trees are home to a large variety of birds in the spring and summer (watch for the extremely rare elegant trogan). The creek offers small pools of water or a rushing stream, depending upon the season and rainfall.

The trail follows along or above the creek bed for the next 2.5 miles. The trail passes old stone foundations and a cement tank within a wire holding pen is an excellent watering opportunity for livestock. It is only a short distance from here to the wilderness boundary and trailhead.

Trip 1-E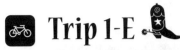

Alternate Bicycle Route Around the Miller Peak Wilderness from Montezuma Pass to Sunnyside Canyon

Bicycles are not allowed within the wilderness area, so we suggest cyclists take this route as the alternate to Trips 1-C and 1-D.

This is a scenic and challenging ride on a winding, rolling, gravel road that offers spectacular views of the Miller Peak Wilderness, Old Mexico, and the San Raphael Valley. From high atop Montezuma Pass, the route swings down around the southern perimeter of the wilderness and rejoins the Arizona Trail in Sunnyside Canyon. Or you have the option of cycling directly to Parker Canyon Lake.

Nature Highlight: Watch for wild turkey and other wildlife in Sunnyside Canyon.

Maps: Coronado National Forest, Sierra Vista Ranger District.

Difficulty: Moderate. The mostly downhill route is narrow, winding, and sometimes steep. Some sections may be very rocky, washboarded, or have loose gravel. Drainages that cross the road may be flooded in rainy weather.

Length: It is 19 miles from Montezuma Pass to Sunnyside Trailhead. It is an additional 5.4 miles to the Parker Canyon Lake (Overlook) Trailhead following the Arizona Trail to the end of this passage.

> or

It is 19 miles from Montezuma Pass to Parker Canyon Lake, staying on gravel roads.

Elevation: 6,575 feet to 5,400 feet.

Recommended Season: All seasons, depending on the weather.

Water: (Treat all water unless noted otherwise. During dry weather, water sources may not be dependable.)

- **Montezuma Pass:** Has potable water that is turned off during the winter months.
- **Bear Canyon:** Has seasonal water and is 13 miles east of Montezuma Pass.
- **Sunnyside Canyon Creek:** Water is seasonal.
- **Parker Canyon Lake:** Has potable water.

Camping: Camping is not allowed within the national memorial. There are primitive camping opportunities along FR 61.

- **Sunnyside Canyon:** Has primitive camping.
- **Parker Canyon Lake (Overlook) trailhead:** Has primitive camping.
- **Parker Canyon Lake:** Has a developed campground. (See the Canelo Hills Passage.)

Directions to Montezuma Pass: See directions provided in Trip 1-A or 1-C.

ROUTE DESCRIPTION

From the scenic overlook at Montezuma Pass, take FR 61 as it travels west. As it passes from the Coronado National Memorial boundary into the Coronado National Forest, the road makes a steep and winding descent.

Watch for a sign for Copper Canyon 1.3 miles from the pass as FR 61 crosses a wash, which may hold water. (To the left [south] is the alternate bicycle and equestrian route to the Mexico border.)

Four and two-tenths miles from the pass, FR 61 passes FR #771 on the right and a sign for Oversight Canyon.

FR 61 crosses the bridge over Bear Creek 6.2 miles from Montezuma Pass. A little farther on the left, Bear Canyon offers some nice swimming holes seasonally and flat areas to camp. This is a popular local camping spot, so firewood is scarce.

The oak and juniper of the Huachuca Mountain foothills give way to the Chihuahuan grasslands of the San Raphael Valley. The road travels along the edge of a golden rolling savanna, rimmed by distant mountains and the blue Arizona sky. At 8.9 miles from the pass you meet a junction with FR 48. Turn onto FR 48 and follow it toward Parker Canyon Lake. (FR 61 curves left and parallels the U.S.-Mexico border for 42 miles to Nogales, Arizona, an international port of entry.)

Twelve miles from Montezuma Pass, FR 48 passes a junction with FR 227 and travels a short distance farther to a junction with FR 228 on the right. Here you have two options:

1) You can continue on FR 48 for 3 miles to Parker Canyon Lake, which offers a small store and a developed campground,

   or

2) You can take FR 228 3 miles to Sunnyside Canyon and pick up the Arizona Trail as it exits the Miller Peak Wilderness.

Option 1): Follow FR 48 as it makes a steep, winding descent toward the lake. There is a sign on the left for South Lake Drive 1.5 miles past the FR 228 turnoff. (South Lake Drive does not take you to Parker Canyon Lake, but it does take you 0.5-mile to the Arizona Trail trailhead, which overlooks the lake and marks the end of the Huachuca Mountains Passage. There is primitive camping here, with no water.) Continue following FR 48 0.5 mile to the junction with SR 83. Turn left to access the lake and the campground.

Option 2): Turn north on FR 228 and travel 1 mile to an *unsigned* junction. Go left down a rocky, rutted dirt road for 1.7 miles to a T junction. Turn right on FR 204 to Sunnyside Canyon. FR 204 curves left and crosses Sunnyside Creek to another unsigned T junction. The Miller Peak Wilderness (Arizona Trail) trailhead is to the left about 0.5 mile. From the Miller Peak Wilderness border, following the Arizona Trail through Scotia Canyon, it is 5.4 miles to the Parker Canyon Lake (Overlook) trailhead (see Trip 1-F).

Trip 1-F
Sunnyside Canyon to Parker Canyon Lake (Overlook) Trailhead

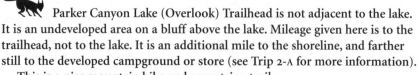 Parker Canyon Lake (Overlook) Trailhead is not adjacent to the lake. It is an undeveloped area on a bluff above the lake. Mileage given here is to the trailhead, not to the lake. It is an additional mile to the shoreline, and farther still to the developed campground or store (see Trip 2-A for more information).

This is a nice mountain bike and equestrian trail.

Beginning in Sunnyside Canyon at the Miller Peak Wilderness boundary, the Arizona Trail travels to a trailhead located on a hill above Parker Canyon Lake.

The Arizona Trail travels through a sycamore-shaded canyon and grassy meadows with views of the Canelo Hills and the Huachuca Mountains. The area offers multiple trails through the foothills of the Huachucas, and opportunities for observing birds and wildlife are abundant. Fishing supplies, boat rentals, and a developed campground are available at Parker Canyon Lake.

Nature Highlight: Watch for small coues deer, wild turkeys, hummingbirds, and the rare elegant trogan in Sunnyside and Scotia Canyons. Parker Canyon Lake is a haven for waterfowl and nesting bald eagles.

Difficulty: Easy.

Length: 5.4 miles, one way.

Elevation: 5,940–5,600 feet.

Recommended Season: Year-round, depending on the weather.

Water: (Treat all water unless noted otherwise. During dry weather, water sources may not be dependable.)
- **Sunnyside Canyon:** Water may be seasonal.
- **Scotia Canyon:** Water may be seasonal.

If the canyons are dry, follow FR 228 toward Gate #7 to some ponds on the right side of the road.

Maps: Coronado National Forest, Nogales and Sierra Vista Ranger Districts.
- USGS Quad: Huachuca Peak.

Camping:
- **Sunnyside Canyon:** Primitive. Flat, shady areas to camp, and water is seasonal.
- **Scotia Canyon:** Primitive. There is a large parking area on the west side of FR 228. Unless it is a very dry year, water is less than 0.25 mile north in Scotia Canyon.
- **Parker Canyon Lake (Overlook) trailhead:** (See Trip 2-A.)
- **Lakeview Campground:** (See Trip 2-A.)

Livestock: There is usually water in upper Sunnyside Canyon (the southern route of the Arizona Trail into the Miller Peak Wilderness. You can pull off FR 204 and park, but do not attempt to pull a trailer to the wilderness boundary.

A more accessible area is in Scotia Canyon, FR 228, where it may be possible to pull a horse trailer up the very steep hill. It is only 0.2-mile to a nice primitive campsite on the left, where the Arizona Trail intersects the road. If the road is deeply rutted you may need to unload livestock first and walk them up the hill. There is ample parking at the top for up to six trucks and trailers. There are two small wire corrals approximately 20 feet in diameter. Water is usually available where FR 228 crosses Scotia Creek, 0.25 mile north.

Parker Canyon Lake (Overlook) trailhead has a good horse or llama corral 200 feet east of the trailhead.

Directions to Sunnyside (Miller Peak Wilderness) Trailhead: High-clearance vehicles are recommended for the last 3 miles, although they may be passable by passenger car, depending on when the road was last graded. Do not attempt to drive the last 0.5 mile to the wilderness boundary. There are no gas stations after leaving Sonoita or Sierra Vista.

If traveling from Tucson, take Interstate 10 east to Sonoita exit 281. The Sunnyside Canyon trailhead is approximately 60 miles south of Interstate 10. From Sonoita, SR 83 takes a sharp left, then travels south 29 miles toward Parker Canyon Lake. As it enters Coronado National Forest the pavement ends and SR 83 becomes a graded dirt road.

If you are coming from Sierra Vista through the west gate of Fort Huachuca, you will need a valid driver's license, vehicle registration, and proof of liability insurance. Call (520) 533-7373 or (520) 538-7111 for information. When you stop at the main gate for your pass, ask for directions to the west gate. From the west gate, follow the graded dirt road #827 approximately 5 miles to SR 83. Turn left (south) toward Parker Canyon Lake, traveling another 10 miles.

SR 83 ends at the lake turnoff junction of 48 and 48D. Turn left (south) on Forest Road 48. This narrow, dirt road winds uphill for 2.2 miles (passing South Lake Drive on the left—the access road to Parker Canyon Lake [Overlook] trailhead) to a junction with FR 228 to Sunnyside. Turn left (north) on FR 228 and proceed one mile to an unmarked junction. Go left down a rocky, rutted dirt road for another 1.7 miles to a T junction. FR 204 goes right to Sunnyside Canyon, the Miller Peak Wilderness boundary, and the Copper Glance mine. Scotia Canyon is to the left on FR 228 toward gate number 7.

From this point there are two ways to access the Arizona Trail:

• **Sunnyside Canyon and the Miller Peak Wilderness Boundary.** To access the Miller Peak Wilderness trailhead in Sunnyside Canyon follow FR 204 right. At 0.2-mile FR 204 takes a sharp left and continues a short distance, crossing Sunnyside Creek to an unmarked T junction. There are some pleasant, shaded, and relatively level areas for camping in this area. Watch for wildlife in this peaceful riparian setting. The wilderness trailhead is to the left about a half mile. We recommend that you park here and walk to the trailhead. The road in is extremely rough, and there is little room at the trailhead to park or turn a vehicle. At 0.3 mile the Arizona Trail coming from Scotia Canyon on the left (west) joins the road.

• **Scotia Canyon.** You can also access the Arizona Trail by taking FR 228 left, toward gate number 7. It is 0.2-mile up over a very steep and deeply rutted hill to an intersection with the Arizona Trail.

Other Area Trails: Continuing on FR 228 (4WD recommended) will take you to some perennial ponds, Peterson Ranch, and the Lyle Canyon trailhead.

TRAIL DESCRIPTION

Leaving the wilderness boundary in Sunnyside Canyon, the Arizona Trail follows the 4WD dirt road a short distance and then drops off to the right (west), crossing Sunnyside Creek. Watch for brown fiberglass markers with the AT symbol. The trail follows the creek for awhile and then heads west over some low pinyon-, oak-, and manzanita-studded hills. Approximately 0.5 mile from the wilderness boundary the trail crosses FR 228 (the gate #7 road) and enters a large, open parking area with two wire corrals.

Traveling west, the trail crosses the parking area and drops down a rocky trail into sycamore-shaded Scotia Canyon. Although the streambed may be dry at this crossing, water can usually be found up- and downstream from this point. The trail crosses the streambed to an Arizona Trail marker and then parallels the creek as it wanders down the gentle grade of Scotia Canyon. The trail is shaded and almost level, with an abundance of grass. Crossing the small stream frequently, the trail follows traces of an old road through the beautiful sycamore-, oak-, and juniper-lined canyon.

The trail arrives at a grassy area, with a windmill and barbwire corral 1.3 miles from FR 228. Signs are posted here to remind us not to camp within 0.25 mile of water. The trail leaves the windmill, descending to a rocky stream crossing signed with an Arizona Trail marker.

The trail again follows remnants of an abandoned road until it exits the creek bed on the right and follows a winding route through an oak and juniper forest. Pieces of partially buried black, plastic pipe are visible along this section. Scotia Canyon gradually turns to the south, as the trail follows along the right, or west, side. This is a very pleasant, almost level walk. The trail winds down to a wash, crossing to the south and passing a rock cairn. It then follows a small incline and joins an unsigned little-used forest road coming in from the left.

Immediately after this junction the trail crosses Scotia Creek once again, where it is joined by a tiny creeklet coming in from the left. Watch for the trail marker as you cross here, indicating that the trail leaves the road, heading west. The path follows along sparkling Scotia Creek, until it eventually rejoins an abandoned dirt road coming from the left. One hundred feet farther, there is a junction with an unsigned little-used road on the right.

An Arizona Trail marker indicates that the route continues past this junction and drops back down to the streambed. Continue on the abandoned track along the west side of the creek, noticing the beautiful pools created by the rocky walls of the east bank.

The trail arrives at a fence and a gate with an open meadow and picturesque but noisy windmill beyond. The area is surrounded by low foothills dotted with oak. The Arizona Trail does not go through the gate but turns to the left, or south, to a rocky creek crossing. Having crossed the creek, the trail heads west, roller-coastering up and down through a dense oak forest and closely following a barb-wire fence on the right. As you follow the trail, it skirts around the meadow; on a breezy day, you may be accompanied by the windmill's mournful song. The trail crests a hill arriving at a Forest Service gate. Take the opportunity to look back for a view of Huachuca Peak to the east. From here it is a short distance down to Forest Road 48.

Four and one-half miles from the Miller Peak Wilderness trailhead is the junction with Forest Road 48, a graded dirt road. Looking west, you can see the perimeter of the rolling Canelo Hill region. Cross the road heading southwest and look for an Arizona Trail marker as the trail descends through an oak and juniper forest to a pleasant, grassy glen with large oak shade trees.

The trail continues a short distance and intersects a little-used dirt road that comes in from FR 48. The trail continues, paralleling the road on the right and a barbwire fence on the left. It follows the fence line up a steep hill and then veers off to the right. *The trail is faint in places* as it proceeds up a grassy hill marked with rock cairns. To the northeast is a skyline view of the Huachuca Mountains, and if it's not too windy, the white, aerostat balloon will be floating above Fort Huachuca.

At the crest of the hill the path crosses a little-used dirt road, with trail markers on each side, directing you across the junction and down into a shallow drainage. The route curves sharply left, and as it climbs out of the drainage, the pathway is marked by rows of rocks along each side.

As the trail ascends the hill, from FR 48, it approaches an old corral with mesh fencing, suitable for horses and llamas, and a wire gate. The views as you pass through the gate and proceed up the hill are of the Canelo Hills, gently undulating on toward Patagonia. To the east are spectacular views of the Huachucas. Follow the path a short distance until it gains the top of the ridge.

It is 200 feet to the official trailhead overlooking Parker Canyon Lake, with splendid views of the lake below. There is an Arizona Trail sign that states that this is a Heritage Fund project. This trailhead is accessed by taking South Lake Drive from Forest Road 48. For information on Parker Canyon Lake, directions to the Parker Canyon Lake (Overlook) trailhead, and directions on watering livestock at the lake, see Canelo Hills Passage and Trip 2-A.

A view of cattle and the Canelo Hills by a remote water tank as seen along the Canelo Hills Passage.

Dream of the prairie
Dream of the wild wind
Dream of the grasses belly high.
Dream of the old days
Dream of the riders
They lope beneath the endless prairie sky.

All that I can do is dream my dream,
And in my mind there's one more ride.
A good strong horse between my legs,
We roam the prairie stride by stride.

— **"Dream of the Prairie," by John A. Ryberg II**
(Used with permission.)

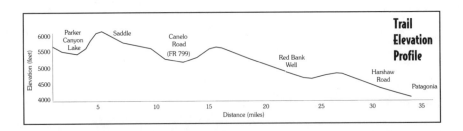

2 Canelo Hills Passage
Parker Canyon Lake to Patagonia

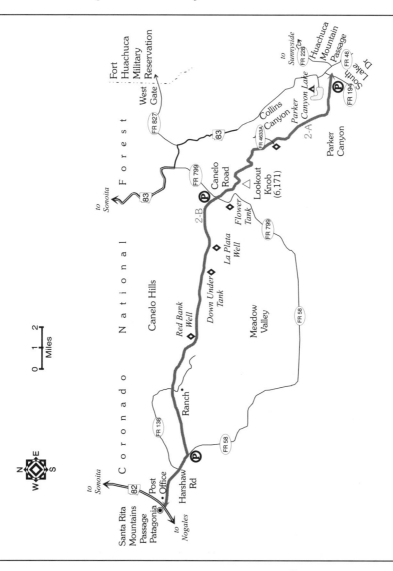

Fort Huachuca Military Reservation

West Gate

FR 827

Forest

83

to Sonoita

to Sunnyside

FR 228

Huachuca Mountain Passage

FR 48

South Lake Dr

FR 194

Collins Canyon

Parker Canyon Lake

FR 4634A

83

2-A

Parker Canyon

FR 799

Canelo Road

2-B

Lookout Knob (6,171)

Flower Tank

La Plata Well

FR 799

FR 58

Canelo Hills

National

Red Bank Well

Down Under Tank

Meadow Valley

Coronado

Ranch

FR 138

FR 58

Miles
0 1 2

N
E
W
S

to Sonoita

82

Post Office

Harshaw Rd

Santa Rita Mountains Passage

Patagonia

to Nogales

	Forest Road		Boundary		Trailhead and Parking
	Paved Road		River, Stream, or Wash		Trailhead, no Parking
	State/Interstate		Canyon Rim		Parking
	Arizona Trail		Campground		Town or City
	Trip Access Trail		Water		Point of Interest
	Other Trail Area		Ranger Station		Mountain Peak

THIS 33-MILE PASSAGE comprises two trips. Trip 2-A travels for 13.4 miles, from Parker Canyon Lake (Overlook) to Canelo Pass (FR 799). Trip 2-B travels 20 miles, from Canelo Pass to Patagonia.

This passage features rolling oak- and pine-covered hills that blend into a rolling grassland savanna. Bordered by the Huachuca Mountains on the east and the Santa Ritas on the north, they extend almost to Mexico, spanning part of two counties. This passage offers magnificent views of surrounding mountain ranges and the vast, rolling grasslands of Meadow and San Rafael Valleys.

Nestled in the oak woodland foothills at the southeastern perimeter of the Canelos is Parker Canyon Lake. The 80-acre lake offers multiple recreation opportunities: fishing, boating, camping, and a hiking trail around the shoreline. Birding is especially good for ducks, bald eagles, osprey, and several varieties of hummingbird. This is an excellent area to spot wildlife; coatimundi are frequently seen.

Three springs located in a narrow valley probably account for why John Parker chose to build the old Parker homestead where Parker Canyon Lake is today. The homestead was established in 1882. When the last owner, Jim Hathaway, died the homestead was unoccupied for many years. The U.S. Forest Service and the Arizona Game and Fish Department began negotiations in 1960 to acquire the area for a dam and lake. The dam was completed in 1962, creating a lake that eventually covered the site of the homestead.

The route of the Arizona Trail passes near the small community of Elgin, renowned for its vineyards and winery, and ends in the charming little town of Patagonia. Both communities were established in the late 1800s. A railroad line was constructed in 1882, from Benson to Nogales. This line connected to a railroad line from Guaymas, Mexico, on the Gulf Coast to Nogales. One of the stations on the line is north of the Canelo Hills on the Babocomari River at Elgin. The train carried freight, cattle, and passengers, which helped the extensive ranching in this area. The last train came to Elgin in 1958. Many television and movie productions are filmed in this scenic area. One of the best-known films of the past is the musical Oklahoma, and more recently, the movie Tombstone was filmed here.

Gold, silver, lead, and copper attracted thousands to the area in the late 1880s. This is part of a historic mining district that included towns of up to 2,000 residents. Sunnyside, Mowry, Duquesne, and Harshaw are some of the mining towns that once flourished in the area. In most cases, little remains except the shafts, some quite treacherous. The towns are considered ghost towns today.

The town of Patagonia is nestled in the valley at 4,044 feet elevation. The population of 1,000 creates a small and quaint town atmosphere. This picturesque cattle town, with a distinct mining flavor, is situated on the Arizona Trail between two of the mountain passages: the Santa Rita Passage and the Canelo Hills Passage. Patagonia was also a railroad town. The abandoned railroad line is part of the National Rails to Trails system. You will find it in the Patagonia–Sonoita Creek Preserve used as a scenic walk through the preserve.

The Sonoita Creek runs near town and supports dense and varied riparian cottonwood-willow forest. The Patagonia-Sonoita Creek Sanctuary is managed by the Nature Conservancy as a wildlife sanctuary, which is open for tours. There are at least three hundred species of birds, native fish, and animals. Songbirds are prevalent as well as rare hawks and kites.

For Arizona Trail travelers Patagonia offers the convenience of a post office, shopping, feed store, horse boarding, restaurants, hotels, and guest ranches. A Patagonia Affair, a fall festival, is presented annually the third week of October. In 1995 the opening of two passages of the Arizona Trail, the Canelo Hills Passage and the Santa Rita Mountain Passage, was celebrated during the fair. The opening and dedication were attended by hikers, mountain bike groups, equestrians, and the Llama and Alpaca Association of Arizona.

GOVERNING AGENCIES

Coronado National Forest, Sierra Vista Ranger District, 5990 S. Highway 92, Hereford, AZ 85615. (520) 378-0311.

FOR MORE INFORMATION

The Patagonia Tourist Information Office, P.O. Box 214, Patagonia, AZ 85624. (520) 394-0060.

"A Self-Guided Auto Tour of Scenic Southern Arizona, The Patagonia Adventure," 1994, M & K Associates.

The Nature Conservancy, P.O. Box 815, Patagonia, AZ 85624, (520) 394-0060.

NEAREST SERVICES TO PARKER LAKE

Parker Lake store, Sierra Vista, or Sonoita. (See Trip 1-f, Directions To Trailhead and Appendix A).

Trip 2-A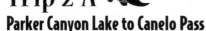
Parker Canyon Lake to Canelo Pass

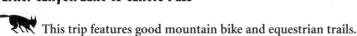 This trip features good mountain bike and equestrian trails.

From beautiful Parker Canyon Lake, nestled in the foothills of the Huachuca Mountains, Trip 2-A travels through the rolling, golden landscape of the Canelo Hills to Canelo Pass and FR 799. The route follows newly built trail and abandoned dirt roads through a hilly terrain dotted with oak, juniper, manzanita, and pine. Opportunities for viewing wildlife from two very distinct habitats are excellent, as the trail travels from lake side into a desert grassland environment. Ridgelines afford fine vistas of the surrounding southern Arizona mountain ranges.

Nature Highlight: Entering the bottom of a dry arroyo, we startled a small group of javelina. Tiny hooves clattering on the loose rocks, they disappeared into the brush.

Maps:
* Coronado National Forest Recreation Map.
* USGS Quads: Huachuca Peak, Canelo Pass, O'Donnell Canyon.

Difficulty: Moderate to difficult.

Length: 13.4 miles, one way.

Elevation: 5,230–6,100 feet.

Recommended Season: Year-round, depending on the weather.

Water: (Treat all water unless noted otherwise. During dry weather, water sources may not be dependable.)
* **Parker Canyon Lake:** Potable water available.
* **FR 4633A:** Dirt tank.
* **Canelo Pass Road:** Dirt tank.

Camping: Trailhead at Parker Canyon Lake (Overlook): There is a parking area that will accommodate several cars, trucks, and trailers. There are primitive camping possibilities near the trailhead and along South Lake Drive with views of the lake below. If you will be driving in, bring your own firewood and water.

Lakeview Campground: There is a developed campground at Parker Canyon Lake. The campground is open year-round, with sixty-five single-unit sites. The campground does not allow livestock. This is a fee campground with drinking water available. There is also a convenience store with fishing supplies, and boat rentals. There is no lodging available at the lake.

Livestock: Livestock are not allowed at Lakeview Campground. Parker Canyon Lake (Overlook) trailhead has two good, smooth-wire corrals 200 yards east, just below the parking area. There is no water, and grazing is limited. It is approximately 1 mile down to the lake to water livestock (see the trail description). This trip is strenuous, and availability of water depends on rainfall. There is a dirt stock tank 8 miles north along the route.

Directions to Trailhead: The trailhead can be accessed by passenger car. There are no gas stations after leaving Sonoita or Fort Huachuca. If traveling from Tucson, take Interstate 10 east to Sonoita exit 281. Parker Canyon Lake is approximately 55 miles south of Interstate 10. From Sonoita, SR 83 takes a sharp left, then travels south 29 miles toward Parker Canyon Lake. As SR 83 enters Coronado National Forest, the pavement ends and it becomes a graded dirt road.

If you are coming from Sierra Vista through the west gate of Fort Huachuca, you will need a valid driver's license, vehicle registration, and proof of liability insurance. Call 533-7373 or 538-7111 for information. When you stop at the main gate for your pass, ask for directions to the west gate. From the west gate, follow dirt road 827 approximately 5 miles to SR 83. Turn left (south) toward Parker Canyon Lake and travel another 10 miles.

SR 83 ends at the lake turnoff junction of 48 and 48D. Turn left on FR 48. This narrow dirt road winds uphill 0.5-mile to South Lake Drive on the right, just before a cattle guard. Turn right and follow South Lake Drive 0.5-mile to the large parking area for the Arizona Trail.

Other Area Trails: The 4.5-mile **Lakeshore Trail** travels around the perimeter of Parker Canyon Lake. Lakeshore Trail provides access from the AT to both the Lakeview Campground on the east side of the lake and the marina and store at the southeastern end of the lake.

TRAIL DESCRIPTION

The Canelo Hills East/Arizona Trail travels downhill to the west, following an abandoned dirt road with excellent views of the lake. Approximately 1 mile from the trailhead, the route passes a "no vehicle" sign and an abandoned road that leads down to the lake. (Turn right and follow this route to water livestock, or access the 4.5-mile Lakeshore Trail.) The Canelo Hills/Arizona Trail continues up a steep hill to a vantage point that offers excellent views of the surrounding mountain ranges.

The route travels northwest along a level ridge, then winds through low hills dotted with oak and juniper.

Two miles from the trailhead the trail arrives at a Forest Service gate and a junction. Rock cairns direct the route east. The trail winds down through trees into riparian Parker Canyon. Down-canyon from the earthen dam is Parker Canyon Lake, large Arizona ash trees and pools of water suggest that this may be a dependable water source. The trail crosses the canyon then travels uphill to a gate.

As the trail becomes faint in places, watch closely for rock cairns directing the trail northwest. The route meanders in and out of a minor drainage and the trail occasionally disappears in the sand and rocks of the wash. Chihuahua Pines provide some shade here. Leaving the drainage, the well-signed trail rolls over the hills. Heading northwest, the route gains 300 feet as it follows a steeply ascending ridgeline, offering wide open views.

The trail arrives in a saddle marked by an Arizona Trail sign and an old metal trough, 4.2 miles from the trailhead. The route leaves the saddle, skirting around some high hills, then ascends a very steep ridgeline to an elevation of 6,100 feet.

Six miles from the trailhead, a high saddle affords expansive views of the vast grasslands of the San Rafael Valley and Mexico. The descent from the ridge is steep as the trail switchbacks down through oak into the rugged and beautiful upper Collins Canyon. Shaded by tall pines, the path travels toward a distinctive, weathered rock wall. A signed junction indicates a left (west) turn through a gate.

The trees open to frame a vista of the Santa Rita Mountains and Mount Wrightson, as the trail travels northwest through the gate. The trail threads through a wooded canyon to a gate, where it abandons the shade of big trees to travel along the exposed, south-facing drainage. Leaving the canyon, the trail intersects an abandoned dirt road and comes to an Arizona Trail marker. Following the old road as it curves uphill to the left, there are fabulous views of the Rincons, Santa Ritas, Huachucas, and the Whetstones. An Arizona Trail marker indicates that the route turns west, following an abandoned road and a fence line. The route passes what appears to be an old engine atop a rusted tank on the right.

Eight and two-tenths miles from the trailhead, the route intersects FR 4633A, a 4WD road leading near the Canelo Ranger Station. The route passes through a gate, making a U-turn to the southwest, then travels steeply downhill. Off the trail to the left is a dirt tank at the bottom of the hill. The quality and quantity of water in the tank varies, depending on rainfall.

The Arizona Trail continues to a gate in a lovely drainage with grass, oaks, and mixed evergreens. This is a pleasant lunch site, with ample shade. The trail continues a short distance, under the shade of the forest, to an intersection with another abandoned dirt road. The route turns left (south), climbing manzanita-covered hills with views of the Whetstones and Huachucas. The trail then descends into a rocky canyon.

In the canyon you come to a junction where the trail leaves the road to the right (west), climbs a ridge, then drops into another little rocky canyon that may have pools of water, depending upon how recently it has rained. As the trail leaves the canyon and ascends a steep hill, there are views of rugged canyons on both sides, with wonderfully sculpted rock. Here you can find pretty pieces of quartz along the trail. A prominent landmark, Lookout Knob, stands like a sentinel above the trail. The destination of the trail is a saddle to the right of the knob. Several switchbacks and spectacular views later the trail arrives at a saddle of 5,720 feet elevation.

The trail leaves the saddle north of Lookout Knob 11.9 miles from the trailhead, and follows a long, high ridgeline with scenic far-reaching views. The distant Dragoon Mountains near Tombstone are visible to the east, the Mustang Mountains, the Whetstones, and Santa Ritas are visible to the north, and the San Rafael Valley, to the west. The trail travels through a gate, then continues along the ridgeline to a view overlooking Canelo Pass Road. From here it is a steep and rocky descent into Canelo Pass and FR 799. Pass through the gate, turn right, and follow FR 799 0.8-mile to the Canelo Pass trailhead on the left (west) side of the road.

(If you need to water livestock, turn left on FR 799 and travel a short distance to a dirt track on the west side of the road, which leads to a dirt stock tank within a corral. Be sure to leave gates as you find them.)

Trip 2-B

Canelo Pass to Harshaw Road to Patagonia

Some sections of this trail pass through areas of whitethorn (known locally as the "wait-a-minute bush"). The plant is well named, for it snags passersby, causing them to have to stop and disengage themselves. Although pruned back from the trail, it grows quickly. Wear long pants or chaps on this trail.

This trip ends at Harshaw Road, and it is another 3 miles to Patagonia. As of this writing, no off-road route has been identified. We have included directions to Patagonia for through-travelers.

Harshaw Road is an excellent route for mountain bikes. The dirt road system south of the trailhead is extensive, going all the way to the Mexican border.

Trip 2-B travels from Canelo Pass (FR 799) to the Harshaw Road trailhead. It is another 3 miles to Patagonia, following a paved road.

Originating in the heart of the Canelo Hills, this trip winds through shallow canyons and rolling hills, with excellent vantage points for viewing distant mountain ranges. The route passes through a riparian area rich with trees displaying colorful foliage, depending upon the season. The cliffs and bluffs of the canyons exhibit striking colors. The main feature of this trip is Red Bank, a spectacular red wall in Red Rock Canyon.

The end of this trip features a visit to the charming, small community of Patagonia, as the Arizona Trail passes the small post office.

Nature Highlight: A solitary coatimundi dashes up into an oak tree then eyes us suspiciously from behind his long, pointed nose.

Maps: Coronado National Forest, Nogales and Sierra Vista Ranger Districts.
* USGS Quads: Mt. Hughes, O'Donnell Canyon.

Difficulty: Moderate. A long trip with some steep grades.

Length: 17 miles, one way, to Harshaw Road. 20 miles, one way, to Patagonia.

Elevation: 4,670–5,720 feet.

Recommended Season: Year-round, depending on the weather.

Water: (Treat all water unless noted otherwise. During dry weather, water sources may not be dependable.)
* **Dirt stock tank:** 0.8-mile south of the trailhead on FR 799.
* **La Plata Tank.**
* **Down Under Tank.**
* **Red Bank stock tank.**
* **Redrock Canyon** has an intermittent stream.

Camping:
* **Canelo Pass trailhead:** The trailhead has signs indicating no camping. There are primitive camping areas in the national norest along FR 799. One-half mile north of the trailhead on FR 799, is an area with ample room for several trailers or cars. The site offers the shade of many large oaks.
* **Harshaw Road trailhead:** There are no developed campgrounds at the trailhead or in the town of Patagonia. Primitive camping is allowed within the national forest.

Livestock:
* **Canelo Pass trailhead:** There is a hitching post here, and a dirt tank 0.8-mile south on FR 799 on the west side of the road. There is water along the trail for livestock. The trip has several steep grades, and animals need to be well conditioned for this long trip.
* **Harshaw Road trailhead:** There is a hitching post here and some grass but no water. There is a feed store in Patagonia, and a local outfitter may have corrals available. (See appendix B for information on boarding and transporting livestock.) Use caution and watch for traffic if crossing from the trailhead or following Harshaw Road into Patagonia.

Directions to Canelo Hills Trailhead: You can access the area by passenger car. The road is paved from SR 83 in Sonoita to within 3 miles of the trailhead. From Sonoita take SR 83 south toward Parker Canyon Lake to the junction of FR 799. Take FR 799 south (straight) toward Lochiel. Travel 2.6 miles on this graded dirt road to the Arizona Trail sign on the west side of the road. There is a small circular drive for 3–4 trailers and several cars.

Directions to Harshaw Road (FR 58) Trailhead: From SR 82 turn left (south) at the Patagonia post office. Turn left at the stop sign, onto paved Harshaw Road. Travel 2.9

miles to a cattle guard and national forest boundary. The trailhead, located between the cattle guard and the large Coronado National Forest sign on the west side of the road, offers a circular drive and a large, shaded parking area.

TRAIL DESCRIPTION

The Canelo Hills West/Arizona Trail follows an abandoned dirt road behind the large heritage sign. Traveling west along the base of some large hills, the road narrows to a trail. The trail winds through a small oak and juniper forest in a minor drainage. Several switchbacks take the route up a steep hill to a ridge and through the first of many gates. The route leaves the pass and weaves its way down toward Meadow Valley, with views of San Rafael Valley to the southwest. These valleys are extensive grasslands, with large ranches that have been used for grazing livestock since Spanish missionaries first brought cattle into the area in the late seventeenth and early eighteenth centuries.

The rocky trail on the side of the mountain has good footing. At the bottom of the mountain is a junction with a little-used dirt road; the route turns left (south) as indicated by a sign. Meadow Valley Tank is visible to the south. Approximately 0.25 mile from the previous sign you will see two more signs indicating a right turn (north) over a low, grassy hill with rock cairns marking the way. *The trail is faint here* where it leaves the road. Watch carefully for the signs. At the next dirt road, turn right (north) toward a gate at 5,500 feet elevation.

Three miles from the trailhead the Arizona Trail passes through the gate at the top of a ridge that affords a vantage point with views of the distant mountains and the cinnamon-colored, wrinkled hills. Descending from the ridge on FR 4632 , the country is open with low-growing chaparral. Watch out for the whitethorn. In the wash below, you will travel among small junipers and oaks meandering in and out of the drainage. The AT follows this drainage to La Plata well, where there are two stock tanks for watering livestock. Passing a junction with a fainter track, the route continues up a hill on FR 4632.

At the next junction with a 4WD dirt road, the signs indicate a left (south) turn. The route descends a hill to the Down Under Tank, a dirt tank for watering livestock and an excellent photo opportunity. The trail follows FR 4632 road traveling right (west) into Redrock Canyon that is very rocky in places. The route ambles through this riparian canyon displaying ash and walnut trees. The amount of water found in the canyon is dependent upon the rainfall. Intersecting FR 4631, the Arizona Trail continues down the canyon on FR 4632, past the remains of an old homestead.

Eight miles from the trailhead you come to a confluence of two major drainages. Turn right (north) across the drainage to Red Bank Well and a windmill inside of stock corrals. This is an inviting area for a picnic, camping, watering livestock, or a rest under one of the many large oaks. After passing through the corral, *the trail is indistinct in areas,* disappearing in the grass and a profusion of cow paths in the area. Traveling northwest through grassy mesquite bosquet, watch for faded plastic ribbons. The route will leave the canyon through a gate in a barbed wire fence. The trail traverses above the canyon, circumventing Gate Spring, which has an environmentally sensitive species of fish. Watch out for whitethorn as the trail travels above the canyon.

As the route drops into the canyon again, it rolls in and out of a sandy wash, alternating with mesquite woodland. The colors of the mineral-rich cliffs and rocks are interesting. Watch carefully for trail markers. Just past some old metal tanks there is a confluence of two large drainages. Drop down a steep bank and travel north, directly across the junction of washes to an abandoned dirt road on the left bank.

At a junction of abandoned dirt roads turn right (north) to a gate. Trail markers indicate that the route travels west, uphill, away from the wash. The trail meanders over rolling, grassy hills of oak and ocotillo, and mesquite forest to another gate. Red Mountain, with its fire lookout, is visible to the west. The route arrives at Red Rock Canyon Road (FR 138), which may be unsigned. Crossing the road, the trail travels 0.5 mile to another gate. Pass through the gate and follow the trail into and across Red Rock Canyon.

After crossing the rocky creek bed, which may have water, the trail turns south, leaves the canyon, and follows switchbacks up a steep hill. The route descends and climbs several steep, grassy, oak-dotted hills and drainages. This area has many mines, including the San Simon Mine. At the last high saddle Harshaw Road is visible. It is a steep descent to a sacaton grass meadow bordering Harshaw Road at 4,470 feet elevation. Cross Harshaw Road to the trailhead and parking area.

It is three miles from the trailhead to the Patagonia post office. Use caution and watch for fast-moving traffic. All cattle guards have gates for livestock. A bridge on a curve in the road is a bad spot for livestock. The road passes through a rural residential area into Patagonia. As you enter town, the post office and SR 82 are to the right. See the Canelo Hills Passage description (pages 68–69) for information on Patagonia.

3 Santa Rita Mountain Passage

Patagonia to Oak Tree Canyon/Empire-Cienega

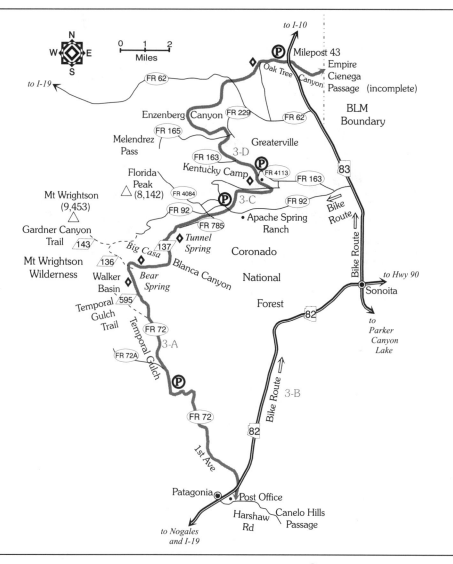

to I-10

Milepost 43
Empire
Cienega
Passage (incomplete)

Oak Tree Canyon

FR 62

to I-19

BLM
Boundary

Enzenberg Canyon   FR 229

FR 62

FR 165

Greaterville

Melendrez
Pass

3-D

FR 163

Kentucky Camp

FR 4113

83

FR 163

Florida
Peak
(8,142)

Mt Wrightson
(9,453)

FR 4084

3-C

FR 92

FR 92

Bike Route

Gardner Canyon
Trail   143

FR 785

Apache Spring
Ranch

Mt Wrightson
Wilderness

Tunnel
Spring

Big Casa   137

Coronado

136

Blanca Canyon

National

to Hwy 90

Walker
Basin

Bear
Spring

Sonoita

Forest

82

Temporal
Gulch
Trail   595

to
Parker
Canyon
Lake

FR 72

3-A

FR 72A

Temporal Gulch

3-B

Bike Route

FR 72

82

1st Ave

Bike Route

Patagonia

Post Office

to Nogales
and I-19

Harshaw
Rd

Canelo Hills
Passage

FR102	**Forest Road**	
	Paved Road	
	State/Interstate	
	Arizona Trail	
	Trip Access Trail	
122	**Other Trail Area**	

.— ..— ..—	**Boundary**
	River, Stream, or Wash
	Canyon Rim
▲	**Campground**
◆	**Water**
	Ranger Station

Ⓟ	**Trailhead and Parking**
○	**Trailhead, no Parking**
P	**Parking**
◉	**Town or City**
●	**Point of Interest**
△	**Mountain Peak**

Photo by Kelly Tighe

An old adobe building in the ghost town of Kentucky Camp, which hikers can visit along the Santa Rita Mountain Passage.

> *When the July lightnin' gleams*
>   *This brown range will start to workin',*
> *Hills be green and tricklin' streams*
>   *Down each arroyo lurkin';*
>   *Now the sleepy land is shirkin',*
> *Drowzin', smilin' in her dreams.*

—"Southwestern June," Badger Clark, 1915

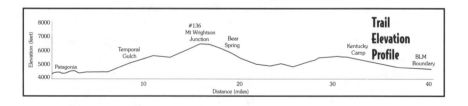

THIS 40-MILE PASSAGE *is divided into four trips:
Trip 3-A follows roads for 6 miles from Patagonia to the Santa
Rita Mountain passage trailhead. From there, the Arizona
Trail heads 15 miles to Gardner Canyon Road. Trip 3-B offers
an alternate bicycle route around the Mount Wrightson
Wilderness. Trip 3-C heads 5 miles from Gardner Canyon to
the ghost town of Kentucky Camp. Trip 3-D travels 13 miles
from Kentucky Camp, under SR 83, to Oak Tree Canyon/Em-
pire Cienega. Cyclists who wish to continue on beyond the
Santa Ritas Mountain Passage should refer to Trip 8-C (page
110), for the route around the Rincon Mountain Wilderness.*

*The distinctive pyramid-shaped profile of Mount Wrightson
is visible throughout most of this passage. The trail enters the
Mount Wrightson Wilderness and encompasses five biotic communities: desert grassland, oak woodland, pine-oak woodland,
pine forest, and mixed conifer forest. Extreme changes in elevation offer the opportunity to see diverse plant and animal life.
The diversity that characterizes this desert oasis serves as a powerful attraction to nature lovers and outdoor enthusiasts. The elegant trogan nests in the riparian canyons that cut deeply into
these mountains. Madera Canyon, located on the north side of
the Santa Rita Mountains, offers excellent bird and wildlife
viewing opportunities. Over two hundred bird species have been
recorded there. A lodge, picnic area, nature walks, and trailhead
to the wilderness are added attractions.*

*The passage offers wide-open vistas across rugged ridges,
miles of foothills, unfolding like fans, spectacular riparian
canyons, and views of historic mining sights.*

*One of the important features of the passage is the historic
mining sites and evidence of past mining endeavors.*

*Sonoita Creek was home to Indians for centuries, and Father
Kino came to the area, established missions, and converted the
area's Native Americans. The Gadsden Purchase made this
United States territory in 1854. The Apaches raided in this area
until Camp Crittenden was built in 1867. From here, soldiers
protected settlers until 1873, when the camp fell into disuse.*

*Surrounding mountains produced various ores that sup-
ported large and small mining camps. The Southern Pacific*

Railroad, Benson-Nogales line, brought growth to the area and served as a shipping medium for ore and cattle. Mining activity and cattle movement developed many of the trails in the Santa Rita Mountains that are used today.

The most prominent historic site on the trail is Kentucky Camp in Kentucky Gulch. Late in the nineteenth century, on the east slope of the Santa Rita Mountains, gold was discovered in the Greaterville mining district. It proved to be the largest and richest placer deposit in southern Arizona.

Placer mining required water, a commodity that was not in great abundance on this eastern slope. A California mining engineer, James Stetson, built a water system that moved water from Bear Spring and other runoffs to a reservoir near the camp. From 1904-1906 the buildings at Kentucky Camp served as headquarters for dam builders, ditch diggers, and miners. Stetson and his partner, George McAneny, died in 1905, and the mining operation ceased. The government sold the buildings and land for back taxes in 1906, after which the site was used as a cattle ranch until the 1960s. Kentucky Camp is being restored and is now a part of the Coronado National Forest.

The grand dedication of this passage was held in conjunction with the A Patagonia Affair, the Patagonia fall festival, in October 1995. Participants included hikers from the Huachuca Hiking Club, mountain bikers from SAMBA, equestrians, and llama trekkers, who traveled on the different trails from Canelo Pass to State Highway 83 at Oak Tree Canyon.

GOVERNING AGENCIES

Coronado National Forest, Nogales Ranger District, 303 Old Tucson Road, Nogales, AZ 85621. (520) 281-2296.

FOR MORE INFORMATION

The Patagonia Tourist Information Office, P. O. Box 241, Patagonia, AZ 85624. (520) 394-0060.

Hiker's Guide to the Santa Rita Mountains, by Betty Leavengood and Mike Liebert, 1994, Pruett Publishing Co., Boulder, Colorado.

NEAREST SERVICES

The passage begins in the town of Patagonia. See Appendix A for further information about available services.

Trip 3-A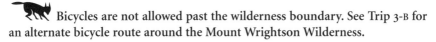

Temporal Gulch Trailhead to Gardner Canyon Road Trailhead

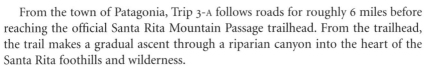 Bicycles are not allowed past the wilderness boundary. See Trip 3-B for an alternate bicycle route around the Mount Wrightson Wilderness.

From the town of Patagonia, Trip 3-A follows roads for roughly 6 miles before reaching the official Santa Rita Mountain Passage trailhead. From the trailhead, the trail makes a gradual ascent through a riparian canyon into the heart of the Santa Rita foothills and wilderness.

Winding through riparian canyons and forests of pine, oak, juniper, and mixed conifer, the route passes mining works and small diggings from the past. Traveling in this remote backcountry the trail follows the course of an old ditch used to transport water from Bear Spring to mining operations farther east in the historic Kentucky Camp.

This route offers views of 9,453-foot Mount Wrightson and accesses several trails in the extensive trail system of the Santa Rita Mountains. There are opportunities for loop trips and peak bagging along the way.

Nature Highlight: Elegant trogans nest in the sycamore groves of riparian canyons.

Maps:
- Coronado National Forest.
- Santa Rita Mountain Trail and Recreation Map, 5th edition, 1996.
- USGS Quads: Patagonia, Mount Wrightson, Helvetia.

Difficulty: Easy to difficult.

Length: 21.4 miles from Patagonia, one way; 15 miles from the trailhead in Temporal Gulch, one way.

Elevation: 4,050–6,560 feet.

Recommended Season: Spring, fall, and winter.

Water: (Treat all water unless noted otherwise. During dry weather, water sources may not be dependable.)
- **Temporal Gulch** has seasonal pools.
- **Bear Spring** has seasonal pools and a tank.
- **Wilderness Boundary (Walker Basin Trail) Spring,** equipped with tank. (If this tank is dry there is another 0.25 mile uphill on the trail.)
- **Tunnel Spring** has a tank.
- **Cave Creek** has seasonal pools.
- **Gardner Canyon Creek** has seasonal pools.

Camping: You may camp alongside of FR 72 before the trailhead. There is a small pull off along the side of the road. There is no camping allowed at the newly developed trailhead, although there is ample room for parking several cars and trucks with trailers. Those in four-wheel-drive vehicles can cross Temporal Gulch after the trailhead and find many camping sites along the creek.

Livestock: This route is suitable for trail animals. There is water at tanks and springs along the route. There is one area on the Chinaman Trail that requires dismounting to pass through a tunnel in a rock. Pack animals must detour this area via a path below the tunnel, which is described in greater detail in the Trail Description section.

Directions to Trailhead: Passenger cars can drive to the trailhead. The Arizona Trail leaves Patagonia and shares the route with State Highway 82 for a short distance then turns left (north) on 1st Avenue next to the high school. This is Gringo Gulch, which is paved as it passes 0.5 mile through a residential area and then becomes FR 72 at the National Forest boundary. At 2 miles, a large sign indicates that the trailhead is 4 miles away. Continue straight on FR 72 past FR 762 on the left. Between this intersection and the trailhead you'll see a couple of wide spots suitable for camping. At the trailhead, a sign indicates it is 4 miles to Temporal Trail and 6 miles to Walker Basin Trail.

Other Area Trails: The **Walker Basin Trail** and the **Temporal Gulch Trail** both access a network of trails within the wilderness. Contact managing agencies for more information.

TRAIL DESCRIPTION

The trail leaves the parking area and crosses the creek immediately; it meanders north in Temporal Gulch, crossing the creek several times. The trail shares the route with FR 72, a 4WD road, for several miles. This riparian canyon nurtures stands of sycamores and ash trees. The creek flows heavily at different times of the year (during snowmelt and monsoons), making this part of the trail difficult to negotiate because of high water.

Approximately 2 miles from the trailhead is a junction of FR 72 and FR 72A. Continue straight ahead (north) on FR 72. At the windmill, Anaconda Spring, the trail touches private property. Please do not trespass.

 The four-wheel-drive road deteriorates 0.5 mile after the windmill, dropping into the middle of the creek. This is a potentially confusing area. Pass through a narrow section of the creek and exit the creek on the left side. Traverse just above the canyon on a hillside sprinkled with oaks and then return to the creek and cross it. The area has several mine shafts on the surrounding hillsides. The road becomes rocky as it gently ascends, crossing in and out of the canyon.

Four miles from the parking area you come to a junction with the Temporal trailhead (#595). This trail leaves the road to the left and follows Temporal Gulch west into the mountains. The Arizona Trail, however, continues to follow FR 72 traveling north into the foothills toward Walker Basin. The gradual and constant ascent becomes strenuous. Take a breather and look south to Red Mountain, which is framed by the foothills.

Six miles from the parking area the trail makes a gentle descent into Walker Basin which is shaded by Chihuahua, Apache, and piñon pines.

The route climbs to a junction with FR 4090 and FR 72. Stay on FR 72 left to the wilderness boundary. Upper Walker Tank, a lovely pond and spillway below the dam, punctuates the boundary. This remote and tranquil place is deep within the Santa Rita Mountains. The elevation here is 5,680 feet and it is 12 miles from Patagonia. The sign indicates it is 2.6 miles to Gardner Canyon Trail (do not go that far); travel only another 1.1 miles to the junction of the newly constructed Chinaman Trail.

Leaving the pond on an abandoned dirt road, Walker Basin/Arizona Trail climbs steeply for approximately 0.25 mile, until the trail leaves the road and veers left. This is a potentially confusing area because there is no sign indicating that the trail leaves the road. Shortly after you veer left you will see a spring that has been developed into a tank for wildlife and livestock.

As the trail switchbacks steeply to a saddle, the elevation gain affords some of the finest views on this section. The trail passes through an opening in the fence line with no gate, but there is barbwire stretched overhead—beware equestrians. Just beyond the fence you arrive at the saddle and a sign indicating the turn onto the Chinaman Trail. The section of trail from this saddle to the Casa Blanca Creek crossing was completed in 1996. The elevation at the saddle is 6,560 feet, and Gardner Canyon trailhead is 9 miles from here.

At the saddle, turn right (east) and begin a gradual descent on switchbacks through an oak and pine forest. The route slices around the mountains, crossing several minor drainages. As you traverse high above Big Casa Blanca Canyon, listen for the sound of water cascading over small rock waterfalls. Here, steep slopes with loose footing are potentially difficult. Equestrians and those with pack animals should be careful in this section.

On the north side of the canyon, picturesque rock pinnacles covered with green lichen gleam in the sunlight. These formations also stand out in other areas along the route.

Bear Springs is approximately 3.3 miles from the saddle. About 0.2 mile before the Casa Blanca Creek crossing you'll pass a sign along the trail marking the location of the springs. You'll find a wood trough 50 yards downhill from here for watering livestock. Continue down the trail to the Casa Blanca Creek crossing. This area is a small oasis with seasonal pools and an abundance of oak, pine, and sycamore trees. Packers may want to consider this area for camping. There is a level place here for tents and tethering livestock. The elevation is 5,500 feet.

The route from Bear Spring to Tunnel Spring, on the Chinaman Trail, follows the course of an old open aqueduct used to bring water from Bear Spring to mining operations east at Kentucky Camp. The ditch and the original trail are said to have been constructed by Chinese laborers at the turn of the twentieth century. The ditch/trail cuts a level path around Ditch Mountain to Tunnel Spring. The trail traverses above Big Casa Blanca Canyon, affording the sights and sounds of the stream below. The bluffs of the canyon loom above it and accent the rugged course of this major drainage, which slices through the heart of the Santa Rita foothills.

The hillsides open up with less vegetation. One mile from Bear Spring, the trail passes through a tunnel formed by two large boulders that have shifted together. The short tunnel is tall enough for most animals, but riders must dismount. Pack animals cannot get through and must use a detour below the tunnel. The detour is about 336 feet back on the trail and is a faint, crude path that traverses the hill below the tunnel and returns to the trail about 236 feet down the trail from the other side of the tunnel.

The rock in this area is a pale green and white with a loose texture, which, when combined with the steep grade of the hill, calls for careful travel for livestock the next 0.5 mile.

The route turns northeast around Ditch Mountain, leaving Big Casa Blanca Canyon. The mountain ranges to the southeast are visible on this now open trail. Approximately 1 mile from the tunnel, a sign marks the wilderness boundary. One mile from this boundary is Tunnel Spring, at approximately 5,510 feet elevation, where there is a tank for livestock. The Forest Service has installed an impressive interpretive sign indicating your location and elevation and providing the following historic information: "This section of the Arizona Trail follows a water system built a century ago for a short lived hydraulic mining venture. In hydraulic mining, power uses water to blast away hillsides to reach gold deposits. In the Santa Rita Mountains gold deposits and water did not occur in the same valleys. In 1904 the Santa Rita Water Mining Company built ditches, pipes, and tunnels to carry water from springs near here to the dry gold bearing gravels near Greaterville." The water pipe traveled underground from here to Gardner Canyon Road.

The trail leaves the spring and climbs a steep grade north to a gate. Pass through the gate and descend steeply to FR 785. Turn right (east) at the trail sign and follow the road to another gate. There is a large water trough here fed by Tunnel Spring. Trail users with 4WD vehicles can drive to this spot from the Gardner Canyon Road Trailhead and park. There is room for several vehicles. Primitive camping spots dot the road intermittently at the side of the creek. It is not recommended or even possible to pull trailers to this site.

 From the water tank, the trail shares FR 785 for approximately 1 mile and crosses the creek a few times. Gardner Canyon is a major riparian drainage. High waters during snow runoff and the summer monsoons may interfere with creek crossings. Junipers, sycamores, and oaks provide a shady trip and inviting camping along the creek.

The trail turns left and leaves the road approximately 1 mile from the tank. Immediately after crossing the creek, you will see a sign that indicates a right (east) turn. There are two interpretive signs along the creek that give a brief history of mining and the ditch connected with it. The trail traverses above the creek providing views of the rugged walls below. Oaks and junipers grow sparsely on the hillsides. To the south in the distance lay the Canelo Hills.

The trail passes around the tunnel that carried the water and then drops back to FR 785. After crossing the road, you enter a lovely open meadow. This meadow may have a blanket of yellow flowers, depending upon the rainfall and the season. A corral provides excellent level camping for packers. There may be water in Cave Creek 0.25 mile down the hill. Pass the corral and go a short distance through two gates. After the second gate, the trail is loose, rocky, and steep as it descends to Cave Creek. Cave Creek is a major drainage that may offer a gentle or a torrential stream, depending upon the snow and rain. Cross the canyon and pass through another gate; the trail climbs out of the canyon to Gardner Canyon Road (FR 92). At the road, turn right (east) and cross to a trailhead with parking.

Trip 3-B

Alternate Bicycle Route Around the Mount Wrightson Wilderness from Patagonia to Gardner Canyon Road

Because bicycles are not allowed in the wilderness area, we suggest this alternate route that follows paved highways for the first 17 miles. The trip begins in the quaint town of Patagonia, which has facilities for eating, sleeping, and restocking supplies. Trip 3-B follows the scenic State Highway 82 to Sonoita, a ranching and horse-raising area. From the small town of Sonoita the route travels north through rolling grasslands to Gardner Canyon Road, which it follows into the foothills of the Santa Rita Mountains.

Nature Highlight: From the road we spot the white rump patches of a small band of pronghorn antelope grazing on a grassy hillside.

Maps:
* Arizona highway map.
* Arizona Atlas and Gazetteer.
* Coronado National Forest Map.

Difficulty: Easy.

Length: 22.6 miles, one way.

Elevation: 4,044–5,050 feet.

Recommended Season: All year, depending on weather (summer temperatures can reach 100 degrees Fahrenheit).

Water: (Treat all water unless noted otherwise. During dry weather, water sources may not be dependable.) Potable water is available in the communities of Patagonia and Sonoita.

Camping: The nearest developed camp is at Patagonia Lake State Park, 10 miles south of Patagonia on route 82. This is a fee area with water, hook-ups, a campsite, showers, boat launching, and boat rentals. The Coronado National Forest surrounds Patagonia, and it has many primitive areas suitable for camping.

Directions to Trailhead: This trip begins in the town of Patagonia. Patagonia is approximately 60 miles southeast of Tucson on State Highway 82. Travel from Sonoita at the junction of State Highways 83 and 82 approximately 12.5 miles west to Patagonia.

ROUTE DESCRIPTION

Leave Patagonia and travel east on State Highway 82. The road climbs gently for 9.6 miles, at which point there is a Historic Marker for Camp Crittenden on the left (north) side of the highway. Camp Crittenden, a military post from 1867–1873 used as a base from which to protect the area from Apaches, was located in this general area.

Continue west on SH 82 2.9 miles to Sonoita. Rolling hills and grasslands surround Sonoita, an area known for horse breeding and horse racing. In Sonoita you will find a fairground, stores, restaurants, post office, and a gas station.

In Sonoita, turn left (north) on SH 83 and follow 4.5 miles of rolling terrain to Gardner Canyon Road (FR 92). Turn left (west) onto Gardner Canyon Road. Follow the first 5.6 miles on Gardner Canyon Road on a graded dirt road until you come to a cattle guard. Just 0.1 mile past the cattle guard is a trailhead on the north side of the road, where you can begin your trip on the Arizona Trail to Kentucky Camp, State Highway 83, and Oak Tree Canyon (see Trips 3-C and 3-D).

Trip 3-C

Gardner Canyon Trailhead to Kentucky Camp

This trip uses abandoned dirt roads connected by new trail to travel from Gardner Canyon, over a ridge and down into Fish Canyon, to the historic 1904 mining operation of Kentucky Camp. There are spectacular views of surrounding mountain ranges as the trail trecks through rolling, grassy, oak- and juniper-studded hills.

Nature Highlight: A coyote trots across the ridgeline. One nervous glance in our direction, and he is gone.

Maps: Coronado National Forest.
* Santa Rita Mountain Trail and Recreation Map, 5th edition, 1996.
* USGS Quads: Sonoita.

Difficulty: Easy to moderate.

Length: 5.2 miles, one way.

Elevation: 5,400–5,000 feet.

Recommended Season: All year, depending on the weather.

Water: (Treat all water unless noted otherwise. During dry weather, water sources may not be dependable.) There is a spigot at Kentucky Camp.

Camping: There is a primitive camping area on Gardner Canyon Road near the trailhead, with ample room for several campers and horse trailers. The land south of the road is private and is fenced. Majestic oaks shade this site just above Gardner Canyon Creek, which may have seasonal water.

Livestock: This is an excellent trail for livestock, because it is easy and has minimal elevation gain and good footing.

Directions to Trailhead: Passenger cars can drive on this rocky, graded road to the trailhead. Traveling on highway 83 from Interstate 10, or Sonoita, turn west on

Gardner Canyon Road (FR 92), which is a graded dirt road. After traveling 4.4 miles, you will pass Apache Springs Ranch on the left. Proceed another mile to a cattle guard. Cross over the cattle guard and within 0.1 mile the Arizona Trail intersects the road. The parking area is on the right (north) side of the road at the trailhead.

Other Area Trails: A number of trails from this trailhead lead into the foothills, including Aliso Springs, Florida Saddle, and Mount Wrightson Wilderness. Refer to the hiking trail map for further information. There is also an extensive network of old mining roads that access the old Greaterville cemetery, mine sites, a cave, and trailheads into the Mount Wrightson Wilderness Area. Contact the Forest Service or refer to maps for more information.

TRAIL DESCRIPTION

From the trailhead, the Arizona Trail crosses through a grassy area with large oaks, then heads north. There is a steep climb to the top of the hill, then the trail intersects a four-wheel-drive road. Turn left, go a few yards, and look for where the trail leaves the road, traveling northeast. This route crosses a metal pipe and follows an old aqueduct that was designed and built to channel runoff for a reservoir at Kentucky Camp.

After passing through a gate at the crest of a hill, enjoy the views of the Huachuca and Whetsone Mountains. This is the high point at 5,400 feet. Follow the trail markers in this area, as the route gradually descends in a northeasterly direction, following the old waterline. When the route intersects with a seldom-used dirt road, turn right (east) onto the road, following the ridgeline. The vegetation of this area is characteristic of many ridges in the extensive foothills of the Santa Ritas, with native grasses, oak, manzanita, juniper, bear grass, yucca, and piñon pines. Here the elevation and open vegetation combine to offer panoramic views. Looking north from this ridge, you can see the adobe buildings at Kentucky Camp.

Keep an eye out for a trail marker that indicates a left turn, where the trail leaves the ridge and begins a steep descent on switchbacks, through a lovely grove of oaks, into Fish Canyon. At the bottom of the canyon there is a gate. Past the gate, the trail enters a grassy meadow and may be faint in areas because of the grass. The trail crosses FR 163 then turns left onto an abondoned dirt road to another gate. After passing through the gate, stay along the fence line for a short distance to Kentucky Camp. As you approach Kentucky Camp, you'll see a large adobe building through the trees. This impressive building, once headquarters for the mining company, is being stabilized and restored by the Forest Service with help from volunteers. This and other buildings in the area are old and potentially dangerous. Do not enter them or remove or destroy anything in the area.

The road to Kentucky Camp is closed with a locked gate 0.5 mile north of the camp, and a caretaker resides at the site.

The Arizona Trail leaves Kentucky Camp going north on a closed dirt road, up a steep hill approximately 0.5 mile to a fence and gate. This is the trailhead for Trip 3-D.

Trip 3-D

Kentucky Camp to Oak Tree Canyon/Empire-Cienega

Trip 3-D follows a complex network of linking dirt roads and trails with frequent junctions. Watch carefully for Arizona Trail markers.

The trip leaves the historic ghost town of Kentucky Camp on a long, open ridge and gently climbs to the southeastern slope of the Santa Rita Mountains. It then winds in and out of the foothills in oak woodland vegetation, passing some mines and topping out on high ridges providing for excellent views of the surrounding mountains. The route passes close to the historic location of Greaterville. Little remains of Greaterville, save the cemetery, which sports hundreds of yellow iris in the spring. The last part of the trip is in an open canyon filled with majestic oaks. The trail follows the course of the canyon, making use of a large culvert, and passes under State Highway 83 to the east. The Arizona Trail passes from National Forest to Bureau of Land Management land, where the Santa Rita Passage ends.

Nature Highlight: A blacktail jackrabbit hops across the trail in front of us, as a gray-breasted jay looks on from above in the branch of an oak.

Maps: Coronado National Forest.
* USGS Quads: Helvitia, Empire Ranch.

Difficulty: Easy.

Length: 13.3 miles, one way.

Elevation: 5,600–4,900 feet.

Recommended Season: All year, depending on the weather.

Water: (Treat all water unless noted otherwise. During dry weather, water sources may not be dependable.)
* **Kentucky Camp,** spigot.
* **Oak Tree Canyon,** metal stock tank.

Camping: There is primitive camping allowed along the whole trail segment in Oak Tree Canyon 0.5 mile west of State Highway 83 on a graded dirt road that is passable by passenger car. There is a seasonal stock tank in the canyon on the road, and the canyon provides large level areas shaded by great oaks. To access this area from Highway 83, see Trip 8-C.

   Fish Canyon on FR 163 also offers primitive camping. Refer to the Directions to Trailhead section in this trip for specific directions. This area has large level spots and shade trees; however, there is no water.

Livestock: This trip is excellent for livestock travel, because it has easy roads and a good trail, with minimal elevation changes.

Directions to Trailhead: Passenger cars and trailers can drive to within 0.5 mile above Kentucky Camp.

Traveling on highway 83 from Interstate 10, it is 21.5 miles south or, from Sonoita, it is 4.2 miles north to the turn off. Turn west on Gardner Canyon Road (Forest Road 92), which is a graded dirt road. Go 0.8 mile to a sign indicating that Kentucky Camp is 5 miles to the right on FR 163. Turn right and drive another 0.8 mile to a junction, where you should continue on FR 163 to the right. Approximately 2 miles from FR 92, there are several good primitive campsites with level areas and shade trees. Travel on to an unmarked junction and bear left. At 3.1 miles, pass over a cattle guard and you will find more excellent campsites. At 4.4 miles there is a junction with FR 4113. Take this to the right over a cattle guard and travel 1 more mile to a fence and a gate. Park to the side of the road outside the fence. At this point, the road becomes the Arizona Trail. Going down, the route leads to Kentucky Camp; going up, you'll have a gradual climb, and panoramic views await you.

TRAIL DESCRIPTION

The parking area is on the Arizona Trail, and there are signs indicating the direction of travel. At the parking area, you are approximately 0.5 mile north of Kentucky Camp. The trail shares the route with a well-used, rocky, dirt road. Go north on the road approximately 1.5 miles to the first gate and cattle guard. Proceed to the junction with FR 163, which heads left or straight. Head straight (north) on FR 163 to the next gate. Here, the road deteriorates and becomes increasingly rugged and steep, for it is at the base of Granite Mountain.

At the next junction turn right (north), staying on FR 163 as it travels around the mountain. Turn left at the next junction, again staying on 163, and begin to descend on the road through a wooded area. The next junction is not marked, but bear left and continue to descend into the drainage. At the floor of the canyon is a sign indicating a left (west) turn onto FR 165. The sign indicates that you are 2 miles from Kentucky Camp. (FR 165 originates at the Greaterville Road and goes to Melendrez Pass, which is the site of a group of radio towers and also the beginning of a trail to Aliso Springs.)

Travel about 0.75 mile on FR 165 and turn right (north) at the signed turnoff onto an abondoned road. As the route ascends a hill, look west down through the trees at a lovely stock tank. Resume climbing through the oak and juniper forest to a saddle. A rock cairn indicates that the trail turns right (east) and ascends another hill to a gate. The views here are worth a pause: an oak forest surrounds this spot, which is nestled in the foothills. After the gate, at 5,730 feet, turn left (north) then wind through the hills on a trail that descends into the floor of Enzenberg Canyon on gentle switchbacks.

Enzenberg Canyon offers a small meadow and a dry creek. Cross the drainage to a sign and turn left (west) onto a little-used dirt road. Notice the power line overhead in this area. The road becomes more defined and intersects a well-used 4WD road. Turn right (east) on the well-used road. At the next gate a sign indicates a turn to the north to another gate approximately 1/8 mile away. After the gate, the road descends gently to an open meadow with impressive oaks and native grasses.

Here the road narrows to a trail that can be difficult to follow in this area because of several cross trails. Look carefully for the carsonite trail signs guiding you toward the east. At the last sign in the meadow there is an arrow pointing left (north) up a steep hill. As you climb the hill, you will see an Arizona Trail sign. Continue to climb to the crest, where you will see FR 62 below. The trail drops down the slope on a few well-graded switchbacks to FR 62 (Box Canyon Road).

Cross FR 62, go through a gate, and follow the trail (northeast) along a gentle ascent to an abandoned dirt road. Turn left, pass through the next gate, and follow the road, which turns into a trail and ascends steeply, topping out on a hill with fine vistas. Descend to a gate and travel through a forest of small oaks. At the next intersection, turn left onto a 4WD road and ascend a high hill. Before the summit, the trail leaves the road to the left, traverses the side of the hill, and meets the road again. Turn left. The road drops steeply from the hill to a gate. Continue through the gate and go approximately 1/16 mile and veer left to a walk-through opening. At the fork in the trail, turn right, go up through a second walk-through for a short distance. Here the trail turns left before topping a hill (at the time of this writing, the trail cutoff is unmarked). The trail traverses the side of the hill, veers left, and ascends a ridge to another walk-through. After this walk-through, go left onto a 4WD road and just before you reach a large metal tank, turn right. Follow the road down to a cattle guard and gate in Oak Tree Canyon. It is easy to understand how this canyon obtained its name. The oaks are truly magnificent and abundant.

The canyon is large with grassy level areas for picnicking, camping, or parking. Travel approximately 1 mile on the road through the canyon to State Highway 83. The trail continues east under the highway through a large culvert. On the east side, the trail markers direct you down the road. Stay on the 4WD road through the canyon to the Forest Service and Bureau of Land Management boundary, approximately 1.25 miles east of SH 83.

Cyclists: Those wishing to continue on from the end of the Santa Ritas Mountain Passage should refer to Trip 8-C (page 110) for the route around the Rincon Mountain wilderness.

4 Empire-Cienega Passage
Oak Tree Canyon/Empire-Cienega to Interstate 10

As of this writing, sections of the Arizona Trail in this passage are not yet completed. This description outlines the *proposed route* of the Arizona Trail through this passage; it is not intended to be used as a trail guide. Much of the information included here is taken from an Arizona Trail management guide designed not for recreational use but for use in planning, developing, and managing the trail. Contact the governing agency or The Arizona Trail Association for more information on the route, signage, availability of water, and completion status of this passage.

WHEN COMPLETE, *this 20+-mile passage will connect the National Forest/Bureau of Land Management boundary at Oak Tree Canyon with Interstate 10. The high desert grasslands and majestic canyons are predominant features of the Empire-Cienega Resource Conservation Area. The Sonoita Basin, at 4,500 feet elevation, with 15 inches of annual rainfall, support some of the finest examples of native grasses in Arizona. Another dominant feature is the riparian Cienega Creek. The creek is a leafy oasis of giant Fremont cottonwoods, Godding willows, velvet ashes, and Arizona walnuts, with an understory of grass, seep willow, and rushes. The vegetation and water attract a variety of rare birds and animals. Headwaters of the creek bubble to the surface 3 miles east of the historic adobe ranch house. The stream meanders for 10 miles before disappearing underground. The narrow water course is 6-8 inches deep and joins Pantano Wash at the foot of the Rincon Mountains, 20 miles north of the ranch.*

The quality of the water in the creek is excellent and supports three native fish species. A portion of the creek within the preserve has been designated "Unique Water of Arizona" because of the excellent surface water.

Wildlife thrives in this nearly pristine area; pronghorn antelope play in the grassy hills along with many other species of mammals, birds, and reptiles. The rolling grasslands offer magnificent vistas of the Whetstone, Mustang, Huachuca, Santa Rita, and Empire Mountains.

The heritage of Native American peoples in the area dates back at least 5,000 years, to the recent presence in the 1880s of the Apache Indians.

The Butterfield Overland Mail Line operated along Cienega Creek until 1861 and was followed by the Southern Pacific Railroad in 1880. There are currently two operating rail lines through the Cienega Creek Natural Preserve.

Ranching began in the 1870s and continues today on the Empire and Empirita Ranches. Walter L. Vail and a partner bought the ranch house, corral, 612 head of cattle, and 160 acres in 1876. Mr. Vail expanded the operation, and by 1905 the Empire Ranch had spread over Pima and Santa Cruz Counties for 1,000 square miles. Walter Vail was involved in state and local politics. He and partners operated the Total Wreck Silver Mine and mill on the ranch in the Empire Mountains. The mine was in operation from 1880 to 1885 and had as many as three hundred people residing there.

Mr. Vail died in 1906 and the family continued to run the ranch until 1928. It was sold to the Chiricahua Cattle Company. Jack Greenway bought a portion of the ranch in 1949 and named it the Cienega Ranch. Mr. and Mrs. Frank Boice bought out their partners and operated the Empire until 1960. Gulf American Corporation bought it for a real estate development. The development never occurred, and the Anamax Mining Co. bought the Empire Ranch in 1974 and the Cienega Ranch in 1977. The public became interested in preserving the ranches and their natural resources. A series of land exchanges in 1988 put the property into public ownership under the administration of the Bureau of Land Management.

Pima County Flood Control District purchased the Empirita land and ranch house along the Cienega Creek in the 1990s. Their ownership extends north to Colossal Cave. This became known as the Cienega Creek Natural Preserve.

This passage incorporates the southern portion of the Cienega Creek Natural Preserve. The preserve is north of the Empire-Cienega and is a 3,979-acre parcel of land located along Cienega Creek and owned by Pima County Flood Control District.

PROPOSED ROUTE

This passage begins 1.25 miles east of SH 83, at the Forest Service and Bureau of Land Management boundary and ends at Interstate 10 near the Marsh Station interchange. The trail is approximately 23 miles long, but its exact route has not been determined. Trail routes were researched in the field and included alignments near the Empire Ranch and Cienega Creek. Respect for archeological sites, environmentally sensitive Cienega Creek, and state trust lands must be given when routing the trail.

Interim routes are usable at this time on dirt roads passing near the ranch from the national forest boundary at Oak Tree Canyon on the west to the narrows at the Cienega Creek Natural Preserve boundary, approximately 16 miles. At the narrows the proposed trail will travel approximately 7 miles along the creek, north to Interstate 10 at the Marsh Station Road interchange.

The gently sloping, dissected, old alluvial fans and a nearly level, broad valley floor makes this area excellent for mountain biking. The best seasons are winter, spring, and fall. Be cautious during heavy rains because of the danger of flooding in the creek and deep drainages. Equestrians need to be cautious of bogs and quicksand in the creek.

The Empire-Cienega is not a park; there are no campgrounds, rest rooms, grills, trash pickups, parking lots, or concession stands. The goal is to retain and enhance the area's pristine, natural setting while making it available for use by a responsible and environmentally conscious public.

The Cienega Creek Natural Preserve will accommodate public use with certain restrictions. The goals are to protect natural resources, reduce the need for extensive capital improvements, and reduce the need for facility maintenance. There are plans for future development of a county park, campground, and equestrian staging area. A system of trails is proposed, including an alignment for this segment of the Arizona Trail. The plans must be studied and reviewed before the trail is finalized.

GOVERNING AGENCIES

Empire-Cienega, Bureau of Land Management, Tucson Office, 12661 E. Broadway, Tucson, AZ 85748. (520) 722-4289. Contact them for information on camping.

Cienega Creek Natural Preserve, Pima County Parks and Recreation Department, 1204 W. Silverlake Rd., Tucson, AZ 85713. (520) 740-2690. Permits are required for access into the preserve and may be obtained at no cost from the preceding address.

FOR MORE INFORMATION

Contact the Arizona Trail Association, P.O. Box 36736, Phoenix, AZ 85067.

NEAREST SERVICES

Beginning of Passage: Sonoita, AZ, 7 miles south on SH 83.

5 Cienega Creek Passage

Interstate 10 to Colossal Cave Mountain Park
(Western Alignment to the Rincon Mountains)

As of this writing, sections of the Arizona Trail in this passage are not yet completed. This description outlines the *proposed route* of the Arizona Trail through this passage; it is not intended to be used as a trail guide. Much of the information included here is taken from an Arizona Trail management guide designed not for recreational use but for use in planning, developing, and managing the trail. Contact the governing agency or The Arizona Trail Association for more information on the route, signage, availability of water, and completion status of this passage.

The Arizona Trail has two proposed routes to the Rincon Mountains. Both western and eastern routes are being considered. Two passages, Cienega Creek and Rincon Valley, travel on the west side of the Rincon Mountains and will offer an urban trail experience. Happy Valley and Rincon Mountain Passages, travel to the Rincons from the southeast offering a primitive wilderness trip.

W*HEN COMPLETE, the Cienega Creek Passage will link Empirita Ranch near Interstate 10 with Colossal Cave Mountain Park. The route will travel through the Cienega Creek Natural Preserve, an oasis that is barely visible from surrounding hills. The oasis occurs because of a stream that nurtures cottonwoods, willows, velvet ashes, and the Arizona walnut. The stream goes underground at Interstate 10 and surfaces again north of Interstate 10. The preserve is an excellent example of a desert riparian environment.*

Pima County Department of Transportation and Flood Control is managing this area to encourage the natural processes to occur. Their future goals include reestablishing native plant cover and improving habitat on disturbed areas. The objectives of the county are to preserve and protect the perennial stream and biological resources and to provide opportunities for public use and education.

The north extremity of the passage has a quite different feature called Colossal Cave. This popular tourist attraction, 20 miles southeast of Tucson, is one of the world's largest dry limestone caverns. There are tours of areas in the cave having stalagmites and stalactites. The Colossal Cave Mountain Park offers a developed campground.

PROPOSED ROUTE

Beginning at Interstate 10 and ending at Colossal Cave Mountain Park, the route crosses state trust land. The proposed route will parallel Cienega Creek from Marsh Station Road and Interstate 10 to Colossal Cave Mountain Park. Trailheads are planned near I-10 and at Colossal Cave Mountain Park. As of this writing, mileage has not yet been determined.

GOVERNING AGENCIES

Pima County Parks and Recreation Dept., 1204 W. Silverlake, Tucson, AZ 85713. (520) 740-2690.

FOR MORE INFORMATION

Colossal Cave Mountain Park, Post Office, Vail, AZ 85641. (520) 647-7275.

NEAREST SERVICES

Benson, Arizona.

6 Rincon Valley Passage
Colossal Cave Mountain Park to Saguaro National Park
(Western Alignment to the Rincon Mountains)

As of this writing, sections of the Arizona Trail in this passage are not yet completed. This description outlines the *proposed route* of the Arizona Trail through this passage; it is not intended to be used as a trail guide. Much of the information included here is taken from an Arizona Trail management guide designed not for recreational use but for use in planning, developing, and managing the trail. Contact the governing agency or The Arizona Trail Association for more information on the route, signage, availability of water, and completion status of this passage.

W<small>HEN</small> <small>COMPLETED</small>, *this passage will travel from Colossal Cave Mountain Park to Saguaro National Park. It begins at the unique natural feature known as Colossal Cave. Colossal Cave is on the National Register of Historic Places. It is one of the world's largest dry limestone caverns. Prehistoric people used the cave for shelter and storing food. Recent discovery of the cave was in 1879. Train robbers used it as a hideout. The cave is nestled in the southern foothills of the Rincon Mountains. Pima County owns the cave and adjoining property. A foundation leases and manages the cave and surrounding acreage. The Civilian Conservation Corps built buildings, walkways, and lighting in the 1930s. The managers maintain a free campground and picnic area with water and rest rooms. The first tours of the cave began in 1923 and are still given daily, year-round.*

Saguaro National Monument is at the northern end of the passage. The saguaro cactus is the supreme symbol of the Sonoran Desert. The cactus has a personality, with each plant having a unique shape, with arms that sometimes give it an almost human-like appearance. Since 1933 this giant cactus has been protected within Saguaro National Park. The Sonoran Desert elevations range from 2,000 to 2,700 feet. This lower elevation sustains a lushness and variety of life that surpasses all other North American deserts. It is one of the hottest

and driest regions on the continent, with summer tempera-
tures typically above 100 degrees Fahrenheit and fewer than 12
inches of annual rainfall. The monument visitor center offers
rest rooms, a bookstore, a small museum, 128 miles of trails,
scenic drives, and picnic areas.

PROPOSED ROUTE

This passage will travel from Colossal Cave to Saguaro National Park. A
trailhead is proposed in the area of the cave.

There are two proposed routes: 1) Cienega Creek to Camino Loma Alta
to Saguaro National Monument and then linking to Madrona Ranger Station, and 2) Cienega Creek to Pantano Wash to Rincon Creek to Coyote
Wash. The mileage and the exact route are unknown at this time.

GOVERNING AGENCIES

Pima County Parks and Recreation Department, 1204 W. Silverlake, Tucson, AZ 85713, (520) 740-2690.

Saguaro National Monument, 3693 S. Old Spanish Trail, Tucson, AZ 85730,
(520) 733-5153.

Colossal Cave Mountain Park, Post Office, Vail, AZ 85641, (520) 647-7275.

FOR MORE INFORMATION

Arizona Trail Association, P.O. Box 36736, Phoenix, AZ 85067, (602)
252-4794.

NEAREST SERVICES

Tucson, Arizona, 17 miles northwest.

7 Happy Valley Passage
Interstate 10 to Miller and Turkey Creek Trailheads
(Eastern Alignment to the Rincon Mountains)

As of this writing, sections of the Arizona Trail in this passage are not yet completed. This description outlines the *proposed route* of the Arizona Trail through this passage; it is not intended to be used as a trail guide. Much of the information included here is taken from an Arizona Trail management guide designed not for recreational use but for use in planning, developing, and managing the trail. Contact the governing agency or The Arizona Trail Association for more information on the route, signage, availability of water, and completion status of this passage.

WHEN COMPLETE, *the Happy Valley Passage will travel from Interstate 10 to Miller Creek and Turkey Creek, two trailhead sites on the eastern side of the Rincon Mountain Wilderness. This passage features a high desert pass between the Rincon Mountains and the Whetstone mountains at the 3,000- to 4,000-foot elevation. The vegetation is desert grassland, Chihuahua desert types, with open views of surrounding countryside and mountain ranges. The last part of the passage goes through Ash Creek, a scenic area with seasonal water, large sycamores, and ash trees. There are picnicking opportunities along the creek.*

A special feature on FR 35 *is "Old Tucson East," a movie set that has been used for such films as* Young Guns, Tombstone, The Quick and the Dead, *and the TV series* Young Riders.

PROPOSED ROUTE

This passage begins where the Arizona Trail crosses under Interstate 10 at Marsh Station Road and ends at the Miller Creek and Turkey Creek trailheads.

Research and planning continues on providing a connection from Cienega Creek to the Happy Valley area. Access across private lands is needed to connect the various alignments. In the interim, there are enough roads to make connections. This is the most logical temporary connection for long-distance users wanting to travel from Cienega Creek to the Rincon Mountains. Travel east 7.7 miles on I-10 from Marsh Station Road. Take exit 297 at J-Six and Mescal Road. Turn north onto Mescal Road. The road passes through a rural community on 4 miles of pavement and becomes FR 35 as it enters the national forest. It is 12.3 miles from the pavement to the Miller Creek Trailhead. It is another 0.7 mile to the Turkey Creek Trailhead. The forest road is graded with rocky areas and a few steep climbs.

GOVERNING AGENCIES

Coronado National Forest, Santa Catalina Ranger District, 5700 N. Sabino Canyon Road, Tucson, AZ 85715, (520) 749-8700.

FOR MORE INFORMATION

The Arizona Trail Association, P.O. Box 36736, Phoenix, AZ 85067, (602) 252-4794.

NEAREST SERVICES

Benson, Arizona, 6.5 miles east on Interstate 10.

A rider and his pack mule heading into the Rincon Mountains Passage of the Arizona Trail.

Photo by Kelly Tighe

Just a-ridin', a-ridin'
Desert ripplin' in the sun,
Mountains blue along the skyline
I don't envy anyone
When I'm ridin'.

—"Ridin'," Badger Clark, 1906

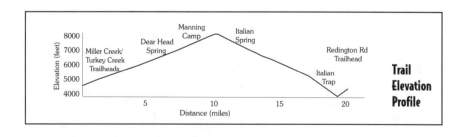

Trail Elevation Profile

8 Rincon Mountains Passage

Miller and Turkey Creek Trailheads to Redington Road
(Eastern Alignment to the Rincon Mountains)

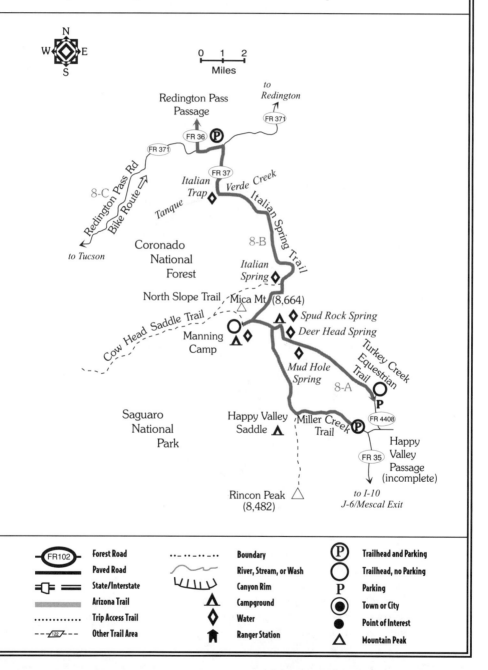

FR102 Forest Road	**........** Boundary	**Ⓟ** Trailhead and Parking
Paved Road	River, Stream, or Wash	**◯** Trailhead, no Parking
State/Interstate	Canyon Rim	**P** Parking
Arizona Trail	**▲** Campground	**◉** Town or City
.... Trip Access Trail	**◆** Water	**●** Point of Interest
-- 122 -- Other Trail Area	**⌂** Ranger Station	**△** Mountain Peak

Map labels:
N W E S

0 1 2 Miles

to Redington

Redington Pass Passage

FR 371

FR 36 Ⓟ

FR 371

Redington Pass Rd Bike Route ⇒

8-C

FR 37

Italian Trap ◆

Tanque Verde Creek

Italian Spring Trail

to Tucson

Coronado National Forest

8-B

Italian Spring ◆

North Slope Trail

Mica Mt (8,664) △

◆ Spud Rock Spring

Cow Head Saddle Trail

◯ ◆ ▲ ◆
▲ ◆

◆ Deer Head Spring

Manning Camp

Turkey Creek Equestrian Trail

Mud Hole Spring

8-A

◯ Ⓟ

Saguaro National Park

Happy Valley Saddle ▲

Miller Creek Trail Ⓟ

FR 4408

Happy Valley Passage (incomplete)

FR 35

to I-10 J-6/Mescal Exit

Rincon Peak △ (8,482)

O N THE ARIZONA TRAIL *divides this 20-mile passage into two trips. Trip 8-A travels 8.7 miles from Turkey Creek trailhead (FR 4408) to Manning Camp, a site within the wilderness that is not accessible by vehicle. Trip 8-B travels 11 miles from Manning Camp to Redington Pass Road.*

The Rincon Mountain Wilderness is rugged with deep canyons and rocky ridges. Many areas are difficult to reach on foot and virtually impassable on horseback. Because of the rugged terrain and lack of vehicle access this passage remains pleasantly remote, offering a quality opportunity for solitude. In this trip, the Arizona Trail climbs almost 4,000 feet from hot Sonoran Desert to a historic log cabin dating back to 1905.

At this time there are two Arizona Trail routes to Manning Camp: a hiking route, Miller Creek, and an equestrian route, Turkey Creek, travel to Manning Camp from Happy Valley on the east side of the wilderness. We have chosen to describe the Turkey Creek equestrian route, because it may also be hiked.

Overnight camping within the park is restricted to designated campgrounds and requires a (free) permit. Contact Saguaro National Park for information. Bicycles are not allowed within the wilderness. Llamas, pack goats, and dogs are not allowed within the national park, and at this time, an alternate route has not been identified. Horses are allowed within the park if a permit has been obtained, and pipe corrals may be available at Manning Camp. If you are staying overnight with stock, follow all permit procedures and use regulations—stock are prohibited on some of the trails. Ten head is the maximum permitted overnight at Manning Camp, and they must be kept in the corral facility. The maximum number of stock at any other campground is five head. Picket ropes are required. Contact Saguaro National Park for information.

From Manning Camp, a backcountry campground and fire crew station at 8,000 feet, an extensive trail system offers a variety of treks through beautiful forests and meadows. The area affords wonderful bird watching opportunities for higher-elevation species and numerous scenic overlooks with fabulous views. A variety of loop trips are possible throughout the wilderness and the park.

Although there are not many saguaro cactus in the Happy Valley area, this passage offers an opportunity to visit a unique national park, with a forest that is different from any other in

North America. Saguaro National Park, established in 1933 to protect these unique and picturesque plants, offers two visitor centers, guided tours, nature walks, scenic drives, picnic areas, and hiking and equestrian trails (see Trip 8-C for directions).

The history of the passage dates back to ancient Native American inhabitants. Ancestors of Tohono O'odham people harvested the saguaro cactus fruit and seeds. The cactus frames or "ribs" were used to build shelters and fences. The area was claimed by Spain in 1598. Tucson, originally a fort, was founded by the Spanish in 1775. In the 1600s Spanish missionaries brought agriculture and cattle to the area. When the Mexican-American War ended in 1848 with the signing of the Treaty of Guadalupe Hidalgo, this part of the Sonoran Desert became property of the United States. With the Gadsden Purchase came ranchers, army forts, miners, and towns.

Levi Howell Manning moved to Tucson in 1884. He had a diverse and prosperous career as a reporter and surveyor, followed by ventures in real estate, mining, and ranching. For a short time, he had his hand in politics and was the mayor of Tucson in 1905. In 1904, Levi homesteaded 160 acres in the Rincon Mountains. He built a summer cabin in the cool, high country of the Rincons in 1905. A wagon road was constructed to the cabin, and his family used the cabin as a retreat from the summer heat of Tucson. The homestead rights were revoked in 1907 when that area became part of the Coronado National Forest. The National Park Service began to use the cabin in 1922 for fire crews and work parties. They began repair on the structure in 1946. The cabin is used today by a seasonal fire crew.

GOVERNING AGENCIES

Coronado National Forest, Santa Catalina Ranger District, 5700 N. Sabino Canyon Road, Tucson, AZ 85715. (520) 749-8700.

Saguaro National Park, Rincon Mountain District Visitor Center, 3693 S. Old Spanish Trail, Tucson, AZ 85730. (520) 733-5153.

FOR MORE INFORMATION

Tucson Hiking Guide, Second Edition, by Betty Leavengood, 1997, Pruett Publishing, Boulder, Colorado.

NEAREST SERVICES TO MILLER AND TURKEY CREEK TRAILHEADS

Benson. From the junction of Mescal Road (exit 297) and I-10 travel east on I-10 6.5 miles to Benson.

Trip 8-A

Turkey Creek Trailhead to Manning Camp

The end of Trip 8-A is not accessible by vehicle. This is the first part of a two (or more) day trek. All overnight campers must obtain a (free) permit from Saguaro National Park.

A fire in 1994 burned large sections of the eastern slopes after our trip. We have been told that the fire did not affect the route of the Arizona Trail through the Rincons.

The route of the Arizona Trail within the park is not signed with the Arizona Trail logo. There is an extensive network of trails in the area around Manning Camp. Pay close attention to the route description in this guide. There are many different routes to Manning Camp, offering opportunities for loop trips.

Mountain bikes are not allowed past the park boundary. See Trip 8-C, alternate bicycle route around Rincon Mountain Wilderness.

Trip 8-A travels from Turkey Creek Trailhead (FR 4408) 8.7 miles to Manning Camp. This is a strenuous climb from the upper Sonoran Desert foothills of the Rincons to the cool shade of conifers at Manning Camp, a historic park service log cabin in the heart of the high country.

The route offers excellent views of the San Pedro River Valley as it follows a steep trail, sparkling with mica flakes. Once at Manning Camp, there are many side trip opportunities within the Rincon Mountain Wilderness. Several days can be spent in the high country exploring the well-marked trails.

Nature Highlight: Large barrel cactus along the trail lean south, pointing the way back to the Mexico border.

Maps: Coronado National Forest, Santa Catalina Ranger District.
- Rincon Mountain Hikers' Map, Southern Arizona Hiking Association.
- Saguaro National Park, Arizona, featuring: Tucson Mountain District, Rincon Mountain District, and Tucson mountain Park, "Trails Illustrated," 1996.
- USGS Quads: Happy Valley, Mica Mountain.

Difficulty: Difficult. A long, steep climb.

Length: 8.7 miles, one way.

Elevation: 4,200–8,100 feet.

Recommended Season: All year, depending upon the weather. In the winter there may be snow in the higher elevations. In the summer temperatures may be above 110 degrees Fahrenheit in the lower elevations.

Water: (Treat all water unless noted otherwise. During dry weather, water sources may not be dependable.)

- Turkey Creek.
- Mud Hole Spring.
- Deer Head Spring.
- Spud Rock Spring.
- Manning Camp.

Camping:

- **Forest Route 35:** On the way in, FR 35 offers some nice primitive areas, including one 8 miles from I-10, just after the road crosses a creek bed.
- **Miller Creek:** 15.8 miles from I-10 is the turnoff for the Miller Creek Trailhead, where you'll find nice, shady, flat areas, seasonal water, and primitive camping. If you are driving in, bring your own water and firewood.
- **Turkey Creek:** 16.2 miles from I-10 is the turnoff for Turkey Creek trailhead. (See Directions to Turkey Creek Trailhead.) Just after the gate are spacious, flat, open areas, offering the shade of large sycamore trees. This primitive area, bordering the major drainage of Turkey Creek, has seasonal water. If you are driving in, bring your own water and firewood.

  Overnight camping within the park is restricted to designated campgrounds and requires a permit.
- **Spud Rock Cabin Site:** This is a beautiful grassy area with a rest room, and a spring 6.8 miles from the trailhead. A permit is required for overnight camping.
- **Manning Camp:** Here there is a park service cabin, privies, water, developed campsites, and corrals. A permit is required for overnight camping.

Livestock: If you are staying overnight with livestock within the national park, follow all permit procedures and use regulations. Be forewarned that this trail may pose problems for inexperienced trail animals. Some sections of this trail are very steep and have stone erosion checks and water bars set into the trail. Other sections are deeply worn and narrow. Remember that heat exhaustion can kill livestock. Allow animals frequent rest stops.

Spud Rock Campsite has water, and up to five horses are allowed with a permit. Manning Camp has horse corrals and a campground. Contact Saguaro National Park for information on obtaining a permit.

Livestock travel is prohibited on Miller Creek Trail. Turkey Creek is the recommended trail for livestock. This steep and strenuous trail is recommended for experienced and well-conditioned animals only. There is ample room for trucks and horse trailers 0.2-mile before the Turkey Creek trailhead; however, grazing is limited.

Miller Creek trailhead has dirt pull-ins for parking trucks and trailers and more grazing opportunities than Turkey Creek. It is less than a mile on horseback from Miller Creek to the Turkey Creek trailhead.

Directions to Turkey Creek Trailhead: (Note: As of this writing, the Happy Valley Passage has not been developed. The Arizona Trail temporarily follows Mescal Road.)

Passenger cars and trailers can drive to within 0.2-mile of the trailhead, depending on road conditions. There are 14 miles of narrow dirt road, which may be washboarded. The route crosses drainages that could be a problem in wet weather. High-clearance vehicles are preferable. From I-10 take the Mescal, J-Six Ranch exit (297), and travel north on Mescal Road. The pavement ends after 2.5 miles, and the road becomes FR 35. As the pavement ends, look to the left for a glimpse of a Western movie set that is owned by Old Tucson Studios. Many films, including *The Quick and The Dead, Lightning Jack, Tombstone,* and the TV series *Legends* have been filmed here. A Keep Out sign has been posted.

From I-10 it is 15.8 miles to a signed turnoff for the Miller Creek trailhead. (See Other Area Trails, below.) Continue on FR 35 past the Miller Creek turnoff 0.4 mile to the junction with FR 4408. This junction may be unsigned except for a small carsonite Arizona Trail marker. Turn left on FR 4408 and travel 0.3 mile to a gate. From the gate to the trailhead, another 0.2 mile, are open, level areas in which to camp and park. Between the gate and the trailhead, seasonal pools of water may be found to the right of the road.

Other Area Trails: Miller Creek Trail: This steep trail affords access to Happy Valley Campground, Rincon Peak, and Manning Camp. (See directions to trailhead above.)

There is a network of trails within the wilderness that access the Arizona Trail. Refer to maps and local guide books or contact governing agencies for more information on Miller Creek Trail and other trails in the area.

TRAIL DESCRIPTION

From the Turkey Creek Trailhead the route of the Arizona Trail climbs north on an old 4WD road. The road is steep, ascending a long, open ridge, with views of the surrounding foothills. The area is landscaped with barrel cactus, mesquite, and treacherous patches of shin dagger. On the left the massive Rincon Mountains rise before us. (To the northwest a distinctive cliff face known as Reef Rock is visible. Just below Reef Rock a patch of bright green aspen trees mark the site of Spud Rock Spring. To the right of Reef Rock is a prominent rock formation known as Mica Secondary. To the left is the long ridgeline of Heartbreak Ridge and 8,482-foot Rincon Peak.)

At 1.5 miles from the trailhead the road ends at an altitude of 4,500 feet and becomes a trail. This area is rocky, and the trail could be missed here, so look carefully for the Arizona Trail marker. You will resume climbing along a ridge, then the trail descends into and across a small valley, passing a junction with a faint and rarely used trail to Fox Mountain.

A gate announces the border of Saguaro National Park. This area of Upper Sonoran chaparral was affected by the July 1994 fire and has recently been described as a "moonscape." At the park boundary a long, steep 1-mile climb begins to Mud Hole Spring. A series of stone water bars and checks have been set into the trail. Watch for sparkling pieces of mica along the trail.

At 5,700 feet, the spring is a welcome sight, especially to livestock after the steep climb. The spring is small, but offers a delightfully shady and level area for a welcome break. After Mud Hole Spring watch for yellow or red metal tags on trees marking the route, as the trail makes a steep switchbacking ascent. Equestrians may want to lead their animals through some of the narrow, deeply worn sections of trail. The route passes through a pretty area of grass, ferns, and wildflowers.

Large oak and pine trees announce our arrival at Deer Head Spring, 6.2 miles from the trailhead. The area around the spring is blanketed with grass, colored with flowers, and shaded by ponderosas. At 7,160 feet, this is an excellent rest spot. A short distance above Deer Head Spring is a signed junction of trails. Travel north on Deer Head Spring Trail toward the Spud Rock Campground, climbing through an oak and ponderosa forest. There will be opportunities to see the valley below. Entering a grove of aspen, the trail intersects a junction with trails to Mica Secondary, Reef Rock, and Spud Rock Campground.

The Arizona Trail follows East Slope Trail 0.2-mile to Switchback Trail. Turn right (west). Switchback Trail climbs through a pretty area of ferns, shady pine and oaks, and interesting rock outcroppings. Look for the occasional view to the east of Paige Canyon, the San Pedro River Valley, Galiuro Mountains, and Dos Cabezas in the distance.

At the next junction, 0.3-mile from the last, veer right for 0.7 mile on the Heartbreak Ridge Trail to the Fireloop Trail. Continue to follow the metal trail markers attached to trees along the trail. The long climb is over as the route travels through more level terrain in the high country perfumed with the fresh scent of pine. You will pass a small seasonal creek with yellow columbine.

At the next junction with Mica Meadow and Reef Rock Trail, continue west on the Fireloop Trail 0.7 mile to Manning Camp. At 8,100 feet the path crests a ridge with a fabulous view to the southwest of the Santa Rita Mountains and then begins an easy descent.

One-tenth of a mile from camp our route joins Mica Mountain Trail, which it follows west into Manning Camp. Entering the camp at 8,000 feet, we are greeted by the old cabin used by firefighters in the summer months, and a campground. Be sure to visit the charming waterfall beyond the cabin.

Trip 8-B
Manning Camp to Redington Pass Road

The beginning of this trip is not accessible by vehicle. This is the second part of a two (or more)- day trek. All overnight campers must obtain a (free) permit from Saguaro National Park. See the Rincon Mountain Passage description for more information. There are many different routes to Manning Camp, offering opportunities for loop trips. Note that the Arizona Trail within the park is not signed. There is an extensive network of trails in the area around Manning Camp. Pay close attention to the route description in this guide.

A fire in 1994 burned large sections of the eastern slopes; however, the fire did not affect the route of the Arizona Trail through the Rincons.

Mountain bikes are not allowed past the park boundary. See Trip 8-C, Alternate Bicycle Route Around the Rincon Mountain Wilderness.

Trip 8-B travels from the historic Park Service log cabin at Manning Camp to Italian Spring, a small but generally dependable water source in the heart of the Rincon Mountains. From Italian Spring, the trip follows a steep descent to Redington Pass Road. The mixed conifer-topped summit of the Rincon Mountains near Manning Camp has a delightful park-like atmosphere. Well-signed trails offer a variety of treks through cool woodlands and meadows. There are seasonal streams and pools, and scenic overlooks with fabulous views in all directions.

From Italian Spring the trail drops steeply, passing from pine forest, to pine-oak woodland, and ending in the high desert grasslands. The views are breathtaking as the route descends to the major drainage of Tanque Verde Creek. This route is remote and peaceful in a less-visited area of the Rincons.

Nature Highlight: In the summer months, listen for the haunting, flute-like song of the hermit thrush echoing through the trees. This elusive bird is frequently seen at Manning Camp.

Maps: Coronado National Forest, Santa Catalina Ranger District.
* Rincon Mountain Hikers' Map, Southern Arizona Hiking Association.
* Saguaro National Park, Arizona, Featuring: Tucson Mountain District, Rincon Mountain District, and Tucson Mountain Park, "Trails Illustrated," 1996.
* USGS Quads: Happy Valley, Mica Mountain, Piety Hill.

Difficulty: Moderate to Difficult—mostly downhill, with some difficult spots. Very steep and brushy in places.

Length: 11 miles, one way.

Elevation: 8,500–4,300 feet.

Recommended Season: All year, depending upon the weather. In the winter there may be snow in the higher elevations. Summer temperatures may be above 100 degrees Fahrenheit in the lower elevations.

Water: (Treat all water unless noted otherwise. During dry weather, water sources may not be dependable.)
* **Manning Camp.**
* **Italian Spring.**
* **Stock tank:** at junction of Italian Spring Trail and FR 37, south of Redington Pass Road.

Camping: Within the park, overnight camping is restricted to designated campgrounds and requires a permit. See Trip 8-A and the Rincon Mountain Passage for more information on camping in the park.

At the junction of Italian Spring Trail and FR 37, south of Redington Pass Road, there are primitive camping possibilities. The area has a stock tank, corrals, and large shade trees.

Livestock: Manning Camp has corrals. See Trip 8-A for information on taking livestock into the park.

The section of trail from Italian Spring to Tanque Verde Wash is extremely steep and brushy. It is recommended only for experienced and well-conditioned animals. Tanque Verde Wash features a windmill and tank, corral and shade.

Directions to Manning Camp: Manning Camp is not accessible by vehicle. On the east side of the range, Manning Camp is accessed by two routes of the Arizona Trail: Miller Creek Trail and Turkey Creek Trail (see Trip 8-A).

Other Area Trails: Manning Camp may be reached from the west side of the mountains on **Douglas Spring Trail** or **Tanque Verde Trail** (no livestock). There is a network of trails in the Rincon Mountain Wilderness, offering multiple opportunities for loop trips. Refer to the maps listed or contact Saguaro National Park for more information on trails in the area.

TRAIL DESCRIPTION

The Arizona Trail leaves Manning Camp heading northeast following the Fire Loop Trail, 0.1 mile to the junction with Mica Trail. Turn left at this junction onto the Mica Mountain Trail. The trail passes through deep ponderosa forest, intermingled with lacy ferns and large oak trees and is signed with red metal rectangles attached to trees.

At 1.4 miles from Manning Camp you meet a junction. Take the right fork, which is Fire Loop Trail East. The trail switchbacks up 300 feet to a trail junction with a spur trail that leads 0.1-mile to the top of Mica Mountain. (The spur trail offers an interesting and short side trip to view the Tucson Valley from 8,666 feet. Remains of concrete pilings mark the site of the old fire tower.)

The route continues east through an area that in early summer is awash with colorful wildflowers. The path makes a gentle descent through pine forest, with ferns blanketing the forest floor, then passes through a lovely mountain meadow, to a junction with the North Slope Trail. Turn left and follow the North Slope Trail to Italian Spring. The North Slope Trail makes a moderate 500-foot descent to Italian Spring in 0.6 mile at 7,980 feet.

Italian Spring is 2.2 miles from Manning Camp. It is small but adequate for filtering drinking water and perhaps for watering livestock. This spot provides shade and tranquility before the long descent. Leaving the spring, traveling north on the Italian Spring Trail, the descent on narrow switchbacks is steep. There are extensive views to the north of the Catalina Mountains. Pine forest gives way to the mixed pine, oak, and manzanita of the Transition life zone. The trail is very steep and rocky in places. This rugged trail offers fabulous views of the Santa Catalinas. The (at times) snowcapped peaks near Mount Lemmon (the northern route of the Arizona Trail) are visible to the north. After you pass a pretty little seepage with wild geraniums, a sign and a panoramic view of Redington Pass and the San Pedro River Valley announce your arrival at the national park border.

One and six-tenths miles from Italian Spring and 3.8 miles from Manning Camp, the trail leaves the national park boundary and drops steeply down a wash. Orange metal disks on trees mark the route. Watch carefully for the place where the route veers to the left, away from the drainage it has been following. As it drops down a ridgeline, the route is badly eroded, rough, and steep.

Approximately 1 mile from the park border the trail enters an area of prominent boulders. Watch carefully for rock cairns because the route becomes faint amid the rocks. As the trail travels along the left (west) side of a steep and rugged canyon, there are picturesque, weirdly eroded cliffs and rock formations, that have been sculpted by wind and water. Depending upon the time of year, you may hear the sound of rushing waterfalls. The trail enters a densely vegetated area of small oak and manzanita, winding down the narrow trail to a creek crossing.

There is a lovely pool 2.3 miles from the national park boundary. This is a nice place for a picnic amid the trees, at an elevation of 5,000 feet. After the creek crossing, the trail ascends a hill that offers views of the massive foothills of the Rincons behind and the northern route of the journey to come. Past the creek crossing the Arizona Trail is an abandoned dirt road that the Forest Service has replanted and reclaimed as a one-track trail. The route rolls in and out of drainages that cut through the swelling northern foothills of the Rincons. The vegetation here is Upper Sonoran chaparral, grasses, and cactus.

The route makes a final, very steep descent into the upper Tanque Verde Wash. This is a prominent wash in the lower foothills of the Rincon Mountains, carving a deep canyon with the spectacular Chiva and Tanque Verde waterfalls. The wash continues into the Tucson Valley. Upon entering the wash, the route turns left (west) and travels past an Arizona Trail sign and on to a windmill and corral.

Five and three-tenths miles from the park and 9 miles from Manning Camp, this lovely riparian area is a welcome sight. This is an excellent camping spot, and the stock tank and grass make it especially inviting to travelers with livestock. Leaving Tanque Verde Wash the route travels north on FR 37, a rocky 4WD road, in a 2-mile, moderate ascent to Redington Road.

 # Trip 8-C

Alternate Bicycle Route Around the Rincon Mountain Wilderness: Santa Rita Mountain Passage to the Redington Passage

As of this writing the Empire-Cienega and Cienega Creek Passages are in the planning stages. Official Arizona Trail routes through them have been proposed but not finalized. Public scoping has begun through the Sonoita Valley Planning Partnership, and the Arizona Trail is being addressed within this process. Because these passages are not completed this trip bypasses them and begins where the Santa Rita Mountain Passage crosses State Highway 83. See pages 91–99 for more information on the proposed routes through these passages.

This 60.9-mile bicycle route begins at Oak Tree Canyon at the end of the Santa Rita Mountains Passage. It bypasses the Rincon Mountain wilderness (where bicycles are prohibited) via paved highways, service roads, city streets, and ends with a steep switchbacking ascent on a graded dirt road. The terrain is like a roller-coaster, beginning in the oak woodlands, then traveling through the beautiful Sonoran Desert, and rising to the desert grasslands. This scenic trip passes the natural wonders of Colossal Cave and Saguaro National Monument, and vendors on the streets of Tucson offer refreshments.

Nature Highlight: Saguaro cactus stand like sentries, silhouetted by the setting sun.

Maps:
* Arizona road map.
* Coronado National Forest.

Difficulty: Moderate to difficult.

Length: 60.9 miles, one way.

Elevation: 2,500–4,900 feet.

Recommended Season:
Fall, winter, and spring.

Water: (Treat all water unless noted otherwise. During dry weather, water sources may not be dependable.)
* **Colossal Cave.**
* **Saguaro National Monument.**
* **Gas stations on Houghton Road.**

Camping:
* **Coronado National Forest:** The trip begins on SH 83 in the Coronado National Forest, where there are primitive campsites.
* **Colossal Cave:** Has developed campsites.
* **BLM:** Empire-Cienega Resource Area has primitive camping.

Directions to Trailhead: Travel SH 83 south from I-10 16 miles to mile post 43 at Oak Tree Canyon. There is no sign for this canyon. Watch for a culvert under the highway and a gate on the right (west) just before the culvert. (If you pass the canyon, the next road you come to is The Old Sonoita Highway to the right [west], at mile post 41. Turn around and travel approximately 2 miles back on SH 83, north to Oak Tree Canyon to the northwest of the culvert.) Pull off the highway and through the gate where there is parking.

ROUTE DESCRIPTION

Travel SH 83 north through rolling hills and canyons. Approximately 9 miles north, the highway parallels Davidson Canyon for a few miles. Davidson canyon lies between the Santa Rita and Empire Mountains. Apaches raided this area in the 1860s and 1870s. Mail carriers traveled between Fort Crittenden (see Trip 3-B) and Tucson through this area. They had to travel with care and sometimes did not always finish their trip.

East of Davidson Canyon in the Empire Mountains is the ghost town of Total Wreck. This was a silver mine in the 1880s. The town had as many as three hundred people with saloons, stores, and hotel and saw gunfights and Apache raids. Today little remains of the town.

Continue on SH 83 approximately 7 more miles north to Interstate 10. Cross over I-10 to the north side onto the frontage road and travel west for 2 miles. The frontage road joins the Vail road and turns north. It is approximately 2 miles to the town of Vail at 3,323 feet elevation. This very small rural town has a school and feed store. It was named after Walter E. Vail, who developed the Empire Ranch to the south. The Southern Pacific Railroad passes through Vail, and, beginning in 1880, Vail served as a shipping point for local mines and other commerce.

The Vail Road winds through low mountains. Travel about 5.6 miles to the Colossal Cave Mountain Park turnoff. Colossal Cave is a large, dry limestone cave, and the park has a campground and picnic area. At the turn to the cave, bear left (west) on Old Spanish Trail for about 12 miles to Saguaro National Monument. You will pass a market at the Rocking K. Ranch. The road will cross Rincon Creek, a major drainage from the Rincon Mountains. Saguaro National Monument, on the east side of Old Spanish Trail, features a visitor center, complete with rest rooms, water, and a small bookstore.

Leave Saguaro National Monument on Old Spanish Trail traveling northwest and ride for 3 miles to Houghton Road, where you should turn right (north). There are several quick markets and gas stations along Houghton Road. Travel about 3.9 miles to Tanque Verde Road and turn right. It is about 4 miles on Tanque Verde Road to the first mile post marker on Redington Pass Road. The pavement will end and the name of the road becomes Redington Pass Road. Three miles from mile post marker 1 the pavement ends and the road starts switchbacking steeply up the hills. You travel through lush desert growth of saguaros and ocotillo.

Seven and one-half miles from mile post 1 there is a parking area on the right (south) and a trail to Chiva Falls. This fall is on the Tanque Verde Creek, which cuts its way through the foothills to the valley below. Along the way the creek creates beautiful waterfalls.

Ten miles from mile post 1 on the left (north) is Bellota Ranch Road (FR 36) and the Arizona Trail. Here you intersect the Arizona Trail toward Molino Basin. Turn left (north) on this four-wheel-drive road to follow the Arizona Trail into the foothills of the Santa Catalinas.

9 Redington Pass Passage

Redington Road to Molino Basin

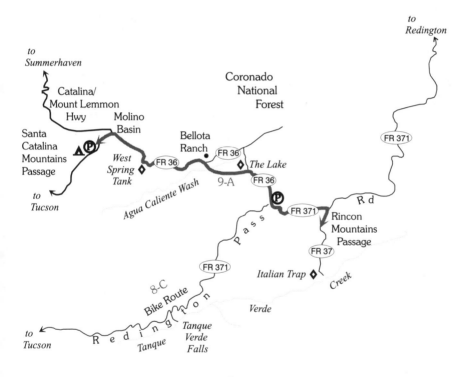

N W E S

0 1 2
Miles

to
Summerhaven

Catalina/
Mount Lemmon
Hwy   Molino
Basin

Santa
Catalina
Mountains
Passage

West
Spring
Tank

Agua Caliente Wash

Bellota
Ranch

Coronado
National
Forest

FR 36

FR 36

The Lake

9-A   FR 36

FR 371

FR 371

to
Tucson

Pass

Rincon
Mountains
Passage

R d

FR 37

FR 371

8-C
Bike Route

Italian Trap

Creek

R e d i n g t o n

Verde

to
Tucson

Tanque

Tanque
Verde
Falls

to
Redington

Saguaro
National
Park

Forest Road	·········· Boundary	Trailhead and Parking
Paved Road	River, Stream, or Wash	Trailhead, no Parking
State/Interstate	Canyon Rim	P Parking
Arizona Trail	Campground	Town or City
··········· Trip Access Trail	Water	Point of Interest
---- Other Trail Area	Ranger Station	Mountain Peak

Photo by Susan Moran

A rider enjoys a view of the Rincon Mountains as seen from Redington Pass.

> *I love you Arizona;*
>   *Desert dust on the wind;*
> *The sage and cactus are blooming,*
>   *The smell of the rain on your skin.*

—**"Arizona," Rex Allen Jr., 1981,
Arizona State song, reprinted courtesy
of the Arizona State Capitol Museum.**

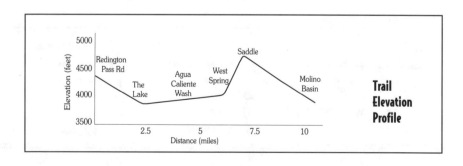

**Trail
Elevation
Profile**

THIS 10.7-MILE LONG PASSAGE *requires only one trip, which begins on Redington Pass Road and ends at Molino Basin.*

This is a high desert pass between two significant mountain ranges, the Santa Catalinas on the north and the Rincons on the south. The vegetation is desert grass lands, with occasional oaks, junipers, and manzanitas. A prominent feature is Agua Caliente Wash, which is lined with cottonwood and ash trees. The creek quickly becomes a rugged canyon as it descends into the desert below. The canyon lies on the southeastern edge of the Catalina Mountains and is a graphic example of erosion.

Padre Francisco Kino traveled through the San Pedro Valley in 1706 and encountered 2,000 Sobiapuri Indians living in villages and successfully farming the area. Apache Indians drove the Sobiapuri out of the area as they did white people who tried to settle here. The raids ended in the 1880s.

Originally the pass was called Cebedilla Pass, but it has been renamed after the small hamlet of Redington on the east side of the pass. Lem Redfield founded Redington in 1877, building a log home. Later a post office, school, and agriculture fields composed the town of Redington, which became the scene of many gun battles and killings. Redington was also plagued by natural disasters such as an earthquake, floods, and droughts, which eventually drove many of the settlers from the area.

Redington had protection from Fort Lowell, a military fort in Tucson. The fort sent wagons and troops over the Cebadillo Pass from Tucson. The road was heavily used by people traveling over the pass in buckboards and on horseback. The military abandoned the road in 1895, which made the trip to Tucson quite long for the residents of Redington. They had to travel 100 miles through Benson or 70 miles through Oracle, both routes going around the mountain instead of over the pass. The trip was shortened to 45 miles in 1936, when a new road was built over the pass to Tucson. This road is now a graded dirt road linking the San Padro Valley with the Tucson Valley.

The Redington Pass area has been dominated by cattle ranching. The Arizona Trail passes near Bellota Ranch, which is 4 miles off the main road, nestled in a grove of trees on the Agua Caliente Wash. The original ranch was built in 1890 and changed ownership several times. It remains an active cattle ranch at this time.

GOVERNING AGENCIES

Coronado National Forest, Santa Catalina, 5700 N. Sabino Canyon Road, Tucson, AZ 85715. (520) 749-8700.

FOR MORE INFORMATION

Coronado National Forest, Santa Catalina District.

NEAREST SERVICES

Tucson is 8 miles west on Redington Pass Road. See appendix A for further information on available services.

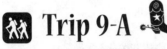

Trip 9-A

Redington Pass Road to Molino Basin

 As of this writing, 2 miles of Redington Pass Road connects the southern route (FR 37) with the northern route (Bellota Ranch Road, FR 36) of the Arizona Trail. There are plans to build a trail that will eventually take the route off Redington Pass Road.

Trip 9-A begins at the junction of Bellota Ranch Road (FR 36) and Redington Pass Road, 2 miles west of the FR 37 trailhead.

Trip 9-A travels 8.7 miles from Redington Pass Road to Molino Basin on the Catalina Highway. This popular mountain cycling route crosses Redington Pass, a high desert pass between two large sky islands, the Rincon Mountains, and the Santa Catalina Mountains. The journey travels through a major drainage, Agua Caliente Creek.

The majority of the trip is through desert vegetation mixed with oak, juniper, and manzanita. The end of the route requires a steep climb to a saddle, culminating in a technically challenging (if you're on a bike) 500-foot descent to the Catalina Highway and the lovely canyon of Molino Basin.

Nature Highlight: A pair of mallard ducks paddle about in The Lake, a beautiful pond rimmed with white sand and desert willow.

Maps: Coronado Forest, Santa Catalina Ranger District.
* Santa Catalina Mountains, A Trail and Recreation Map. Tenth edition. 1995.
* USGS Quad: Agua Caliente Hill.

Difficulty: Moderate, with one very steep climb.

Length: 8.7 miles, one way.

Elevation: 3,920–4,900 feet.

Recommended Season: Year-round, depending on the weather. Temperatures exceed 100 degrees Fahrenheit in the summer.

Water: (Treat all water unless noted otherwise. During dry weather, water sources may not be dependable.)
- **The Lake.**
- **Agua Caliente Creek.**
- **West Spring Tank.**

Camping:
- **Redington Road** offers primitive camping. At the FR 37 junction with Reding-ton Road (the southern route of the Arizona Trail) there is limited space for parking and camping.
- **Bellota Ranch Road** has a place to pull off about a mile north of the junction.
- **The Lake and Agua Caliente Wash** have good primitive camping possibilities with shade and water. A 4WD vehicle is required to travel FR 36 to The Lake.

Livestock: This trip is "livestock friendly," with accessible water, good footing, and little use. The last part is steep and narrow, necessitating experienced and well-conditioned animals. Watch out for cyclists.

    The best camping places for livestock are probably near the windmill south of Redington Pass Road (See Trip 8-B), or near a large pond known as The Lake (remember to camp 0.25 mile away from water). Molino Basin Campground does not allow livestock. (See Trip 10-A for information on camping with live-stock at Old Prison Camp.)

Directions to Redington Pass Trailhead: You can access the trailhead by passenger car. From Tucson travel east on Tanque Verde Road. As it nears the mountains, Tanque Verde Road becomes Redington Pass Road. About 3 miles past the be-ginning of Redington Pass Road the pavement ends as the graded gravel road climbs steeply with many sharp turns and switchbacks. Traveling up through the foothills, the route passes a turnout for Tanque Verde Falls parking.

    Bellota Ranch Road is on the left, marked by a white metal sign for the ranch headquarters, 7.4 miles from where the pavement ends. Turn left here to travel north on the Arizona Trail to Molino Basin.

    To access the Arizona Trail traveling south toward Saguaro National Park (Trip 8-B), continue east on Redington Pass Road 2 miles, to FR on the right. This is the southern route of the Arizona Trail from Redington Pass Road to Manning Camp.

TRAIL DESCRIPTION

At the junction of Redington Pass Road and Bellota Ranch Road (FR 36), there is a wooden post with an Arizona Trail symbol and a white metal sign for the ranch headquarters. Beginning at 4,400-feet elevation the route travels north, following a 4WD road. The road descends through rolling hills dotted with piñon pine, man-zanita, oak, and juniper. The views of the Catalinas are expansive from here. There is a large Arizona Trail sign, and the Arizona Trail leaves the ranch road here and follows a sandy wash a short distance to a welcome surprise: The Lake.

Two and four-tenths miles from Redington Pass, this beautiful pond is complete with waterfowl and white sandy shores. At an elevation of 3,980 feet, this lush area is an oasis, surrounded by Sonoran Desert. The area offers good primitive camping and great photo opportunities.

From The Lake the Arizona Trail follows Bellota Trail #15 as it travels west, winding through rocks, juniper, and manzanita. The trail ambles through low hills and the sometimes slick rock of a creek bed, with occasional small pools of water. The area is decorated with barrel cactus, ocotillo, bear grass, and beautiful wildflowers. Depending on the time of year, verbena, Indian paintbrush, and penstemon may be blooming, or snakeweed may carpet the hills in yellow. After traveling 0.5 mile look north and you will see the Bellota Ranch on the Agua Caliente Wash. The wash is lined with cottonwoods and Arizona ash, which weave a colorful ribbon through the desert. Depending upon the season, you will be treated to brilliant green or the bright yellow of fall.

The trail passes through a gate 3.2 miles from Redington Pass, then it travels through a scenic area of large, granite boulders and oak trees.

The route descends into a large riparian canyon, Agua Caliente Wash, 4.2 miles from Redington Pass. The amount of water to be found here will depend upon rainfall. The sandy banks and huge trees offer a restful area for camping or lunch. The Agua Caliente flows into Tucson, and as it descends to the Sonoran Desert below, it carves a spectacular canyon, before it becomes a level, wide wash in Tucson. From the wash it is a slight ascent up the bank to a junction where the route again joins FR 36.

Trail markers indicate a left (west) turn onto FR 36. Traveling on 4WD road again, the Arizona Trail follows a wash that originates at West Spring. Traveling is quite easy here, as the route dips in and out of the creek bed, through upper Sonoran vegetation of manzanita, oak, and mesquite.

Six and two-tenths miles from Redington Pass Road, FR 36 ends at West Spring at an elevation of 4,070 feet. This spring has been developed for livestock and wildlife use. There are solar panels powering a pump that fills a large, concrete tank. The Arizona Trail follows West Spring Trail, climbing northwest toward a large saddle. There is no sign here, but the trail is well used and easy to spot. The hillside is open with low desert vegetation. Looking back to the south, you have unobstructed views of the Rincons. The trail continues in a long, steep, switchbacking 830-foot ascent, with sheer drop-offs.

Seven and three-tenths miles from Redington Pass, at an elevation of 4,900 feet, the trail arrives at the saddle and a gate. Passing through the gate the trail enters a new mountain range—the Santa Catalina Mountains. The Mount Lemmon Highway and the impressive rock walls above the Molino Basin parking area are visible from here.

The trail makes a steep switchbacking descent from the saddle to the canyon bottom below. The route crosses the creek to a large, metal Arizona Trail sign, then veers left, traveling a short distance to the Mount Lemmon Highway and the Molino Basin Campground beyond at an elevation of 4,380 feet. Use caution crossing to the parking area, as this road is heavily used. If you are planning to park in this popular area, you should get here early on weekends during the fall, winter, and spring months.

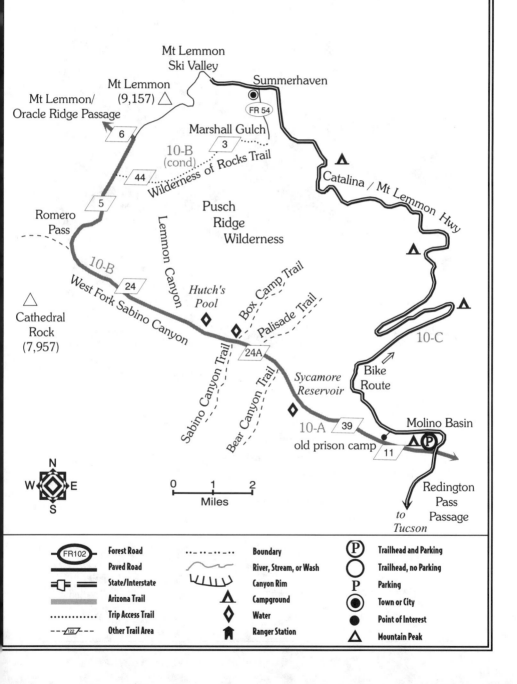

10 Santa Catalina Mountains
Passage Molino Basin to Mount Lemmon

Mt Lemmon
Ski Valley

Summerhaven

Mt Lemmon
(9,157) △

Mt Lemmon/
Oracle Ridge Passage

FR 54

6

Marshall Gulch

3

10-B
(cond)

44

Wilderness of Rocks Trail

Catalina / Mt Lemmon Hwy

5

Romero
Pass

Pusch
Ridge
Wilderness

10-B

24

West Fork Sabino Canyon

Lemmon Canyon

Hutch's
Pool

Box Camp Trail

Palisade Trail

△
Cathedral
Rock
(7,957)

10-C

24A

Sabino Canyon Trail

Bear Canyon Trail

Sycamore
Reservoir

Bike
Route

Molino Basin

10-A
old prison camp

39

11

△ Ⓟ

N
W   E
S

0   1   2
Miles

Redington
Pass
Passage

to
Tucson

Symbol	Description	Symbol	Description	Symbol	Description
FR102	Forest Road	·—··—··—·	Boundary	Ⓟ	Trailhead and Parking
	Paved Road	～～	River, Stream, or Wash	◯	Trailhead, no Parking
	State/Interstate	⊔⊔⊔⊔	Canyon Rim	P	Parking
	Arizona Trail	△	Campground	◉	Town or City
122	Trip Access Trail	◆	Water	●	Point of Interest
122	Other Trail Area	🛖	Ranger Station	△	Mountain Peak

A yucca plant at the start of the Molino Basin Trailhead that continues on to Mount Lemmon.

> *The dust-devil dances and staggers*
> *And the yucca flower daintily swaggers*
> *At her birth from a cluster of daggers*
> *And ever the heat ripples run.*

—"The Border," Badger Clark, 1911

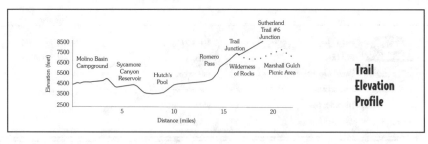

Trail Elevation Profile

ON THE ARIZONA TRAIL *details two trips from this 19-mile passage. Trip 10-A travels 9.4 miles from Molino Basin, on the Catalina Highway, to Hutch's Pool, a site within the wilderness that is not accessible by vehicle. Trip 10-B links to 10-A, traveling 7 miles to a junction with the Wilderness of Rocks Trail, where Trip 10-B exits the Arizona Trail and follows the Wilderness of Rocks Trail another 5.3 miles to Summerhaven. The Santa Catalina Mountains Passage continues another 2.5 miles to a junction with the Mount Lemmon/Oracle Ridge Passage and a utility line road below Mount Lemmon.*

The rugged pinnacles and majestic ridgelines of the Santa Catalina Mountains dominate Tucson's eastern skyline. The epitome of mountain islands, this 250-million-year-old rock pile rises from a 2,200-foot Lower Sonoran Desert to the lofty, 9,157-foot Mount Lemmon, an ascent of almost 7,000 feet. The Santa Catalina Passage offers a fascinating view of vertical plant and animal communities as the route climbs from sweltering saguaro-dotted bajadas, through oak woodland, then pine forest, on its journey to the Canadian Zone.

The area offers magnificent vistas, campgrounds, Mount Lemmon Ski Valley, and the charming community of Summerhaven. One hundred seventy miles of trail lead to some of the most beautiful and remote country in Arizona. Larger mammals include white tail deer and black bear, and there is a dwindling population of bighorn sheep in the Pusch Ridge Wilderness.

Hohokam sites from 1,200 years ago have been found in the Santa Catalina Mountains. Later, the area was frequented by the Tohono O'odham and Apache. It is believed that the Santa Catalinas were named by Father Kino, who first visited the area in 1692. In the 1870s and 1880s Soldier Camp, located south of Summerhaven, was used by Fort Lowell during campaigns against Apache Indians. Mount Lemmon was named for the wife of botanist John Lemmon after they climbed to its summit in the spring of 1881. In 1920 the dirt road (Old Mount Lemon Road) was built from Oracle to Summerhaven. The Catalina (also called the General Hitchcock Highway and the Mount Lemmon Highway) Highway was completed in 1950.

GOVERNING AGENCIES

Coronado National Forest, Santa Catalina Ranger District, 5700 N. Sabino Canyon Rd., Tucson, AZ 85715. (520) 749-8700. Contact the Santa Catalina Ranger District for information on trail conditions, campgrounds, or other hiking and riding opportunities in the area.

FOR MORE INFORMATION

Tucson Hiking Guide, 2nd edition, by Leavengood.

Trail Guide to the Santa Catalina Mountains, by Glendening and Cowgill.

(See reference list for full bibliographic information on these titles.)

Arizona Historical Society Museum, 949 E. Second Street, Tucson, AZ 85719. (520) 628-5774.

Arizona-Sonoran Desert Museum,Tucson Mountain Park, 2021 N. Kinney Road, Tucson, AZ 85743. (520) 883-2702.

NEAREST SERVICES TO MOLINO BASIN

From Molino Basin Campground follow the Catalina Highway south 10 miles to Tanque Verde Road. Follow Tanque Verde Road west into the city of Tucson.

Trip 10-A

Molino Basin Campground to Hutch's Pool

Bicycles are not allowed past the wilderness boundary. See Trip 10-C for an alternate bicycle route.

The end of Trip 10-A is not accessible by vehicle. This is the first part of a two (or more) day trek. Hutch's Pool is a popular destination, which may be accessed by several different trails from both the east and west sides of the range.

Because of the low elevation this is a fabulous winter trek, but a warning for long-distance travelers: You need to time your trip to avoid snow on Mount Lemmon.

The Forest Service has renumbered some trails in this area, so older maps may not correspond to this text.

Trip 10-A travels from Molino Basin to a scenic, natural swimming hole in the heart of the Pusch Ridge Wilderness. The wilderness is defined by steep-walled, deeply eroded canyons and ragged ridgelines. The cliff-bound heights conceal serene willow- and sycamore-lined streams and lovely canyon pools. This mostly downhill route intersects other popular trails leading into Sabino Basin, offering opportunities for alternate routes out of the wilderness.

Nature Highlight: Giant armed saguaro cactus, famous symbol of the American Southwest, mingle with riparian sycamores in Sabino Canyon.

Maps: Coronado National Forest Map, Santa Catalina Ranger District.
- Trail and Recreation Map, Santa Catalina Mountains, Rainbow Expeditions.
- USGS Quads: Sabino Canyon and Mt. Lemmon.

Difficulty: Moderate to difficult, with steep, rocky descents. (Remember that difficulty ratings are from south to north. If you return by the same route, you will have some very long, steep climbs.)

Length: 9.4 miles, one way.

Elevation: 5,000–3,900 feet.

Recommended Season: Year-round. Caution: In warm weather when temperatures can exceed 110 degrees Fahrenheit, travel in the early morning and carry a minimum of one gallon of water per person per day. Sunscreen and protective clothing is also recommended.

Water: (Treat all water unless noted otherwise. During dry weather, water sources may not be dependable.)
- **Seasonal creek at Old Prison Camp.**
- **Sycamore Canyon Reservoir.**
- **Sabino Canyon.**

Camping:
- **Molino Basin Campground:** This picturesque, developed campground in a Sonoran Desert setting offers grills, picnic tables, and privies. It is a fee area with no water, and you should bring your own firewood. The campground is closed during the hottest months of the year.
- **Old Prison Camp:** Watch for a signed road on the left, 1.7 miles north of Molino Basin on the Catalina Highway. The area offers a developed campground and a spacious, shaded area for large groups. If you will be driving in, bring your own water and firewood.
- Along the route there are some good primitive camping possibilities.
- **Hutch's Pool:** In this area, flat spots are difficult to come by, especially on a weekend. There are some heavily used areas just below the pool. Firewood is scarce, and insects aren't—carry bug repellent.

Livestock: The authors recommend that livestock travel this passage no farther than Trip 10-A, which ends at Hutch's Pool. Use caution taking livestock on this section of the route, which is rugged, with narrow, cliff-hanger trails (which may not accommodate horses carrying panniers), and can reach temperatures above 100 degrees Fahrenheit. Take only experienced trail animals that are acclimated to the heat (and not afraid of heights). If you wish to make a loop route, check with the Forest Service regarding which, if any other trail can accommodate horses or llamas.

An alternate route has not been determined. We recommend that long-distance travelers have their animals transported from the Old Prison Camp north of Molino Basin to Red Ridge or Oracle Ridge trailheads above Summerhaven. Both connect to the Arizona Trail (Oracle Ridge is the easier of the two). (See appendix B for information on transporting or boarding livestock.)

The recommended place to unload and camp with livestock is the Old Prison Camp, located 1.7 miles northwest of Molino Basin Campground. Prison Camp may be reached either by driving (do not attempt to ride livestock up the highway), or by following the Arizona Trail west. A spacious area with big shade trees makes this an ideal horse camp, with easy access from the highway and plenty of room for turning and parking trailers. Seasonal water and grass may be available as you follow the dirt road west a short distance beyond the rock walls. If you will be driving in, bring your own water and firewood.

There are no suitable camping areas near Hutch's Pool for livestock. There is a flat, grassy area near the creek, 0.5 mile southeast of the pool (before the final, rocky, creek crossing). Bring insect repellent for your animals.

You may unload livestock in the Molino Basin Campground parking lot, but clean up manure. Livestock is not allowed in the campground.

Directions to Molino Basin Trailhead: You can access the trailhead by passenger car. From Tucson, take the Catalina Highway from Tanque Verde, or Houghton Road. Follow the Catalina Highway 9.7 miles to the Molino Basin Campground.

Directions to the Old Prison Camp: Continue past the Molino Basin Campground 1.7 miles. Watch for a road on the left that is signed.

Other Area Trails: The Arizona Trail encounters several trails on the way to Hutch's Pool that offer other routes out of the wilderness. **Palisade Trail** and **Box Camp Trail** climb northeast approximately 8 miles to connect with the Catalina Highway.

Bear Canyon Trail travels 7 miles southeast to the Sabino Canyon Visitor Center. **Sabino Canyon Trail,** one of the most popular routes into the Santa Catalinas, travels 2.5 miles to the upper Sabino Recreation area, with an optional 4.7-mile shuttle to the visitor center parking lot.

TRAIL DESCRIPTION

The Arizona Trail leaves the Molino Basin campground parking lot and heads south and then west as it bypasses Molino Campground, following Molino Trail #11. Paralleling the Catalina Highway (also called the Mount Lemmon or the General Hitchcock Highway), the trail traverses rolling chaparral of scrub oak, manzanita, shin dagger, and prickly pear cactus.

Two miles from the Molino Basin trailhead, is the site of a federal prison camp, which once supplied labor for construction of the highway. The Forest Service is developing this area for use by larger groups and equestrians. The Arizona Trail travels southwest as it skirts the campground and passes through a charming area of grassy meadows, colorful wildflowers, and an intermittent stream; the Trail eventually joins an abandoned road.

A brown marker indicates where the old 4WD road begins a steep, uphill grade to the wilderness border, 1.3 miles from the old prison camp. The route is exposed and rocky as it leaves the meadow for the hot, chaparral-covered slopes above. As the route gains a saddle it encounters a large metal Arizona Trail sign and magnificent views of the Pusch Ridge Wilderness and Mt. Lemmon to the north. This is the wilderness boundary, and the beginning of the Sycamore Reservoir Trail #39 (shown on some maps as #339).

About 3.3 miles from Molino Basin Trailhead, the Sycamore Reservoir Trail drops steeply from the Pusch Ridge Wilderness Boundary along a rough, narrow, rocky, 600-foot descent. If on horseback, watch for knee-banger rocks. The route levels for a brief respite and then swoops again toward the canyon floor, passing thickets of manzanita, oak, shin dagger, and bear grass. One steep mile from the wilderness boundary the trail alights beside a metal mileage sign and Sycamore Canyon Reservoir, hidden behind a thick growth of desert willow, alder, and sycamore trees. Turn left and follow the narrow path along an old stone wall, leading to a cement foundation. The old foundation makes a wonderful overlook, offering a dramatic view of beautiful and rugged Bear Canyon, the dam, and a waterfall dropping to a pool below. This is the confluence of Bear and Sycamore Canyons.

Backtrack to the sign, and continue northeast, paralleling the stream. The path may be overgrown by grass and wildflowers as you make your way a short distance upstream to an unsigned crossing. The Arizona Trail lies to the west, across the stream and up Sycamore Canyon. Watch for a small rock cairn and the most obvious place to cross—there is a rocky little hill on the opposite side that might be used as a landmark. Once you have crossed the shallow stream and the dense vegetation of the opposite bank, the trail is well defined.

Traveling west along the right side of Sycamore Creek the Arizona Trail continues to follow the route of Sycamore Reservoir Trail #39 for another 0.75 mile. The trail takes a pleasant, gentle, uphill grade away from the riparian sycamores and into a nice mix of oak, Arizona cypress, and alligator juniper, interspersed with yucca and manzanita. There are some grassy camping possibilities along the creek. Occasional rock cairns mark the route as the trail plays tag with the creek before climbing to a saddle, and junction.

At 5 miles from Molino Basin you come to junctions with Bear Canyon Trail #29 and East Fork Trail #24A. Note that there may not be Arizona Trail markers at these junctions. The Arizona Trail follows East Fork Trail to the right (north) as it makes a steep, narrow, switchbacking descent into Sabino Basin. Equestrians, this is a cliff-hanger! There are spectacular views down-canyon, as the trail drops to a junction with Palisade Trail #99 to the right (Palisade Trail climbs 7.5 miles to Showers Point Campground, 0.25 mile south of the Mt. Lemmon Highway).

Continue to follow the East Fork Trail #24A as the route travels a gradual, westward descent along the east fork of Sabino Canyon, to a signed junction with Box Camp Trail #22. Just beyond the signs, to the right, are some lovely, cool pools of water in Palisade Creek. Shade and some level areas offer camping possibilities. A short distance from here, the trail meets the Sabino Canyon Trail #23.

The junction with Sabino Canyon Trail, one of the most popular trails into this region, is 8.7 miles from the Molino Basin trailhead. You may meet other travelers who have hiked up the approximately 2.5 miles from the Sabino Canyon Trailhead. The East Fork Trail #24A becomes *West* Fork Trail #24 at the junction with Sabino Canyon Trailhead.

Continuing west on West Fork Trail #24/AT, the route crosses rocky Box Camp Creek. Equestrians may want to dismount and lead their animals through the boulders. The route proceeds at a fairly level grade, along a bank above the beautiful pools of Sabino Creek, offering an interesting mixture of plant communities. This is a desert oasis of large sycamore and oak trees mingling with giant saguaro, prickly pear, ocotillo, teddy bear cholla, and barrel cactus. Watch out for poison ivy along the creek.

Less than a mile from the junction, the trail passes an open, grassy area dotted with mesquite trees. This is the recommended place for camping, especially with livestock. From here it is a short distance to a rough and bouldery stream crossing. After scrambling through rocks, the trail climbs west along the side of the stream. The large canyon opening up to the right is Lemmon Canyon.

It is a short climb up a wooded hillside to Hutch's Pool, located below the confluence of Sabino and Lemmon Canyons. The pool, hidden by trees, is awesome: a larger-than-Olympic size, rectangular swimming hole with a small waterfall at the north end and sheer rock sides. As the narrow trail cuts uphill, watch for pathways on the right that drop down to the stream. This is rugged, rocky country with few level places to camp. If you follow the small paths, you will come to some heavily used, flat camping areas below the pool.

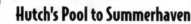

Trip 10-B

Hutch's Pool to Summerhaven

The beginning of Trip 10-B is not accessible by vehicle. This is the second part of a two (or more) day trek. In the heart of the wilderness, Hutch's Pool is not near any road. This popular destination is accessible from several different trails from both the east and west sides of the range.

The Arizona Trail now bypasses the small community of Summerhaven. However, after this difficult section of trail, some travelers may opt to exit the Arizona Trail, as we did, via Wilderness of Rocks in order to resupply or end their hike in Summerhaven. Though the route of the Arizona Trail continues north, passing to the west of Mt. Lemmon via Mt. Lemmon Trail #5 (shown on some maps as #8), Trip 10-B exits the Arizona Trail via Wilderness of Rocks Trail to Summerhaven.

Contact the Forest Service for trail conditions before traveling the final Mt. Lemmon Trail section of the Arizona Trail.

We do not recommend taking livestock on this trip.

Trip 10-A travels from Hutch's Pool to Summerhaven. This trip is a mostly uphill climb from a hidden desert treasure: a rock-walled swimming hole in the West Fork Sabino Canyon. A steep ascent to Romero Pass affords far-reaching views of

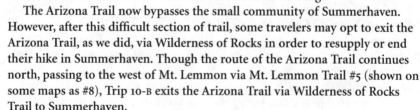

The Pusch Ridge Wilderness, Cathedral Rock, and the southern route of the Arizona Trail. From Romero Pass it is a challenging climb to a junction below Mount Lemmon, which offers the choice of continuing north on the Arizona Trail or exiting through Wilderness of Rocks to the charming community of Summerhaven.

Nature Highlight: We enjoyed the antics of a small, freshwater turtle, as he paddled about in Hutch's Pool. Watch for desert bighorn sheep; although now quite rare, there was once a healthy population living in the Pusch Ridge Wilderness.

Maps: Coronado National Forest Map, Santa Catalina Ranger District.
- Santa Catalina Mountain Trail Map, published by Rainbow Expeditions.
- USGS Quads: Sabino Canyon and Mt. Lemmon.

Difficulty: Very difficult. Long, steep, rocky ascents.

Length: 7 miles, one way to the junction with Wilderness of Rocks Trail (through-travelers); 12.4 miles one way to Summerhaven.

Elevation: 3,900–8,000 feet.

Recommended Season: All year, depending on the weather at Mount Lemmon. Use caution; in warm weather, temperatures at Hutch's pool may exceed 110 degrees Fahrenheit. In winter, the trails around Mount Lemmon may be blocked by snow.

Water: (Treat all water unless noted otherwise. During dry weather, water sources may not be dependable.)
- **West Fork Sabino Canyon** (Hutch's Pool).
   No other reliable water source for many miles. (There is usually water in the Wilderness of Rocks area, and Lemmon Creek, which is not part of the AT, but is part of this trip, traveling to Summerhaven.)

Camping:
- **Hutch's Pool:** See Trip 10-A.
- There are some nice primitive camping opportunities along **Wilderness of Rocks Trail** (which is not part of the AT).
- **Summerhaven:** There are a lodge and bed-and-breakfast establishments in Summerhaven. Reservations are recommended. For further information about services, see appendix A.

Livestock: We do not recommend this trip for livestock because the Romero Pass area is extremely steep and rocky. Both of our experienced trail horses fell here (luckily with no injuries). If you are using llamas, you may have to remove packs to get the animals up over the boulders.

Directions to Hutch's Pool: There is no vehicle access to Hutch's Pool. (See Trip 10-A for the route of the AT from Molino Basin.) This popular site may be accessed by several different trails from both the east and west sides of the range.

Other Area Trails: Romero Canyon Trail is an extremely rugged trail that travels west from Romero Pass 7 miles to Catalina State Park. There are many hiking and biking opportunities in the area around Summerhaven. Contact the Santa Catalina Ranger District for more information on the Arizona Trail or other trail opportunities in the area. See also camping information in Trip 10-A.

TRAIL DESCRIPTION

There are no Arizona Trail markers along this trip. The route of the Arizona Trail, following West Fork Trail #24, climbs steeply from Hutch's Pool, switchbacking up 0.25 mile to a saddle. As the trail winds, there are spectacular views into the deep and rocky cleft of Lemmon Canyon to the north. The trail becomes a narrow cliffhanger, washed out in places.

For the next 5 miles the route climbs toward Romero Pass, following the south side of the long, east/west defile of West Fork Sabino Canyon. The grade levels, then drops as it crosses the drainage, continuing west on the other side, through oak and juniper chaparral. As the trail wanders back and forth across the dry bottom of the canyon, it disappears now and then in the rocky floodplain. The canyon deepens, bound by granite boulder cliffs as the path follows along the floor of the drainage.

Three miles from Hutch's Pool, approaching the western end of the drainage, the trail makes several crossings as it wanders up-canyon. Watch for occasional rock cairns. The route passes a small (apparently seasonal) pool, the first water since Hutch's Pool and the last for many miles. Approximately 0.5 mile farther is a faint, easily missed junction with Cathedral Rock Trail #26, marked by a small wooden sign to the left of the trail. (Cathedral Rock Trail passes to the east of Cathedral Rock, linking to other trails on the front range of the Santa Catalinas.) Both routes may be hidden here by fallen leaves. Immediately after this junction, the Arizona Trail makes a final crossing of West Fork Sabino Canyon and begins a switchbacking ascent of the north slope.

The steep, narrow trail is overgrown with manzanita in places, but passable. The route affords spectacular views across the vast expanse of Sabino Basin to the eastern edge of the wilderness boundary and beyond. The southern route of the Arizona Trail lies below us; beyond the Catalinas, the distant Rincons, and farther still, the Santa Ritas, fading blue into the skyline. Across the canyon to the east, the fortressed spires of Cathedral Rock rise starkly from the ragged ridgeline looming above us. Cathedral Rock is a distinctive landmark that is visible from many areas, including Tucson and I-10. The narrow trail continues its steep ascent to Romero Pass.

About 5.2 miles from Hutch's Pool is a junction with Romero Canyon Trail #8, and Mount Lemmon Trail #5. The Arizona Trail turns right (northeast) and follows the Mount Lemmon Trail #5. For the next 1.75 miles the route makes a steep, boulder-scrambling ascent as it follows the crest of a jagged ridgeline. At length, the route levels briefly, affording an impressive view to the west of a deep defile: wild and remote Romero Canyon. Beyond, Interstate 10 and Picacho Peak are visible. The trail continues to climb steeply through a mixed cover of ponderosa pine, oak, alligator juniper, and madrone, finally topping out with a view of Mount Lemmon. At this point the unsigned trail is indistinct in places. Watch for rock cairns as the route heads downhill.

Seven miles from Hutch's Pool the trail arrives at the junction with Wilderness of Rock Trail #44. The Santa Catalina Mountains Passage continues north approximately 2.5 miles, gaining over 1,000 feet as it follows Mount Lemmon Trail

#5 to the Pusch Ridge Wilderness boundary. The passage ends at a junction with Sutherland Trail #6, and a utility road below Mount Lemmon.

If you wish to exit the Arizona Trail for Summerhaven, turn right (east) on the Wilderness of Rocks Trail. There are small creeks and some nice camping possibilities as the Wilderness of Rocks Trail travels through pine forest and, in less than a mile, enters Wilderness of Rocks. It is 5.3 miles to Marshall Gulch, which is within easy walking distance (0.75 mile) of Summerhaven. Wilderness of Rocks is an intriguing jumble of gigantic boulders, weirdly eroded pinnacles, and balanced rocks—impossible shapes silhouetted against the blue Arizona sky. This area is made even more appealing by wind-carved boulders intermixed with some huge old ponderosas and lovely little pools of water. A tiny, striped water snake tells us that these pools may be a reliable water source.

Continuing along the trail through pine and oak woodland, the path crosses Lemmon Creek frequently. The route passes through a small copse of aspen and then returns to a lovely oak and pine woodland mixed with fern, columbine, Indian paintbrush, and other wildflowers. After boulder-hopping across some deep pools, the trail begins the steep ascent to Marshall Saddle.

Four miles from the junction with Mount Lemmon Trail #5 (the Arizona Trail), the Wilderness of Rocks Trail tops out in Marshall Saddle and a signed junction. Take Marshall Gulch Trail #3 east. This well-maintained trail makes an easy descent 1.3 miles to the Marshall Gulch Picnic area. Turn left for an easy, 0.75-mile stroll into Summerhaven.

Trip 10-C
Alternate Bicycle Route Around the Pusch Ridge Wilderness from Molino Basin to Summerhaven

This trip is potentially dangerous because of the high-speed traffic on the Catalina Highway (also known as the Mount Lemmon or General Hitchcock Highway), especially on weekends. A safer option would be to transport your bicycle to the Red Ridge trailhead, and continue with Trip 11-A.

This is a steep but popular ride on a paved, winding, mountain road that takes you on a climatic journey that is the equivalent of going from Mexico to Canada in 20 miles. As the elevation increases and the temperature drops, you abandon the heat of the Sonoran Desert for coniferous forests, cool mountain air, and stunning views.

Nature Highlight: Gigantic ponderosa pine trees announce the cooler elevations of the Transition life zone; next stop, Canada.

Maps: Coronado National Forest Map.

Difficulty: Difficult. This is a long, steep, uphill climb.

Length: 19.3 miles, one way from Molino Basin.

Elevation: 4,370–7,840 feet. Mount Lemmon, 9,000 feet.

Recommended Season: All year, depending on the weather. In warm weather, the temperature can exceed 100 degrees Fahrenheit in the lower elevations. In winter, upper sections of the highway may be closed because of snow.

Water:
- Rose Campground.
- Summerhaven.

Camping:
- **Molino Basin Campground:** A picturesque campground in a Sonoran bajada setting that offers grills, picnic tables, and privies. A fee area. There is no water. Bring your own firewood. It is closed during the hottest months of the year.

    There are several campgrounds along the route of the Mt. Lemmon Highway. Check with the Santa Catalina Ranger District for camping information and availability of water (see Governing Agencies section in this passage for address and phone number).
- **Summerhaven:** This small community offers a variety of accommodations, ranging from a lodge to bed-and-breakfast establishments. Reservations are recommended.

Directions to Molino Basin Trailhead: See Trip 10-A, page 124.

ROUTE DESCRIPTION

Following the paved road west through the Molino Basin Campground, travel the first 2 miles of Trip 10-B to the site of an abandoned federal prison camp. Turn right and ride 0.25 mile to the Catalina Highway and turn left. Between mileposts 8 and 10 are pullouts on the left with views of Bear Canyon. Shortly thereafter, the highway passes through a shady riparian area of Bear Canyon.

Six and a half miles from Molino Basin, at 6,000-foot elevation, is the General Hitchcock Campground, which has no water. Passing the campground, the road climbs through a mixture of desert chaparral and pine forest to Windy Point, an overlook with far-reaching vistas. From Windy Point the route travels through some weirdly eroded granite rock formations.

Milepost 17 marks the entrance to Rose Canyon Campground, which offers a panoramic view of the San Pedro River Valley and the Galiuro Mountains beyond. This is a fee campground that has water available.

Fourteen miles from Molino Basin, Palisades Ranger Station is a good spot for a break. Visit the visitor center and bookshop.

You'll come to a fork in the road 19.3 miles from Molino Basin. Turn left to go into Summerhaven, or you can continue straight up the highway to Mount Lemmon.

11 Mount Lemmon/Oracle Ridge Passage

Mount Lemmon to American Flag Trailhead

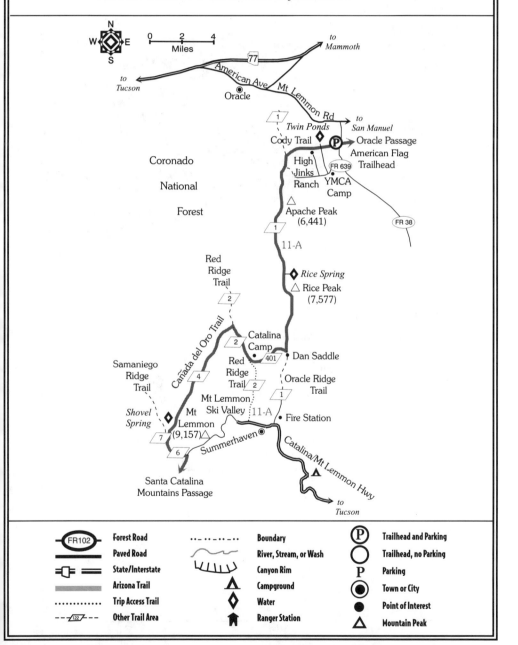

Legend:

FR102	Forest Road	∙−∙∙−∙∙−	Boundary	Ⓟ	Trailhead and Parking	
	Paved Road		River, Stream, or Wash	◯	Trailhead, no Parking	
	State/Interstate		Canyon Rim	P	Parking	
	Arizona Trail	▲	Campground	⊙	Town or City	
∙∙∙∙∙∙∙	Trip Access Trail	◆	Water	●	Point of Interest	
−−122−−	Other Trail Area	♦	Ranger Station	△	Mountain Peak	

A view of the abandoned Catalina Camp along the Mount Lemmon/Oracle Ridge Passage.

The yellow stuff! The yellow stuff!
   All day his steel would tinkle
And when the blast roared out at last
   He scanned each rocky wrinkle.

— **"The Yellow Stuff," Badger Clark, 1917**

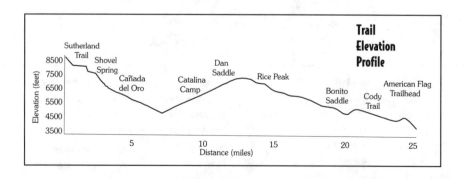

T*HIS PASSAGE OF THE Arizona Trail highlights Arizona's mining history. Beginning with the pick and shovel days of abandoned mining camps and ending with views of San Manuel's copper smelter and Biosphere 2, the route offers an extraordinary contrast between life in the 1800s and that of modern day Arizona.*

The only trip in this passage, Trip 11-A does not start at the beginning of the passage. To access the beginning of this passage, head west from Summerhaven past the Mount Lemmon ski area. Passenger cars can continue up a dirt road to the radio towers and parking area (in winter months this road may be closed due to snowfall). A closed utility road (Mount Lemmon Trail #5) is accessed from the west side of the parking area. This road travels west approximately 1.5 miles to connect with Sutherland Trail #6, the beginning of the Mount Lemmon/Oracle Ridge Passage of the Arizona Trail.

From the junction of Mt. Lemmon Trail #5 and the Sutherland Trail #6, the Arizona Trail follows the Sutherland Trail 0.8-mile to Samaniego Ridge Trail #7. Here the Arizona Trail turns right and follows Samaniego Ridge Trail 0.6-mile to a junction with Cañada del Oro Trail #4 on the right (east). The Arizona Trail follows Cañada del Oro Trail 6.1 miles to a junction with Red Ridge Trail #2. The Arizona Trail turns right on Red Ridge Trail and travels south 1.9 miles to connect with Catalina Camp Trail #401 and the beginning of Trip 11-A. This opening section of the Mount Lemmon/Oracle Ridge Passage is steep and we recommend that you contact the governing agency listed below for updated information on it. Trip 11-A joins the Arizona Trail at Catalina Camp and travels north.

In Cañada del Oro (Canyon of Gold), at the old mining camp of Catalina, the trail passes a little mine shack. A handwritten note tells travelers to "Respect the shelter from the storm. Eat your fill, leave the rest for others. Put bedding on the walls because of mice." Signed, The General.

The mostly downhill trek affords panoramic views of the San Pedro River Valley, the Galiuro Mountains, Biosphere 2, and Picacho Peak, as it follows long, sweeping ridgelines from

Canadian zone conifers to Sonoran Desert chaparral. Imagine Buffalo Bill riding the Cody Trail segment, from his High Jinks Mine to the post office at American Flag. The route offers several opportunities for loop trips.

Picacho Peak is the distinctive volcanic pinnacle visible to the northwest from Oracle Ridge. It overlooks the site of a conflict between Confederate and Union troops in 1862, the westernmost battle of the Civil War.

The American Flag Ranch became Oracle's first post office in 1880. It is one of Arizona's oldest existing territorial post office buildings and has been placed on the National Register of Historic Places. The building, now privately owned, is just south of the trailhead.

Buffalo Bill Cody was a pony express rider, cavalry scout, and in the late 1800s and early 1900s he starred in his own Wild West Show. Featuring cowboys riding bucking broncos and roping wild steers, Native American warriors, Buffalo Soldiers from the Fifth and Tenth Cavalries, pony express riders, western prairie girls, Annie Oakley, and other famous sharpshooters, Buffalo Bill's Wild West show romanticized the West. He took the show to Europe and was a huge success, the guest of royalty wherever he went. Buffalo Bill came to Arizona in 1910, interested in the gold mines at Campo Bonito. He staked the High Jinks Mine Claim in 1912, and he was treated as a celebrity when he visited Oracle. There is a photograph in the museum of Buffalo Bill playing Santa Claus with miners' children. Buffalo Bill spent his last winter at High Jinks in 1916. He died in 1917 in Colorado.

High Jinks Ranch, perched high on the slopes below Oracle Ridge, is an amazing structure. Dean Prichard, a local historian and segment steward for this passage of the Arizona Trail, owns High Jinks and has maintained the character of the building and mementos of Buffalo Bill's life there. The building is being considered for placement on the National Register of Historic Places. A tour of the ranch may be arranged by calling Dean at (520) 896-2005.

The Arizona Trail passes above Biosphere 2, a somewhat controversial 3-acre, airtight "mini-world" that offers a visitor center, hotel, restaurant, and tours. Eight men and women lived sealed in the glass structure for two years. Their goal was to replicate different ecosystems found on Earth (Biosphere 1), and create a self-sufficient system that would sustain plant and animal life in space. Biosphere 2 is west of Oracle on SR 77. (P.O. Box 689, Oracle, AZ 85623. [520] 896-6200.)

GOVERNING AGENCIES

Coronado National Forest, Santa Catalina Ranger District, 5700 N. Sabino Canyon Road, Tucson, AZ 85715. (520) 749-8700.

FOR MORE INFORMATION

Oracle Chamber of Commerce, P.O. Box 1886 Oracle, AZ 85623. (520) 896-9322

Oracle Historical Society, Acadia Ranch Museum, located on American Avenue, is only open on Saturdays from 1:00 to 5:00 P.M. P.O. Box 10, Oracle, AZ 85623.

NEAREST SERVICES TO MOUNT LEMMON

Summerhaven has a post office, lodge, and restaurants (see Appendix A).

Through-travelers who need to resupply or access the post office in Oracle may opt to stay on the Oracle Trail (rather than exiting on the Cody Trail). The Oracle Ridge Trail travels to a residential area on the south side of Oracle.

Trip 11-A

Summerhaven to Catalina Camp to American Flag

The Arizona Trail bypasses the small community of Summerhaven. However, some travelers may opt to exit the Arizona Trail in order to resupply or end their trip in Summerhaven.

Trip 11-A is a long, one- or two-day trip. It uses a connecting trail, Red Ridge, to travel north from Summerhaven to connect with the Arizona Trail at Catalina Camp. Note that there are no gas stations after you leave Tucson.

Trip 11-A travels 17.5 miles from Summerhaven to American Flag trailhead near Oracle. Trip 11-A is a long, one- to two-day descent following ridgelines from the Canadian life zone of Mount Lemmon to the Sonoran Desert setting of one of Arizona's oldest territorial post offices. The route, which affords unlimited views in all directions, highlights Arizona's mining history. Beginning with a visit to an old mining shack, the route passes High Jinks Mine, once owned by Buffalo Bill Cody, and ends with a view of San Manuel's copper smelter.

Nature Highlight: A pretty, long-eared Abert's squirrel peers at us from the safety of his ponderosa pine tree.

Maps: Coronado National Forest, Catalina Ranger District. USGS Quads: Mount Lemmon and Campo Bonito.

Difficulty: Moderate. Mostly downhill with a few steep climbs. (Remember that difficulty ratings are south to north. Were you to reverse this trip, it would be a very long climb.)

Length: Catalina Camp to American Flag (through-travelers): 14.5 miles, one way. Summerhaven to Catalina Camp to American Flag: 17.5 miles, one way.

Elevation: 8,673–4,250 feet

Recommended Season: All year, depending on the snowfall on Mount Lemmon.

Water: (Treat all water unless noted otherwise. During dry weather, water sources may not be dependable.)
- **Catalina Camp.**
- **Rice Spring.**
- **Twin Ponds.**
- **Creek by American Flag.**

Camping:
- **Red Ridge Trailhead:** There is no camping here. The closest developed campground is Spencer Canyon, south on the Catalina Highway. (Primitive camping is allowed in the national forest.)
- **Catalina Camp** offers primitive camping possibilities.
- **Twin Ponds** also offers primitive camping. Beware if you are driving in, for the road is quite rough; 4WD vehicles only. Bring your own firewood and drinking water. Directions to Twin Ponds: continue past American Flag Trailhead 0.8-mile to FR 639 on the right. Turn right and drive past the Triangle Y Ranch gate. Take the first junction to the right, which is a 4WD road leading to the ponds.
- **American Flag Trailhead:** There is a parking area at the trailhead and primitive camping is available. If you are driving in, bring your own firewood and water.

Livestock:
- **Red Ridge Trailhead:** There is limited space at the trailhead to park; it will accommodate four trucks and trailers at the most. Livestock is not allowed in developed campgrounds, but you may camp with livestock in the national forest.
- **Summerhaven:** Has a bed-and-breakfast with a corral. (See appendix B for information.)
- **American Flag Trailhead:** There are three large, wooden corrals at the trailhead and some grass. Water is turned on by appointment with the caretaker at the American Flag building (see appendix B).

- **Triangle Y Camp,** 0.8-mile south of American Flag, may have corrals available. (See appendix B for information on boarding facilities and outfitters in the area.)

Directions to Red Ridge Trailhead: You can access the trailhead by passenger car. From Tucson follow the Catalina Highway 25 miles to a fork in the highway. The left fork goes to Summerhaven. Stay right, continuing 0.5 mile toward the Mount Lemmon ski area. *(If you are walking up from Summerhaven be wary of traffic on this narrow road.)* There is no sign on the highway indicating the trailhead, so watch closely for a pullout marked by reflective markers. A rusted steel sign denoting the trailhead is set back off the road and difficult to see.

Other Area Trails: It is possible to make a loop trip back to Summerhaven from Dan Saddle using the **Oracle Ridge Trail.**

Four-wheel-drive or abandoned dirt roads that access the Oracle Ridge/AT from the **Old Mount Lemmon Road** afford numerous other possibilities for loop trips. Contact the Santa Catalina Ranger District for more information.

TRAIL DESCRIPTION

From the Catalina Highway, the Red Ridge Trail cuts steeply up the bank through dense pine forest. Cresting the ridge, the route follows a gentle downgrade that soon steepens. As the trail passes through a small grove of aspen, the trees open to a spectacular view, the first of many on this route. The long ridgeline to the right is Oracle Ridge, a route we will eventually be following.

The trail curves east, downhill, and then heads north along Red Ridge, in a gentle descent through a conifer forest mixed with occasional oak. As you pass a huge dead ponderosa, the gradient steepens into switchbacks. Following the ridgeline through shady forest, the trail levels, traveling between two prominent ridges. Oracle Ridge is to the east, and Reef of Rock, with its impressive white rock cliffs parallels us to the west. As the trail drops in elevation, pine blends into oak and madrone, yucca, and cactus. The Red Ridge Trail, which is well-maintained and easy to follow, curves east, abandoning the ridgeline for the drainage that divides the two ridges.

Three miles from the Red Ridge trailhead, the trail crosses the east fork of the Canada del Oro, marked by a small, lovely stream, and a junction of trails. (Except for Rice Spring, *this is the only water* until High Jinks Ranch, or Twin Ponds, near the American Flag trailhead.) Just beyond the creek is the junction with the route of the Arizona Trail, though the route may not be signed with the Arizona Trail symbol. Turn right (east) following Catalina Camp Trail #401 (it may also be signed as East Fork of the Canada del Oro). Follow the trail toward Dan Saddle, which winds up the east side of the canyon through oak and pine woodland. The trail turns into what appears to be an abandoned road, traveling a short distance to a tin shed.

Here you are in the old mining settlement of Catalina Camp. A short distance up the trail is a little mine shack. The windows are screened and the door is propped shut with a big rock. Take a moment to visit. Inside the small, one-room cabin are metal cots, a woodstove, a small table, and even first aid supplies. On the wall is a sign-in roster and a note: "Welcome to the Canyon of Gold. There's very few sacred spots left in this world, please refrain from making a mess and enjoy." There are other interesting notes and comments from people who have stayed here. Who has gone to the trouble of maintaining this charming retreat? It's a mystery! There are some nice spots to camp in the area, and if you use the cabin, do as the note says and "please respect the shelter from the storm."

The Arizona Trail follows a 4WD road above the cabin, in a steep climb, heading east to connect with Dan Saddle. This shadeless stretch offers wonderful views back to Red Ridge, Reef of Rock, and the long slope of Samaniego Ridge beyond.

There is a junction with a mining road and Oracle Ridge Trail 1.7 miles from Catalina Camp. A loop back to Summerhaven can be made here by following the Oracle Ridge Trail back to the Catalina Highway (contact the Santa Catalina Ranger District or local guides for details). The Arizona Trail joins the Oracle Ridge Trail at this junction. Turn left (north), passing to the left of the cattle guard. The trail cuts uphill staying to the west of the crest. The trail passes through a shady oak woodland, intermixed with bear grass and yucca, then begins a moderate climb through some granite outcroppings to a fine vista of Biosphere 2 far below.

Traveling along the west side of Oracle Ridge for 2.5 miles, the well-pruned trail passes a huge alligator juniper as it winds through rocks in a gradual climb to the crest of the ridge. The ridgeline, topped by a barbed wire fence, offers a superb first view to the east of the San Pedro River Valley, and the Galiuro Mountains beyond. The trail continues to parallel Oracle Ridge. As the trail crosses to the east side of the ridge, the stacks of San Manuel's copper smelter appear in the distance. Rice Peak is visible due north.

At 4.2 miles from Catalina Camp (7.2 miles from the Red Ridge trailhead) the route passes through a gate to a dirt road, FR 4483. The Arizona Trail turns left (north) here and follows the road to a junction at the base of Rice Peak. The junction offers a side trip up the short, steep road to the top of the peak. The views aren't any better than from the ridgeline, but there are some interesting conglomerate type rocks on top! Continuing on the Arizona Trail, follow the dirt road to the northwest as it travels around Rice Peak. The road makes a switchbacking descent to a Y junction with FR 4475, the road to Rice Spring. Look for big trees and a cement stock tank 0.25 mile down FR 4475 below the road on the left.

Approximately 3 miles after the Arizona Trail picks up FR 4483, it abandons it. Watch carefully for a place where the road, which has been comparatively level, curves to the right heading downhill. To the left is a wire fence and a gate, the route of the Arizona Trail. The gate may not be signed. Pass through the gate and follow the trail north along Oracle Ridge for another 4.5 miles. This section of trail is really nice, level, and well maintained. To the northwest, Picacho Peak is visible.

A mile after leaving the road the trail passes through a gate, into a saddle just south of Apache Peak. The trail turns left, travels a short distance, and passes back to the west through another gate. The route circles Apache Peak on the west, traveling through a pretty area that in late spring is splashed with beautiful blue larkspur and Indian paintbrush. The trail follows the fence to Bonito Saddle and an abandoned mining road. (The Campo Bonito road, which drops 1 mile to the remains of the mining camp, leads eventually to the Old Mount Lemmon Road and can be used along with the Cody Trail to make a loop hike from the American Flag trailhead. Contact the Santa Catalina Ranger District for more information.)

From Bonito Saddle the trail continues north, climbing a steep, chaparral-clad hillside. Cresting a rise, the trail passes a junction with a dirt road on the right (which also connects with FR 639 to the Old Mount Lemmon Road) and continues uphill. After a series of long, steep hills, watch for a brown carsonite Arizona Trail marker on the right.

At 10.8 miles from Catalina Camp, the Arizona Trail leaves the Oracle Ridge Trail and follows the Cody Trail #9 to the right. Watch for the brown carsonite Arizona Trail markers. The Oracle Ridge Trail continues north, passing out of the national forest near a residential area on the south side of Oracle.

The Cody Trail curves to the east, twisting steeply down through rolling chaparral-covered hills that give way to grassy slopes and a mix of cholla cactus, scrub oak, sotol, and bear grass. Two miles from American Flag trailhead the route passes High Jinks Ranch on the right, property once owned by Buffalo Bill Cody. Soon after, the trail arrives at an intersection with a 4WD road. If you turn left, it is a short distance down the road to an area called Twin Ponds and some nice, primitive camping spots. A right turn leads to FR 639 and the Old Mount Lemmon Road.

The Arizona Trail, signed with carsonite markers, continues straight across the road and drops down an eroded drainage. The trail wanders down a very pretty gulch, between wonderfully sculpted granite boulders shaded by large trees. In late spring hedgehog cactus are blooming, and as the path crosses a small flowing creek, desert verbena and delicate penstemon are also in bloom. The trail crosses the little creek several times then follows along its right bank. This sandy wash, with large oaks on either side, looks like a delightful place to camp. Leaving the wash, the trail ascends a grassy hillside to the east, and tops out to a view of San Manuel's copper smelter. It is an easy downhill walk to the Old Mount Lemmon Road and the trailhead below.

Photo by Kelly Tighe

The American Flag Trailhead, near Oracle.

> *So the trail it led him southward all the day,*
>   *Through the shinin' country of the thorn and snake,*
> *Where the heat had drove the lizards from their play*
>   *To the shade of rock and bush and yucca stake.*

—"A Ranger," Badger Clark, 1909

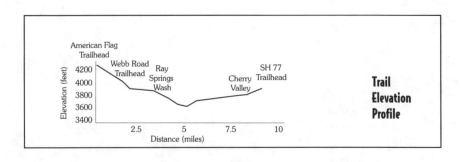

Trail Elevation Profile

12 Oracle Passage
American Flag Trailhead to Highway 77

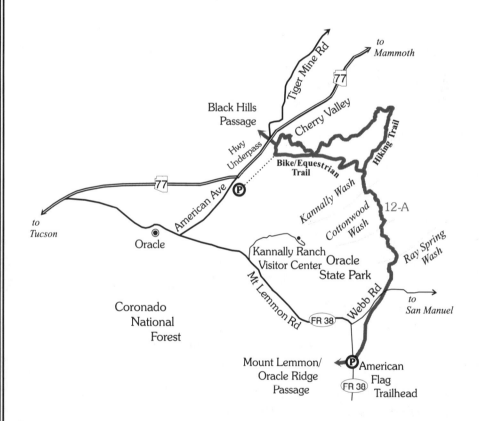

N W E S

0   1/2   1
Miles

to Mammoth

Tiger Mine Rd

77

Black Hills
Passage

Cherry Valley

Hiking Trail

Hwy
Underpass

Bike/Equestrian
Trail

77

Kannally Wash

12-A

American Ave

to Tucson

Cottonwood
Wash

Ray Spring
Wash

Oracle

Kannally Ranch
Visitor Center

Oracle
State Park

Mt Lemmon Rd

Coronado
National
Forest

FR 38

Webb Rd

to San Manuel

Mount Lemmon/
Oracle Ridge
Passage

American
Flag
Trailhead

FR 38

FR102	Forest Road		··············	Boundary		P	Trailhead and Parking
	Paved Road		〜	River, Stream, or Wash		P	Trailhead, no Parking
=◻=	State/Interstate		⊔⊔⊔⊔	Canyon Rim		P	Parking
	Arizona Trail		▲	Campground		◉	Town or City
··············	Trip Access Trail		◇	Water		●	Point of Interest
--◁122▷--	Other Trail Area		♦	Ranger Station		△	Mountain Peak

T HIS 9-MILE-LONG *passage is one trip beginning at the American Flag trailhead southeast of Oracle and ending at American Avenue. A 1-mile segment of trail has been constructed across state trust Land to connect the National Forest and Oracle State Park. The projected completion date was to be within 1997. Contact the Oracle State Park for the current status of this portion.*

The passage is in the northern foothills of the Santa Catalina Mountains near the community of Oracle in Southern Pinal County. Gently rolling hills, slopes, and canyons, dominate the landscape. The vegetation is primarily open oak woodland, riparian woodland, and desert grassland. The diversities of vegetation, slope, and elevation contribute to the presence of abundant wildlife. The route offers panoramic views of the Santa Catalina Mountains to the south and the San Pedro River Valley and Galiuro Mountains to the north and east.

The most prominent feature in the passage is the 4,000-acre Oracle State Park, which was donated to the Arizona State Parks Board in 1986. The park contains various native plant communities, interesting geologic formations, and the historic Kannally Ranch House.

The town of Oracle is on the northern slope of the Catalina Mountains, 4 miles northwest of the trailhead. The town was named for a ship built in Bath, Maine, and launched in 1876. The ship survived a terrible storm at sea, and a grateful passenger who later traveled to Arizona in search of gold, named his first mine claim "The Oracle." Guest ranches became popular in Oracle because of the scenery and healthful climate. Many famous people, including royalty from Europe and an infamous female bandit, stayed at the Mountain View Hotel. In 1899 Pearl Hart, who had robbed a stagecoach near Riverside, stayed at the hotel in custody of the sheriff, following her capture.

Ancient cultures once inhabited and visited this area. The Clovis people occupied the San Pedro River Valley and possibly the park site as long as 10,000 years ago, and there is evidence that the Hohokams also resided in the area of the park, using the area for hunting and food gathering.

This area grew with ranching and farming when the Apache raids ceased in the late 1880s. Neil Kannally, who came to the area for his health, homesteaded his ranch in 1902. Members of his family joined him through the years and the ranch grew. Lucille Kannally, the last surviving member of the family, donated the ranch to the Defenders of Wildlife in 1976. The Defenders of Wildlife deeded the 4,000-acre ranch to the Arizona State Parks in 1986. The purpose of the park is for a wildlife refuge, recreation, and environmental learning. The park's plan is to preserve the natural and cultural resources and to offer educational programs based on ecological principles and safeguarding natural resources. The park is not currently open to the public on a drop-in basis, but they do schedule educational programs by reservation. Picnic and parking areas are built and will be open to the public sometime soon.

GOVERNING AGENCIES

Coronado National Forest, Santa Catalina Ranger District, 5700 N. Sabino Canyon Road, Tucson, AZ 85715. (520) 749-8700.

Oracle State Park, Center for Environmental Education, P. O. Box 700, Oracle, AZ 85623. (520) 896-2425.

FOR MORE INFORMATION

Oracle Chamber of Commerce, P. O. Box 1886, Oracle, AZ 85623. (520) 896-9322.

NEAREST SERVICES

Oracle. From the American Flag trailhead, follow the Old Mt. Lemmon Road northwest 4 miles. See appendix A for further information.

Trip 12-A

American Flag Trailhead to American Avenue

This trip links two passages: Mount Lemmon/Oracle Ridge and Black Hills. The trip begins amidst the oaks outside the town of Oracle at the American Flag trailhead. Sections of this trail pass areas of whitethorn—wear long pants. The route winds through hills in Coronado National Forest for 1 mile. The next mile of the route crosses state trust land. The next part of the trail is a 7-mile route across Oracle State Park. This is a clear trail and well maintained. The first 2.6 miles of rolling hills is a multiuse trail. At Kannally Wash the route divides into a trail for hikers and a power line road for equestrians and mountain bikers.

This 4,000-acre Oracle State Park is in the northern foothills of the Santa Catalina Mountains. The trip winds north through foothills in and out of drainages, through high desert grasslands with mesquites, junipers, and oaks dotting the hills and washes. The trail drops 4.6 miles into Kannally Wash and meanders down-canyon. Eventually, you abandon the canyon and follow a series of ridges to the northern trailhead at American Avenue.

Nature Highlight: Two mule deer spot us and quickly seek refuge among the junipers.

Maps:
- Coronado National Forest.
- USGS Quads: Camp Bonito, Mammoth.
- Oracle State Park trail map.

Difficulty: Moderate.

Length: 9 miles for hikers, one way.
6.4 miles for bikers and equestrians, one way.

Elevation: 4,250–3,660 feet.

Recommended Seasons: Fall, winter, and spring.

Water: (Treat all water unless noted otherwise. During dry weather, water sources may not be dependable.) There is no water at this time, but the park plans to develop water at Kannally Wash windmill.

Camping: There is no camping at the park, but there are primitive camping areas in the Coronado Forest. The nearest developed campsites are in Catalina State Park, 20 miles south on SH 77, and Peppersauce Campground, 5 miles south on Mount Lemmon Road (FR 38).

Livestock: This route is suitable for trail animals; there are two large corrals at the trailhead. There is a separate route for equestrians and mountain bikes from Kannnally Wash north, which follows a powerline road to the northern trailhead, approximately 1.8 miles. See appendix B for horse and llama boarding facilities in this area.

Directions to Trailhead: Passenger cars can drive to the trailhead. From the town of

Oracle, take Mount Lemmon Road 3.1 miles to the first fork in the road and bear right where the road becomes a well-graded dirt road. Travel 1 mile to the American Flag trailhead on the right side of the road. There is a large AZ Trail sign, a corral, and pull-off areas on both sides of the road.

Oracle State park has developed a parking area on the north end of the trip on American Avenue, 0.25 mile from SH 77. (American Avenue is the second exit in Oracle if traveling north on SH 77.)

TRAIL DESCRIPTION

Leave American Flag trailhead at 4,250 feet elevation and cross the Mount Lemmon Road to the east. The archway guides you to the trail, and AZ Trail signs indicate the route through the low hills dotted with oaks, chaparral, prickly pear, mesquite, and low catclaw. Clusters of boulders jut up from the hills and harbor small gardens of cactus. To the east you can see the Galiuro Mountains and get occasional glimpses of the copper smelter in the valley. The route proceeds in a northerly direction across national forest about 1 mile. The trail encounters a fence at the state trust land. The mile of unfinished trail through state trust land is fairly level, roller-coastering in and out of small drainages. At Webb Road, a well-used dirt road, the route follows the fence line east to a gate, then crosses the road and reenters state trust land for a short distance to the Oracle Park boundary, at 4,130 feet elevation. The distance between the national forest boundary and the park boundary is approximately 1 mile.

The park trail was dedicated on National Trails Day in June 1994. Volunteers did most of the trail routing and building, using decomposed granite, which provides excellent footing. The route follows existing animal trails and is well marked with 4x4 wooden posts bearing the Arizona Trail brand.

Proceed in a northerly direction through low, exposed foothills with blooming fairy duster and grassland chaparral vegetation. The first major drainage is Ray Springs Wash. After the wash you pass over the buried El Paso Gas Line. You travel through several miles of burned area, the result of a burn in 1994 that scarred the vegetation. The fire burned 1,400 acres, but new growth and the return of wildlife indicate recovery.

Thread your way through low hills dipping in and out of washes. The washes run west to east into the San Pedro River below. The larger drainages offer shade trees—a relief after the shadeless hillsides. You will come to two intersecting trails (under construction) that come from the visitor center, but proceed north to Kannally Wash. At 4.6 miles from the American Flag trailhead, the route weaves down the grassy canyon side to the floor of Kannally Wash. You will encounter a sign in the floor of the canyon indicating that the multiuse trail ends here. At this point, equestrians and bikers should cross the wash (west) onto the power line road. It is 1.8 miles to the trailhead on SH 77. At this point, the hiking trail turns right (north) down-canyon.

A windmill and shade trees stand out in this prominent canyon. The windmill is not working at this time, but the spring is reliable below the windmill, with a small stream above ground for 0.25 mile that supports small stands of trees and vegetation. Hikers should strike off northeast down the canyon approximately 1 mile. The trail follows an abandoned wagon road, with rock cairns marking the route in the sandy areas. There is a signed turn just before a large hackberry tree in the canyon. Scramble out of the canyon to the top of a hill, where the trail makes a 90 degree turn to the west, and climb on a long ridge to the high point. The views at the top of the Galiuros in the east and the Santa Catalina Mountains in the south are unobstructed. Traveling will be more strenuous for the rest of the journey, because of several steep, deep drainages that you will have to cross.

Three miles from Kannally Wash the trail intersects the power line road. There is a sign here indicating that equestrians and bikers should go straight (west) on the road and that the hiking trail leaves the road to the right (northwest). As you weave in and out of the deep canyons, look for the trail signs or large rock cairns indicating the direction of the route through the canyons. The burn did not affect this northern portion of the park, so green trees dominate the drainage.

The last canyon you descend into is Cherry Valley, a major drainage cutting through the hills to the San Pedro River. Cherry Valley provided a natural path for SH 77. The trail turns left (west) in the wash and travels up the canyon paralleling SH 77. Travel a short distance past a culvert that will lead the way to the Black Hills Passage. The Arizona Trail will continue north under the road when the next passage is complete. At this time travel up the wash about 0.25 mile, crossing a power line road. Continue along Cherry Valley Wash about 0.25 mile farther to the parking area on American Avenue.

13 Black Hills (Sonoran Desert) Passage Highway 77 to Freeman Road

As of this writing, sections of the Arizona Trail in this passage are not yet completed. This description outlines the *proposed route* of the Arizona Trail through this passage; it is not intended to be used as a trail guide. Much of the information included here is taken from an Arizona Trail management guide designed not for recreational use but for use in planning, developing, and managing the trail. Contact the governing agency or The Arizona Trail Association for more information on the route, signage, availability of water, and completion status of this passage.

WHEN COMPLETED, *this twenty-plus-mile passage will connect SR 77 north of Oracle with the Freeman Road in the Tortilla Mountains west of Dudleyville and will follow an alignment roughly 10 miles west of the San Pedro River. The Arizona Trail crosses rolling hills of cactus and juniper within the Black Hills. In late March this Sonoran Desert landscape is dotted with wild mariposa lily, desert marigold, and Indian paintbrush. There are views to the east of the Galiuro Wilderness.*

PROPOSED ROUTE

This passage of the Arizona Trail will cross state trust land, requiring a special land use permit. In early 1995 a group of ten equestrians scouted this corridor, which includes the Tortilla Mountain Passage, over the course of three days, identifying water sources and trailhead locations.

From mile post #105 on SR 77, an easement may be needed to cross private land along the Tiger Mine Road, where a potential trailhead location has been identified. The route will skirt the western slopes of the Black Hills, pass near the Tunnel Ranch (Camp Grant Wash), and link to Freeman Road, an ideal location for a trailhead, because it is midway between Oracle and Kelvin.

This route is currently in the planning stage. It will be built with the assistance of Heritage Funds and juvenile community-service crews. Because of low elevations and lack of water, travel is not recommended May through September.

GOVERNING AGENCIES

Pinal County Department of Civil Works, P.O. Box 727, Florence, AZ 85232. (520) 868-6411.

FOR MORE INFORMATION

Arizona Trail Association, P.O. Box 36736, Phoenix, AZ 85067. (602) 252-4794.

NEAREST SERVICES

Nearest services are in Oracle.

14 Tortilla Mountains (Sonoran Desert) Passage
Freeman Road to the Gila River

As of this writing, sections of the Arizona Trail in this passage are not yet completed. This description outlines the *proposed route* of the Arizona Trail through this passage; it is not intended to be used as a trail guide. Much of the information included here is taken from an Arizona Trail management guide designed not for recreational use but for use in planning, developing, and managing the trail. Contact the governing agency or The Arizona Trail Association for more information on the route, signage, availability of water, and completion status of this passage.

WHEN COMPLETED, *this twenty-plus mile passage will connect Freeman Road in the Tortilla Mountains west of Dudleyville with the Kelvin-Riverside Bridge on the Gila River. As the Arizona Trail travels north the topography becomes more rugged, and drops to a Lower Sonoran elevation, characterized by a variety of cacti, including the giant saguaro. This remote segment of the trail will appeal to those searching for a backcountry experience far from civilization. This passage features views of the Pinal and Superstition Mountains.*

PROPOSED ROUTE

This passage of the Arizona Trail will cross state trust land, requiring a special land use permit. The route also crosses several miles of BLM land.

From Freeman Road the route will travel north, passing to the west of Eagle and Hackberry Washes. Paralleling The Tortilla Mountains, the trail will pass to the west of Ripsey Peak, and parallel Ripsey Wash to the Florence-Kelvin Highway, a possible trailhead location.

This route is currently in the planning stage. It will be built with the assistance of Heritage Funds and juvenile community-service crews. Because of the low elevations and lack of water, travel is not recommended from May through September.

GOVERNING AGENCIES

Pinal County Department of Civil Works, P.O. Box 727, Florence, AZ 85232. (520) 868-6411.

FOR MORE INFORMATION

Arizona Trail Association, P.O. Box 36736, Phoenix, AZ 85067. (602) 252-4794.

NEAREST SERVICES

Nearest services are in Oracle.

15 White Canyon Passage
Gila River to Telegraph Canyon Road

As of this writing, sections of the Arizona Trail in this passage are not yet completed. This description outlines the *proposed route* of the Arizona Trail through this passage; it is not intended to be used as a trail guide. Much of the information included here is taken from an Arizona Trail management guide designed not for recreational use but for use in planning, developing, and managing the trail. Contact the governing agency or The Arizona Trail Association for more information on the route, signage, availability of water, and completion status of this passage.

WHEN COMPLETED, *this twenty-mile passage will connect the Gila River to Telegraph Canyon Road in Tonto National Forest, south of U.S. 60 near Superior. After crossing the Gila River at Kelvin, the Arizona Trail will pass through a corner of the wild White Canyon Wilderness. This passage features some of the most spectacular Sonoran Desert along the entire route of the Arizona Trail.*

PROPOSED ROUTE

The northernmost part of this passage is open and accessible via the Alamo Canyon Passage. A planning team is researching and identifying a route that will connect with the bridge at Kelvin-Riverside and use cattle trails and an existing primitive road through the White Canyon Wilderness to connect to the Tonto National Forest. A proposed land exchange with ASARCO Corporation will determine the route of the Arizona Trail.

GOVERNING AGENCIES

Bureau of Land Management—Phoenix Resource Area, 2015 W. Deer Valley Rd., Phoenix AZ 85027. (602) 780-8090.

FOR MORE INFORMATION

Arizona Trail Association, P.O. Box 36736, Phoenix, AZ 85067. (602) 252-4794.

NEAREST SERVICES

Nearest services are in Kelvin.

16 Alamo Canyon Passage

Telegraph Canyon Road to Picketpost Trailhead/ Highway 60

This description outlines the route of the Arizona Trail through this passage; it is not intended to be used as a trail guide. Much of the information included here is taken from an Arizona Trail management guide designed not for recreational use but for use in planning, developing, and managing the trail. Contact the governing agency or The Arizona Trail Association for more information on the route, signage, availability of water, and completion status of this passage.

T*HIS 10.5-MILE PASSAGE connects Telegraph Canyon Road in Tonto National Forest to the Picketpost Mountain trailhead south of U.S. 60 near Superior. This passage has recently been completed and is accessible by traveling south from Picketpost trailhead. This area has been described as the "Sonoran Desert at its best."*

DESIGNATED ROUTE

From Telegraph Canyon Road the Arizona Trail begins a gradual ascent following primitive roads and new and existing trails. It descends through the Alamo Canyon drainage via two routes. One route uses the streambed, where cairns mark the route. This route may not be suitable for horses because of dropoffs. Another route is possible along the 4WD road that parallels Alamo Canyon. Look for two 4x4 wood posts bearing the AT symbol.

GOVERNING AGENCIES

Tonto National Forest, Globe Ranger District, Rt. 1, Box 33, Globe, AZ 85501. (520) 425-7189.

FOR MORE INFORMATION

Arizona Trail Association, P.O. Box 36736, Phoenix, AZ 85067. (602) 252-4794.

NEAREST SERVICES

Nearest services are in Superior.

17 Picketpost Mountain/Reavis Trail Canyon Passage

Picketpost Mountain Trailhead to Rogers Trough Trailhead

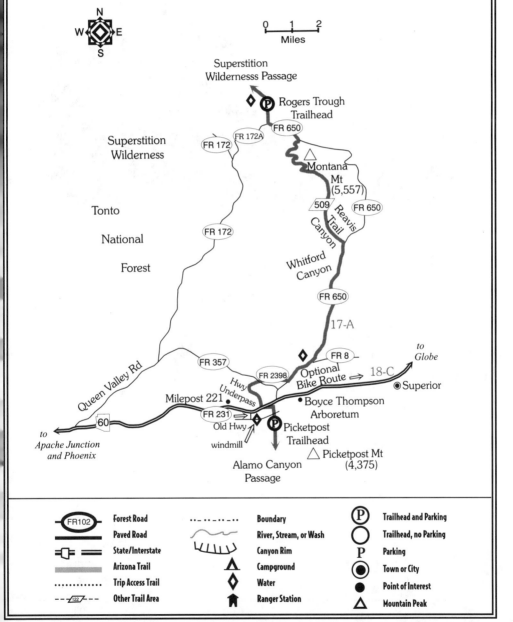

N W E S

0 1 2
Miles

Superstition
Wildernesss Passage

Rogers Trough
Trailhead

FR 172A

FR 172

FR 650

Superstition
Wilderness

Montana
Mt
(5,557)

509
FR 650

Tonto

Reavis
Trail
Canyon

FR 172

National

Whitford
Canyon

Forest

FR 650

17-A

to
Globe

FR 8

Queen Valley Rd

FR 357

Optional
Bike Route

18-C

FR 2398

Superior

Hwy
Underpass

Boyce Thompson
Arboretum

Milepost 221

60

FR 231

Old Hwy

Picketpost
Trailhead

to
Apache Junction
and Phoenix

windmill

Picketpost Mt
(4,375)

Alamo Canyon
Passage

FR102	Forest Road	
	Paved Road	
	State/Interstate	
	Arizona Trail	
....	Trip Access Trail	
122	Other Trail Area	

....	Boundary
	River, Stream, or Wash
	Canyon Rim
⛺	Campground
◊	Water
🏠	Ranger Station

Ⓟ	Trailhead and Parking
◯	Trailhead, no Parking
P	Parking
◉	Town or City
●	Point of Interest
△	Mountain Peak

Sunlight on Picketpost Mountain as seen along the Picketpost Mountain/Reavis Trail Canyon Passage.

The rhythm of the seasons
The wind, the snow, the rain,
The tune of rhyme and reason,
The song bird's sweet refrain.
These were all he ever needed,
God was helping him along.
Listening for the cowboys' last song.

—"The Cowboys' Last Song," Skelly Boyd
(Used with permission.)

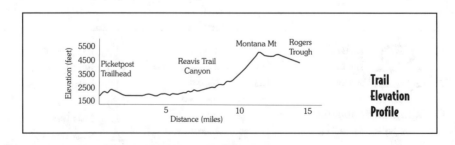

T_HIS PASSAGE CONTAINS_ one 15-mile trip. From Picketpost Trailhead south of U.S. 60 between Superior and Florence Junction, the Picketpost Mountain/Reavis Trail Canyon
Passage travels north to Rogers Trough trailhead, a gateway
into the Superstition Wilderness.

From beneath the towering ramparts of Picketpost Mountain the Arizona Trail travels into the heart of the rugged and
remote Superstition Wilderness. Glimpses of the landmark
Weaver's Needle remind us that the jagged ridgelines and
deep canyons of the Superstitions are the setting of one of Arizona's greatest mysteries: the Lost Dutchman Mine.

This passage affords the opportunity to visit a unique 35-
acre botanical garden that was established in the 1920s. Boyce
Thompson Southwestern Arboretum is just 1.5 miles east of
Picketpost Trailhead, on U.S. 60.

The legends that surround the Lost Dutchman Mine are
abundant. The story has been featured on the television program Unsolved Mysteries and has been the subject of many
books. Jacob Waltz, "the Dutchman," was a mysterious
prospector who appeared periodically in Phoenix in the late
1800s with high-grade gold ore. According to some accounts,
Waltz was secretive about the location of his mine, and those
who attempted to track him back to his treasure did not return. Weaver's Needle, a towering rock monolith visible for
many miles, is said to be the key to the location of Waltz's
mine. Legends say that the shadow cast by the landmark at a
certain time of day, pointed to the location of the mine. The
Dutchman died in 1891, taking his secret with him. The town
of Apache Junction has a Lost Dutchman Museum and holds
a Lost Dutchman Days celebration in February.

The 124,000-acre Superstition Wilderness was designated
in 1964. It is managed by three different Ranger Districts of
the Tonto National Forest. Up until the 1960s, untold numbers of treasure hunters searched for gold in the Superstitions,
and the stories of murder and intrigue continued. The
Wilderness Act closed all wilderness areas to new mining activity after 1984. Prospecting and treasure hunting are now
regulated by the Forest Service.

William Boyce Thompson was a successful mining engineer who made his fortune in the copper mines of Globe and Superior. Colonel Thompson led a Red Cross expedition to Siberia in 1917 and became interested in the scientific study of arid land plants. In 1923 he established the Boyce Thompson Southwestern Arboretum, in a picturesque canyon beneath Picketpost Mountain. The arboretum was intended to be a "living museum" where plants from the world's deserts could be collected and studied. Early work at the arboretum led to the development of the U.S. Soil Conservation Service. The goal of the facility is to study, display, and introduce arid land plants, distribute seeds to other agencies, and offer educational services dealing with plant science.

GOVERNING AGENCIES

Globe Ranger District, Tonto National Forest, Rt. 1, Box 33, Globe, AZ 85501. (520) 402-6200.

Mesa Ranger District, Tonto National Forest, 26 North MacDonald, Room 120, Mesa, AZ 85211-1161. (602) 379-6446.

FOR MORE INFORMATION

Superior Chamber of Commerce, 151 Main St., Superior, AZ 85273 (520) 689-2441.

Apache Junction Chamber of Commerce, P.O. Box 1747, 1001 N. Idaho Rd., Apache Junction, AZ 85217-1747. (520) 982-3141.

Superstition Mountains/Lost Dutchman Museum, Apache Junction. (520) 983-4888.

Boyce Thompson Southwestern Arboretum, U.S. 60, 3 miles west of Superior. The arboretum offers a visitor center, gift shop, and 35 acres of fabulous nature trails and gardens. (520) 689-2811.

NEAREST SERVICES TO PICKETPOST TRAILHEAD

Superior: It is 4.5 miles east on U.S. 60 to Superior.

Trip 17-A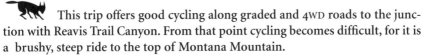

Picketpost MountainTrailhead to Rogers Trough

This trip offers good cycling along graded and 4WD roads to the junction with Reavis Trail Canyon. From that point cycling becomes difficult, for it is a brushy, steep ride to the top of Montana Mountain.

Primitive roads lead to the wilderness border at Rogers Trough. Bicycles are not allowed in the wilderness. From there a long loop can be made using FR 172A and 172 back to U.S. 60. Bicyclists can refer to Trip 18-C for an alternate bicycle route around the Superstition Wilderness.

From the picturesque spires of Picketpost Mountain, Trip 17-A travels north to Rogers Trough Trailhead, a gateway into the Superstition Wilderness. This trip affords a glimpse of Weaver's Needle, a famous Superstition landmark, as it travels north from U.S. 60. The trail follows primitive dirt roads through riparian canyons and cholla cactus–covered hills to a junction with a historic trail once used by Elisha Reavis. The ascent of Montana Mountain provides spectacular views. You can take an interesting side trip to Boyce Thompson Southwestern Arboretum, only 1.5 miles east of Picketpost Trailhead on U.S. 60.

Nature Highlight: On Montana Mountain a small coues whitetail buck bounds away across the hillside, his large feathery tail a white flag behind him.

Maps: Tonto National Forest.
- USGS Quads: Picketpost Mountain, Iron Mountain.

Difficulty: Moderate, with one long, steep 2,400-foot climb.

Length: 15 miles, one way.

Elevation: 2,300–5,340 feet.

Recommended Season: All seasons. Remember that temperatures may rise well above 100 degrees Fahrenheit in the summer months and there could be snow in the winter months.

Water: (Treat all water unless noted otherwise. During dry weather, water sources may not be dependable.)
- **Picketpost Trailhead:** None. Water may be found a little over a mile west, behind the old windmill on FR 231. (See Directions to Trailhead.)
- FR 8: After passing under power lines, watch for cottonwood trees marking a seasonal spring to the left of the road.
- FR 650: Crosses seasonal water intermittently.
- **Reavis Trail Canyon:** Crosses seasonal water intermittently the first two miles.

Camping:
- **Picketpost Trailhead** has flat areas for primitive camping. There are plans to develop a parking and equestrian staging area here.
- FR 650 offers some nice primitive camping spots.

Livestock: Sections of this passage are rough, steep, and rocky, requiring experienced trail animals in good physical condition. Animals need to be acclimated to hot weather and able to handle themselves safely on narrow, steep, rocky trails. We traveled this passage in April and found grass and water.

There are plans to create an equestrian staging area at the trailhead. There are corrals and a spring near the old windmill on FR 231. If you utilize this area be sure not to block the permitee's corrals or loading chutes and don't close gates that will block cattle access to water.

Along the route there are corrals on FR 650 approximately 3 miles north of the junction with FR 8. In dry conditions this area is accessible to trucks and trailers.

Directions to Picketpost Mountain Trailhead: You can access the trailhead by passenger car: The road to Picketpost trailhead is 4.5 miles west of Superior and 9 miles east of Florence Junction on U.S. 60. FR 231, just east of milepost #221, is not signed on the highway. Watch carefully for the dirt road, located on the south side of the highway.

Travel 0.5 mile past a windmill to a junction with an abandoned paved road. Turn left and travel 0.7 mile to the turnoff for Picketpost Trailhead on the right. Wooden markers indicate where the Arizona Trail crosses the road at this point.

TRAIL DESCRIPTION

Traveling northwest, the Arizona Trail crosses an abandoned paved road. Watch closely for the trail, which is faint in places, as it ascends a ridgeline, winding through prickly pear, cholla, saguaro cactus, and small palo verde trees. As you reach the top of the ridge, you will see a rock cairn. The trail curves to the left (west), offering views of U.S. 60 below and the distinctive landmark, Weaver's Needle, a jagged pinnacle rising from the Superstition Wilderness to the northwest. Traveling west to a large drainage, the trail drops down into the wash, which it follows north to a highway culvert.

The culvert is large enough to accommodate pack horses. After traveling under U.S. 60 the trail follows the wash for a short distance. Watch carefully for a rock cairn marking where the trail leaves the wash on the left bank then follows above the drainage. Then watch for a second small rock cairn that may be partially obscured by the brush, marking where the route of the Arizona Trail leaves the trail we have been following to curve uphill to the left.

As it gains the top of the ridgeline the trail turns north, following occasional rock cairns up the hill. As you crest the hill and follow a high ridgeline above Queen Creek Wash, you will enjoy panoramic views. To the north is the Superstition Wilderness and Weaver's Needle, and behind to the south, the massive, jagged form of Picketpost Mountain. The trail winds through Sonoran Desert chaparral and cactus as it descends to the wide wash, which is marked on both sides by 4x4 posts branded with the Arizona Trail symbol. The trail goes directly across the wash heading east. Watch for rock cairns as the trail winds through a sandy, grassy area then crosses another small drainage to a gate.

The route makes a hairpin turn as it passes through one gate, then immediately back through another on the right. The route is level as it travels southeast, winding through chaparral and a forest of large cholla cactus. Although faint on the hard ground, the trail is well-marked with rock cairns. The trail follows a fence line east, passes through a gate, and travels north under a power line.

One and a half miles from the trailhead the trail crosses FR 357, signed with 4x4 posts. After crossing FR 357, the route follows FR 2398 east, paralleling the railroad tracks for 0.5-mile and crossing junctions with two abandoned dirt roads. The road travels east with U.S. 60 and Picketpost Mountain to the right and a ridge-line with a power line to the left.

Two miles from the trailhead the Arizona Trail joins FR 8, a graded dirt road signed with 4x4s. FR 8 crosses the railroad tracks as it travels northeast. After crossing under a major power line, look to the left for cottonwood trees marking a seasonal spring.

At 3.6 miles from the trailhead is a junction with FR 650, a graded dirt road, which may not be signed with an Arizona Trail marker. Turn left (north) and follow FR 650 for 4 miles, to a junction with Reavis Trail Canyon. The road travels over low, rolling hills studded with saguaro cactus, mesquite, palo verde, and desert broom. In the area of Happy Camp the road crosses a cattle guard (with gate) and a streambed with seasonal water.

Ignore junctions with roads to the left and follow FR 650 north through an area of "teddy bear" cholla (jumping cactus), with distinctive light, fuzzy-looking thorns. At the base of a large hill the road drops into the gravel wash of Whitford Canyon and curves east. Approximately 3 miles after the junction with FR 8, FR 650 passes corrals on the right. Large shade trees and water in the creek make this an inviting place to camp. The road may be passable by high-clearance vehicles to this point in dry weather. After the corral the road becomes narrower and rockier as it dips in and out of Whitford Canyon, eventually ascending a hill on the east side of the drainage to 4x4 markers and a junction.

At 7.6 miles from Picketpost Mountain Trailhead the Arizona Trail leaves FR 650 traveling left, downhill a short distance to a large metal Arizona Trail sign and map. This is the beginning of Reavis Trail Canyon, which climbs 4.7 miles to a junction where it again picks up FR 650. The Reavis Trail Canyon route drops in and out of a creek bed several times, following it to a confluence of two drainages.

Here, the route for the Reavis/Arizona Trail goes up the canyon to the left. Follow rock cairns as the trail curves above the drainage, dropping in and out of the small canyon bottom as it narrows. The canyon and the trail above curve to the west, then north. The bottom of Reavis Trail Canyon has pools of water and cottonwood trees; a riparian habitat surrounded by Sonoran Desert. At times the trail disappears among the rocks on the canyon floor. Follow rock cairns up-canyon through areas of large cottonwood and sycamore trees mixed with saguaro cactus and cholla. The rocky, eastern slopes of the canyon display bare cliff faces dotted with saguaro, and on the west are chaparral-covered hills. As the canyon narrows the trail is overgrown in places with thorny underbrush. Watch carefully for rock markers as the route travels in or along the west side of the canyon.

The trail eventually leaves the canyon for the last time, curving left (west), then north toward Montana Mountain. Following the cairns, the trail drops into a drainage and crosses a rocky shelf with pools of water. Watch carefully for rock markers here as the trail turns west heading uphill over a grassy cactus-dotted hill. This marks the beginning of the long, switchbacking 2,400-foot ascent of Montana Mountain. The switchbacks are moderate, with level places to rest. With the gain in elevation there are great views to the south of Picketpost, the town of Superior, and the mountains beyond. At 5,340 feet the trail tops out at a gate. Rock cairns direct us down a long ridgeline to meet the road. To the left are breathtaking views of the wild and rugged country, defined by ragged ridgelines and sheer cliffs. Apache Junction is visible to the southwest.

There is an unsigned junction with FR 650 12.3 miles from the trailhead. Turn left (northwest) and follow the road along a high ridgeline to an unsigned T junction and a gate. The Arizona Trail route goes left (west) through the gate. The road winds through a pleasant, shady, wooded area, curves uphill to the left, then begins a long descent to a signed junction with FR 172A.

At 14.7 miles from the Picketpost Trailhead, carsonite markers indicate that the route is to the right, following FR 172A 0.3-mile to Rogers Trough trailhead.

18 Superstition Wilderness Passage Rogers Trough Trailhead
to Forest Road 83 Junction with Cottonwood Canyon

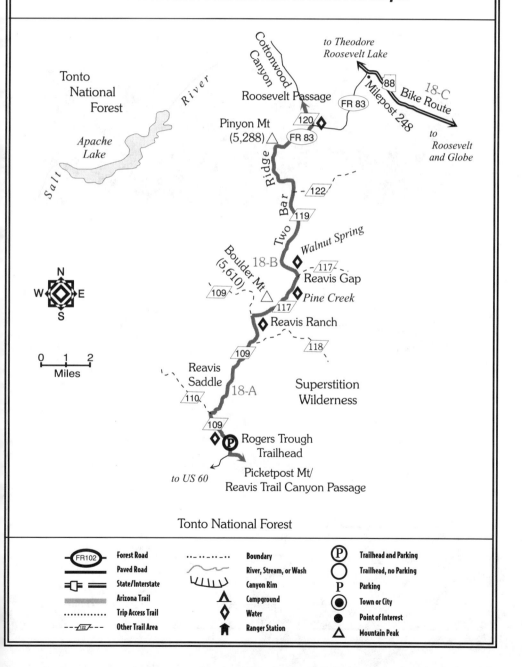

Tonto
National
Forest

River

Salt

Apache Lake

Cottonwood Canyon

to Theodore Roosevelt Lake

Roosevelt Passage

88

Milepost 248

18-C Bike Route

FR 83

to Roosevelt and Globe

Pinyon Mt
(5,288) △

120 ◆

FR 83

Ridge

122

119

Two Bar

Walnut Spring

Boulder Mt
(5,610) △

18-B

117

Reavis Gap

109

Pine Creek

117

Reavis Ranch ◆

118

109

N
W E
S

Reavis
Saddle

110

18-A

109

◆ P Rogers Trough
Trailhead

Superstition
Wilderness

0 1 2
Miles

to US 60

Picketpost Mt/
Reavis Trail Canyon Passage

Tonto National Forest

FR102	Forest Road	
	Paved Road	
	State/Interstate	
	Arizona Trail	
	Trip Access Trail	
122	Other Trail Area	
	Boundary	
	River, Stream, or Wash	
	Canyon Rim	
△	Campground	
◆	Water	
	Ranger Station	
P	Trailhead and Parking	
	Trailhead, no Parking	
P	Parking	
	Town or City	
	Point of Interest	
△	Mountain Peak	

A scenic view in the Superstition Wilderness Area as seen from Two Bar Ridge.

Photo by Kelly Tighe

From a world of unfenced room
    Just a breath of breeze is strayin',
Triflin' with the yucca bloom
    till its waxy bells are swayin'.

—**"Southwestern June," Badger Clark, 1915**

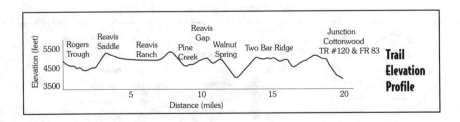

Trail Elevation Profile

O N THE ARIZONA TRAIL *divides this 20 mile passage into two Trips. From Rogers Trough trailhead, a gateway into the Superstition Wilderness, Trip 18-A travels north for 6 miles to Reavis Ranch. From Reavis Ranch, Trip 18-B travels 14 miles to the FR 83 junction with Cottonwood Canyon. Cyclists should refer to Trip 18-C.*

This passage offers the opportunity to experience the solitude and desolate beauty of some of Arizona's most remote and inaccessible backcountry. The Arizona Trail travels to the site of a historic homestead, once owned by an eccentric nineteenth century hermit.

From the lush riparian canyon and apple orchards of Reavis Ranch it is a challenging journey through jagged, windswept ridgelines and canyons into the heart of the Superstition Wilderness. The passage ends with spectacular vistas of Apache Lake, the Four Peaks Wilderness, and Theodore Roosevelt Lake.

Reavis Trail Canyon, Reavis Saddle, Reavis Ranch, Reavis Creek, Reavis Gap, Reavis Falls; all named for the man who probably knew the Superstitions better than anyone else. Elisha Reavis established his 60-acre homestead in the early 1870s. The location he chose for his farm was a pristine riparian canyon bordered by ponderosa and juniper-forested hills. Reavis raised vegetables, which he packed out periodically to sell in Phoenix or Florence.

Elisha Reavis was a wild-looking character. His long hair and beard, his reclusive lifestyle, and ultimately the circumstances of his death, led to much speculation and more "Superstition" stories. Elisha Reavis's body was found along the trail in 1896, the cause of his death, unknown. The Arizona Trail (Trip 18-A), passes near the unmarked grave site. Hiker's Guide to the Superstition Wilderness *by Jack Carlson and Elizabeth Stewart has a wonderful cover photograph of Elisha Reavis.*

Following Reavis's death the homestead had a succession of owners. The apple orchards were planted in the 1950s. Reavis Ranch was purchased by the Forest Service in the 1960s and incorporated into the 124,000-acre Superstition Wilderness, designed in 1964. The Arizona Wilderness Bill of 1984 added another 30,000 acres. It is managed by three different Ranger Districts of the Tonto National Forest.

GOVERNING AGENCIES

Mesa Ranger District, Tonto National Forest, 26 North MacDonald, Room 120, P.O. Box 5800, Mesa AZ 85211-1161. (602) 379-6446.
Tonto Basin Ranger District, HC 02, Box 4800, Roosevelt, AZ 85545. (520) 467-3200.

FOR MORE INFORMATION

Hiker's Guide to the Superstition Wilderness, by Carlson and Stewart (see reference list for complete information for this title).

NEAREST SERVICES TO ROGERS TROUGH

Superior: From Rogers Trough it is approximately 18 miles south to U.S. 60, following FR 72A to FR 72 to FR 357 East. Follow U.S. 60 east 4.5 miles to Superior.

Trip 18-A
Rogers Trough to Reavis Ranch

There is no vehicle access to Reavis Ranch. This is the first part of a two (or more)-day trip. Trip 18-A ends at Reavis Ranch, a popular destination within the Superstition Wilderness, where there is usually water and good camping. The site can be accessed by several different trails. Trip 18-A links with Trip 18-B for those who wish to do a transmountain trek through the Superstition Wilderness.

Bicycles are not allowed in the wilderness. See the alternate route described in Trip 18-C.

From Rogers Trough, a popular trailhead east of Apache Junction, Trip 18-A enters the Superstition Wilderness and on to a historic homestead site. The Arizona Trail travels through riparian canyons, upper Sonoran Desert chaparral, and pine and juniper forest to the apple orchards of Reavis Ranch. The variety of life zones and opportunities for loop or side trips make Reavis Ranch an appealing destination.

Nature Highlight: In late spring hedgehog cactus present a stunning display of pink blossoms along the trail.

Maps: Tonto National Forest.
- USGS Quads: Iron Mountain, Pinyon Mountain.

Difficulty: Moderate, with one long climb.

Length: 6 miles, one way.

Elevation: 4,420–5,140 feet.

Recommended Season: All year, depending on the weather. There may be snow in the winter months, and the temperature may exceed 100 degrees Fahrenheit in the summer.

Water: (Treat all water unless noted otherwise. During dry weather, water sources may not be dependable.)

Before you begin your trip, check with governing agencies regarding availability of water.
- **Rogers Trough:** Creek below the north side of the parking area.
- **Rogers Canyon:** Reavis Ranch Trail crosses water intermittently.
- **Reavis Ranch:** Reavis Creek.

Camping: Rogers Trough has a spacious parking lot and offers primitive camping.

Livestock: This trip is rough, steep, and rocky, requiring experienced, well-shod trail animals in good physical condition. Animals need to be acclimated to hot weather and able to handle themselves safely on narrow, steep, rocky trails. Be prepared to meet backpackers and hikers. We traveled this trip in April and still found water.
- **Rogers Trough:** There is a hitching post at Rogers Trough. Look for water along the Reavis Ranch Trail west of the trailhead.
- **Reavis Ranch:** There is water and two barbed wire corrals and a hitching post below the foundation of the ranch house.

Directions to Rogers Trough Trailhead: Four-wheel-drive vehicles are required for the last three miles. From Florence Junction east of Phoenix take U.S. 60 east to Queen Valley Road on the left. Follow Queen Valley Road to Hewitt Station Road (FR 357). Travel right (east) 3 miles to FR 172 on the left. Traversing FR 172 requires a high-clearance vehicle. Follow FR 172 10 miles to a junction with FR 172A. Turn right on FR 172A and travel 3 miles on a rough 4WD road to Rogers Trough.

If coming from the Picketpost Trailhead, turn right on U.S. 60 and travel 1 mile to FR 357, just past Queen Creek, on the left. Follow FR 357 west to the junction with FR 172.

Other Area Trails: There is an extensive network of trails within the Superstition Wilderness. Contact governing agencies for more information.

West Pinto Trail #212 travels east to Miles Ranch trailhead near a mining area west of Miami.

Rogers Canyon Trail is a scenic trail that passes ancient Salado Indian cliff dwellings on its way to a junction with several other trails.

TRAIL DESCRIPTION

The Arizona Trail leaves the north side of the parking area following Reavis Ranch Trail #109 west. Crossing Rogers Creek, it is a short distance to a junction with the Pinto Trail #212 to the right. Continue west following Rogers Creek. The route leaves the creek, dropping steeply down a deeply worn trail bordered by oak, juniper, and manzanita, to the rocky bottom of Rogers Canyon.

As the trail leaves the drainage and climbs, clinging to the rocky slopes, it affords a view into the beautiful and dramatic canyon below. The drainage is narrow and deep, with large sycamore and juniper trees and inviting pools of water. The south side of the canyon is composed of picturesque, rocky cliffs. The route affords great views of the Superstition Wilderness to the north and west. The rocky trail dips in and out of the canyon, sometimes passing small pools of water. Climbing the north side of the canyon, the trail passes through a brushy area overgrown with manzanita to a junction.

At 1.5 miles from the trailhead, watch carefully for the junction with Rogers Canyon Trail to the left. It is very brushy, and signs may be difficult to see. This is a confluence of Rogers Canyon and a tributary canyon. The Reavis Ranch/Arizona Trail leaves Rogers Canyon heading northeast. The trail travels up the drainage through a brushy area mixed with oak and sycamore trees. Verbena and other wildflowers may be blooming. The terrain is rocky as the trail dips in and out of the creek bed. The route climbs moderately, passing occasional small seasonal pools of water.

A little over 2 miles from the trailhead, the Reavis Ranch/Arizona Trail leaves the canyon on the west side and switchbacks up chaparral-covered slopes rimmed by jagged cliffs. The switchbacks are moderate, curving up through manzanita, oak, juniper, and cactus, in an ascent of over 700 feet.

Three miles from Rogers Trough the trail tops out in Reavis Saddle, a grassy, level area with views to the south. The trail travels north, through piñon pine, juniper, and oak woodland. The route drops down through a rocky bouldery area, and as it descends the northern-facing slope of the ridge, it passes the first big ponderosa pines.

This pleasant stretch of trail is an easy downhill, traveling under large ponderosa and alligator juniper, mixed with grassy areas. As the trail follows the drainage of Reavis Creek, it passes a very large alligator juniper and sycamore trees. As the trail rambles down the creek bed there are occasional small pools of water. The descent is easy, almost level, through pine-oak forest. The trail leaves the creek bed, winding through a dense and thorny undergrowth, as it leaves the forest and enters a grassy, open area. This was the site of a forest fire thirty years ago. The blackened remains of some huge trees are still standing, scattered among the hills.

Five miles from Rogers Trough the trail follows along the left bank of a wide gravel wash, passing through a very pretty grassland dotted with oak trees and rimmed by rolling hills. Soon large ponderosa pine replace the oak trees, and as the trail leaves the grassland, entering the forest, there is a huge ancient alligator juniper to the right of the trail.

The trail travels between grassy park-like areas and ponderosa forest, to a junction with Fireline Trail #118. The Fireline Trail goes right, and Reavis Ranch Trail continues to the left, crossing the creek. As it gains the other bank, the trail passes through a large open meadow toward orchard trees. Beyond the trees, atop a small rise is the remains of the Reavis ranch house, marked by rubble that was once the foundation. Below the foundation to the right is a level grassy field with corrals and a hitching post.

Trip 18-B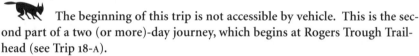

Reavis Ranch to FR 83 Junction
with Cottonwood Canyon Trail #120

The beginning of this trip is not accessible by vehicle. This is the second part of a two (or more)-day journey, which begins at Rogers Trough Trailhead (see Trip 18-A).

This trip travels into a remote and formidable land of rugged, steep ridgelines and canyons. The solitude and inaccessibility of this trip offer a wonderful wilderness experience, but be sure that you are physically and emotionally prepared for this very difficult trip. In some areas the trail is poorly defined or overgrown with cactus. Canyons are extremely steep and water is scarce; in fact, there is no water the last 9.5 miles. Temperatures may climb well above 100 degrees Fahrenheit in the summer months. Carry a minimum of one gallon of water per person per day. Wear protective clothing.

Large sections of this trip are not signed with the Arizona Trail symbol. Pay close attention to trail descriptions. Those who wish to exit the Arizona Trail at the end of this Trip via FR 83, add 4 miles to SR 88.

From Reavis Ranch, site of a historic homestead in the heart of the Superstition Wilderness, Trip 18-B travels north 14.3 miles to a junction with Cottonwood Canyon and FR 83, south of Roosevelt Lake. This scenic but extremely rugged trip travels from a lush setting of apple orchards, sycamore, and ponderosa pine to high, windswept ridges and steep canyons. Following a series of long interlinking ridgelines, the trail affords panoramic views of the Four Peaks Wilderness, Roosevelt Lake, Apache Lake, and the Salt River.

We dubbed the steep canyon south of Two Bar Mountain "Beanie Burrito Canyon" for Beanie, a pack burro who slipped off the trail and landed upside down on her pack (unhurt) in the rocks below.

Nature Highlight: Dropping down Boulder Mountain we heard the pretty song of the little canyon wren, a series of clear, descending notes, echoing from the rocky walls.

Maps: Tonto National Forest.
- USGS Quads: Pinyon Mountain, Two Bar Mountain.

Difficulty: Very difficult.

Length: 14.3 miles, one way to FR 83 junction with Cottonwood Canyon (through-travelers). Those exiting to SR 88, add 4 miles.

Elevation: 5,070–3,820 feet.

Recommended Season: All seasons, depending on the weather. Temperatures may exceed 110 degrees Fahrenheit in the summer. Beware of lightning storms when traveling exposed ridgelines.

Water: (Treat all water unless noted otherwise. During dry weather, water sources may not be dependable.) The last 9.5 miles of this trip have no water.
- **Reavis Ranch:** Water is usually to be found in Reavis Creek.
- **Pine Creek** has a small pool.
- **Walnut Spring:** This is the last water for 9.5 miles. We found water here in April, after a dry winter, and an area rancher told us that there is usually water here.
- **Klondike Spring:** Warning! This spring has proven impossible to find. Although it is shown on the Forest Service map, don't depend on it as a water source.
- There is a dirt stock tank on the west side of FR 83. (Cleaner water may be found in a cement tank 0.5 mile down FR 83 toward Black Brush Ranch.)

Camping:
- **Reavis Ranch:** There is delightful, primitive camping in the vicinity of the old ranch and orchard.
- **FR 83:** There are flat areas for primitive camping along the road.

Livestock: This Trip is rough, steep, and rocky, requiring experienced, well-shod trail animals in good physical condition. Animals need to be acclimated to the heat and able to handle themselves safely on narrow, steep, rocky trails. We traveled this trip in April and still found water.

Reavis Ranch: There is water and two barbed wire corrals and a hitching post below the foundation of the ranch house.

Reavis Gap Trail #117 has some tight but passable spots for pack animals. For cactus, protective leg boots are recommended, or carry a tool for removing thorns.

Directions to Reavis Ranch Trailhead: Reavis Ranch is not accessible by vehicle. There are several trails within the Superstition Wilderness that lead to Reavis Ranch. For the route of the Arizona Trail from Rogers Trough, see Trip 18-A.

Other Area Trails: There is an extensive network of trails within the Superstition Wilderness. Contact governing agencies for more information.
- **Fireline Trail #118:** Travels east, connecting with other trails within the wilderness. Fireline Trail is a route that has been used to access Circlestone, a mysterious prehistoric ruin that may have astrological significance. See the Superstition Wilderness Passage (under "For More Information"), or contact the Mesa Ranger District for information on how to find Circlestone.

- **Reavis Ranch Trail #109:** Continues north from Reavis Ranch for 9 miles to the Reavis trailhead. Reavis trailhead is accessed from SR 88 (the Apache Trail) on the north side of the wilderness.

TRAIL DESCRIPTION

The Arizona Trail follows Reavis Ranch Trail #109 north. There are numerous paths crisscrossing the orchard. Stay to the left of the orchard on the Reavis Ranch Trail or you may miss the signed junction ahead.

At 0.3 miles north is a signed junction with Reavis Gap Trail #117 on the right. The Arizona Trail abandons Reavis Ranch Trail here, turning right (east) on Reavis Gap Trail. If you happen to miss the signs, the route travels east between two rows of metal fence posts as it crosses an open field toward some large sycamore trees and Reavis Creek. Turning left, cross the creek to a slanted rock shelf on the opposite bank. The trail turns right, following the rock shelf up the bank and through the trees heading east. The trail makes a steep ascent of Boulder Mountain, following a long upended rock shelf. Traveling above a tributary drainage of Reavis Creek, the route affords a nice view back down into the area of Reavis Ranch.

Having gained almost 400 feet, the trail levels in a saddle, winding through oak, piñon, and juniper beneath a scenic wall of balanced rocks and sculpted cliffs. As the trail leaves the saddle, beginning a 600-foot descent to Pine Creek, there are spectacular views. The distant high saddle to the north is Reavis Gap, the route of the Arizona Trail. The trail is bouldery but well worn and signed with occasional rock cairns. There are some tight but passable spots for experienced pack animals. The scenic trail winds down through boulders, intermixed with bear grass, twisted old juniper trees, pinyon, and manzanita. Looming above the trail on the left are the dramatic high rocky cliffs and sheer eroded pinnacles of Boulder Mountain. The trail levels at the base of the mountain, entering a shady woodland of oak and juniper on its way to Pine Creek.

The Reavis Gap/AT crosses water in Pine Creek 2.8 miles from Reavis Ranch. The trail climbs a rocky hillside northeast toward Reavis Gap, at length topping a high saddle with stunning views in all directions. The large mountain to the west is Four Peaks, a landmark that will be visible intermittently during the rest of this trip. (The Four Peaks Wilderness, north of the Salt River and west of Roosevelt Lake, is part of the northern route of the Arizona Trail.) The trail curves east on an extensive saddle, with multiple drainages falling away in different directions. This is Reavis Gap, at an elevation of 4,740 feet. Watch for the signed junction with Two Bar Ridge Trail #119. The trail is faint in places.

The trail junction is 4.1 miles from Reavis Ranch. The Arizona Trail turns left here and follows Two Bar Ridge Trail #119. (Reavis Gap Trail #117 continues northeast, eventually connecting to other trails within the wilderness.) The Two Bar Ridge #119/Arizona Trail travels northwest down through a large, open, grassy drainage. Following occasional rock cairns, it is 0.5-mile to Walnut Spring.

At 4.6 miles from Reavis Ranch the trail enters a small drainage marked by sacaton-like bunchy grass and a wet seep across the trail. The spring is to the right of the trail hidden in the deep grass. The spring's namesake, an ancient Arizona walnut tree to the left of the trail provides shade for a welcome break. *Walnut Spring is the last water for almost 10 miles.* Local wildlife are dependent upon this water. Do not wash anything in the spring or waste water. If you camp in the area, make sure that you are far enough away (0.25 mile) that wildlife can access the spring.

The trail continues northwest, uphill, almost immediately passing through another sacaton-like area. The route levels here but is boulder-strewn and thick with prickly pear and hedgehog cactus. Some sections of the trail are quite faint, or disappear altogether among the rocks and cactus. Watch carefully for the occasional rock cairns. Approximately 0.5 mile from the spring, the trail begins to climb a grassy hill that offers impressive views as the trail gains the top. From the high ridge, look below to the most difficult section of this trip: "Beanie Burrito Canyon." (This canyon is unnamed on the topo.) If you are on horseback, check your cinches!

The trail makes a precipitous and rocky descent, without the benefit of switchbacks, for almost 800 feet. Stay to the right at the unsigned junction. (A short distance from the bottom of the canyon, a sign propped against a tree on the left side of the trail points west to Klondike Spring. Following a faint spur trail through almost impenetrable brush, we were unable to locate the spring.) After crossing the narrow bottom of the canyon, it is a steep and laborious ascent of 880 feet to reach the saddle atop Two Bar Ridge. The trail switchbacks steeply up a hillside that is abundantly adorned with rocks and large prickly pear cactus. Just before topping the saddle you have a brief, first glimpse of Theodore Roosevelt Lake to the east.

At 7.7 miles from Reavis Ranch the trail adjoins Two Bar Ridge, which it follows along a succession of linking ridgelines for approximately 5 miles. As the trail travels north, paralleling a barbed wire fence along the high, narrow, windswept ridgeline, the views are outstanding in all directions. Roosevelt Lake and the Sierra Ancha Wilderness to the east, Four Peaks, the Salt River, and Apache Lake to the west.

Nine miles from Reavis Ranch is a junction with Tule Trail #122, at an elevation of 4,800 feet. (Tule Trail travels east to FR 449, which leads to SR 88.) The Two Bar Ridge/Arizona Trail continues uphill, heading north. Still following ridgelines, the route curves a horseshoe around a deep basin to the west. The windy, exposed ridgeline is overgrown with cactus in places, as the trail dips and climbs along the backbone of Two Bar Ridge. Watch for rock cairns marking the route.

Shortly after the trail travels down over some erosion bars and levels in a saddle, watch for an unsigned junction. Our route takes a sharp right and drops downhill, north. Watch for cairns. As the trail skirts around an unnamed peak to our left, it is easy to follow, but overgrown in spots with cactus and shindagger. As the trail gains a small saddle and drops down the other side, it disappears in the drainage. Watch for the rock cairns as the route travels uphill to the north.

Following a barbed wire fence on the left, the trail makes a scrambling, switchbacking ascent of a high ridgeline. After gaining the top of the hill the trail follows the long ridge, curving east as it circles around Pinyon Mountain on the left. Although the trail is narrow and "edgy" it is almost free of cactus and rocks and seems like a super highway compared to what we have traveled today. It is an easy, moderate descent to the wilderness boundary.

The Superstition Wilderness boundary is 12.8 miles from Reavis Ranch, marked by a fence and a gate. Located in a saddle at 4,790 feet, the boundary gate affords a bird's-eye view of Roosevelt Lake and SR 88. Far below to the right, a dirt stock tank and road (our destination) are visible.

From the gate an old 4WD road travels steeply down a ridgeline to a saddle and an unsigned junction. Stay on the more-traveled road as it curves to the left. Less than 0.5 mile from the boundary gate is a junction with a dirt road to the left. Continue straight (north). The scenic old road drops at a very steep rate as it winds down to the dirt tank and an unsigned junction with a dirt road traveling south through a gate. Our route, FR 83, curves to the left (north) past a dirt tank on the left. (Cleaner water may be found in a little over a mile at a cement stock tank approximately 0.5 mile east of the Cottonwood Canyon junction, following FR 83 toward SR 88. Or continue north following Cottonwood Canyon.) It is 0.5-mile to the junction with Cottonwood Canyon Trail #120 to the left (north).

Continue on the Arizona Trail as it follows Cottonwood Canyon (see Trip 19-A), or exit via FR 83 as it tops a ridge then travels downhill 4 miles to SR 88.

Trip 18-C 🤠

Alternate Bicycle Route Around the Superstition Wilderness from Picketpost Trailhead to Theodore Roosevelt Bridge

This trip follows paved highways that are steep, narrow, winding, and may have a lot of traffic. In many sections there are no shoulders, with guard rails adjacent to the pavement, and blind curves. A safer option is to transport bicycles around the Superstition Wilderness.

This trip provides access to Trip 19-A (steep and rocky for bicycles), or cyclists may opt to continue on the highway to Roosevelt Lake. Snow and ice may be present in the winter months.

Trip 18-C begins at the Picketpost trailhead, travels east through the mining towns of Superior and Miami, and ends at Roosevelt Bridge (the northern end of Roosevelt Passage). The scenic route is steep and winding as it follows canyons and traverses high, rugged, boulder-strewn passes. This trip offers an opportunity to visit a "living museum," Boyce Thompson Southwestern Arboretum, and also passes Tonto National Monument, the site of a fascinating 700-year-old village.

Nature Highlight: The bizarre Boojum tree, a huge succulent native to Baja California, resembles an upsidedown turnip. It is one of many plants on display at the Boyce Thompson Southwestern Arboretum.

Maps:
- Arizona road map.
- Tonto National Forest Map.

Difficulty: Very difficult, with some long, very steep up-hills.

Length: 56 miles, one way.

Elevation: 2,200–4,600 feet.

Recommended Season: Depending on the weather. Temperatures can exceed 100 degrees Fahrenheit in the lower elevations. The higher passes may have snow and ice in the winter months.

Water (potable):
- Boyce Thompson Arboretum.
- Superior.
- Miami.
- Roosevelt Lake Complex.

Camping:
- **Oak Flats campground** east of Superior (no water).
- **Roosevelt Lake Complex:** Developed campsites, fee, shower.

ROUTE DESCRIPTION

From the Picketpost trailhead turn left on the abandoned paved/gravel road and travel 0.7 mile to a junction with FR 231. Turn right onto FR 231 and travel 0.4 mile to U.S. Highway 60. Turn right (east) on U.S. 60 and travel toward Superior.

At 1.5 miles is the entrance to Boyce Thompson Southwestern Arboretum, on the south side of the highway (see the Picketpost Mountain/Reavis Trail Canyon Passage for more information on this "living museum"). If you don't stop at the arboretum, look to the right as the highway climbs, for a glimpse into the dramatic canyon of Queen Creek. Some of the arboretum's exotic vegetation is visible from the highway.

It is an easy downhill grade into the mining town of Superior. At 4 miles the route passes a sign for tourist information on the left, and a laundromat on the right. This is a full-service community with markets, gas stations, and lodging. As U.S. 60 leaves Superor it begins a long, winding, steep climb through rocky, rugged terrain.

At 6 miles the highway travels on a high, narrow bridge over scenic Queen Creek Canyon. A mile later it passes through Queen Creek Tunnel, built in 1952. A passing lane and occasional pull-outs aid the long, scenic, 3-mile, 1,000-foot climb up the canyon.

At 9 miles, as the highway tops out, the road to Oak Flats campground is on the right side of the highway. It is approximately 0.5 mile down the dirt road to the campground (which has no water). The highway begins a steep 6 percent grade drop into Devil's Iron Canyon. Then, aided by a passing lane, the road climbs steeply through an area of picturesque rock pinnacles and spires, to top out 3 miles from the Oak Flat turnoff at 4,600 feet.

At 15 miles, the highway passes a roadside rest area, then heads down a very steep grade, through an interesting landscape of white, eroded boulders. To the left, the route offers a first glimpse of the vast white-colored mine tailings that form the periphery of Miami.

At 19 miles, the highway crosses a bridge over Pinto Creek with dramatic views of the deep canyon on either side. After a short climb, the highway begins a very steep descent into the town of Miami. The massive mine tailings form the skyline as the highway wanders for almost 5 miles through the old mining community, to a junction with SR 88.

Trip 18-C leaves U.S. 60 at 26 miles and turns left (north) onSR 88, toward Roosevelt Lake. For the next 6 miles SR 88, a narrow winding road, travels in a gentle downhill grade through several small communities. Then the terrain changes as the highway rolls through an area of small but steep, rocky hills.

At 35 miles, the highway begins a long, steep 4-mile climb up a series of tall saguaro-studded hills. Once on top there is a fabulous first view of Theodore Roosevelt Lake. The Superstition Wilderness is to the left, and to the northwest is the distinctive silhouette of the Four Peaks Wilderness (the faraway route of the Arizona Trail as it travels north). It is a long, steep 9 percent grade drop down toward the lake. At the junction with SR 288, stay left on SR 88.

At mile 45, the highway crosses Pinto Creek and passes through the small community of Roosevelt. This is home to the closest post office and gasoline for the lake complex, which is 9.5 miles to the north.

At 50.6 miles, the highway passes the turnoff for FR 83, which accesses the Arizona Trail as it exits the Superstition Wilderness (see Trip 19-A). FR 83 is not signed on the highway. It is directly opposite milepost 248, on the left (south) side of the highway. Turn onto FR 83 here if you wish to pick up the Cottonwood Canyon section of the Arizona Trail. Trip 19-A is steep and rocky; bicyclists may opt to continue on the highway to Roosevelt Lake.

At 52.5 miles, you'll see the road into Tonto National Monument, and its prehistoric cliff dwellings (see Roosevelt Passage). One mile farther is the signed turnoff for Frazier Trailhead, located behind an electrical substation. This is the recommended trailhead for equestrians.

At 54.5 miles is the Roosevelt Lake complex. To the right of the highway is the marina store. Beyond the store, the blue roof of the Roosevelt Lake visitor center is visible. On the left side of the highway is Lake View (trailer) Park, and the long-abandoned Roosevelt cemetery. The Roosevelt cemetery trail affords the easiest access to the Arizona Trail from the Roosevelt complex. (Turn into Lake View Park and take an immediate right turn into the cemetery trailhead parking lot. The blacktopped trail travels 250 yards to the cemetery. From there it is 0.25 mile to the Thompson/Arizona Trail.)

At 56 miles, you reach the northern end of the Thompson/Arizona Trail, marked by a curve in the highway and a jumble of highway signs (a 35 mph sign, a sign for the junction of SR 88 and SR 188, and a green mileage sign for Phoenix and Payson). Look for the green gate on the left (south) side of the highway. There is nowhere to park here. It is 0.1 mile to Theodore Roosevelt Bridge. There is a view of Roosevelt Dam and the Salt River Canyon to the left as you cross over the bridge to the parking area on the other side.

19 Roosevelt Passage

Forest Road 83 to Theodore Roosevelt Lake

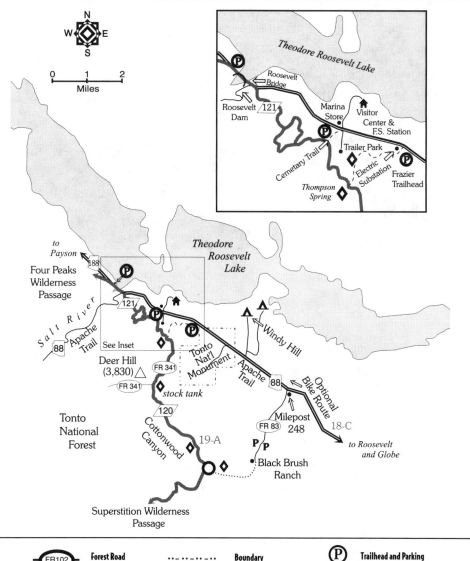

N
W E
S

0   1   2
Miles

Theodore Roosevelt Lake

Roosevelt Bridge

Roosevelt Dam /121/

Marina Store

Visitor Center & F.S. Station

Cemetary Trail

Trailer Park

Electric Substation

Frazier Trailhead

Thompson Spring

to Payson

/188/

Four Peaks Wilderness Passage

/121/

Theodore Roosevelt Lake

Salt River

/88/ Apache Trail

See Inset

Deer Hill (3,830)△

FR 341

FR 341

Tonto Nat'l Monument

stock tank

Windy Hill

Apache Trail

88

Optional Bike Route

18-C

Tonto National Forest

/120/

Cottonwood Canyon

19-A

Milepost 248

FR 83

P P

• Black Brush Ranch

to Roosevelt and Globe

Superstition Wilderness Passage

⊸FR102⊸	**Forest Road**	·-·-·-·-· **Boundary**
	Paved Road	∿∿∿ **River, Stream, or Wash**
⊏⊐⊏⊐	**State/Interstate**	⊔⊔⊔⊔ **Canyon Rim**
	Arizona Trail	▲ **Campground**
··········	**Trip Access Trail**	◇ **Water**
--/122/--	**Other Trail Area**	⌂ **Ranger Station**

Ⓟ **Trailhead and Parking**
◯ **Trailhead, no Parking**
P **Parking**
◉ **Town or City**
● **Point of Interest**
△ **Mountain Peak**

Photo by Kelly Tighe

Cottonwoods and saguaros demonstrate the abundance and diversity of plant life found along the Roosevelt Passage.

> *It's sun and sun without a change*
> *the lazy length o' May*
> *And all the little sun things own the land.*
> *The horned toad basks and swells himse'f;*
> *The bright swifts dart and play;*
> *The rattler hunts or dozes in the sand.*

—"The Rains," Badger Clark, 1917

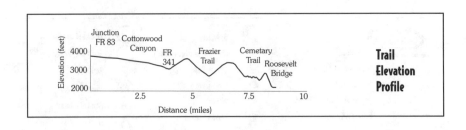

Trail Elevation Profile

THIS PASSAGE CONTAINS ONE TRIP. *The passage itself is only 9 miles long, but a spur trail from* SR *88 connects with the Arizona Trail at the beginning of the passage to add more miles. Trip 19-*A *begins at Black Brush Ranch and connects with the Arizona Trail 2 miles west. Roosevelt Passage begins at the junction of* FR *83 and Cottonwood Canyon and ends on the north side of Theodore Roosevelt Bridge.*

The Arizona Department of Transportation has agreed to allow pedestrian traffic across the bridge. Use extreme caution when crossing the bridge.

From the classic Sonoran Desert and riparian woodlands of Cottonwood Canyon to far-reaching vistas of Theodore Roosevelt Lake and the Tonto Basin, this scenic passage of the Arizona Trail offers great winter hiking and recreational opportunities. There are fascinating side trips to the early-1900s Roosevelt cemetery and the ancient cliff dwellings of Tonto National Monument. Opportunities for boating, fishing, and camping along Roosevelt Lake, or a drive along the historic Apache Trail make this passage even more appealing.

The Tonto Basin is surrounded by mountainous wilderness. The rugged Superstitions are to the south, the Sierra Ancha Wilderness to the east, and the Mazatzal and Four Peaks Wilderness areas to the northwest. The lower elevation and topography of the basin made it a natural setting for the lake, created by Theodore Roosevelt Dam, the world's tallest masonry dam.

Cottonwood Canyon is a beautiful example of an Arizona riparian habitat. It is easy to imagine that the cliff-dwelling Salado Indians, who lived only a few miles to the east in a village that is now Tonto National Monument, might have frequented this canyon almost a thousand years ago. Perhaps they hunted here and gathered the wild grapes and blackberries. Prehistoric Salado Indians (named after Rio Salada—the Salt River) had a well-established culture centuries before Europeans arrived in America. Visit Tonto National Monument (1 mile east of the Frazier trailhead) for a fine example of a seven-hundred-year-old Salado village, built into a hillside above the Tonto Basin.

Roosevelt Dam, initiated by President Theodore Roosevelt in 1905, and completed in 1911, was the first Federal Reclamation project in the West. Its purpose was to provide flood control and irrigation to the Salt River Valley and Phoenix. Thousands of individuals labored for five years to build the world's tallest masonry dam, which stood 283 feet when completed. (Modifications completed in 1996 have increased the dam's height to 357 feet.) It was dangerous work and there were many accidents and over thirty deaths related to the construction of the dam.

The settlement of Roosevelt developed to support the thousands of people involved in the preparation and construction of the dam. Roosevelt at one time had a theater, dance halls, restaurants, and hotels. As water backed up behind the dam creating the lake, most of the original townsite was submerged. Except for some old foundations and the Roosevelt cemetery, little remains today. (There is a town of Roosevelt 11 miles south of the dam on SR 88.)

GOVERNING AGENCIES

Tonto National Forest, Tonto Basin Ranger District. The ranger station has a visitor center, beyond the Roosevelt Lake Marina store. Roosevelt Lake Visitor Center is open seven days a week. Brochures for the cemetery are available as well as books, maps, and camping information. HC 02 Box 4800, Roosevelt, AZ 85545. (520) 467-3200.

FOR MORE INFORMATION:

Tonto National Monument. The visitor center offers exhibits and an audio-visual program and guided and self-guided tours of the cliff dwellings. The monument is 3.4 miles southeast of Roosevelt Dam. (520) 467-2241.

NEAREST SERVICES TO FR 83/ COTTONWOOD CANYON JUNCTION

Roosevelt Lake Marina store: Follow FR 83 4 miles to SR 88. Turn left (north) on SR 88 and travel a little over 4 miles to the Roosevelt Lake Marina store. (See appendix A.) Closest fuel and post office are in the town of Roosevelt, 5 miles south on SR 88.

There is closer access to the Marina store toward the end of this passage, if you stay on the Arizona Trail until the Cemetery Trail junction, marked by a green gate. Take the Cemetery Trail to the parking area and walk across SR 88 to the store. Livestock are not allowed on the Cemetery Trail, and there is a livestock exit at Frazier trailhead. The store is 0.6 mile west on SR 88.

Trip 19-A

Black Brush Ranch, FR 83 to Roosevelt Bridge

Because of the low elevation and associated warmer temperatures, this is a nice winter trek. This trip uses 2 miles of forest road at its south end to access the Arizona Trail. The Arizona Trail covers 9 miles in this passage, but the total length of Trip 19-A is 11 miles.

Bicycles may use this passage; however, there are some very rocky and some very steep sections. (See Trip 18-C for an alternate bicycle route around the Superstition Wilderness.)

Long-distance travelers traveling through the Superstitions should be aware that FR 83 is the first relatively easy access to SR 88.

This trip begins at Black Brush Ranch on FR 83 and travels 2 miles to meet the Arizona Trail as it exits the Superstition Wilderness, and ends at the south side of the Roosevelt Bridge. This is a rocky, mostly downhill route with several steep climbs offering excellent examples of Sonoran Desert vegetation, as the trail plays tag with delightful riparian woodlands along Cottonwood Creek. This scenic trail passes a fascinating, early 1900s cemetery and offers far-reaching vistas as it clings to the contours along the rim of the Tonto Basin, overlooking Roosevelt Lake. The area offers fishing, camping, boating, and trails into the ancient cliff dwellings of Tonto National Monument.

Wildlife Highlight: A colorful, 8-inch-long, orange and black giant desert centipede ambles off the trail, all forty-two legs moving in perfect synchrony.

Maps:
- Tonto National Forest.
- USGS Quads: Pinyon Mountain, Theodore Roosevelt Dam.

Difficulty: Moderate to difficult, with some steep climbs and descents.

Length: 9 miles, one way, from FR 83 junction with the AT to Roosevelt Bridge (through-travelers); 11 miles, one way, from Black Brush Ranch headquarters to Roosevelt Bridge.

Elevation: 3,800–2,200 feet.

Recommended Season: All year, with caution. In hot weather travel in the early morning. Temperatures can exceed 100 degrees Fahrenheit later in the day.

Water: (Treat all water unless noted otherwise. During dry weather, water sources may not be dependable.)
- Stock tanks, FR 83.
- **Cottonwood Canyon Creek.**
- **Thompson Spring.**
- Stock Tank on **trail 0.5** mile south of Frazier trailhead.

Camping: Cottonwood Canyon and Thompson Spring have primitive camping possibilities. The Forest Service has implemented a riparian recovery plan in partnership with the grazing permittee. Trail users are asked to use low-impact camping techniques and to carry animal feed for livestock.

Windy Hill and Cholla are developed campgrounds with showers. (They are near the lake and not on the route of the Arizona Trail.)

Roosevelt Lakeview Park accommodates RV and travel trailers. (520) 467-2203.

Frazier equestrian staging area has no amenities and camping and fires are not encouraged. If you will be staying overnight with livestock, the Forest Service suggests using RVs or sleeping in vehicles.

Livestock: For safety reasons, those traveling with livestock should exit the Arizona Trail at Frazier trailhead. There is no room at the terminus of Thompson/AT, which ends on SR 88, to park a trailer. Traffic on the bridge is fast and furious, making it extremely dangerous to take livestock onto the bridge. No alternative route has been identified at this time.

There is a steep section of trail, between Thompson Spring and Roosevelt Bridge, where wooden steps have been built into the hillside. Taking heavy animals down these stairs could damage the stairs, or worse, cause an accident. The Forest Service has provided an alternate route around the stairs.

Our recommendation to long-distance riders or packers is to have your animals trailered from Frazier trailhead over the bridge. If you are seeking a border-to-border experience and don't want to skip any sections of the trail, then walk this one.

See appendix B for information on boarding and transporting livestock across Roosevelt Bridge.

If you are planning to park trucks and trailers at Black Brush Ranch or Frazier trailhead or to use the corrals at Frazier, the grazing permittee has asked that you call ahead for parking instructions. Call Hayhook Ranch, (520) 467-2354. Do not block loading chutes or pens, or close gates that will deny cattle access to water.

Forest Road 83 trailhead: Don't attempt to pull a horse trailer past Black Brush Ranch headquarters. Call ahead for instruction on where to park.

Frazier trailhead has a pull-through and plenty of room for horse trailers, and two good corrals that the public may use when not being used by area ranchers. There is no grass or water at the trailhead.

Directions to FR 83 Junction with the Arizona Trail (Beginning of passage): Two sand washes make high-clearance vehicles preferable for the first 2 miles. The last 2 miles, from Black Brush Ranch to the Arizona Trail, require a four-wheel-drive vehicle. FR 83 is located on east SR 88, 2 miles south of Tonto National Monument and 5 miles north of the Roosevelt post office at Pinto Creek. Note that FR 83 is not signed on the highway; it is on the south side of the highway, across from mile post 248. Take the fork to the left and drive 2 miles to Black Brush Ranch headquarters, marked by a pull-around and a stock tank. From this point it is approximately 2 miles to the junction with the Arizona Trail and Cottonwood Canyon. Do not park in the pull-around or block the rancher's access to gates and corrals. Pull off the road, where your vehicle will be out of the way.

Directions to Other Trailheads in this Trip: Frazier trailhead can be accessed by passenger car. The trailhead is on the south side of SR 88, just behind an electrical sub-station. If you are traveling from Globe, watch for the turnoff on the left, 1 mile past the entrance to Tonto National Monument. (It is 0.6 mile farther west on SR 88 to the marina store and visitor center.) The dirt road circles around the substation to the right. The 1.3-mile connecting route to the Arizona Trail leaves from the south side of the pull-around.

Roosevelt Cemetery can be accessed by passenger car. This route offers the easiest access to the Arizona Trail (no livestock). The parking lot is reached from the Roosevelt Lakeview Park entrance directly across from the marina store and visitor center. Take the first right after the entrance, to a parking area.

AT/SR 88 junction at the south end of Roosevelt Bridge: The highway passes through a narrow cut with guardrails. There is nowhere to park at this junction, but you can park across the bridge on the north side and walk back (being careful of the heavy traffic) or access the trail from Roosevelt Cemetery parking lot or Frazier trailhead. The narrow path leading from SR 88 to the Arizona Trail (Thompson Trail 121) is easy to miss. Look for it on the south side of East SR 88, near a green highway sign ("Globe 32 miles"), 100 yards east of the three-way intersection of SR 188, West 88, and East 88. Passing behind the guardrail, the path travels to a green Forest Service gate.

Other Area Trails:

- **Lower Cottonwood Canyon** travels from Thompson Spring, 1.3 miles to the Frazier trailhead and equestrian staging area. The authors recommend that livestock exit here.
- **Roosevelt Cemetery Trail** offers the shortest route from the Arizona Trail to the Roosevelt Lake Marina store and the Roosevelt Lake Visitor Center. A tour of the cemetery offers a fascinating glimpse of life at the settlement during the construction of Roosevelt Dam in the early 1900s.
- **Tonto National Monument,** 1 mile east of Frazier trailhead on East SR 88, offers a visitor center, trails, and guided tours of a marvelous, seven-hundred-year-old city.

  Some loop trips using old roads that access the Arizona Trail are possible. Contact the managing agency for more information.

TRAIL DESCRIPTION

(From Black Brush Ranch to the Arizona Trail: FR 83 heads east, up over a steep bank requiring a 4WD vehicle, then turns south. As the road forks, stay to the right, and shortly after, the road passes through a gate. Heading west, it is a steep climb, passing several stock tanks, to a gate at the top of a high ridge. After passing through the gate, follow the road to the left down the ridge to a junction with abandoned dirt road 120, AKA Cottonwood Canyon Trail, and the route of the Arizona Trail.)

The Arizona Trail travels north, following Cottonwood Canyon Trail 120, which is an abandoned, rocky road. Cottonwood Canyon seems to be misnamed, because the route travels down a wide, open, rocky canyon, passing through Lower Sonoran

Desert and Upper Sonoran chaparral. Prickly pear and barrel cactus, Spanish dagger, yucca, low-growing juniper, catclaw, and manzanita dot the landscape. In less than 0.25 mile the old road ends in a clearing with a cement stock tank. A brown carsonite Arizona Trail marker indicates where the trail continues on the west side of the clearing.

A rock cairn marks where the Arizona Trail, now a narrow path, drops into and crosses a gully. As the trail heads down-canyon, the route is well marked by rock cairns. The trail enters the bottom of the drainage, a rocky, dry, brushy creek bed, which it crosses frequently.

Unexpectedly, the path leaves the open chaparral, dropping into a leafy oasis of large oak and sycamore trees sheltering the small pools of Cottonwood Creek. The trail continues west following along the streambed. Crossing the creek, the trail passes through a wire corral, the route marked with rock cairns. Dark and cool, the sycamore-shaded streambed is a welcome relief from the hot chaparral country we left moments ago.

Under its green canopy, the trail passes through thickets of wild blackberry and large trees festooned with wild grapevines. The route is indistinct in places because of accumulated leaves and undergrowth, and a profusion of criss-crossing cow paths. Watch for rock cairns marking the route, which tends to stay close to the streambed.

At 1.4 miles from FR 83 the trail passes Cottonwood Spring, origin of Cottonwood Creek, and the reason for this cool leafy woodland. All too soon the route returns to a shadeless landscape of scrub oak, saguaro, and prickly pear cactus. As the trail exits a thicket of dense brush, the canyon opens up, with views to the northwest. It's an easy downhill grade, the route well-posted with rock cairns as the trail returns to follow a dry creek bed.

One-half mile after leaving Cottonwood Spring, the trail may be blocked by a tangle of impenetrable brush and confused by cow paths, so watch closely for the rock markers.

Passing through a wire gate (always close gates unless they appear to have been deliberately left open) the trail turns right, dropping down and crossing a dry creek bed. Watch for rock cairns as the path travels west down-canyon. The trail enters a shady mesquite grove which soon gives way to a second delightful riparian forest—an arching canopy of sycamore and ash, shading the flowing water of Cottonwood Creek. Big trees give way to mesquite, and then the first ancient cottonwoods, for which the canyon is named, mark the beginning of a fascinating and remarkable section of trail.

Magnificent saguaros and other Lower Sonoran Desert plants intermingle with the huge old trees and the charming pools of Cottonwood Creek, offering an appealing and unusual contrast between the two plant communities. As the route rambles down-canyon, following the shaded creek, glimpses of the canyon walls reveal red sun-baked rocky cliffs, dotted with cactus. Soon, the route abandons the riparian area for the shadeless saguaro-studded hillsides above.

As the trail parallels a barbwire fence on the right, ignore an unsigned junction with a trail that goes through a gate in the fence. Continue west along the fence. A short distance past the gate, the trail, marked by rock cairns, leaves the fence line and follows a pipeline. The trail passes through classic Lower Sonoran Desert as it travels down-canyon, past a cement tank, picking its way through a rocky terrain of Saguaro, prickly pear, and cholla cactus.

The route curves north and descends past several large barrel cactus into the wide, bouldery drainage. The trail disappears in the sand and rocks of the wash. Watch for markers as the route crosses to the west side of the drainage and continues north. In the distance, a dirt road is visible ascending a hill to the north, and beyond the road is a distinctive, slant-topped mesa. The rock formation, Dutch Woman Butte, is on the far side of Roosevelt Lake. The distant road (FR 341) is the route of the Arizona Trail traveling toward Roosevelt Lake.

The trail arrives at a wooden sign and a cattle holding pen 3.8 miles from FR 83. The trail passes through the corral, past a water tank to a T junction with Deer Hill Road (FR 341). Take the route of the Arizona Trail, which is to the right.

Heading east, the Arizona Trail follows FR 341 as it swings around Deer Hill. Turning north, the road makes a steep winding ascent up a shadeless, swelling ridgeline. Topping out in a high saddle, the ridge offers a fabulous first view of Theodore Roosevelt Lake. Tiny boats are visible on the bright blue water of the lake, which is framed by wrinkled brown hills. Rising from the Sierra Ancha Mountains beyond the lake is the massive, slant-topped mesa, Dutch Woman Butte.

CYCLISTS BEWARE! The road drops steeply north toward the lake. To the left of our route, lower Cottonwood Canyon slices deeply through the rolling landscape, a steep and narrow cleft that separates our slope from Deer Hill. The Arizona Trail crosses a junction with dirt road 3404, continuing downhill to a gate. After passing through the gate, the road makes a precipitous descent toward the bottom of the hill and Thompson Spring. Make your descent with caution.

At 5.8 miles from FR 83 (7.8 miles from Black Brush Ranch), the trail arrives at Thompson Spring and a signed junction for Frazier trailhead. For safety reasons livestock should exit here and follow Lower Cottonwood Canyon Trail 1.3 miles to Frazier trailhead. (The trail leaves the road heading north down a drainage on the eastern side of Cottonwood Creek. You may need to dismount and lead horses through a short, boulder-strewn section of creek bed, but beware of flash floods in rainy weather. The route skirts around Roosevelt Lakeview [trailer] Park and swings east. As you top a ridge, you can see the electrical substation and Frazier trailhead in the distance.)

HIKERS and CYCLISTS! It is 3.2 miles to Roosevelt Bridge. Although it may not be signed, the route of the Arizona Trail continues to follow Deer Hill Road (FR 341), an abandoned dirt road, as it crosses the creek and climbs steeply uphill to the west. After you gain a saddle, there is a corral on the left and view of Roosevelt Lake on the right. The old road travels uphill once more, through an area decorated with saguaro cactus, jojoba bushes, and delicate palo verde trees. The road tops out to a great view of the lake.

One mile from Thompson Spring, brown carsonite trail markers indicate the beginning of Thompson Trail #121/AT. Heading west, the trail crosses an abandoned dirt road, and the lake is again visible, with sailboats moored in the marina. The route travels parallel to the lake at a fairly level grade, then begins an easy downhill trip. Curving north toward the lake, the descent steepens, passing above the trailer park on the right. The route is marked with rock cairns.

At 1.7 miles from Thompson Spring (and 1.5 miles to SR 88 and Roosevelt Bridge), the Thompson/Arizona Trail arrives at the junction with the Roosevelt Cemetery Trail, marked by a green, walk-through gate. (Pass through the gate here for an interesting side trip through the small cemetery, or if you wish to exit the Arizona Trail, this route will take you to the marina store and visitor center on SR 88. Livestock are not allowed.)

Continuing west, the path is narrow, clinging to the side of the hill above the highway. Soon after, it turns south to circumvent a drainage, beginning the first of a series of hairpin journeys around steep drainages that funnel rainstorm runoff into the Tonto Basin. The trail becomes a narrow, rocky cliff-hanger in places, as it loses and then gains elevation with each drainage it traverses. In between the curves, it remains relatively level as it travels above the lake and the highway.

Cresting a hill, the route encounters a sign: "steep trail ahead." Looking down to the right, the highway is visible, bridging a major drainage dropping down before us, from the left. The route is so steep that the Forest Service has put in wooden steps! (The Forest Service also provides an alternate bypass around the steps. Watch for signage.) After going down the steps, the trail turns left (south) as it crosses the drainage.

The Thompson/Arizona Trail climbs a hill that is studded with saguaro cactus and crowned with a power line. The final switchbacking ascent is narrow and rocky. As the trail gains the top of the hill and heads down the other side, Roosevelt Bridge is visible. It is all downhill from here as the trail circles one last gully, then drops steeply toward the bridge, ending at a green metal Forest Service gate. Be careful as you exit onto SR 88 to go across the Roosevelt Bridge to the parking area.

20 Four Peaks Wilderness
Passage Roosevelt Bridge to Lone Pine Saddle

As of this writing, sections of the Arizona Trail in this passage are not yet completed. This description outlines the *proposed route* of the Arizona Trail through this passage; it is not intended to be used as a trail guide. Much of the information included here is taken from an Arizona Trail management guide designed not for recreational use but for use in planning, developing, and managing the trail. Contact the governing agency or The Arizona Trail Association for more information on the route, signage, availability of water, and completion status of this passage.

WHEN COMPLETED, *this 15-mile passage of the Arizona Trail will link Roosevelt Lake Bridge to Lone Pine Saddle Trailhead, just north of the Four Peaks Wilderness boundary.*

From Theodore Roosevelt Bridge, a new trail will travel west through the Three Bar Wildlife Area. Beginning in the lower Sonoran Desert life zone, the passage climbs to pine forest of the Transition life zone, as it passes through the eastern edge of the Four Peaks Wilderness. The Four Peaks are visible over a large section of central Arizona and have been a major landmark since prehistoric times. This area is thought to have the highest concentration of black bears in Arizona.

PROPOSED ROUTE

A 4.5-mile trail (Vineyard Trail) needs to be built to connect Theodore Roosevelt Dam to the Mills Ridge Road (FR 429) trailhead, near the beginning of Trail #130. This section of trail is within the Three Bar Wildlife Area. The route will then travel north on Trail #130 for 8.5 miles to Pigeon Trail #134. Trail #134 travels 2 miles to Lone Pine Saddle (FR 648) trailhead.

GOVERNING AGENCIES

Tonto National Forest, Tonto Basin Ranger District, HC 02, Box 4800, Roosevelt, AZ 85545. (520) 467-3200.

FOR MORE INFORMATION

Arizona Trail Association, P.O. Box 36736, Phoenix, AZ 85067. (602) 252-4794.

NEAREST SERVICES

Roosevelt Lake Marina store.

21 Pine Mountain/Boulder Creek Passage Lone Pine Saddle to Sunflower

As of this writing, sections of the Arizona Trail in this passage are not yet completed. This description outlines the *proposed route* of the Arizona Trail through this passage; it is not intended to be used as a trail guide. Much of the information included here is taken from an Arizona Trail management guide designed not for recreational use but for use in planning, developing, and managing the trail. Contact the governing agency or The Arizona Trail Association for more information on the route, signage, availability of water, and completion status of this passage.

WHEN COMPLETE, *this 17.5-mile passage of the Arizona Trail will link Lone Pine Saddle trailhead, just north of the Four Peaks Wilderness boundary, with Sunflower Trail near SR 87. Traveling through the Mazatzal Mountains, the passage provides far-reaching vistas of Roosevelt Lake and the Sierra Ancha Mountains to the east, and Phoenix metropolitan area to the west. The route features ponderosa pine forest and some beautiful riparian canyons. There is little water.*

PROPOSED ROUTE

At time of publishing, although portions of this passage are complete, plans are under way to reroute the trail away from FR 22, which is heavily used by ATVs. Boulder Creek Trail is undergoing reconstruction with the help of volunteers from Arizona Boy's Ranch and Arizona Mule and Donkey Association. Also, highway construction on SR 87 will change the northern access.

From Lone Pine trailhead, the passage travels north on FR 648 to FR 143, and FR 143 travels to FR 422. The route turns left on FR 422 and continues 9 miles to the junction of Boulder Creek Trail #73. Boulder Creek Trail #73 travels through a scenic canyon, eventually linking to FR 22 near a corral. FR 22 travels to the Sunflower area.

GOVERNING AGENCIES

Tonto National Forest, Tonto Basin Ranger District, HC 02, Box 4800, Roosevelt, AZ 85545. (520) 467-3200.

FOR MORE INFORMATION

Arizona Trail Association, P.O. Box 36736, Phoenix, AZ 85067. (602) 252-4794.

NEAREST SERVICES

Lake Roosevelt Marina store.

22 Saddle Mountain Passage
Sunflower to Mount Peeley

This description is not intended to be used as a trail guide. Much of the information included here is taken from an Arizona Trail management guide designed not for recreational use but for use in planning, developing, and managing the trail. Contact the governing agency or The Arizona Trail Association for more information on the route, signage, availability of water, and completion status of this passage.

THIS 14-MILE PASSAGE travels from Mormon Grove trailhead, FR 25, to the Mount Peeley trailhead on FR 201. This scenic passage travels through the Mazatzal Mountains, along the border of the wilderness. The route follows some canyon streams and affords some nice views.

DESIGNATED ROUTE

This passage is signed with the Arizona Trail symbol from SR 87 to Mount Peeley. The Arizona Trail symbol is branded on the BACK of existing signs; look for it at junctions!

The passage begins at FR 25, on the west side of SR 87, at mile post 218. FR 25 (4WD) leads to the Mormon Grove trailhead. The route follows Little Saddle Mountain Trail #244 to Saddle Mountain Trail #91 to Sheep Creek Trail #88, to Thicket Spring Trail #95, to Cornucopia Trail #86 to the Mount Peeley trailhead. Mount Peeley Rd., FR 201, is a 4WD road. Contact the managing agency for more information regarding the route and mileages.

GOVERNING AGENCIES

Tonto National Forest, Tonto Basin Ranger District, HC 02, Box 4800, Roosevelt, AZ 85545. (520) 467-3200.

FOR MORE INFORMATION

Arizona Trail Association, P.O. Box 36736, Phoenix, AZ 85067. (602) 252-4794.

NEAREST SERVICES

Nearest services can be found in Payson.

23 Mazatzal Wilderness Passage
Mount Peeley to East Verde River

This description is not intended to be used as a trail guide. Much of the information included here is taken from an Arizona Trail management guide designed not for recreational use but for use in planning, developing, and managing the trail. Contact the governing agency or The Arizona Trail Association for more information on the route, signage, availability of water, and completion status of this passage.

T*HIS APPROXIMATELY 31-mile passage travels from Mount Peeley to the East Verde River. The Mazatzal Wilderness Passage follows a complex series of trails within the wilderness. At time of publishing this passage is being signed with the Arizona Trail symbol branded on wood plaques that will be attached to existing signs. This is one of the longest and most remote passages of the Arizona Trail. Trail users need to be prepared to spend three to four days to travel this passage.*

The Mazatzal Wilderness (pronounced "Mata-zel") is the largest wilderness area in Arizona. It was established in 1940 and is composed of 252,000 acres of extremely remote and rugged terrain. Yavapai Indians called the vast expanse of desert and mountains encompassed by the wilderness "mazatzal" or the land of the deer. Sections of the route travel through ponderosa pine forest, and the trails afford spectacular views. Life zones in this passage of the Arizona Trail vary from Upper Sonoran chaparral to small pockets of Douglas Fir representing the Canadian zone.

DESIGNATED ROUTE

This passage begins at the Mount Peeley trailhead (the road in is in poor condition). The route follows the Mazatzal Divide Trail #23 north for 22 miles, to Trail #262. It takes Red Hills Trail #262 west for 2 miles, to Brush Trail #249. Trail #249 travels west and then north a little over 4 miles to Bull Spring Trail #34. Trail #34 travels 2.5 miles to 406 Road, which travels 0.3 mile north to the East Verde River.

GOVERNING AGENCIES

Tonto National Forest, Payson Ranger District, 1009 East Highway 260, Payson, AZ 85541. (520) 474-7934.

FOR MORE INFORMATION

Arizona Trail Association, P.O. Box 36736, Phoenix, AZ 85067. (602) 252-4794.

NEAREST SERVICES

Nearest services are in Payson.

---

24 Whiterock Mesa/ Hardscrabble Mesa Passage
East Verde River to Pine Trailhead

As of this writing, sections of the Arizona Trail in this passage are not yet completed. This description outlines the *proposed route* of the Arizona Trail through this passage; it is not intended to be used as a trail guide. Much of the information included here is taken from an Arizona Trail management guide designed not for recreational use but for use in planning, developing, and managing the trail. Contact the governing agency or The Arizona Trail Association for more information on the route, signage, availability of water, and completion status of this passage.

A T THE TIME OF THIS WRITING *portions of this passage have not been signed with the Arizona Trail symbol, so route-finding skills may be required. Following a series of trails and old roads, the Arizona Trail crosses the East Verde River and then traverses the little-visited areas of Whiterock and Hard-scrabble Mesas. The terrain is rugged and remote, with boulder outcroppings and great views. The route passes within 2 miles of Tonto Natural Bridge State Park, site of the largest natural travertine bridge in the world. The park is not accessible from the Arizona Trail at this time; however, an alternate route that would link to the park is being considered.*

PROPOSED ROUTE

Beginning at the East Verde River this passage follows Saddle Ridge Trail #14 north 9.5 miles across Whiterock Mesa to Hardscrabble Mesa. The route then follows Saddle Ridge Road (FR 154) 2 miles to Twin Buttes Road (FR 194). FR 194 travels a little over a mile to Powerline Trail #540. Powerline Trail travels southeast for 4 miles to Walnut Trail #251. The route follows trail #251 north a little over a mile to Oak Spring Trail #16. Oak Spring Trail travels 2.2 miles to the Pine trailhead.

GOVERNING AGENCIES

Tonto National Forest, Payson Ranger District, 1009 East Highway 260, Payson, AZ 85541. (520) 474-7900.

FOR MORE INFORMATION

Arizona Trail Association, P.O. Box 36736, Phoenix, AZ 85067. (602) 252-4794.

NEAREST SERVICES

Nearest services are in Payson.

25 Highline Passage

Pine Trailhead to Forest Road 300

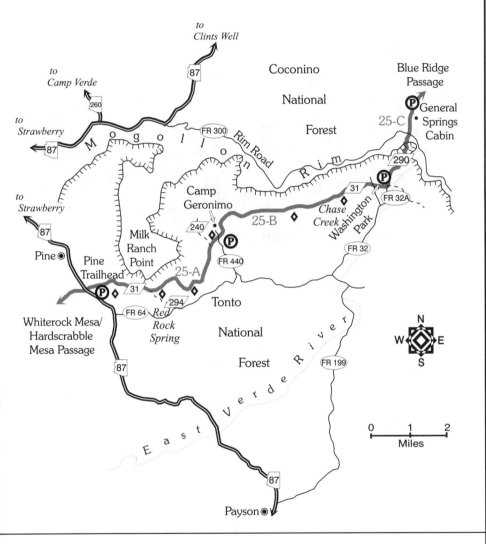

to Clints Well

to Camp Verde

Coconino

National

Forest

Blue Ridge Passage

87

260

87 to Strawberry

FR 300

Rim Road

Mogollon Rim

25-C

General Springs Cabin

290

to Strawberry

87

Camp Geronimo

Chase Creek

31

FR 32A

Pine

87

Milk Ranch Point

240

25-B

Washington Park

FR 32

Pine Trailhead

31

FR 440

25-A

Whiterock Mesa/ Hardscrabble Mesa Passage

FR 64

294

Red Rock Spring

Tonto

National

Forest

East Verde River

FR 199

87

N
W E
S

0   1   2
Miles

87

Payson

	Forest Road
FR102	Forest Road
	Paved Road
	State/Interstate
	Arizona Trail
	Trip Access Trail
122	Other Trail Area

··············	Boundary
	River, Stream, or Wash
⊔⊔⊔	Canyon Rim
⛺	Campground
◇	Water
⌂	Ranger Station

Ⓟ	Trailhead and Parking
◯	Trailhead, no Parking
P	Parking
⊙	Town or City
●	Point of Interest
△	Mountain Peak

A view of the Mogollon Rim, a lengthy band of cliffs forming a high bluff along the Highline Passage.

> *We crossed the rugged Mogollon where tall pine forest grow.*
> *The grass was in abundance and rippling streams did flow.*
> *Our packs were always turning, of course our gait was slow*
> *On the crooked trail to Holbrook, in Arizon-i-o.*

—"The Crooked Trail To Holbrook,"
Anonymous, circa 1887

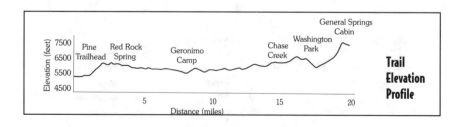

Trail Elevation Profile

THIS 20-MILE PASSAGE, *which begins in the Tonto National Forest and ends in the Coconino National Forest, is divided into three trips. Trip 25-A travels 8 miles from Pine Trailhead to Geronimo Camp. Trip 25-B travels 9.5 miles from Geronimo Camp to Washington Park. Trip 25-C travels 2.5 miles from Washington Park to General Springs Cabin near the Rim Road (FR 300), north of Pine.*

The sheer 2,000-foot ramparts of the Mogollon Rim, stretching for 200 miles across central Arizona, mark the southern edge of the Colorado Plateau. The Arizona Trail follows the historic Highline Trail east along these dramatic cliffs for 17 miles. Several trailheads and spur trails offer opportunities for traveling in segments and loops.

The route offers fabulous vistas of the Tonto Basin—rugged, remote land of the Apaches and the inspiration for many of Zane Grey's novels. The last 2 miles are the grand finale; a dramatic ascent up a deep crevasse, offering a side trip to a never-completed railroad tunnel and ending at a historic log cabin.

The Mogollon (pronounced Mug-ee-own) Rim was named for Juan Ignacio Flores Mogollon, a Spanish governor. The Highline Trail, designated a national recreation trail in 1979, was established in the late 1800s to link various homesteads and ranches under the Mogollon Rim.

This passage of the Arizona Trail was once Apache country. As prospectors and settlers moved into the area, conflicts arose. Lieutenant Colonel Devin was sent to Arizona in 1868, in command of troops in northern and central Arizona. In May 1868, while leading troops on an expedition against Apache Indians, Colonel Devin took his cavalry and infantry troops, which included one hundred horses and fifty pack mules, down over the Mogollon Rim. Although the campaign was unsuccessful, his impressive feat, which became known as "Devin's Jump Off" is remembered. The Colonel Devin Trail, which scales the buttressed face of the rim, marks the end of this passage of the Arizona Trail.

In the late 1800s the Arizona Mineral Belt Railroad Company developed plans to build a major rail route from Flagstaff to the mines near Globe. Tunneling under the Mogollon Rim to link with railroad lines in Flagstaff, the route would have provided the mines with easier access to national markets. The ambitious plan had the support of investors and miners who volunteered their own time to labor in the tunnel. Ultimately the project failed. The entrance to the tunnel is 0.5 mile below the rim and is accessed by the Colonel Devin Trail.

Zane Grey first visited the Mogollon Rim country in 1918. Grey fell in love with the area and eventually built a cabin beneath the rim. The beautiful remote country and the people who lived in the area inspired characters and settings for his novels. Unfortunately his cabin, a historical site, was destroyed by a forest fire in 1990.

GOVERNING AGENCIES

Tonto National Forest, Payson Ranger District, 1009 East Highway 260, Payson, AZ 85541. (520) 474-7900.

FOR MORE INFORMATION

The Highline Trails Guide is available from the Payson Ranger District, or the Payson Chamber of Commerce.

Museum of the Forest is open Wednesday through Sunday. 1001 W. Main Street, Payson, AZ 85541. (520) 474-1541.

Zane Grey Museum is closed on Wednesdays. 408 W. Main St., Suite 8, Payson Az 85541. (520) 474-6243.

Payson Chamber of Commerce, Main Street and the Beeline Highway, P.O. Box 1380, Payson, AZ 85547. 1-800-6-PAYSON.

Pine-Strawberry Chamber of Commerce, Highway 87, Old Country Road. P.O. Box 196, Pine, AZ 85544. (520) 476-3547.

NEAREST SERVICES TO PINE TRAILHEAD

Pine: From the Pine trailhead travel 0.25 mile north on SR 87 to Pine, or 15 miles south to Payson, a larger community.

Trip 25-A

Pine Trailhead to Geronimo Camp

This easily accessible and popular section of the Arizona Trail offers multiple opportunities for side trips or loops.

Beginning at the Pine trailhead south of Pine and ending at Geronimo Camp east of Pine, the Arizona Trail heads into Zane Grey country, following the historic Highline Trail beneath sheer, 200-foot cliffs of the Mogollon Rim. This rocky trail is well signed and easy to follow, as it alternates between sunny, exposed ridgelines with spectacular views of the Mazatzal and Sierra Ancha Wilderness areas and shady forested ravines.

A sign at the trailhead describes the Highline Trail system. Highline Trail #31 follows the Mogollon Rim for 51 miles, from SR 87 east to SR 260. The Arizona Trail adjoins the Highline Trail for 17 miles and then abandons it to ascend the Mogollon Rim via the Colonel Devin Trail.

Nature Highlight: A coyote symphony was the highlight of the evening, as we sat by our small campfire.

Maps:
* Highline Trails Guide. USDA, Payson Ranger District.
* Tonto National Forest. USDA.
* USGS Quads: Pine, Kehl Ridge.

Difficulty: Moderate.

Length: 8 miles, one way.

Elevation: 5,500–6,200 feet.

Recommended Season: All year, depending on the weather. There may be snow in the winter months.

Water: (Treat all water unless noted otherwise. During dry weather, water sources may not be dependable.)
* **Pine Trailhead:** dirt stock tank.
* **Red Rock Spring.**
* **Pine Spring.**
* **Geronimo Camp:** Webber Creek.

Camping: Pine trailhead. This heavily used trailhead offers flat, shady areas to park and camp. There is one rest room and an information board, but no other amenities. If you will be driving in, bring your own water and firewood.

Livestock: Highline is a good horse trail, and there is ample room to park and turn trailers. Two log corrals for horses or llamas receive heavy use, especially on weekends. To water livestock follow the trail past the rest room and through the gate. Take the right fork a short distance to a dirt tank.

Directions to Pine Trailhead: You can access Pine Trailhead by passenger car. The Pine trailhead is just east of SR 87 on FR 297. It is reached by traveling 15 miles north of Payson, or 0.25 mile south of Pine. The turnoff to the trailhead is marked by a sign on the highway. As you pull into the parking area, the trailhead for the Highline Trail is to the left, past the rest room.

Other Area Trails:

- **Pine Canyon Trail #26** is accessed a short distance up the Highline Trail; #26 climbs north over the Mogollon Rim to FR 6038, eventually linking to SR 87 north of the Camp Verde turnoff.
- **Donahue Trail #27** is a steep trail that climbs to Milk Ranch Point and can be accessed from the Highline Trail, 1.5 miles from the trailhead.

Contact the Payson Ranger District for more information on these, or other trails in the area. (See Highline Passage for telephone number and address.)

TRAIL DESCRIPTION

This recently signed passage of the Arizona Trail follows the existing Highline Trail markers, which are diamond-shaped silver symbols attached to trees along the route. The trail passes through a gate and immediately forks. The well-worn path to the right leads to a dirt stock tank. Continue straight on the Highline Trail. A short distance further is another junction. To the left is Pine Canyon Trail #26, Dripping Springs, and SR 87.

Stay to the right on Highline Trail #31, as it passes through a shady mixed forest of pine and oak. The trail makes a gradual ascent and then follows along a dry creek bed crossing back and forth. The rocky trail is well worn and easy to follow, with frequent markers. The route passes some big old junipers, following along the edge of a bouldery, dry creek bed.

One mile from Pine trailhead is a junction of trails. Pineview Trail #28 and Pine Canyon Trail #26 are to the left. Stay to the right toward Redrock Spring. Immediately after taking the right fork the trail turns east, crossing down into the creek bed. Watch for the markers. After crossing the creek bed, the trail enters an area of small juniper and more open country. The rocky outcrop to the left is Milk Ranch Point.

 Watch carefully here for easily missed rock cairns. A deeply worn trail made by a local stable joins the Highline Trail in this area, coming in from the right at an unmarked junction. (If the trail you are on parallels a barbwire fence and passes a large pond on the right, you are on the wrong trail! Backtrack to rock cairns, which indicate where the Highline Trail continues east.) The Highline/Arizona Trail begins to climb up through manzanita, juniper, and oak. The gradient steepens as the trail switchbacks up the rocky hillside. As you top out, a large juniper on the right with a diamond marker is a welcome sight.

At 1.5 miles from Pine trailhead is a junction with Donahue Trail #27 to the left. The trail, well worn and somewhat eroded in places, resumes climbing through a juniper forest. Gaining a saddle, we are offered a fine view of Payson in the

distance to the south, and to the west, is a view of Pine. The trail veers left (northeast), heading uphill along the ridgeline. There are occasional trail markers as the trail ambles east, below the edge of the Mogollon Rim. This section of trail affords scenic views to the south of the Tonto Basin and the vast expanse of the Sierra Ancha and Mazatzal Wilderness areas.

The trail, which has been rocky but comparatively level, drops into a ponderosa-forested drainage, a short but shady respite before the trail begins a steep switchbacking ascent up and out. Still well worn and easy to follow, the trail levels again, as it passes through upper Sonoran woodland, midway between the looming cliffs of the Mogollon Rim and the flatlands below. Watch for rock cairns. The trail drops in and out of two more drainages before reaching Redrock Spring.

At 3.4 miles from the Pine trailhead a water-filled trough marks Redrock Spring. The date October 26, 1934, has been scratched into cement. Redrock Spring was once an important source of water for Apache Indians and early settlers. If your trek ends at Geronimo Camp, this lovely grassy area makes a nice halfway point. Just beyond the spring is a trail junction. Redrock Trail 294, which travels a steep 1.5 miles to FR 64, 2.4 miles east of SR 87, is to the right. A diamond marker indicates that the Highline Trail continues straight ahead.

A short distance past the trail junction, the terrain opens up with a far-reaching view of the Mogollon Rim fading into the northeastern skyline. The trail turns north as it begins to angle around the massive granite bulk of Milk Ranch Point. The Highline Trail has a southern exposure, and traversing the mostly exposed, rocky face of the rim can become hot. The trail remains comparatively level, threading its way through scrubby oak, juniper, and manzanita.

About 4.5 miles from the trailhead is a gate and a sign for Pine Spring. (Do not take livestock through the gate for water. Follow the fence line right, down to a very unusual and nicely made wooden trough.) The route of the Arizona Trail continues through the gate. There is a wooden box accessing the spring, next to the trail where you can find cleaner water for drinking. (Thanks to the Copper Country Mountaineers and the Young Adult Conservation Corp for this 1981 project!)

After leaving the sycamore-shaded oasis of Pine Spring, the trail is again comparatively level, with intermittent ups and downs, meandering along below the Mogollon Rim. The route is quite pleasant as it alternately traverses sunny exposed areas with scenic views, then drops down into inviting ravines that are shady and cool.

At 7.3 miles from Pine Spring is a junction with Geronimo Trail #240, which provides access to several other trails in the area. The Highline Trail takes a sharp right and joins what appears to be an old road. The route is badly eroded in places and has erosion bars placed across it. Follow the diamond-shaped markers. After passing under a power line, the trail drops down and crosses a bouldery, dry creek bed, then continues downhill, following along the left bank. After crossing the creek the road becomes a trail picking its way down through rocks and large pine trees, marked by diamond markers. The trail passes a large metal drainage pipe on the right and a dirt track on the left. Follow the trail as it curves to the right, watching for double diamond markers.

A quarter-mile after the Geronimo Trail junction the route encounters a sign indicating Geronimo Trailhead, 100 yards to the left. To the right is Webber Creek and a level, grassy area with big shady trees. Continuing to the left, it is 100 yards to the streambed crossing and FR 440. It is easier to water livestock by the road, because the bank is not as steep there. Beside the road is a sign for Geronimo Trailhead and Highline Trail #31. Across the road to the left is the Boy Scout facility, Geronimo Camp.

Trip 25-B

Geronimo Camp to Washington Park

Trip 25-B links to other trails near the Geronimo trailhead, offering some interesting side trips.

Beginning at Geronimo Camp and ending at Washington Park, the Arizona Trail follows the historic Highline Trail just below the towering cliffs of the Mogollon Rim. The route affords far-reaching views as it alternates between an Upper Sonoran life zone of oak and mesquite chaparral and the pine forests of the Transition life zone.

Nature Highlight: Four wild turkeys wandered across the trail ahead of us, and disappeared in the brush.

Maps:
* Highline Trails Guide. USDA, Payson Ranger District.
* Tonto National Forest. USDA.
* USGS Quads: Kehl Ridge, Dane Canyon.

Difficulty: Moderate.

Length: 9.5 miles, one way.

Elevation: 5,500–6,500 feet.

Recommended Season: All year, depending on the weather. There may be snow in the winter months.

Water: (Treat all water unless noted otherwise. During dry weather, water sources may not be dependable.)
* **Geronimo Camp:** Webber Creek.
* **Bray Creek.**

- Chase Creek.
- East Verde River.

Camping: **Geronimo Camp** offers primitive camping and there is no developed trailhead. There are some nice camping opportunities along Webber Creek.

Livestock: Highline is a good horse trail, although feed is limited.

Directions to Geronimo Camp Trailhead: The trailhead can be accessed by passenger car. The Geronimo Camp trailhead is reached by taking SR 87 approximately 13.5 miles north of Payson, to FR 64. Turn east on FR 64 and travel 6 miles to FR 440. Turn north on FR 440 and travel 2 miles. Watch for a sign on the road where the Highline/AT crosses FR 440 just before the Boy Scout camp.

Other Area Trails:
- **Geronimo Trail #240** is 0.25 mile west on the Highline Trail. This 3-mile trail links to three other trails:
- **East Webber Trail #289** climbs 3 miles to a spring below the rim.
- **Turkey Springs Trail #217** and **West Webber Trail #228** both make a steep ascent of Milk Ranch Point.

  For more information on these trails or the Highline Trail, contact the Payson Ranger District (see Highline Passage for Telephone number and address).

TRAIL DESCRIPTION

The Arizona Trail crosses FR 440 following the Highline Trail northeast. Geronimo Camp, a boy scout camp, is visible on the left. As the route makes a moderate ascent, following an abandoned dirt road, watch for rock cairns and Highline/Arizona Trail markers.

The gradient steepens, and logs have been placed across the trail for erosion control. As the trail crests a wooded hill, the Highline/Arizona trail markers cue us to bear right at a junction. A short distance farther there are two more junctions with abandoned roads. Stay to the left for both, watching for trail markers. The trail winds uphill through a juniper, mesquite, and pine woodland, the ascent becoming quite steep in places. At the next unmarked junction stay to right. The angle of ascent steepens, and as the trail tops out, it affords a spectacular view of the Mogollon Rim. Leaving the ridge, the trail drops steeply.

You meet a gate 4.8 miles from the trailhead. To the right, downhill, is a very nice and unusual wooden water trough. After passing through the gate, follow the trail markers as the route bends right. The trail follows a wire fence line on the right for a short distance and then dips in and out of some drainages. The path traverses an open area of interestingly eroded red sandstone shelves. Watch for the rock cairns as the trail crosses this sparsely vegetated area and heads back into the tall pines.

The route continues through a forest of pine and fir, then crosses pretty little Sycamore Creek, identified by a small wooden sign on a tree. Immediately after crossing the creek, the trail veers to the right and follows along the left bank. The route passes through a lovely open area with ferns and tall pines. The trail crosses Chase Creek 7.8 miles from the trailhead. It is approximately 1.7 miles to Washington Park from here.

The trail crosses a creek bed, then scrambles up a steep and rocky grade. Having crested the ridge, the path bends to the right, following a barbed wire fence on the left. As the trail switchbacks down into a canyon, a private residence is visible to the left. Follow the rock cairns as the trail descends steeply through the trees to FR 32.

There are no directional signs where the Arizona Trail exits onto the road. Follow the road to the right a short distance, watching for the place where the path continues, up the eastern road bank. The trail skirts around the side of a hill, then makes a long, easy descent, passing beneath a power line, into Washington Park.

Trip 25-C
Washington Park to General Springs Cabin

 An extremely steep trail that is difficult for cyclists.

The Arizona Trail abandons Highline Trail to follow the historic Colonel Devin Trail, paralleling the East Verde River. The trip, which affords impressive views, climbs a deep cliff-bound defile and then makes a steep switchbacking ascent to the top of the Mogollon Rim. An abandoned railroad tunnel 0.5 mile from the rim makes an interesting side trip.

Nature Highlight: A Steller's jay, a noisy flash of blue in the trees above, tells the forest that we are here.

Maps:
- Highline Trails Guide. USDA, Payson Ranger District.
- Tonto National Forest. USDA.
- USGS Quad: Dane Canyon.

Difficulty: Difficult. A very steep climb.

Length: 2.5 miles, one way.

Elevation: 5,840–7,250 feet.

Recommended Season: Spring, summer, and autumn, depending on snowfall.

Water: (Treat all water unless noted otherwise. During dry weather, water sources may not be dependable.)
- **Washington Park:** The East Verde River is accessible 100 yards east of the trailhead.
- **General Springs Cabin:** there is a pond behind the cabin.

Camping: **Washington Park** offers primitive camping, with some nice camping places along the road, just south of the park.

Livestock: There is some grass and a tiny pole corral, large enough for one horse or llama, at the trailhead. This trip is steep but traversable by animals in good physical condition. Water livestock at the East Verde River, east of the park.

Directions to Trailhead: The trailhead can be accessed by passenger car. Washington Park is reached by taking SR 87 north of Payson to FR 199. Turn east on FR 199 and travel 10.3 miles to FR 64. (If you are coming from the north, you can also pick up FR 64 from SR 87 south of Pine.) Turn west on FR 64 and travel 0.7 mile to FR 32. Turn north on FR 32 and travel 3.3 miles to FR 32A. The trailhead is 0.5 mile north on FR 32A.

Other Area Trails: The **Highline Trail** continues for another 32 miles, terminating at SR 260 east of Payson.

* **Tunnel Trail #390** is 1.5 miles north of the trailhead. Tunnel Trail travels 0.25 mile to the site of an abandoned 1800s railroad tunnel.

TRAIL DESCRIPTION

At the Washington Park trailhead is an Arizona Trail marker, along with a sign for Colonel Devin Trail #290 and Tunnel Trail #390. (Volunteers and dedicated U.S. Forest Service staff made Washington Park and the Colonel Devin Trail a National Trails Day project in 1994. Thanks to all who helped to rebuild this wonderfully picturesque trail.)

The Arizona Trail follows the Colonel Devin Trail as they share the route of an abandoned power line road heading north toward the Mogollon Rim. The road climbs steadily at a moderate rate, paralleling the route of the East Verde River, a deep watercourse to the right. You can hear the sound of the rushing river and can glimpse it through the trees, as the old road winds uphill through a pine forest. Following below the power line, the route enters a narrow cliff-bound crevice that cuts in toward the Rim.

One mile from the trailhead is the junction, where the Colonel Devin/Arizona Trail leaves the road, veering up to the right. The trail cuts steeply through pine woodland, and the route is marked by rock cairns. The trail passes through a burned area, the western edge of the Dude Fire of 1990. Some of the trees are noticeably scorched. Alternating long, uphill climbs with runs of switchbacks, the ascent is steep and laborious. As it traverses the canyon, this highly scenic trail affords wonderful views to the south.

One and one-half miles from the trailhead is a junction with Tunnel Trail 390 to the right. (Tunnel Trail leads 0.25 mile to an old, abandoned railroad tunnel— a failed attempt to construct a railroad route from Flagstaff to Globe.) The Colonel Devin/Arizona Trail continues to the left, ascending a steeply slanted rock escarpment. Although it is a natural rock shelf, upended millennia ago and clinging to the canyon wall, the sides have been built up with rocks, giving it the appearance of a charming, old stone road.

Two miles from the trailhead the trail passes through a gate, and FR 300 signals the end of the climb and the border of the Coconino National Forest. Directly acros FR 300 is the monument to the Battle of Big Dry Wash, the last encounter between Apache Indians and the United States Cavalry, which occurred July 17, 1882.

This is the junction of FR 300 (Rim Road), the Colonel Devin Trail, which ends here, and the beginning of Fred Haught Trail #22. Fred Haught/Arizona Trail heads north past the monument, following a little-used dirt road, 0.5 mile to General Springs Cabin.

26 Blue Ridge Passage

Forest Road 300 to Highway 87

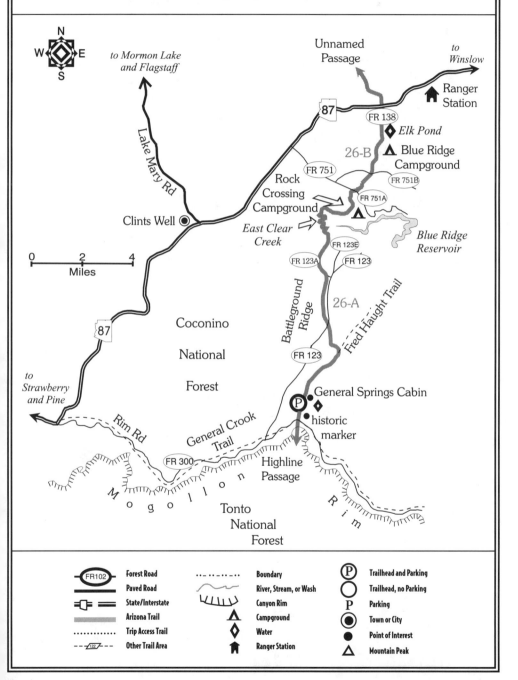

N W E S

to Mormon Lake
and Flagstaff

Unnamed
Passage

to
Winslow

Ranger
Station

87

FR 138

Elk Pond

26-B

Blue Ridge
Campground

FR 751

FR 751B

Rock
Crossing
Campground

FR 751A

Lake Mary Rd

Clints Well

East Clear
Creek

Blue Ridge
Reservoir

FR 123E

FR 123A   FR 123

Coconino

National

Forest

Battleground Ridge

26-A

Fred Haught Trail

FR 123

87

to
Strawberry
and Pine

General Springs Cabin

P

historic
marker

General Crook Trail

Rim Rd

FR 300

Highline
Passage

M o g o l l o n

R i m

Tonto
National
Forest

0   2   4
Miles

FR102 — Forest Road	· · – · · – · · Boundary	Ⓟ Trailhead and Parking
—— Paved Road	River, Stream, or Wash	◯ Trailhead, no Parking
State/Interstate	Canyon Rim	Ⓟ Parking
Arizona Trail	▲ Campground	◉ Town or City
· · · · · · Trip Access Trail	◇ Water	● Point of Interest
– – 122 – – Other Trail Area	⛫ Ranger Station	△ Mountain Peak

The tranquil General Springs Cabin on the Mogollon Rim.

I want to ride way up high in the mountains
  At the edge of the Mogollon
To feel those coolin' breezes, breathe the pine-scented air
  No place else I've been to can even compare

—**"Arizona Mountain Home," Earl T. "Slim" Tighe, 1996**
(Used with permission.)

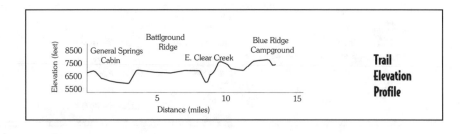

THIS 13.5-MILE PASSAGE *is divided into two trips. Trip 26-A travels 10.3 miles from General Springs Cabin to Rock Crossing Campground. Trip 26-B travels 3.2 miles from Rock Crossing Campground to Blue Ridge Campground. This passage of the Arizona Trail highlights the 19th century conflict between Apache Indians, settlers, and the United States government. The Colonel Devin Trail and General Springs were both named for officers who led troops in pursuit of the Apache near the site of the last conflict between the U.S. Cavalry and Apache Indians.*

Traveling from a historic log cabin on the Mogollon Rim, the route traverses lush canyon meadows and pine-clad ridges along the 7,000-foot-high Mogollon Plateau. This section of the Arizona Trail offers access to the long-distance General Crook Trail, the Cabin Loop System, which links several early 1900s fire guard stations, two developed campgrounds, and trout fishing at nearby Blue Ridge Reservoir.

General George Crook was sent to Arizona Territory by the United States Army to subdue Apache Indians and establish forts for the protection of troops and settlers. General Crook left Fort Apache, near the present town of Show Low, in August 1871. His goal was to find a route for supply trains to travel between Fort Apache and Fort Whipple near Prescott, the Territorial Capital of Arizona. Crook built a 200-mile trail, much of it following along the Mogollon Rim. Some of the mileages that General Crook recorded on rocks and trees, by counting the revolutions of a wagon wheel, are still visible today.

In 1882 Indians from the San Carlos Apache Reservation attacked some ranches in the area, killing several settlers. Cavalry and Indian scouts were dispatched immediately, and on July 17, five troops of cavalry and one troop of Indian scouts surrounded the Apaches at Big Dry Wash. After four hours of fighting it was over: two soldiers were lost, and the Indians suffered over twenty casualties. This was the end of an era; the last battle ever fought between Apaches and U.S. soldiers.

General Springs Cabin was built in 1918 by Luis Fischer and used for many years as a fire guard station by rangers who patrolled the Mogollon Rim. It is one of three cabins that make up the Cabin Loop System. The cabin is a historical site, and is not available for use.

Fred Haught moved to the Tonto Basin area from Texas in the early 1800s. He was soon followed by other members of the Haught family, including a nephew, "Babe" Haught, who became known as a lion and bear hunter, and at one time worked as a guide for Zane Grey.

The Blue Ridge Reservoir was built in 1962 by Phelps Dodge Corporation, a giant in the Arizona mining industry. Phelps Dodge uses water from the Salt River to support its copper mine in Morenci. In exchange, Phelps Dodge built the reservoir, pipeline and pumping stations to channel water back to the Salt River, via the East Verde River.

GOVERNING AGENCIES

Coconino National Forest, Blue Ridge Ranger District, HC 31, Box 300, Happy Jack, AZ 86024. (520) 527-3670.

FOR MORE INFORMATION

(See the Highline Passage for a listing of museums in Payson.)

NEAREST SERVICES TO GENERAL SPRINGS CABIN

Pine: From General Springs Cabin travel 12.5 miles west on FR 300 (Rim Road) to SR 87. Turn left (south) on SR 87 and travel to Pine or Payson.

Trip 26-A

General Springs Cabin to Rock Crossing Campground

 East Clear Creek has a steep section that may be difficult for bicyclists and livestock.

Trip 26-A travels from Rim Road (FR 300) north of Strawberry to SR 87 east of Lake Mary Road. From a historic log cabin near the Mogollon Rim, the Arizona Trail travels north through meadows, forests, and canyons to the top of Battleground Ridge, the site of the last conflict between U.S. Cavalry and Apache Indians. After traversing the steep walls of beautiful East Clear Creek Canyon it's an easy final mile to Rock Crossing Campground.

Nature Highlight: We fell asleep to the bugling songs of bull elk.

Maps:
- Coconino National Forest. USDA.
- USGS Quads: Dane Canyon, Blue Ridge Reservoir.

Difficulty: Moderate to difficult, with some steep climbs.

Length: 10.3 miles, one way.

Elevation: 6,740–7,400 feet.

Recommended Season: Spring, summer, autumn, depending on the weather.

Water: (Treat all water unless noted otherwise. During dry weather, water sources may not be dependable.)
- **General Springs Cabin:** a pond located behind the cabin.
- **General Springs Canyon.**
- **Dirt stock tank on Battleground Ridge.**
- **East Clear Creek (seasonal).**

Camping: General Springs Cabin area offers primitive camping, where there is room to park and flat areas with large trees near the cabin. If you will be driving in, bring your own firewood and water. The cabin is not available for use.

Livestock: There are some grassy areas and plenty of room to pull in and turn trailers. Water livestock at the pond beyond the cabin. This route is possible for experienced trail animals in good physical condition.

There is no water between East Clear Creek and Rock Crossing Campground. The next place to camp with livestock would be Elk Tank, north of Blue Ridge Campground on FR 138. See Trip 26-B.

Directions to General Springs Cabin: The cabin can be accessed by passenger car. FR 300 is a rough, narrow, winding dirt road. From the junction of SR 87 and SR 260, north of Strawberry, travel 2.7 miles north. Turn east on FR 300 (Rim Road), and travel 12.5 miles to the Battle of Big Dry Wash Monument. Turn left (north) traveling 0.5 mile to General Springs Cabin.

Other Area Trails: Fred Haught Trail #28 is part of the historic Cabin Loop System, which links three old fire guard stations dating back to the early 1900s.

The General Crook Trail dates back to 1872. It travels east 114 miles from Camp Verde to State Highway 260 east of Payson. Along the Mogollon Rim, FR 300 frequently intercepts the route of the General Crook Trail, which passes near the General Springs Cabin and the Battle of Big Dry Wash Monument.

For more information on these or other trails in the area, contact the Blue Ridge Ranger District.

TRAIL DESCRIPTION

 The road from FR 300 to General Springs Cabin appears to be a utility road for a power line and a water pipeline that originate at the Blue Ridge Reservoir. If an old wooden sign remains here indicating that the Fred Haught and Arizona Trail proceed up this road, IGNORE IT. That is the old route.

The Arizona Trail follows a dirt driveway that skirts the cabin to the left and ends at the wooden rail fence. The trail passes through the rail fence and follows the rock cairns traveling north across a meadow. At the north end of the meadow the trail crosses the little stream to a brown carsonite Arizona Trail marker. The trail continues north following along the right bank of a drainage, the upper end of General Springs Canyon. Watch for blazes on the trees and Arizona Trail markers.

The trail follows rock cairns as it traverses a charming area of little rocky outcroppings intermingled with ferns and big pines. As the trail drops down a rocky bank, the small creek bed has narrowed and deepened, on its way to becoming a canyon. After crossing the creek, watch carefully. Although it may appear that the trail continues along the left side of the creek, a stairway has been cut into the bank immediately to the right. The trail goes down the steps, crosses the creek again, and continues on the right side.

For the next 2 miles the trail ambles down this serene and lovely canyon, occasionally crossing the creek. Following rock cairns, blazes, and carsonite markers, the trail descends, alternating between small grassy meadows, ferns, and areas of big shady trees. It follows the creek, most often along the west bank, frequently passing small clear pools of water. There are large elk tracks along the trail, as it passes the remains of a rock fireplace on the left.

Three miles from the trailhead, traveling along the west side of the canyon, the route forks. Only a rock cairn marks this unsigned junction to signal that the Arizona Trail abandons General Springs Canyon and the Fred Haught Trail to cut uphill to the west. Following rock cairns, the Arizona Trail begins a steep switchbacking ascent of Battleground Ridge. Once past the switchbacks the trail continues, a bit less strenuously, uphill following rock cairns in a southwesterly direction.

Having ascended the pine-covered flank of the ridge, the trail passes through a wire gate and continues along an old dirt road due north. A short distance down the road is an unsigned junction with FR 123, a graded dirt road, and the same power line we saw back at General Springs Cabin. The Arizona Trail crosses FR 123, and a short distance down the trail, you can see rock cairns. Before long the trail again encounters the huge cement waterline and power line. The power line, the pipeline, and the Arizona Trail play tag for the next couple of miles, as they traverse the long, grassy, pine-clad back of Battleground Ridge.

 Approximately 1 mile after crossing FR 123 the trail crosses an abandoned dirt road, the route prominently marked with rock cairns. The trail disappears at this junction. Continue heading northwest, cutting through grass and pine trees, following rock cairns. You have to watch carefully for rock piles and blazes along here, as the route follows along the right bank of a fairly deep drainage. This trek along Battleground Ridge parallels FR 123 to the east and Battleground Canyon to the west.

The route arrives at a gate. To the right, before you go through the gate, a grassy-sided dirt tank for watering livestock is hidden by trees. Continue through the gate following rock markers north, connecting again with the power line.

Following blazes and rock markers, the route intersects an abandoned logging road. Follow the road a couple of yards, watching closely for a pile of rocks and some trees with blazes. From here the route continues north following rock cairns. There has been logging in this area, and this section of the Arizona Trail may be minimally marked and difficult to follow. If you lose the route, head east a short distance to FR 123 and turn north. Follow FR 123 until you see a corral on the left side of the road. An unsigned dirt road traveling past the corral is FR 123A. Follow 123A a short distance west to an intersection with the Arizona Trail on the left, marked by a rock cairn and an arrow carved into a ponderosa.

The Arizona Trail comes out of the forest onto FR 123A 6.5 miles from General Springs Cabin. This may be an unsigned junction. Turn left (west) and follow the road 1.5 miles.

Eight miles from General Springs Cabin, the Arizona Trail passes through a gate at the end of FR 123A. BICYCLISTS AND EQUESTRIANS: Leaving Battleground Ridge, the trail careens down a series of very steep switchbacks into the canyon of East Clear Creek. This steep-sided, wide-bottomed canyon is quite unusual and appealing. The perfectly flat bottom is covered with remarkably white gravel. There are some small, clear pools of water, and rocky cliffs loom above the northwest side.

The trail traverses the opposite side of the canyon following a series of exceptionally steep switchbacks and then levels out. The route, lined with old logs and rocks, is deceptively easy. The most difficult part of this trek—the final climb out of the canyon—is yet to come.

After leaving the canyon it's an easy final mile. The trail is level and well defined, heading east through a pine, juniper and oak woodland interspersed with grassy, open areas. The trail travels above the canyon with some nice views to the south. The route turns north, crosses a shallow drainage, and enters Rock Crossing Campground.

Trip 26-B

Rock Crossing Campground to Blue Ridge Campground

Trip 26-B travels from Rock Crossing Campground near Blue Ridge Reservoir to Blue Ridge Campground south of SR 87. This short, easy ramble across Blue Ridge is a nice respite after some of the more rigorous sections of trail to the south. The well-marked, almost level route offers a fine view of the San Francisco Peaks north of Flagstaff.

Nature Highlight: A small cottontail rabbit flashes away from our path.

Maps:
- Coconino National Forest. USDA.
- USGS Quads: Dane Canyon, Blue Ridge Reservoir.

Difficulty: Easy.

Length: 3.2 miles, one way.

Elevation: 7,000–7,400 feet.

Recommended Season: Spring, summer, and autumn, depending on the weather.

Water: (Treat all water unless noted otherwise. During dry weather, water sources may not be dependable.)
- **Rock Crossing Campground:** Potable water is turned off in the winter.
- **Blue Ridge Campground:** Potable water is turned off in the winter.
- Elk Tank, north of **Blue Ridge Campground,** has a pond.

Camping: Clear Creek and **Blue Ridge Campgrounds** offer developed campgrounds with water, rest rooms, picnic tables, and campground hosts. If you will be driving in, bring your own firewood. Livestock is not allowed, and this is a fee area. The campgrounds are closed from early September until the end of May.

Livestock: Camping with livestock is not allowed at Rock Crossing Campground or Blue Ridge Campground. The best place to camp with livestock is Elk Tank, north of Blue Ridge Campground on FR 138. Take the animals through the campground, following the road approximately 0.5 mile north to an unsigned dirt road on the right (west) side of the road, which leads to a pond. Remember to camp at least 0.25 mile away from water so that the wild residents of the area may also access it.

Directions to Rock Crossing Campground: The campground can be accessed by passenger car. From the junction of SR 87 and Lake Mary Road (Clints Well), travel 5 miles northeast to FR 751, which goes to Blue Ridge Reservoir. Turn right and travel 2.5 miles to the turnoff for Rock Crossing Campground on the right.

Directions to Blue Ridge Campground: From the junction of SR 87 and Lake Mary Road (Clints Well), travel 8 miles northeast to FR 138. Turn right on FR 138 and travel 1 mile to the campground.

TRAIL DESCRIPTION

The Arizona Trail leaves Rock Crossing Campground following the campground road out to FR 751, which travels southeast to Blue Ridge Reservoir. Turn right and follow FR 751 a short distance to an Arizona Trail sign on the left (north) side of the road. The trail is well marked, with boulders along each side as it travels northeast, across the Mogollon Plateau. In a little less than 0.5 mile the trail crosses a dirt track, and passes under a power line. Traveling through a nice mix of pine and oak, with intermittent open, grassy areas, the route is fairly level and well marked, with rocks lining both sides of the trail.

About 0.75 mile from the campground the trail crosses FR 751B and continues north. Very well signed with brown carsonite markers and logs and rocks lining the trail, this almost level ramble is perfect for bicyclists or hikers who prefer a gentler trek. The trail crosses an abandoned dirt road and then makes an easy ascent of Blue Ridge, affording a far-reaching vista of the San Francisco Peaks to the north of Flagstaff. The route bends to the east, following along the ridge with continuing views to the north.

At 1.75 miles from the campground, the trail begins a gentle descent, winding down through some brushy vegetation and scrub oak, which quickly give way to a shady, wooded glen. As the trail passes through a gate, the gradient levels. Passing a huge, old, dead ponderosa, the trail crosses a small drainage and enters the Blue Ridge Campground.

27 Unnamed Passage
Highway 87 to Lake Mary Road

As of this writing, sections of the Arizona Trail in this passage are not yet completed. This description outlines the *proposed route* of the Arizona Trail through this passage; it is not intended to be used as a trail guide. Much of the information included here is taken from an Arizona Trail management guide designed not for recreational use but for use in planning, developing, and managing the trail. Contact the governing agency or The Arizona Trail Association for more information on the route, signage, availability of water, and completion status of this passage.

T*HIS PASSAGE is completed and signed to Jack's Canyon. The remainder of the route is still being researched and developed.*

PROPOSED ROUTE

From SR 87 (near FR 138 and west of the Blue Ridge ranger station), the Arizona Trail is signed as it travels into Jack's Canyon. From Jack's Canyon, the proposed route travels past the Turkey and Hutch Mountain areas to Lake Mary Road (FR 3), north of Happy Jack.

GOVERNING AGENCIES

Coconino National Forest, Blue Ridge Ranger District, HC 31, Box 300, Happy Jack, AZ 86024. (502) 527-3670.
Coconino National Forest, Blue Ridge District, Long Valley District, Mormon Lake District.

FOR MORE INFORMATION

Arizona Trail Association, P.O. Box 36736, Phoenix, AZ 85067. (602) 252-4794.

NEAREST SERVICES

Nearest services are at Clints Well.

As of this writing, sections of the Arizona Trail in this passage are not yet completed. This description outlines the *proposed route* of the Arizona Trail through this passage; it is not intended to be used as a trail guide. Much of the information included here is taken from an Arizona Trail management guide designed not for recreational use but for use in planning, developing, and managing the trail. Contact the governing agency or The Arizona Trail Association for more information on the route, signage, availability of water, and completion status of this passage.

MARSHALL LAKE, *which has a a marsh-like habitat, offers a good chance for seeing bald eagles in winter, osprey in summer, and waterfowl year-round.*

PROPOSED ROUTE

This passage begins at Lake Mary Road (FH 3), north of Happy Jack, and ends at Marshall Lake. The route may use abandoned railroad spurs southwest of Mormon Lake. The railroad bed continues north (staying west of the U.S. Forest Service campgrounds) and connects to the area near Pine Grove Campground, offering access to amenities in Mormon Lake Village. Immediately east of this campground, FR 129A is signed as the Arizona Trail and provides the linkage to the Marshall Lake area, where the Arizona Trail continues.

GOVERNING AGENCIES

Coconino National Forest, Mormon Lake Ranger District, 4373 S. Lake Mary Road, Flagstaff, AZ 86001. (520) 527-3650.

FOR MORE INFORMATION

Arizona Trail Association, P.O. Box 36736, Phoenix, AZ 85067. (602) 252-4794.

NEAREST SERVICES

Nearest services can be found in Mormon Lake Village.

Photo by Kelly Tighe

A mountain biker finds solitude and a challenging ride below Fisher Point along the Walnut Canyon Passage.

Ridin' home when the light is failin'
And the draws are dim and still,
I can hear the coyote wailin'
In the shadows by the hill—
    "Ah-ee-e-e! Ah-ee-e-e!"
With a lonely sort o' feelin'
Through the dusk it comes a-stealin'
Down to me.

—"Cowboy and Coyote," Badger Clark, 1907

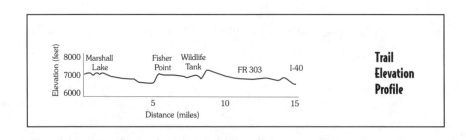

29 Walnut Canyon (Equestrian Bypass) Passage

Marshall Lake to Interstate 40 (Cosnino)

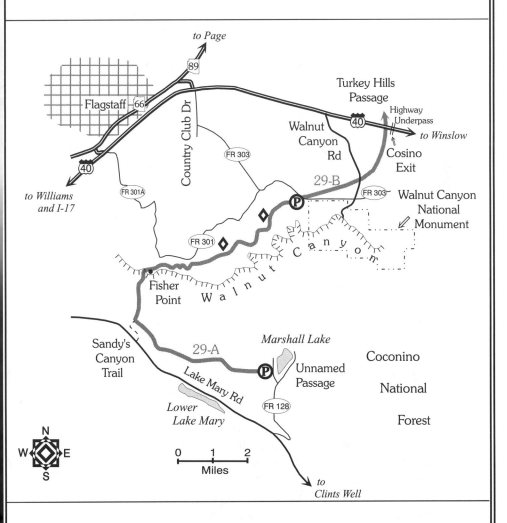

to Page

89

Flagstaff — 66

Country Club Dr

FR 303

40

to Williams and I-17

FR 301A

FR 301

Turkey Hills Passage

Highway Underpass

Walnut Canyon Rd

40

to Winslow

Cosino Exit

29-B

FR 303

Walnut Canyon National Monument

Walnut

Canyon

Fisher Point

Sandy's Canyon Trail

29-A

Marshall Lake

Lake Mary Rd

Unnamed Passage

FR 128

Coconino

National

Forest

Lower Lake Mary

to Clints Well

N W E S

0   1   2
Miles

FR102	Forest Road	

- FR102 — Forest Road
- Paved Road
- State/Interstate
- Arizona Trail
- Trip Access Trail
- 122 — Other Trail Area

- Boundary
- River, Stream, or Wash
- Canyon Rim
- ▲ Campground
- ◆ Water
- ♟ Ranger Station

- Ⓟ Trailhead and Parking
- ◯ Trailhead, no Parking
- P Parking
- ◉ Town or City
- ● Point of Interest
- △ Mountain Peak

THIS POPULAR 15-MILE PASSAGE, *designed as an equestrian bypass around the city of Flagstaff, contains two trips. Trip 29-A begins at the western edge of Marshall Lake, south of Flagstaff, and travels 11.2 miles to FR 303 near the entrance of Walnut Canyon National Monument. Trip 29-B travels 4 miles from FR 303 to I-40 east of Flagstaff. Passage 31 (Flagstaff) also begins at Marshall Lake, offering hikers and cyclists an urban route through the city.*

The shallow waters of Marshall Lake are an important wetlands habitat for area wildlife, waterfowl, and bald eagles in the winter. The Arizona Trail highlights Arizona's early Native American heritage as it traverses the beautiful and intriguing canyon home of people who lived in the area eight hundred years ago. A side trip into Walnut Canyon National Monument offers a visitor center, museum, and dramatic views of prehistoric cliff dwellings built into the walls of a 400-foot-deep gorge.

Walnut Canyon Monument was established in 1915 to protect the prehistoric archeological sites in the canyon. Kaibab limestone and Coconino sandstone form the colorfully sculpted cliffs of this canyon, which holds evidence of human habitation dating back two thousand years. Archeologists using tree ring and ceramic analysis have dated Sinagua sites more than eight hundred years old. The ancient cliff dwellings, built into the limestone cliffs beneath the rim of the canyon, petroglyphs, pottery, and other artifacts give clues to how the Sinagua people lived and farmed.

Traveling through pine forest that fades into piñon and juniper grasslands, the trail has some nice views of Mount Elden and the San Francisco Peaks in the final two-mile descent to Interstate 40 east of Flagstaff. The Flagstaff area offers camping, fishing, skiing, museums, restaurants, brew pubs, Sunset Crater Volcano, an early 1900s mansion, the All-Indian Pow-Wow, and many events and festivals.

GOVERNING AGENCIES

Coconino National Forest, Mormon Lake Ranger District, 4373 S. Lake Mary Road, Flagstaff, AZ 86001. (520) 527-3650.

Coconino National Forest, Peaks Ranger District, 5075 N. Highway 89, Flagstaff, AZ 86004. (520) 527-8225.

FOR MORE INFORMATION

Walnut Canyon National Monument, Walnut Canyon Road, Flagstaff, AZ 86004. (520) 526-3367. Facilities include an information center, museum, rest rooms, overlook, paved trails, and a picnic area. No food or lodging is available, and there is an admission fee. Bicycles are permitted, and horses are not.

Flagstaff Visitor Center, 1 E. Route 66, Flagstaff, AZ 86001. 1-800-842-7293.

NEAREST SERVICES TO MARSHALL LAKE

Flagstaff: Take Lake Mary Road 9 miles north to a junction with I-17. Follow I-17 into Flagstaff.

Trip 29-A

Marshall Lake to FR 303

Trip 29-A is a popular mountain bicycling route that travels from Marshall Lake south of Flagstaff to FR 303 near the entrance to Walnut Canyon National Monument. The Arizona Trail leaves Marshall Lake, a wetlands habitat for waterfowl and other area wildlife, rolling across the western end of Anderson Mesa into beautiful Walnut Canyon. Ascending the rim of Walnut Canyon near Fisher Point, the route travels east, affording spectacular views of the canyon, and the San Francisco Peaks to the north.

Nature Highlight: In the early evening a great blue heron is wading for his dinner among the reeds along the banks of Marshall Lake.

Maps:
- Coconino National Forest.
- USGS Quads: Lower Lake Mary, Flagstaff East.

Difficulty: Easy to moderate, with some steep descents and climbs.

Length: 11.2 miles, one way.

Elevation: 7,100–6,740 feet.

Recommended Season: May through November, depending on the weather.

Water: (Treat all water unless noted otherwise. During dry weather, water sources may not be dependable.)
- Dirt tank: 1 mile west of Marshall Lake.
- Wildlife tank: north rim of Walnut, 7.5 miles from Marshall Lake.
- Wildlife tank: 1.25 miles west of FR 303.

Camping: There is primitive camping at Marshall Lake, where there are flat, shady areas along the west side of the lake near the trailhead. If you will be driving in, bring your own water and firewood.

Livestock: There are flat areas near the Marshall Lake trailhead to turn and park trailers. There is some grass and cattle may be grazing near the lake. Carry a collapsible bucket for accessing water at wildlife tanks, which are usually fenced.

   This trip has great equestrian trails (several steep climbs). There are many livestock boarding facilities in the Flagstaff area. See appendix B for more information.

Directions to Marshall Lake Trailhead: You can access the trailhead by passenger car. Travel southeast from Flagstaff on Lake Mary Road, 9.2 miles to FR 128. Turn left on FR 128 and drive 2.2 miles to Marshall Lake. As you approach the southern end of the lake, take the dirt road to the left that circles the lake to the west. As you approach the western side of the lake, watch for the trailhead on the left, marked by a wooden sign and a brown carsonite trail marker.

Other Area Trails: Sandy's Canyon Trail #137 connects to the abandoned road in Upper Walnut Canyon, four miles from the Marshall Lake trailhead, offering an alternate route back to Lake Mary Road.

   The Flagstaff Passage of the Arizona Trail—the urban route for hikers and bicyclists—will travel from Marshall Lake, across Flagstaff to Buffalo Park, using the **Flagstaff Urban Trail** System. The route was not completed at time this guide went to press.

   Contact the Mormon Lake Ranger District, Peaks Ranger District, or the City of Flagstaff for information on the Arizona Trail or other hiking and riding opportunities in this area.

TRAIL DESCRIPTION

The Arizona Trail leaves Marshall Lake heading west, traveling through a pine and oak woodland. Shortly after you leave the trailhead, the San Francisco Peaks are visible on the right. The well-used path is level, as it travels through open woodland to a junction with an old electric fence and a gate.

   One-half mile from the trailhead, the trail passes through the gate and continues across Anderson Mesa. Eventually the trail starts to drop and the trees become more dense. There are several erosion bars, as the path descends through a forest of oak and pine.

One mile from the trailhead, at the bottom of a drainage, the trail intersects an abandoned dirt road and a wooden Arizona Trail sign. The route turns right (north), passing a fenced, dirt stock tank on the left as it follows the old road down-canyon, winding through pine forest. After a short distance, the trail turns west, crossing the drainage and then crossing an abandoned logging road marked by rock cairns on each side. The gradient steepens and is once more marked by erosion bars, as the route scrambles up the side of the drainage, topping out at an unsigned fork in the trail.

At the unsigned fork, take the more-traveled route to the left. For the next 1.5 miles the trail rolls west through a woodland of scattered oak and pine, as it traverses several minor drainages. The route crosses two more abandoned roads, one right after the other, and a trail sign is visible.

At 1.75 miles from Marshall Lake, the route passes a wooden Arizona Trail sign that states, "no motorized vehicles." The trail begins to drop in elevation, offering a fine view of the San Francisco Peaks. The trail continues in a moderate decline, then contours to the right (north), following the long, sloping, flank of upper Walnut Canyon.

At an unsigned fork, take the trail to the left, which is marked with logs for erosion control. The trail levels out on a grassy plateau, heading north, following the left wall of the canyon. The view from the rim reveals an abundant growth of aspen in the steep, rocky drainage below. As the trail drops to intercept what appears to be a side canyon of Walnut, it is quite narrow in places before the final steep switchbacking descent to the floor of the drainage. A beautifully sculptured pink and gray Coconino sandstone wall on the right highlights our arrival, as the trail enters an open grassy meadow and approaches a junction.

Four miles from Marshall Lake, the trail ends at a T junction with an abandoned road traveling north-south, through the bottom of Upper Walnut Canyon. A wooden sign tells us that the route we have been following is the Arizona Trail. There may be no other signage here indicating which way to go. (Those wishing to make a loop or travel to Lake Mary Road, turn left [south] here. It is approximately 1 mile to Sandy's Canyon trailhead. Check with the Mormon Lake Ranger District for more detailed information on Sandy's Canyon Trail.)

The route of the Arizona Trail turns right (north), following the old road. Passing through a gate, there are nice views of Mount Elden. Motor vehicles are no longer allowed on this road, and logs and rocks have been placed along one track to reclaim it as a trail. The canyon soon opens out into a wide, shadeless, grassy drainage with a gentle downhill grade.

At an unsigned junction of trails, look for Fisher Point, a massive landmark of colorfully eroded sandstone, looming to the east, and follow the path in that direction.

Five miles from Marshall Lake the route of the Arizona Trail may be unsigned as it travels north past Fisher Point. It is an inconspicuous path traveling up a narrow cleft in the canyon wall, just to the west of Fisher Point. The bicyclist in the photo is not on the Arizona Trail. The route makes a sharp left (north) at this point, and enters a narrow, rocky drainage. The trail is well defined as it makes a steep, switch-backing ascent up the rocky crevasse and gains the rim of Walnut Canyon.

As the trail tops out heading east along the rim, a brown carsonite Arizona Trail marker is a welcome sight. The marker indicates the route as the trail crosses an abandoned road, and after some short switchbacks the trail arrives at a junction. FR 303 is toward the left and a view of Walnut Canyon from Fisher Point is to the right. Continuing to the left, the trail turns east, following along the rim. There are occasional glimpses into this pristine canyon that was home to cliff-dwelling Indians nearly a thousand years ago.

The trail angles off to the north away from the rim and then comes to an intersection of abandoned logging roads. Carsonite markers indicate that the trail crosses the first road and then follows the second road to the right (south). A short distance further is another junction. A trail marker indicates that the route turns left. Moments later the road forks, and our route is to the left, approaching a wildlife tank.

At 7.5 miles from Marshall Lake is a wildlife tank, the first water since the dirt stock tank 1 mile west of Marshall Lake. One-half mile after the wildlife tank, the road forks. Carsonite markers direct us to stay to the right. The gradient begins to climb, offering views of Mount Elden and the San Francisco Peaks. Continue east through pine forest (a spur trail to the right offers a view of the canyon). In 0.25 mile farther you meet an unmarked fork. Stay right. A short distance later you meet a carsonite marker at a second fork that tells you to stay to the right. Soon, the trail is back along the rim of Walnut Canyon, heading east.

A wood sign and carsonite marker indicate that the trail abandons the road, striking off to the left (north). (Continuing straight will take you to Walnut Canyon Viewpoint.) The route makes an easy descent through a grove of small oak trees, then wanders down a narrow drainage through an oak and pine forest. Dropping into the drainage, the trail maneuvers a hairpin turn at the bottom and crosses to the east.

The trail is narrow and lined with rock as it follows along the north side of a deep, narrow chasm. As the trail makes a rocky ascent, the defile opens up, becoming wider and deeper, offering a magnificent view of a wild and remote, virtually inaccessible side canyon. After a series of dizzily slanted switchbacks, the trail tops out at an abandoned dirt road.

Ten miles from Marshall Lake a carsonite marker directs us left (west), past a wildlife tank on the left. After a short distance the old road turns north, and then east. The trail is closed to motor vehicles, and logs and rocks have been placed to prevent erosion. The road continues through comparatively level, open grassy areas, dotted with big pines. The route crosses an abandoned road, signed by carsonite markers, then takes an easy downhill grade northeast to FR 303.

Trip 29-B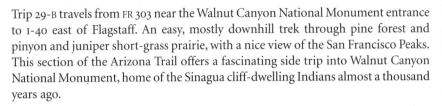

Forest Road 303 to Interstate 40 (Cosnino)

Trip 29-B travels from FR 303 near the Walnut Canyon National Monument entrance to I-40 east of Flagstaff. An easy, mostly downhill trek through pine forest and pinyon and juniper short-grass prairie, with a nice view of the San Francisco Peaks. This section of the Arizona Trail offers a fascinating side trip into Walnut Canyon National Monument, home of the Sinagua cliff-dwelling Indians almost a thousand years ago.

Nature Highlight: A tiny, gray nuthatch clings upside down to the bark of a ponderosa pine as it searches for insects.

Maps:
* Coconino National Forest.
* USGS Quad: Flagstaff East.

Difficulty: Easy.

Length: 4 miles, one way.

Elevation: 6,740–6,490 feet.

Recommended Season: May through November, depending on the weather.

Water: None.

    A fenced wildlife tank 1.25 miles west of FR 303 or the national monument are the only sources of water. Neither is located on this section of trail and both require making a side trip. A fee is charged to enter the monument, and livestock is not allowed.

Camping: **Forest Road 303 trailhead** offers primitive camping and ample parking. If you are driving in, bring your own water and firewood.

    Interstate 40 trailhead offers very limited parking and primitive camping. If you are driving in, bring your own water and firewood.

    There are many developed campgrounds in the Flagstaff area, but none adjacent to this passage of the Arizona Trail.

Livestock: This is a nice equestrian trail. Forest Road 303 trailhead has room for trucks and trailers, some grass, but no water close by.

    I-40 trailhead has no place to turn or park trailers and no water.

Directions to Forest Road 303 Trailhead: You can access this trailhead by passenger car. Travel 4 miles east from Flagstaff on I-40 to Walnut Canyon Monument Road, exit 204. Turn right (south) and travel approximately 2.5 miles to FR 303. Turn right (west) on FR 303 and travel 1.7 miles to the trailhead, which is marked by a wood rail fence.

Directions to I-40 Trailhead: Travel east from Flagstaff on I-40 to Cosnino exit 207. Turn right and drive back (west) on the frontage road 0.7 mile. Watch closely for a small wooden sign to the left, which is set back off the road and may be hidden by brush. If you see a large cement culvert going under I-10 on the right, you have passed the sign. There is no convenient place to park or turn around here, especially with a horse trailer.

Other Area Trails: The Arizona Trail Equestrian Bypass will eventually pass under I-40, using the large cement culvert, and link to the **Elden–Dry Lake Hills** trail system. This route had not been completed as of this writing.

Contact Peaks Ranger District or City of Flagstaff for trail status information.

TRAIL DESCRIPTION

The Arizona Trail crosses FR 303 heading northeast, as it skirts around the northern boundary of Walnut Canyon National Monument. Passing through ponderosa pine forest, the trail crosses a shallow drainage marked by rock cairns and soon after arrives at an unsigned metal gate.

After passing through the gate the route is crisscrossed by a profusion of abandoned logging roads. Fortunately, the Forest Service has done a wonderful job of signing the route of the Arizona Trail through here, and it is easy to follow. Leaving the gate, heading east, the trail crosses five little-used dirt roads. After passing under electrical wires, the trail crosses a sixth dirt road before arriving at a second metal gate. Down the fence to the right, a small white sign declares the fence line the national park boundary.

Two miles from FR 303, the Arizona Trail crosses the paved road into Walnut Canyon National Monument. After crossing the road, the trail heads northeast in an easy descent through a scattered juniper and pine woodland. The path is marked with dead branches placed along the right side of the trail for erosion control. The trail passes through a third metal gate as it exits the national monument, heading northeast.

Still dropping in an easy descent, the land opens up into a rolling grassland with a scattering of small pine and juniper. A power line comes into view as the trail skirts around the west end of an open meadow. Now heading north, the trail climbs a small, grassy hill, dotted with juniper and piñon. The trail passes beneath a power line as it ascends a grassy knob, and when you top out, I-40 is visible in the distance. There is a view of the San Francisco Peaks to the west, and below the Peaks is Mount Elden, crowned with its radio towers. Following a long, grassy ridgeline north, the trail ends at the frontage road below I-40.

30 Turkey Hills (Equestrian Bypass) Passage
Interstate 40 (Cosnino) to Schultz Pass

As of this writing, sections of the Arizona Trail in this passage are not yet completed. This description outlines the *proposed route* of the Arizona Trail through this passage; it is not intended to be used as a trail guide. Much of the information included here is taken from an Arizona Trail management guide designed not for recreational use but for use in planning, developing, and managing the trail. Contact the governing agency or The Arizona Trail Association for more information on the route, signage, availability of water, and completion status of this passage.

WHEN COMPLETED, *this passage (mileage not available) will travel from I-40 (Cosnino) east of Flagstaff to the Mount Elden Trail System north of Flagstaff.*

PROPOSED ROUTE

Planning continues for this passage, which will allow equestrians and other trail users to bypass Flagstaff. From the area near the Cosnino exit the route will pass through a large culvert under I-40. From I-40 the route will travel east to connect to the U.S. 89 underpass immediately south of the Townsend-Winona intersection. A connection to the Sandy Seep Trail of the Mount Elden Trail System is being researched.

GOVERNING AGENCIES

Coconino National Forest, Peaks Ranger District, 5075 N. Highway 89, Flagstaff, AZ 86004. (520) 527-8225.

FOR MORE INFORMATION

The Arizona Trail Association, P.O. Box 36736, Phoenix, AZ 85067. (602) 252-4794.

NEAREST SERVICES

Nearest services are in Flagstaff.

31 Flagstaff Passage
Marshall Lake to Buffalo Park

As of this writing, sections of the Arizona Trail in this passage are not yet completed. This description outlines the *proposed route* of the Arizona Trail through this passage; it is not intended to be used as a trail guide. Much of the information included here is taken from an Arizona Trail management guide designed not for recreational use but for use in planning, developing, and managing the trail. Contact the governing agency or The Arizona Trail Association for more information on the route, signage, availability of water, and completion status of this passage.

WHEN COMPLETED, *this 12.8-mile passage will travel from Marshall Lake through the city of Flagstaff, using a network of trails within the city, to Buffalo Park on the north side of Flagstaff.*

PROPOSED ROUTE

From Marshall Lake this passage uses the same route as the Walnut Canyon (Equestrian Bypass) Passage, as far as Fisher Point. From Fisher Point the passage will travel west to Flagstaff, where it will use the existing Flagstaff Urban Trails Systems to cross the city from south to north. The passage may follow the Rio de Flag under I-40. From there, a route to Enterprise and over Route 66 is being researched. A new pedestrian overpass over the Santa Fe Railroad tracks has been proposed. A connection to McMillan Mesa Trail north of Route 66 is being researched. The McMillan Mesa Trail provides linkage to Buffalo Park.

GOVERNING AGENCIES

City of Flagstaff, Flagstaff Urban Trails System, 211 W. Aspen Ave., Flagstaff, AZ 86001. (520) 779-7632.

Coconino National Forest, Peaks Ranger District, 5075 N. Highway 89, Flagstaff, AZ 86004. (520) 527-8225.

FOR MORE INFORMATION

The Arizona Trail Association, P.O. Box 36736, Phoenix, AZ 85067. (602) 252-4794.

NEAREST SERVICES

Nearest services are in Flagstaff.

32 Elden–Dry Lake Hills Passage
Buffalo Park to Schultz Pass

As of this writing, sections of the Arizona Trail in this passage are not yet completed. This description outlines the *proposed route* of the Arizona Trail through this passage; it is not intended to be used as a trail guide. Much of the information included here is taken from an Arizona Trail management guide designed not for recreational use but for use in planning, developing, and managing the trail. Contact the governing agency or The Arizona Trail Association for more information on the route, signage, availability of water, and completion status of this passage.

W*HEN COMPLETED, this passage (mileage not available) will travel from Buffalo Park to Schultz Pass, using the Oldham Trail.*

PROPOSED ROUTE

Research continues on using existing trails within the system.

GOVERNING AGENCIES

Coconino National Forest, Peaks Ranger District, 5075 N. Highway 89, Flagstaff, AZ 86004. (520) 527-8225.

FOR MORE INFORMATION

The Arizona Trail Association, P.O. Box 36736, Phoenix, AZ 85067. (602) 252-4794.

NEAREST SERVICES

Nearest services are in Flagstaff.

33 San Francisco Peaks Passage
Schultz Pass to Cedar Ranch

As of this writing, sections of the Arizona Trail in this passage are not yet completed. This description outlines the *proposed route* of the Arizona Trail through this passage; it is not intended to be used as a trail guide. Much of the information included here is taken from an Arizona Trail management guide designed not for recreational use but for use in planning, developing, and managing the trail. Contact the governing agency or The Arizona Trail Association for more information on the route, signage, availability of water, and completion status of this passage.

WHEN COMPLETED, *this passage (mileage not available) will travel from Schultz Pass, north of Flagstaff, to Cedar Ranch, north of the San Francisco Peaks. The San Francisco Peaks are the product of the San Francisco volcanic field, an area that has seen volcanic activity for millions of years. Sunset Crater Volcano northeast of Flagstaff erupted only seven hundred years ago. Beautiful Humphreys Peak, with an elevation of 12,670 feet, is the highest peak in Arizona. The Arizona Snow Bowl ski area is on Mount Agassiz and is popular with winter recreationists.*

PROPOSED ROUTE

The two routes of the Arizona Trail (the urban route and the equestrian bypass route) will join each other near Schultz Pass, roughly 5 miles north of Flagstaff. At time of publishing it has not been decided how the AT will traverse the San Francisco Peaks. In determining the route of the trail around the peaks the concerns of Native Americans, for whom the peaks have religious significance, must be considered. Also the wishes of private landowners and wildlife impact concerns have to be taken into account.

GOVERNING AGENCIES

Coconino National Forest, Peaks Ranger District, 5075 N. Highway 89, Flagstaff, AZ 86004. (520) 527-8225.

FOR MORE INFORMATION

The Arizona Trail Association, P.O. Box 36736, Phoenix, AZ 85067. (602) 252-4794.

NEAREST SERVICES

Nearest services are in Flagstaff.

34 Babbitt Ranch Passage
Cedar Ranch to Moqui Stage Station

This description is not intended to be used as a trail guide. Much of the information included here is taken from an Arizona Trail management guide designed not for recreational use but for use in planning, developing, and managing the trail. Contact the governing agency or The Arizona Trail Association for more information on the route, signage, availability of water, and completion status of this passage.

T HIS APPROXIMATELY 19-mile passage is open and was recently signed with branded 4x4 posts. It travels from Cedar Ranch Camp near the northern boundary of the Coconino National Forest to an old stagecoach station in the Kaibab National Forest, south of the Grand Canyon. This passage follows the historic route of the late 1800s Flagstaff to Grand Canyon Stageline. The route travels across rolling short-grass prairie hills dotted with pinyon and juniper. Pronghorn antelope are frequently seen in this area. Babbitt Ranch's vast C O Bar Ranch, a working cattle ranch, is the largest section of private land found along the Arizona Trail.

The route uses a series of little-used dirt roads that offer a quality recreational experience for bicyclists. Since part of the passage lies on state trust lands, trail users will have to obtain a recreation permit or an Arizona hunting license in advance. (See appendix D.) East Cedar Tank, near the beginning of the passage, is a usually reliable water source.

DESIGNATED ROUTE

This passage is accessible by passenger car. From SR 180 near Milepost 247, FR 417 travels east to the Cedar Ranch Camp area. The passage begins east of Cedar Ranch Camp, where FR 416 and FR 417 intersect. The route follows a maintained pipeline road to Tub Ranch Camp. After passing corrals east of some buildings, the route turns west toward Chapel Mountain following little-used dirt roads. Once past the high-voltage power lines, the route travels north to Upper Lockwood Tank. Still following old roads the route travels northeast to Lower Lockwood Tank and then northwest to the Kaibab National Forest boundary. From the forest boundary a trail follows along the west and then the east side of FR 301 to the Moqui Stage Station.

GOVERNING AGENCIES

Babbitt Ranches, Inc., P.O. Box 520, Flagstaff, AZ 86002. (520) 774-6199.

Kaibab National Forest, Tusayan Ranger District, P.O. Box 3088, Grand Canyon, AZ 86023. (520) 638-2443.

FOR MORE INFORMATION

The Arizona Trail Association, P.O. Box 36736, Phoenix, AZ 85067. (602) 252-4794.

NEAREST SERVICES

Nearest services are in Flagstaff.

35 Moqui Stage/Coconino Rim Passage Moqui Stage Station to Grandview Lookout

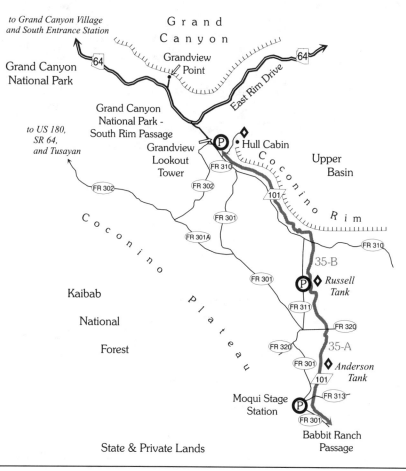

N
W E
S

0   1   2
Miles

to Grand Canyon Village
and South Entrance Station

Grand
Canyon

64

Grandview
Point

64

East Rim Drive

Grand Canyon
National Park

Grand Canyon
National Park -
South Rim Passage

to US 180,
SR 64,
and Tusayan

Grandview
Lookout
Tower

P

Hull Cabin

FR 310

Upper
Basin

Coconino

FR 302

FR 302

101

Rim

FR 301

FR 301A

FR 310

35-B

Coconino

FR 301

P

Russell
Tank

FR 311

Kaibab

National

Forest

FR 320

FR 320

35-A

Plateau

FR 301

Anderson
Tank

101

Moqui Stage
Station

P

FR 313

FR 301

Babbit Ranch
Passage

State & Private Lands

	Forest Road		Boundary		Trailhead and Parking
FR102	Forest Road		Boundary	P	Trailhead and Parking
	Paved Road		River, Stream, or Wash		Trailhead, no Parking
	State/Interstate		Canyon Rim	P	Parking
	Arizona Trail	▲	Campground		Town or City
	Trip Access Trail	◆	Water	●	Point of Interest
122	Other Trail Area	♠	Ranger Station	△	Mountain Peak

From 1892 to 1901, the Flagstaff–Grand Canyon Stagecoach followed the route that is now the Moqui Stage/Coconino Rim Passage of the Arizona Trail. Note the wagon hitched behind the stage. Courtesy of Grand Canyon National Park Museum Collection #4370.

There's a song in the canyon below me
And a song in the pines overhead,
As the sunlight crawls down from the snow-line
And rustles the deer from his bed.

—"The Old Prospector," Badger Clark, 1907

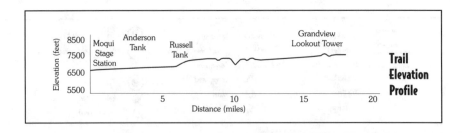

Trail Elevation Profile

THIS 23-MILE PASSAGE *contains two trips. Trip 35-A leaves the ruins of the old Moqui Stage Station and travels 6.7 miles to Russell Tank. Trip 35-B travels 11 miles from Russell Tank to Grandview Lookout Tower, south of the Grand Canyon. Crossing the Coconino Plateau, the Arizona Trail follows the historic route of the stagecoach that traveled between Flagstaff and the Grand Canyon in the late 1800s.*

Passing through piñon pine, juniper, sage, and prairie grasslands, the trail makes a gentle ascent into the Gambel oak and ponderosa pine forest of the Coconino Rim. A small, scenic lake provides delightfully shady campsites and, if you have a current license, fishing for rainbow trout. The last half of the route has enchanting views of the Grand Canyon, the Painted Desert, and the snow-capped San Francisco Peaks north of Flagstaff. This passage offers opportunities for shorter loop trips, and a side trip to view several historic log structures over one hundred years old.

The Moqui Station was one of three rest stops and horse change stations on the stagecoach route between Flagstaff and the Grand Canyon from 1892 to 1901. This popular route, which ended at the Grandview Hotel, was also used by private coaches and horseback riders. The foundation of a building and the remains of a cistern used to store water still exist.

At the station, passengers rested from the rough and dusty ride while fresh horses were harnessed. The day-long trip cost $20.00 and ran three times a week. Four to six horse coaches were used, and if there were too many passengers for one stage, a trailer was added, resulting in a stage train! When the railroad from Williams to the Grand Canyon was completed in 1901 the stagecoach line was abandoned.

One and a half miles northeast of Grandview Lookout, on FR 307, the Hull Cabin Historic District comprises several log buildings constructed by the Hull brothers in 1888. The brothers established a sheep ranch and built a log home and barn. The barn was built of massive hand-squared ponderosa logs, joined by dovetailed notches at the corners. Hull Cabin became a U.S. Forest Service Ranger Station in 1907 and is still in use as a home for seasonal Forest Service crews. Visitors are welcome, but please respect the privacy of personnel living there.

Grandview Lookout Tower was built in 1936 by the Civilian Conservation Corps. The 80-foot, steel tower, topped with a 7-foot square cab, was built to replace an earlier wooden tower. Prior to the wooden structures, fire guards used simple wooden platforms mounted in tall trees to spot fires. The 1930s were an active period for lookout tower construction, and Grandview is typical of towers built during that era.

GOVERNING AGENCIES

Kaibab National Forest, Tusayan Ranger District, P.O. Box 3088, Tusayan, AZ 86023. (520) 638-2443.

FOR MORE INFORMATION

For information on camping within the park: **Grand Canyon National Park,** P.O. Box 129, Grand Canyon, AZ 86023. (520) 638-7888.

NEAREST SERVICES TO MOQUI STAGE STATION

Tusayan: approximatly 16 miles northeast on dirt roads.

Trip 35-A

Moqui Stage Station to Russell Tank

This Trip has good trails for bicycles and equestrians.

From FR 301, Trip 35-A travels to Russell Tank, located southeast of Tusayan on FR 311. The Arizona Trail follows the historic route of the stagecoach that traveled between Flagstaff and the Grand Canyon in the late 1800s. Leaving the site of the old Moqui Stage Station the trail makes a gentle ascent through the open grasslands and pine-forested slopes along Russell Wash, to a small and picturesque lake.

Nature Highlight: We saw a mountain lion dashing across Russell Wash—a tawny streak!

Maps:
- Kaibab National Forest. USDA.
- USGS Quads: Grandview SW, Grandview SE.

Difficulty: Easy to moderate.

Length: 6.7 miles, one way.

Elevation: 6,520–7,000 feet.

Recommended Season: March through early November, depending on the weather.

Water: (Treat all water unless noted otherwise. During dry weather, water sources may not be dependable.)
- **Anderson Tank:** 2.5 miles north of Moqui Stage Station.
- Metal stock tank: 0.3 mile north of FR 320.
- **Russell Tank.**

Camping: Moqui Stage Station offers primitive camping and flat areas to park. If you are driving in, bring your own water and firewood.

Livestock: Moqui Stage Station has room to park and turn trailers, some grass, but no water.

Directions to Moqui Stage Station: The primitive dirt roads are passable by passenger car in dry weather. Use caution in wet weather. We were not able to drive in the last 0.5 mile because of mud holes in the road. Check with Tusayan Ranger District for road conditions. From Highway 64/180 (0.8 mile north of the Grand Canyon Airport entrance and just south of Tusayan) turn east on FR 302. Follow FR 302 to FR 301A and turn right (south) on FR 301A to FR 301. Turn right (south) on FR 301 and follow it south. One-half mile before the Moqui Stage Station, FR 301 passes under a power line and a junction with dirt roads FR 305B and FR 313. After the junction watch for the Moqui Stage sign on the left (east) side of the road.

TRAIL DESCRIPTION

A Kaibab National Forest sign on the east side of FR 301 identifies the Moqui Stage Station and describes the interesting history of the stagecoach journey from Flagstaff to the Grand Canyon. Beyond the sign are ruins of an old building and fireplace and the circular remains of the old stone water tank. Near the ruins is an example of the markers used for the Arizona Trail in this passage, a wooden 4X4 post branded with the Arizona Trail symbol. A spur-trail from the stage station travels east, skirting along the northern edge of a tree-rimmed open prairie for 0.25 mile to a junction with the actual route of the Arizona Trail. (The southern route of the Arizona Trail is to the right, crossing open prairie-like country, on the way to Flagstaff.) It is 6.5 miles north to Russell Tank.

Heading left (north) the Arizona Trail leaves the open grassland and enters a pine forest, following a fairly level pathway lined with rocks. In a little over 0.5 mile the route crosses under a buzzing high-tension line, drops down a bank and crosses FR 313. A sign tells us that we are traveling the Russell Wash section of the

Arizona Trail. The trail enters the beautiful, open, grassy draw that is Russell Wash. Following an abandoned dirt road punctuated at intervals by branded wooden posts, the route continues north. Depending on the season, the wide-open draw may be awash with colorful wildflowers, including Indian paintbrush and yellow burro weed.

Two and one-half miles from Moqui Stage Station the road arrives at a barbed wire fence and the bank of Anderson Tank. This junction may be unsigned. The Arizona Trail passes through the gate to the left. The trail is fairly level as it winds north through the trees, following an abandoned dirt road with occasional Arizona Trail markers. It's a pleasant, gentle ascent as the old road leaves the trees and follows along the west side of Russell Wash, which has the appearance of a grassy meadow bordered by large pines on the east and west. The route arrives at an Arizona Trail marker and a wide gate with cedar posts, with a wire stretched across the top. As you pass through the fence do not continue to follow the dirt road north. The Arizona Trail leaves the old road here to the left (west), following what appears to be a cow path along the fence line, then heads northwest through a pine woodland.

The route intersects FR 320 3.4 miles from the Moqui Stage trailhead. (You can leave the Arizona Trail here, taking FR 320 left 1 mile to FR 301 south, for a loop back to Moqui Stage Station.) The Arizona Trail crosses FR 320 and continues north, sharing the route of a little-used dirt road for 0.3 mile to a cattle tank and gate. This pretty section of trail ambles through ponderosa pines, paralleling a rock bank on the right. The trail passes a stock tank and a large rusty water tank. Just beyond, set between two large boulders is a trailhead sign and a gate.

It is 3 miles to Russell Tank. The route continues up Russell Wash heading north, following the rock outcropping on the right. Leaving the bank that it has followed since FR 320, the route bends west. The trail, still an old roadbed, ascends gently, then more moderately, winding through the pines as it heads north. One mile from Russell Tank the gradient steepens as the trail leaves the old road, cutting up a bank to the left (west). The route becomes a pathway that winds and twists through the pine forest in a northerly direction for the final, moderate ascent to Russell Tank.

Trip 35-B

Russell Tank to Grandview Lookout

This scenic route offers several opportunities for loop trips. It is a great bicycle and equestrian trail, with one steep drainage.

You may climb the lookout if you wish, however the U.S. Department of Agriculture does not assume liability. The tower affords panoramic views of the Grand Canyon, Painted Desert, and San Francisco Peaks.

Trip 35-B travels from Russell Tank on FR 311 to Grandview Lookout, just south of the Grand Canyon National Park boundary. The Arizona Trail leaves a small lake, traveling north through dense pine forest toward the Grand Canyon. Following the rim of the Coconino Plateau, the route offers alluring glimpses of the Grand Canyon, the Upper Basin, and the Painted Desert. It is for the most part a gentle uphill grade with some moderate switchbacks ending at a historic 500-foot tower.

Nature Highlight: We saw a bull elk with an enormous rack drinking from Russell Tank. He faded silently into the forest. Later we saw two more large-antlered elk along the trail.

Maps:
- Kaibab National Forest. USDA.
- USGS Quad: Grandview Point.

Difficulty: Easy to moderate. Traverses one steep drainage.

Length: 11 miles, one way.

Elevation: 7,070–7,490 feet.

Recommended Season: Spring, summer, and autumn, depending on the weather.

Water: (Treat all water unless noted otherwise. During dry weather, water sources may not be dependable.)
Russell Tank, a small lake, is a dependable water source. There is no water along the route or at Grandview. Water nearest to the end of this trip is a stock tank at Hull Cabin, 1.5 miles east of Grandview on FR 307.

Camping:
- **Russell Tank** offers primitive camping. There are ample flat, shady areas to park and camp on the pull-through between FR 311 and Russell Tank. Remember to camp at least 0.25 mile from the water. If you are driving in, bring your own drinking water and firewood.
- **Grandview Lookout** has no camping in the parking area, but primitive camping is permitted 0.25 mile outside the parking area. There is a rest room, and an information kiosk, but no water.
- **Grand Canyon National Park** has developed campgrounds. Contact Grand Canyon National Park for information. (See Passage 35 description for telephone numbers and addresses.)

Livestock: At Russell Tank there is some grass and room to park and turn trailers on the pull-through between FR 311 and the lake. There is no other water along this trip.
At Grandview Lookout there is room to pull in and unload livestock at the trailhead but no water.

Directions to Trailhead: Primitive dirt roads are passable by passenger car in dry weather, but use caution in wet weather. Check with Tusayan Ranger District for road conditions.
- **Russell Tank:** From Highway 64/180 (0.8 mile north of the Grand Canyon Airport entrance and just south of Tusayan) turn east on FR 302 and follow it to FR

301A. Turn right (south) on FR 301A to FR 301. Turn right (south) on FR 301 and follow it to the junction with FR 320 and 311. Turn left (north) on FR 311 and travel 2.5 miles to the signed pull-through for Russell Tank.

- **Grandview Lookout:** From Highway 64/180 (0.8 mile north of the Grand Canyon Airport entrance and just south of Tusayan) turn east on FR 302 and follow the signs along this road for 16 miles to Grandview Lookout Tower.

Other Area Trails: See Grand Canyon National Park—South Rim Passage (page 238).
- **Vishnu Trail** is a 1.1-mile scenic loop that leaves the Arizona Trail heading north, a short distance east of the trailhead.
- **Hull Cabin** is 1.5 miles east on FR 307.

For information on these and other trails in the area, contact the Tusayan Ranger District, or Grand Canyon National Park (see passage description for telephone numbers and addresses).

TRAIL DESCRIPTION

Traveling north from the parking area the Arizona Trail follows a dirt road around the west side of the lake to an aluminum gate and a trail sign. At the north end of the lake the trail passes through a second gate and leaves the lake, entering a pine forest. The trail makes a gentle, winding ascent, following wooden 4x4 posts that have been branded with the Arizona Trail symbol.

At 1.7 miles from Russell Tank the trail crosses FR 310, leaving the Russell Wash segment of the Arizona Trail and beginning the Coconino Rim segment. The trail is well signed on both sides of the road. (It is a short distance west on FR 310 to the junction with FR 311 for those who wish to make a short loop back to Russell Tank.) Leaving FR 310, heading north through ponderosa pine, the trail passes through an aluminum gate. The comparatively level grade begins a moderate descent, as it switchbacks easily down through oak and pine to the grassy bottom of a drainage. The trail ascends the other side, heading north, in a series of easy switchbacks.

As the trail tops out, a trail marker indicates that the path veers left (west), paralleling the 500-foot-high cliff known as the Coconino Rim Escarpment. A little over 0.5 mile from FR 310, there is a gap in the dense forest growth, offering a magnificent vista. Awesome pink ramparts to the north—the distant sculpted domes and spires of the Grand Canyon! To the east, the vast Upper Basin drops away from the Coconino Plateau, offering views of the Painted Desert beyond. For the next 0.75 mile the trail roams through dense pine forest, skirting a drainage, with intermittent glimpses of the Grand Canyon through the trees.

You meet the difficult section of this route 3 miles from the Russell Tank Trailhead. Here, the trail takes a turn to the right (northeast) and begins an easy switchbacking descent to a wooden sign that cautions cyclists to walk their bicycles. After the sign a series of seven steep switchbacks drop into a deep drainage. The steep climb up the other side is just as arduous and is also posted with precautionary signs. After ascending the drainage the trail intersects a dirt road and a sign indicating that this is an alternate route, a return loop via FR 310. (Those coming from the north who don't want to traverse the switchbacks can turn west here, connect with FR 310, and head north back to Grandview. You may also take FR 310 south to FR 311 south, back to Russell Tank.)

The Grand Canyon is no longer visible as the path ambles through shady forest to one of three more aluminum gates. After passing through the gate the trail turns east and heads downhill, skirting a drainage to the second gate. Passing through the gate, the trail follows a fence line on the left for a short distance, before traversing some shallow drainages. The well-marked trail winds through a pleasant mixture of large ponderosa pine and oak, and in the summer, grassy areas with wildflowers. The trail meanders through another shallow drainage, and again the fence is visible as the trail continues north to the third gate.

After the last gate a sign informs us that we have come 5.8 miles from Russell Tank. The trail has been fairly level, rambling along through delightfully shady forest intermixed with wildflower-dotted clearings of yellow chrysanthemum, penstemon, and purple aster. The serenity of this lovely place, unfortunately, is interrupted by the almost constant sound of aircraft, heralding our approach to one of the most popular tourist attractions in the world. Views of the Upper Basin begin to appear as the route again parallels the rim.

Six miles from Russell Tank the trail offers a fleeting view of the San Francisco Peaks to the southeast. A short distance further, as the route bends to the north, a fabulous view of the Grand Canyon lies straight ahead. As the trail follows along the rim, the route offers a succession of vistas.

Nine miles from Russell Tank the trail passes out of the forest and into an open clear-cut area where trees have been removed because of a dwarf mistletoe infestation. An interpretive sign labeled "The Dying Forest" is the first of a series of signs that explain how the Forest Service has removed diseased trees and replanted ponderosa seedlings in an attempt to control the spread of the mistletoe. The trail continues northwest, past an area of newly planted baby ponderosa, and enters an oak and pine woodland. As the path begins to climb, winding up through the trees, the parasitic mistletoe is clearly visible, hanging in yellow-orange clumps from unhappy, sickly looking pines.

One mile from the Grandview Lookout the trail meanders gently downhill to FR 307. (Through-travelers with livestock may wish to turn right and travel 1.5 miles east to water animals at Hull Tank.) The route turns left and crosses a cattle guard (there is a livestock gate) and continues north. In a short distance the trail adjoins a white gravel path that is an interpretive loop explaining dwarf mistletoe. The route continues north, then west on the gravel path to a junction with the Vishnu Trail, and a short distance beyond, the Grandview Lookout and Trailhead.

36 Grand Canyon National Park—South Rim Passage

Grandview Lookout to Bright Angel Trailhead

As of this writing, sections of the Arizona Trail in this passage are not yet completed. This description outlines the *proposed route* of the Arizona Trail through this passage; it is not intended to be used as a trail guide. Much of the information included here is taken from an Arizona Trail management guide designed not for recreational use but for use in planning, developing, and managing the trail. Contact the governing agency or The Arizona Trail Association for more information on the route, signage, availability of water, and completion status of this passage.

WHEN COMPLETED, *this passage will travel from Grandview Tower in the Kaibab National Forest to the Bright Angel trailhead in Grand Canyon National Park. The Arizona Trail is completed to Half Way Trick Tank. From the tank, the route will enter Grand Canyon National Park, steward of one of nature's most spectacular creations.*

There is a fee for entering the park. Visitors planning to backpack anywhere in the park or camp below the rim must obtain a permit from the backcountry office. Reservations can be made up to four months in advance. Grand Canyon National Park oversees more than one million acres of some of America's most scenic, diverse, and historically and geologically interesting terrain. The park has over four million visitors annually, and is one of the most popular tourist attractions in the world. Ninety percent of tourism occurs at the more easily accessed south rim of the canyon.

Eight hundred years ago the Anasazi, or "Ancient Ones," inhabited the area. The Tusayan (Anasazi) Ruins and Museum are 22 miles east of Grand Canyon Village, following East Rim Drive.

In 1540 a member of Coronado's expedition in search of the Seven Cities of Cíbola was the first known European to view the Grand Canyon. The area was set aside as a forest reserve in 1893. The El Tovar Hotel at Grand Canyon Village was built in 1905. Clinging to the rim of the canyon, this beautiful

*old hotel is still in use today. It is now a national historic
landmark. The national park was established in 1919.*

*The railroad station was built in 1909 and is the last re-
maining log railroad depot in the country. The railroad
replaced the stagecoach as the easiest way for visitors to access
the Grand Canyon. Private automobiles replaced the trains,
and rail service was discontinued in 1968. The Grand Canyon
Railway has since been restored and offers round trip excur-
sions from Williams to the Grand Canyon aboard authentic
twentieth-century steam-powered trains.*

PROPOSED ROUTE

New trail has been constructed from Grandview Lookout west to Half Way
Trick Tank. From the tank the route will enter Grand Canyon National
Park. Within the park the route may link to the Long Jim Canyon Trail, follow equestrian trails near the entrance station to Mather Campground, and
eventually connect with the Bright Angel Trailhead.

GOVERNING AGENCIES

Kaibab National Forest, Tusayan Ranger District, P.O. Box 3088, Grand
Canyon, AZ 86023. (520) 638-2443.

Grand Canyon National Park, P.O. Box 129, Grand Canyon, AZ 86023.
(520) 638-7771.

FOR MORE INFORMATION

Grand Canyon Chamber of Commerce, P.O. Box 3007, Grand Canyon, AZ
86023. (520) 638-2901.

Backcountry Office, Box 129, Grand Canyon, Az 86023. (520) 638-7888.

NEAREST SERVICES

Nearest services are found either at Grand Canyon Village or the town of
Tusayan, located on SR 180 south of the park entrance. Showers and laundromats are available at Mather Campground and Trailer Village.

Reservations for National Park Service–operated campgrounds are in
demand and need to be made as early as possible.

Van shuttle service for rim-to-rim travelers is available through Trans
Canyon Van Service (520) 638-2820 and South Rim Travel 1-800-682-4393.

A view of the inner gorge of the Grand Canyon from the South Rim, as seen along the Grand Canyon National Park Inner Gorge Passage.

Cliffs of vermilion,
*   Shadows of blue,*
Feathery pine boughs
*   The wind whispers through.*

—"Arizona August," Gail I. Gardner, 1935
(Used with permission.)

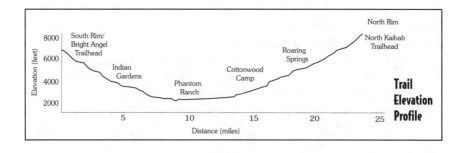

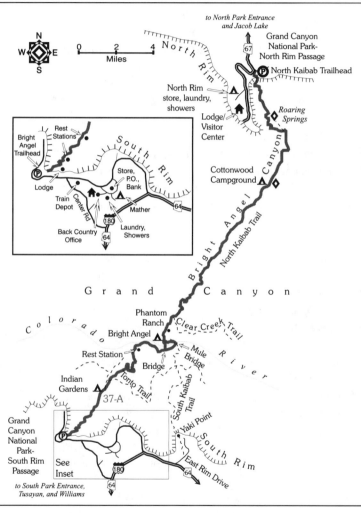

to North Park Entrance
and Jacob Lake

Grand Canyon
National Park-
North Rim Passage

67

North Kaibab Trailhead

North Rim
store, laundry,
showers

Roaring
Springs

Lodge/
Visitor
Center

N
W   E
S

0   2   4
Miles

North Rim

Bright
Angel
Trailhead

Rest
Stations

South Rim

Store,
P.O.,
Bank

Cottonwood
Campground

Bright Angel Canyon

Lodge

Train
Depot

Mather

64

North Kaibab Trail

180

Back Country
Office

Laundry,
Showers

64

Grand   Canyon

Phantom
Ranch

Clear Creek Trail

Bright Angel

Colorado

Rest Station

Mule
Bridge

Bridge

River

Indian
Gardens

Tonto Trail

South Kaibab Trail

37-A

Grand
Canyon
National
Park-
South Rim
Passage

See
Inset

Yaki Point

South Rim

East Rim Drive

180

64

to South Park Entrance,
Tusayan, and Williams

64

Forest Road	··· ─ ··· ─ ··· Boundary	(P) Trailhead and Parking
──── Paved Road	River, Stream, or Wash	◯ Trailhead, no Parking
=◻= State/Interstate	⊔⊔⊔ Canyon Rim	P Parking
Arizona Trail	△ Campground	◉ Town or City
············· Trip Access Trail	◇ Water	● Point of Interest
Other Trail Area	⌂ Ranger Station	△ Mountain Peak

THIS 23.5-MILE PASSAGE *travels from the Bright Angel trailhead on the south rim of the Grand Canyon to the North Kaibab trailhead on the north rim. Trip 37-A travels 9.3 miles from the Bright Angel Trailhead to Phantom Ranch. From Phantom Ranch, the Grand Canyon National Park–Inner Gorge Passage continues north, following the North Kaibab Trail as it climbs for 14 miles and gains over 5,000 feet in elevation.* On the Arizona Trail *does not include a detailed description of this segment of the Passage. Contact the Grand Canyon National Park for more information about trail conditions. See also* Other Area Trails *in* Trip 37-A.

   This 37th passage of the Arizona Trail is certainly one of the most spectacular! The Grand Canyon is awesome; its beauty, vastness, and diversity are inconceivable to those who have not stood on the edge and looked. Layer upon layer of colored rocks, cliffs, and pinnacles fading pink and purple into the distance, drop more than a mile to the Colorado River. The scene and the hues are forever changing as light and shadows, storm clouds, and sunsets play across the monolithic buttes and spires.

   Ancient people inhabited the Grand Canyon as long as four thousand years ago. They were followed two thousand years later by the Anasazi. The first Europeans to see the canyon were explorers from Francisco Vásquez de Coronado's expedition, in 1540. In the years that followed, other Spanish explorers, followed by Americans, explored the huge chasm. To some it was a terrifying spectacle, while others were dazzled by the canyon's beauty. Early descriptions of the canyon range from "a horrid abyss" to Theodore Roosevelt's exclaim: "The Grand Canon fills me with awe. It is beyond comparison—beyond description."

   Probably the most famous exploration of the Grand Canyon was that of Major John Wesley Powell: In May of 1869 ten men with four wooden boats began their expedition to explore the length of the Colorado River. One of Powell's party left before they reached the Colorado. Powell's wooden boats took a beating in the rapids, and many supplies were *lost. On August 15 Powell discovered and named Bright Angel Creek. On August 28 three of the crew, exhausted and discouraged, decided to abandon the expedition. Their plan was to climb up out of the canyon and attempt to make their way across the desert to the nearest settlement, some 70 miles away. They did not survive. On August 30th the remaining 6 voyagers arrived at the Virgin River and the end of the adventure; the first to pass through the Grand Canyon by water.*

The Havasupai people still live in the Grand Canyon area, and have been there since ancient times. Tucked away in a side canyon, they were isolated from the rest of the world for centuries. Havasupai Canyon is captivatingly beautiful. Turquoise-colored water that emerges from a spring at the head of the canyon thunders down over a series of spectacular waterfalls and travertine pools. The abundant water has created a lush riparian habitat. Havasupai has the only post office in the United States where the U.S. mail is still transported by pack animals.

Phantom Ranch was built for tourism in 1903. Originally called Rust's Camp, the name was changed to Roosevelt's Camp following a visit by Theodore Roosevelt in 1913. In 1922 the camp was enlarged and renamed Phantom Ranch. The ranch has a restaurant, dorms, and private cabins.

GOVERNING AGENCIES

Kaibab National Forest, Tusayan Ranger District, P.O. Box 3088, Grand Canyon, AZ 86023. (520) 638-2443.

Grand Canyon National Park, P.O. Box 129, Grand Canyon, AZ 86023. (520) 638-7771.

FOR MORE INFORMATION

Grand Canyon Chamber of Commerce, P.O. Box 3007, Grand Canyon, AZ 86023. (520) 638-2901.

Backcountry office, Box 129, Grand Canyon, AZ 86023. (520) 638-7888.

NEAREST SERVICES TO BRIGHT ANGEL TRAILHEAD

Grand Canyon Village: has a store, post office, and bank. Showers and laundromats are available at Mather Campground and Trailer Village.

Phantom Ranch: has a restaurant, lodging, and a pay phone.

Van shuttle service for rim-to-rim travelers is available through Trans Canyon Van Service (520) 638-2820 and South Rim Travel 1-800-682-4393.

Trip 37-A

Bright Angel Trailhead to Phantom Ranch

The end of this trip is not accessible by vehicle, and permits and reservations are required for overnight stays. Travelers may backtrack, make a loop using the South Kaibab Trail or follow the North Kaibab Trail to the north rim of the canyon.

This trip is extremely strenuous. There is a change in elevation of almost 4,500 feet. Summer temperatures may climb above 110 degrees Fahrenheit and there is little shade. Hikers need to be in condition, acclimated to the heat, and carry plenty of water. We recommend a planning minimum of two days for this trip. Hiking up may take twice as long as hiking down.

The steep, narrow trail is populated with large numbers of hikers, tourists, and the Grand Canyon mule trains. Remember mules have the right-of-way. Step off the trail and stand quietly as they pass. Dogs, llamas, and pack goats are not allowed on inner-canyon trails.

Bicycles are restricted to roads within the park and are prohibited on inner-canyon trails. Although the canyon is less than 20 miles wide, it is more than 215 miles by road from the south to the north rim (see Nearest Services in the Passage information for shuttle services).

Following the Bright Angel Trail, Trip 37-A travels from the trailhead on the south rim of the Grand Canyon to Phantom Ranch and Bright Angel Campground at the bottom of the Grand Canyon.

Framed by sweeping vistas, the Arizona Trail follows the sun-baked ledges of the Bright Angel Trail, one of the most popular hiking trails in the world. The Grand Canyon is another example of stacked biotic communities, and as the trail drops through colorful layers of geologic time, the temperature goes up. Passing through the desert oasis of Indian Gardens, the route continues to the Colorado River. Crossing a suspension bridge, this trip ends at historic, turn-of-the-twentieth-century Phantom Ranch.

Nature Highlight: At Indian Gardens a beautiful collared lizard watches us from atop a rock. His fancy black and white collar and bright blue throat are iridescent in the sun.

Maps:

- Kaibab National Forest, Tusayan Ranger District.
- USGS Quads: Bright Angel, Grand Canyon, Phantom Ranch.

Difficulty: Very difficult.

Length: 9.3 miles, one way.

Elevation: 6,840–2,440 feet.

Recommended Season: All seasons, with caution. In the summer, temperatures may exceed 110 degrees Fahrenheit in the lower elevations of the canyon. In winter, there will be snow on the rims. (The north rim is closed in the winter.)

Water: Potable water is available at shelters and campgrounds within the canyon May through September.

* South Rim.
* Three rest shelters along the route.
* Indian Gardens.
* Bright Angel Campground.

Camping: All campgrounds within the park require reservations, and campgrounds within the inner canyon require a backcountry permit. Camping is restricted to designated areas. Indian Gardens and Bright Angel are developed campgrounds. Reservations for National Park Service–operated campgrounds are in demand and need to be made as early as possible.

Livestock: Dogs, llamas, and pack goats are not allowed on inner-canyon trails. There is a South Rim Horse Camp that accesses the Bright Angel Trailhead. With appropriate permits, which must be obtained from the backcountry reservations office, camping with livestock is possible in designated areas. We recommend careful consideration. Obviously, only well-conditioned, well-trained, gentle, healthy, and properly shod stock should be taken into the Grand Canyon. You will be sharing a steep, narrow trail with large numbers of hikers, tourists, and the Grand Canyon mule trains. An unruly animal could injure not only the rider but other people who are visiting the canyon.

Animals need to be in condition (used to long, steep, switchbacking trails and acclimated to the heat). Wear hiking boots; if you have not adequately prepared your animal you can walk and lead him out. It is inhumane to take an animal that is not in condition on a trip like this. There are regulations regarding feed, water, and manure. A private stock use handout is available from the backcountry office listed in the passage information. (See appendix B for more information.)

Directions to Bright Angel Trailhead: From Flagstaff follow U.S. 180 north approximatly 80 miles to Grand Canyon National Park. Continue to Grand Canyon Village. The trailhead is just to the west of the Bright Angel Lodge.

Other Area Trails: The **South Kaibab Trail** provides the opportunity for a loop trip back to the south rim. There are shuttles available.

The Arizona Trail follows the **North Kaibab Trail** as it travels toward Utah. Note that there are no services or overnight facilities available on the North Rim from October 15th through May 15th because of snow. The roads into the North Rim are also closed at this time. The North Kaibab Trail is an extremely strenuous, 14-mile-long climb that gains over 5,000 feet in elevation. The route follows Bright Angel Creek, offering water access and the chance to explore beautiful Ribbon Falls (5.5 miles from Phantom Ranch). During the spring snowmelt, beware of dangerous flash floods when in rainy weather on the trail. From Phantom Ranch, it is 7.2 miles to Cottonwood Camp (permit required). Contact Grand Canyon National Park for more information about the North Kaibab Trail, the route of the Arizona Trail, and other area trails in the Park.

TRAIL DESCRIPTION

From the rim of the canyon the Arizona Trail follows Bright Angel Trail in a steep, 3,000-foot descent over the first 3 miles. The trail passes through two tunnels cut into the rock. As the elevation drops, the vegetation changes from the large ponderosa and fir along the rim of the canyon to smaller juniper and pinyon of the Upper Sonoran life zone.

One and one-half miles from the trailhead the trail reaches the first of three small shelters along the route. The shelters have emergency phones and drinking water from May until the end of September. Views are breathtaking as the trail continues to switchback down. Watch for the bright green trees of Indian Gardens below. After passing the second shelter, the trail levels along the Tonto Plateau.

The Bright Angel/Arizona Trail arrives at Indian Gardens 4.5 miles from the trailhead. Indian Gardens has a campground, reliable drinking water, a picnic area, and a ranger station. Garden Creek has created a riparian oasis surrounded by desert. This area offers good wildlife and bird watching opportunities and makes a nice halfway rest stop.

From Indian Gardens turn right at a signed junction and follow the Bright Angel/Arizona Trail as it passes the pump house that supplies water to the south rim. At a junction with Tonto Trail, stay left. The route crosses Garden Creek several times then makes a steep descent down a long series of switchbacks to Pipe Creek. The trail follows Pipe Creek to a point near the Colorado River, where the third rest shelter is located, with an emergency phone and restroom.

At 7.7 miles from the trailhead, near the river and the shelter, is a junction. The Bright Angel Trail ends here and the River Trail begins. Turn right (east) and follow the River/Arizona Trail as it travels above the rushing, turbulent water. (The river has a dangerous current and swimming is prohibited.) The trail follows the river for a little over a mile to a steel suspension bridge. Cross the bridge to the Bright Angel Campground and Phantom Ranch.

Through-travelers planning to continue up the North Kaibab Trail, see *Other Area Trails* (Trip 37-A) and contact Grand Canyon National Park for more information.

38 Grand Canyon National Park—North Rim Passage
North Kaibab Trailhead to National Park/ National Forest Boundary

As of this writing, sections of the Arizona Trail in this passage are not yet completed. This description outlines the *proposed route* of the Arizona Trail through this passage; it is not intended to be used as a trail guide. Much of the information included here is taken from an Arizona Trail management guide designed not for recreational use but for use in planning, developing, and managing the trail. Contact the governing agency or The Arizona Trail Association for more information on the route, signage, availability of water, and completion status of this passage.

WHEN COMPLETED, *this passage will travel from the North Kaibab trailhead on the north rim of the Grand Canyon to FR 610 within the Kaibab National Forest. The forests in this area are spectacular, featuring aspen, fir, spruce, and alpine meadows. Kaibab mule deer are frequently seen.*

PROPOSED ROUTE

Planning continues for this passage. The proposed route will follow new trail to an area just east of the north rim entrance station. From there it will leave the park and enter the Kaibab National Forest to a connection with the southern terminus of the Kaibab Plateau Trail #101.

GOVERNING AGENCIES

Kaibab National Forest, North Kaibab Ranger District, P.O. Box 248, Fredonia, AZ 86022. (520) 642-7395.

FOR MORE INFORMATION

Grand Canyon National Park, P.O. Box 129, Grand Canyon, AZ 86023. (520) 638-7771.

NEAREST SERVICES

Nearest services are at North Rim Village.

A rider and his horse take a leisurely walk through an isolated high-alpine meadow on the Kaibab plateau.

I long to see the clear blue skies in the summer,
*   The golden quaking aspen in fall.*
Winter snows cover all, then comes the springtime thaw
*   The season that I love most of all.*

—"Arizona Mountain Home," Earl T. (Slim) Tighe, 1996
(Used with permission.)

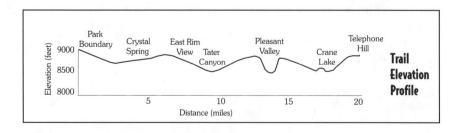

39 Kaibab Plateau Trail— Southern Passage

National Park/National Forest Boundary to Telephone Hill

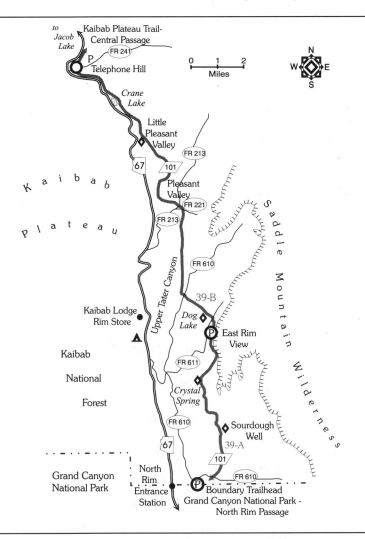

to Jacob Lake

Kaibab Plateau Trail- Central Passage

FR 241

P

Telephone Hill

Crane Lake

0   1   2
Miles

N
W   E
S

Little Pleasant Valley

FR 213

K a i b a b

67   101

Pleasant Valley

FR 221

P l a t e a u

FR 213

S a d d l e

Upper Tater Canyon

FR 610

39-B

M o u n t a i n

Kaibab Lodge Rim Store

Dog Lake

P East Rim View

FR 611

Kaibab

Crystal Spring

W i l d e r n e s s

National

Forest

FR 610

Sourdough Well

39-A

67   101

Grand Canyon National Park

North Rim Entrance Station

P Boundary Trailhead
Grand Canyon National Park - North Rim Passage

FR 610

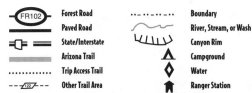

FR102	Forest Road	P Trailhead and Parking
	Paved Road	O Trailhead, no Parking
	State/Interstate	P Parking
	Arizona Trail	▲ Campground
	Trip Access Trail	◆ Water
--122--	Other Trail Area	⌂ Ranger Station
	Boundary	Ⓟ Town or City
	River, Stream, or Wash	● Point of Interest
	Canyon Rim	△ Mountain Peak

T HIS 20-MILE PASSAGE *is divided into two trips. Trip 39-A travels 7 miles from the national park boundary to East Rim View, which is on a forest road east of the Kaibab Lodge. Trip 39-B travels 13 miles from East Rim View to* FR 241.

The Arizona Trail travels north from the Grand Canyon National Park border, following the eastern edge of the Kaibab Plateau, the highest of the five plateaus that make up the north rim of the Grand Canyon. The route offers spectacular vistas of the Saddle Mountain Wilderness, House Rock Valley, the Vermilion Cliffs, and Marble Canyon. The DeMotte burn area showcases the important role that aspen trees play in forest regeneration after a forest fire. The trail winds through spruce, fir, pine, and aspen forest, high grassland parks, and beautiful, lush, alpine meadows. The final ascent of Telephone Hill displays the remains of an original fire lookout tree, a predecessor to the metal fire towers used by forest rangers today.

The roads are closed from November 15 to May 15; however, the Kaibab Lodge provides travel by "Snow Vans" into the area for skiing. Contact the lodge for information and reservations.

Aspen trees are dependent on forest fires for their survival. Forest fires create openings in dense coniferous forests that allow enough sunlight for aspen roots to sprout. After ten to twenty years the young aspen are large enough to shade the soil below them, creating a cooler environment for conifer seeds to sprout. After one hundred to one hundred and fifty years the conifers grow taller than the aspen that "nurse" them, and the aspen die off.

More than ninety species of birds and fifty species of mammals live on the Kaibab Plateau, including several that are found no where else. For example, the Kaibab squirrel is a gorgeous creature, with a dark gray body and a lovely white, feathery, plume of a tail. Its long ears are decorated with tassels at the ends. Unlike some of the noisier species that scold intruders from the tree tops, Kaibab squirrels are quiet and reluctant to show themselves. It is believed that the Kaibab squirrel became isolated from its long-eared Abert's squirrel cousins eons ago and developed its own distinctive coloring.

Renowned for their large size and huge racks, the Kaibab mule deer is another famous inhabitant of the Kaibab Plateau. In 1906 Congress and Theodore Roosevelt created a Grand Canyon Game Preserve for the protection and breeding of game animals. Hunting was prohibited, and predator control was initiated to protect the deer. Wolves were completely eliminated from the area, and mountain lion were also killed in great numbers. This resulted in a population explosion of the deer by 1924 that led to disease, starvation, and a massive die-off of the Kaibab deer. The die-off emphasized to game managers throughout the nation the importance of controlling deer populations in line with the habitat's capacity to produce forage. Since 1948 management of the herd has improved through the reintroduction of hunting, predator population recovery, and direct habitat development. Habitat development, which includes over one hundred water sources and thousands of acres of forage improvement, is funded by the timber industry and by hunting fees.

A Mormon cooperative, the Orderville United Order, ran stock in DeMotte Park in the late 1870s. During the late 1800s, up to thousands of cattle and sheep grazed seasonally on the North Kaibab. Along with the early ranching, there were some attempts at farming in the 1870s. In 1879 wheat was planted in DeMotte Park. Tater Canyon received its name from a potato farm in the area. In addition to the farms, the United Order also established dairy cooperatives. Because of the short growing season, inadequate water, and poor soil, farming experiments on the Kaibab Plateau were never successful.

GOVERNING AGENCIES

Kaibab National Forest, North Kaibab Ranger District. P.O. Box 248, Fredonia, AZ 86002-0038. (520) 643-7395.

FOR MORE INFORMATION

Kaibab Plateau Visitor Center in Jacob Lake. (520) 643-7298.
Kaibab Lodge. (520) 638-2389 for reservations and information.
Grand Canyon National Park. See Grand Canyon National Park—Inner Gorge Passage for information.

NEAREST SERVICES TO BOUNDARY TRAILHEAD

North Rim Country Store: located across from the Kaibab Lodge; open mid-May to mid-November.

Grand Canyon North Rim: has showers, store, and laundromat.

Jacob Lake: Lodge, restaurant, store, gas station, and visitor center are 26.5 miles north on SR 67.

Trip 39-A

Grand Canyon National Park Boundary to East Rim View

This is a great bicycle and equestrian trip, with one very steep climb.

Trip 39-A travels from Boundary Trailhead to East Rim View, approximatly 4 miles east of Kaibab Lodge. This trip is a scenic ramble from Grand Canyon National Park, along the eastern edge of the Kaibab Plateau. Following beautiful, alpine Upper North Canyon, the gently rolling trail passes two small spring-fed ponds. The final steep ascent to East Rim View offers magnificent vistas of the Saddle Mountain Wilderness, House Rock Valley, Vermilion Cliffs, and Marble Canyon.

Nature Highlight: The renowned large-antlered Kaibab mule deer are seen singly along the trail and in greater numbers at dusk, along perimeters of meadows.

Maps:
* Kaibab National Forest.
* USGS Quad: DeMotte Park.

Difficulty: Easy to moderate, ending with a steep climb.

Length: 7 miles, one way.

Elevation: 9,000–8,600 feet.

Recommended Season: Grand Canyon National Park and the roads into this area close from November 15 to May 15.

Contact the Kaibab Lodge for information on winter skiing.

Water: (Treat all water unless noted otherwise. During dry weather, water sources may not be dependable.)
* None at the trailheads.
* **Sourdough Well:** 2 miles north of FR 610.
* **Crystal Spring:** 4.5 miles north of FR 610.

Camping: Grand Canyon National Park boundary trailhead: On FR 610, the trailhead is a pull-through marked by log rail fences. The trailhead offers primitive camping, one rest room, but no water.

DeMotte Campground is the nearest developed campground south of the Kaibab Lodge on SR 67.

Livestock: Grand Canyon National Park boundary trailhead has a livestock staging area with two hitching rails and plenty of room to pull in with rigs. The area has some grass, but no water.

The north rim of the Grand Canyon has a horse camp. See Trip 37-A and Appendix B, or contact Grand Canyon National Park for information.

Directions to Boundary Trailhead: You can access the trailhead by passenger car. Follow SR 67 from Jacob Lake south toward the Grand Canyon. Half a mile south of Kaibab Lodge turn left onto FR 611 and travel to the junction with FR 610. Turn right on FR 610 and travel 4.8 miles to the trailhead, marked by an aspen log fence, on the right side of the road.

Other Area Trails: North Canyon Trail #4: See Trip 39-B.

TRAIL DESCRIPTION

If you wish to start your trip from the actual park boundary, follow the path that leaves from the east side of the trailhead pull-through, between the rest room and the rail fence. This spur trail drops down a hill into a grassy north/south drainage, intersecting the Arizona Trail. It is 0.3-mile south to the national park border, marked by a barbwire fence and a gate.

If you don't care about starting at the park boundary, just follow FR 610 east a short distance to the brown carsonite markers below the roadbed on either side, indicating the route of the Arizona Trail as it crosses FR 610. The Arizona Trail follows the route of the Kaibab Plateau Trail #101 (KPT/AT) as it follows Upper North Canyon. Upper North Canyon is a grassy, flat-bottomed drainage, rimmed on the west and east with mixed conifer trees and aspen. Carsonite markers lead us to an abandoned dirt road, and the route continues on the road heading north. The route takes a gentle downhill grade to a T junction of canyons.

At the junction the route turns left (west), following carsonite markers, and passes the confluence of another drainage coming from the left then continues curving north. Following the grassy canyon, rimmed with aspen and evergreen trees, the route appears to be an abandoned roadbed that is fairly level with a slight uphill grade. As the canyon narrows and the route enters a more wooded area, the trail curves around to the west, traveling through a beautiful area of aspen and evergreen, and grassy meadows.

Two miles from the park boundary, the trail arrives at Sourdough Well and a junction. A large cement well cover is visible to the right of the trail. Although the old road we have been following curves to the left, the Kaibab Plateau Trail/Arizona Trail continues north, passing a pond with water. The trail veers west 0.25 mile beyond the pond and begins climbing out of the canyon. It is a moderate ascent up a grassy drainage with trees on each side. The trail is marked by rock cairns until it enters the trees. Although trail markers are infrequent, the trail is distinct and easy to follow as it winds uphill through a forest of large aspen and fir. The trail tops out and then descends steeply into a grassy ravine. After a steep climb out of the drainage, the trail winds through a forest of golden aspen and evergreens, with open sunny areas.

Three miles from the park boundary the trail crosses two abandoned dirt roads. The first, marked by a rock cairn, and a short distance farther, the second, marked on both sides with carsonite markers. The trail drops down through a forest of small fir and aspen trees to a wooden sign identifying Kaibab Plateau Trail #101. Carsonite markers indicate the route as the trail adjoins FR 612A, traveling north. After passing through a large open meadow ringed with aspen and fir, the road forks. The route continues straight, ignoring the fork to the left.

At 4.5 miles from the park boundary the trail arrives at Crystal Spring, and a very pretty, large pond. The Kaibab Plateau Trail/Arizona Trail continues north past the pond, following the canyon. An intermittent little stream runs through this lovely tree-rimmed meadow. At 0.5 mile from Crystal Spring our route intersects a path to the left. (North Canyon Trail #4 travels approximately 1 mile west to FR 611. For information on North Canyon Trail #4, see Trip 39-B.) There may be some discrepancies in posted mileages in this area.

Just past the junction with North Canyon Trail #4, the route begins the most difficult part of this trek, as it abandons North Canyon for the long ascent to East Rim View. The trail climbs a short distance to a signed junction. North Canyon Trail #4, which has been paralleling our route since the last junction, cuts off to the right. There are no Arizona Trail markers here. Stay to the left, following signs for East Rim View.

After a moderately steep climb the trail tops out, offering scenic views of Upper North Canyon and the Saddle Mountain Wilderness. As the trail resumes its ascent through a dense fir and aspen forest, the views are hidden by the trees. After a long climb the trail levels out with some great views of Marble Canyon to the northeast. The trail passes some interesting rock outcroppings that frame a view of the distant Vermilion Cliffs. To the east you can see the pink walls of Marble Canyon, below Lee's Ferry. Alternating between dense forest and the rim of the canyon, the trail goes a short distance to a carsonite marker and a sign announcing the end of this trip at East Rim View.

Trip 39-B

East Rim View to Telephone Hill

This one- or two-day trip offers nice camping opportunities along the trail and is a great bicycle and equestrian route.

Trip 39-B travels from a scenic overlook east of Kaibab Lodge to FR 241 south of Jacob Lake. From splendid, sweeping views of House Rock Valley, the Vermilion Cliffs, and Marble Canyon, the Arizona Trail passes through a peaceful and unfrequented landscape of high grassland parks, fir, pine, and aspen forests and secluded alpine meadows. Passing charming little Crane Lake, the Arizona Trail follows SR 67 a short distance, before ascending Telephone Hill to the site of a historic fire lookout tree.

Nature Highlight: Beautiful "quaking aspen" with their graceful white trunks and shimmering foliage decorate the trail.

Maps:
- Kaibab National Forest map.
- USGS Quad: DeMotte Park, Jacob Lake.

Difficulty: Easy to moderate.

Length: 13 miles, one way.

Elevation: 8,800–8,300 feet.

Recommended Season: Grand Canyon National Park and the roads into this area close from November 15 to May 15.

Water: (Treat all water unless noted otherwise. During dry weather, water sources may not be dependable.)
- Trailheads: None
- **Dog Lake:** 0.5 mile north of East Rim View (shortly after crossing FR 611).
- **Little Pleasant Valley Pond.**
- **Crane Lake:** A wildlife pond that is fenced and not accessible to livestock. There is no other water for many miles.

Camping: East Rim View offers lots of great places to camp in. There are flat areas with shade, fire pits, two privies, but no water and no other amenities. If you will be driving in, bring your own firewood and water.

Along the route you will find primitive camping opportunities. The nearest developed campground is DeMotte Campground, south of the Kaibab Lodge.

Livestock: East Rim View has plenty of room to park and turn trailers. There is some grass, but the closest water is Dog Lake, 0.5 mile north on the Arizona Trail, shortly after crossing FR 611. Carry a collapsible bucket for accessing wildlife tanks.

Directions to East Rim View Trailhead: The trailhead can be accessed by passenger car. Follow SR 67 from Jacob Lake south toward the Grand Canyon. One-half mile south of Kaibab Lodge, turn left onto FR 611 and travel 4 miles to East Rim View.

Other Area Trails: East Rim Trail #7 is a steep 1.5-mile trail that drops down off the rim, connecting with North Canyon Trail #4.
- **North Canyon Trail #4** is a scenic trail that enters the Saddle Mountain Wilderness Area. It is accessed from FR 611, 2.7 miles from Highway 67. It may also be accessed by heading south on the Arizona Trail (Kaibab Trail #101) for 2 miles, or by taking East Rim Trail #7.

For more information on these or other trails in the area, contact the Kaibab Ranger District.

TRAIL DESCRIPTION

Entering East Rim View from the road, there are hiking symbols indicating hiking trails to the north and south. Proceed directly ahead to the overlook and admire the spectacular view. You are on the Arizona Trail.

The Arizona Trail follows Kaibab Plateau Trail 101 (KPT/AT) along the edge of the Kaibab Plateau. Turn left (north) and follow along the rim to a place where logs have been placed across to block traffic and the dirt road turns left. Do not follow the road. Go around the logs, following a path along the rim. It is a short distance to signs identifying Kaibab Plateau Trail #101 and a junction with trail #7 heading into the Saddle Mountain Wilderness. Continuing along the rim, the trail adjoins an abandoned dirt road, winding through a pretty aspen forest to a brown carsonite Arizona Trail marker. Here, the route leaves the road, cutting left to FR 611.

There is a carsonite marker as the route crosses FR 611 heading west on an abandoned dirt road that has been barricaded to vehicle use. Traveling through aspen, fir, and ponderosa on a gentle downhill grade, it is a short distance to Dog Lake. One-half mile from East Rim View is a jewel: the beautiful little aspen-ringed pond called Dog Lake. There is a feeling of stillness and serenity in this quiet, secluded place.

The route continues west, entering a large, rolling, grassy park ringed with aspen and fir. Crossing a faint junction, the road continues west to a carsonite marker where the meadow ends and the old road heads into the trees. Just after the trail enters the trees, a marker indicates that it leaves the road to the left, beginning a gentle uphill climb through a dense forest of large aspen, fir, and ponderosa.

The junction with FR 610 is 1.6 miles from FR 611. The trail crosses FR 610 heading west. After crossing the road the trail descends moderately and then more steeply, culminating in a series of switchbacks, to the bottom of Tater Canyon. Carsonite markers indicate that the Arizona Trail adjoins an abandoned road traveling north up Tater Canyon for 2.5 miles. Tater Canyon is an appealing, wide, prairie-like valley, several miles long. After 1.5 miles the road forks. The route of the KPT/AT stays to the right, continuing to follow Tater Canyon. As the route takes a sharp left, curving uphill toward the trees, a series of carsonite markers indicates where the KPT/AT abandons the road, striking off to the right, and continues to follow the canyon in a northwest direction. A short distance farther the trail joins another abandoned road it follows to the right (north).

The trail drops down a hill over aspen logs that have been placed for erosion control. Curving left over some small grassy hills, the route, marked by rock cairns, travels west. To the left is an area of burned aspen trees, as the trail begins a gradual climb out of Tater Canyon. Rock cairns and erosion-control logs mark the route, as the trail ascends a grassy slope. Views of Tater Canyon disappear as the trail crests a small hill, leaving the grassy shoulder of the canyon, for a gradual timbered climb to FR 213A.

You meet FR 213A, announced by an aspen rail fence 5.2 miles from East Rim View. FR 213A is closed to the public. There is no vehicle access from SR 67.

The trail crosses FR 213A heading northwest and traverses a small drainage. Topping out at a carsonite marker, the trail enters an open woodland of aspen, fir, and ponderosa, then descends to the bottom of a ravine that shelters a tiny pond, the only water since Dog Lake. The trail leaves the ravine, climbing up a small drainage, to an intersection with FR 221. After crossing FR 221, the trail enters an area of new growth aspen, and soon after crosses FR 213. A short distance farther the trail crosses another well-used but unsigned dirt road, and then follows an abandoned road curving uphill to the northwest. This is the DeMotte burn area, site of a large fire in 1977.

The trail climbs through new growth aspen and small evergreens, topping out on a hill with beautiful views to the left of aspen-covered hills. This is a nice view of the burn area and how it is recovering from the fire. First the aspen appear, and then, small evergreens, the groves of young trees punctuated randomly by the huge burned snags of giant trees that perished in the fire.

The KPT/AT drops downhill toward a barbwire fence and then veers to the right (north), beginning a gradual climb into an older part of the forest. The route follows a forested rolling ridgeline above Pleasant Valley. The trail leaves the forest to descend a grassy, bush-covered slope marked by rock cairns. Grass and vegetation could hide the path as it turns east. The trail continues in a moderate descent through aspen and fir woodland, with views to the left of Pleasant Valley.

The trail enters another burn area and in this area is not as clearly defined. Watch for logs and rocks that have been placed to mark the route as the trail takes a sharp left (west), dropping down an old grassy roadbed toward Pleasant Valley. The grade continues, but the path is unsigned. The KPT/AT veers to the right. Watch for a log across the old roadbed and some rocks piled on the right. Passing a carsonite marker, the path drops out of the trees, affording a grand view of Pleasant Valley. It is an easy descent down the grassy slope to the dirt road and signs below. The view to the west is impressive; the golden grasslands of the valley rolling away to meet distant conifer-covered ridges.

Seven miles from East Rim View, the KPT/AT leaves Pleasant Valley, following the dirt road north as it ascends the shadeless hillside, curving up toward the forested ridge above. The road tops out in a potentially confusing junction of old logging tracks. A carsonite marker indicates that the route leaves the road it has been following, to turn left at the first intersection with a fainter road coming from the left. Follow this abandoned road a short distance to another junction with old logging roads coming in from both directions. Watch carefully for carsonite markers. The trail continues north, straight across those roads, into a canopy of aspen trees, following a faint path that may be difficult to see.

The trail travels through big ponderosa, fir, and aspen trees. The route traverses a drainage and soon after makes an easy descent into the beautiful, green, alpine meadow of Little Pleasant Valley. Crossing to an abandoned dirt road, the KPT/AT turns west, following the road as it skirts the north side of the meadow. There is water here; a pond to the left of the trail. At the west end of the park the road enters the forest, passing an old wooden corral on the left. The trees soon give way to a second lush alpine meadow. This lovely park also has a pond, complete with waterfowl.

Nine miles from East Rim View is a junction. The KPT/AT continues as a narrow path, traveling around the east side of the pond. (The old road we have been following turns left [west], traveling the south side of the park and entering the trees at the western end, where it terminates at Highway 67.)

At the north end of the pond, an Arizona Trail marker indicates that the trail turns east into the trees, then north as it begins to climb out of the deepening drainage that provides water to the pond below. As the trail winds through the trees, the ascent steepens, climbing through a shady forest of huge ponderosa, to top out in an area of obscure logging roads. A carsonite marker shows the way as the trail curves to the northwest, roller coasters several shallow drainages, then turns west for the descent to SR 67.

Ten miles from East Rim View the KPT/AT skirts a meadow and then, leaving the trees, parallels SR 67 for a short distance. Abandoning the highway and heading north through a pretty aspen and fir woodland, the trail makes a short climb to an old wooden corral. The trail passes through the corral, and it is an easy descent to the vast and beautiful alpine park that harbors Crane Lake.

Eleven miles from East Rim View, Crane Lake is nestled in the center of a large, open park, bordered on the east and west by forest-clad ridges. The lake is completely fenced and not accessible to livestock. SR 67 and the KPT/AT both traverse this high mountain grassland in a north-south direction. Continuing north, following markers and rock cairns, the trail enters a stand of ancient aspen trees at the north end of the park. One tree near the trail bears the inscription "Emron Robinson 1934." It is 2 miles to Telephone Hill and FR 241. The trail ascends, then ambles down a small hill, passing through a beautiful old-growth canopy of ponderosa, aspen, and fir. A carsonite marker indicates where the route joins an abandoned dirt road dropping downhill to the north, and then takes a sharp left (west), toward the highway.

Again paralleling the highway, the trail is indistinct in places, concealed by the grass. After a short distance, the highway curves off to the west and the trail continues north, marked periodically by rock cairns. As the trail returns to the trees and begins to climb, it veers to the left, ascending the ridgeline above the highway. As the angle of ascent steepens, the route offers occasional glimpses of the highway below. The path levels off, then climbs again, following a barbed wire fence to a gate. The trail passes through the gate and then turns west following the ridgeline of Telephone Hill. In places the route is marked by long sticks placed end to end.

One-half mile from the gate, watch for a wooden marker identifying a historic forest service lookout tree. Beyond the sign the huge dead tree has fallen, the remains of the ladder still attached. Just beyond the wood sign is a marker identifying where the KPT/AT leaves the road it has been following and swings to the right. From here, it is an easy descent through the forest to FR 241.

40 Kaibab Plateau Trail— Central Passage

Telephone Hill to Orderville Trailhead

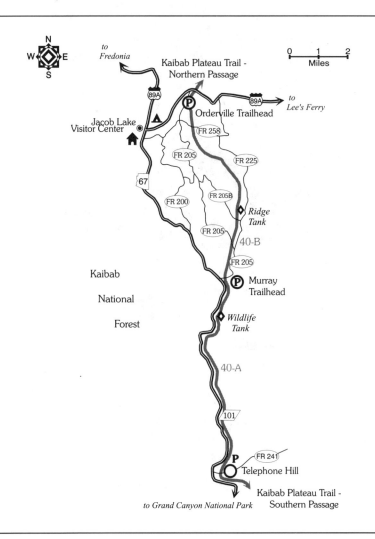

N
W E
S

to Fredonia

Kaibab Plateau Trail - Northern Passage

0 1 2
Miles

89A

89A

to Lee's Ferry

P

Orderville Trailhead

Jacob Lake Visitor Center

FR 258

FR 205

FR 225

67

FR 200

FR 205B

Ridge Tank

40-B

FR 205

FR 205

P Murray Trailhead

Wildlife Tank

Kaibab

National

Forest

40-A

101

P

FR 241

Telephone Hill

Kaibab Plateau Trail - Southern Passage

to Grand Canyon National Park

FR102	Forest Road	·· — ·· — ··	Boundary
	Paved Road	~~~~	River, Stream, or Wash
	State/Interstate		Canyon Rim
	Arizona Trail		Campground
··········	Trip Access Trail	◆	Water
− −122− −	Other Trail Area		Ranger Station

P Trailhead and Parking
O Trailhead, no Parking
P Parking
◉ Town or City
● Point of Interest
△ Mountain Peak

A ladder from a fallen fire lookout tree as seen on Telephone Hill along the Kaibab Plateau Trail–Central Passage.

Photo by Kelly Tighe

Gone—the years fly on, old pardner,
And the last, faint wheel tracks fade;
We are scattered like the ashes
Of the campfires that we made.

—**"The Old Trailer," Badger Clark, 1907**

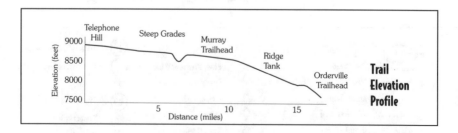

Trail Elevation Profile

THIS 17-MILE PASSAGE *is divided into two trips. Trip 40-A travels 8 miles from Telephone Hill to* FR 205, *south of Jacob Lake. Trip 40-B travels 9 miles from* FR 205 *to U.S. 89A, east of Jacob Lake.*

The Arizona Trail rolls across the Kaibab Plateau, on a mostly downhill route, beneath shady forest canopies of mature aspen and pine. Following a series of charming old logging tracks, the trail parallels the route of SR 67; *however, the highway is almost never in view. Delightfully shady groves of huge, old-growth aspen create a spectacular autumn showing. A short side trip affords magnificent vistas of House Rock Valley and the Vermilion Cliffs, before the trail makes a gentle descent down a serene and pleasantly wooded canyon.*

This portion of the Arizona Trail, the Kaibab Plateau Trail, was the very first segment of the Arizona Trail to be completed and dedicated in 1988. It was a wonderful cooperative effort between Kaibab National Forest, Kaibab Forest Products Company, and the Sierra Club.

There are views from the trail of House Rock Valley. The valley received its name from an early area rancher who spent a night in the shelter of some large boulders. In the morning, using a piece of charcoal from his fire, he printed "House Rock Hotel" on the boulder. As a result, the area became known as House Rock Valley.

Shortly after the Grand Canyon Game Preserve was established in 1906, a mountain man, buffalo hunter and scout, Charles C. Jones, acquired a small herd of buffalo that he brought to the Kaibab Plateau (the American bison is not native to Arizona). Jones had a plan to cross-breed cattle with buffalo and formed a partnership with some local investors. The "cattalo" venture was not a great success, and the animals were sold to the State of Arizona in 1926. Today a free-ranging herd of seventy-five to one hundred buffalo is maintained. These impressive animals are sometimes seen in the area of House Rock Valley Ranch, 41 miles east of Jacob Lake and 21 miles south of U.S. 89A. Contact the North Kaibab Ranger District or visitor center for more information.

Aspen graffiti dating from the 1870s through the 1930s was left by sheep herders and other early travelers on the Kaibab Plateau. Whereas graffiti left by early pioneers is interesting, carving aspen trees today is vandalism, and it is illegal. Please respect our forests and do not scar the trees.

A century ago California condors lived in the area of the Vermilion Cliffs, a 1,500-foot promontory 10 miles east of U.S. 89A trailhead. The Vermilion Cliffs are part of the Paria Canyon–Vermilion Cliffs Wilderness. The endangered birds have recently been reintroduced to this remote area.

GOVERNING AGENCIES

Kaibab National Forest, North Kaibab Ranger District, Box 248, Fredonia, AZ 86022. (520) 643-7395.

FOR MORE INFORMATION

North Kaibab Visitor Center on Jacob Lake. (520) 643-7298.

NEAREST SERVICES TO TELEPHONE HILL

Jacob Lake is 13 miles north on SR 67.
There is a store, a restaurant, a gas station, and a lodge. The closest laundromat and showers are within the national park.

Trip 40-A

Telephone Hill (FR 241) to Murray Trailhead (FR 205)

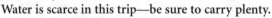 This trip has excellent mountain biking and equestrian trails. The route traverses one steep canyon that may prove difficult for bicyclists and cross-country skiers.

Water is scarce in this trip—be sure to carry plenty.

Trip 40-A travels from FR 241 south of Jacob Lake to Murray trailhead at FR 205. The Arizona Trail follows a delightful old logging route that rolls through a mature pine and aspen forest, as it crosses the Kaibab Plateau. Although a large portion of the route parallels SR 67, the road is almost never in view.

Nature Highlight: A beautiful Kaibab squirrel, with its long, tasseled ears and gorgeous plume of a tail scampers to hide itself on the back side of a ponderosa pine.

Maps:
- Kaibab National Forest Map (North).
- USGS Quad: Telephone Hill, Jacob Lake.

Difficulty: Easy to moderate, with one section of steep switchbacks.

Length: 8 miles, one way.

Elevation: 8,800–8,400 feet.

Recommended Season: Roads are closed from November 15 through May 15 because of snow. Contact Kaibab Lodge for information on winter skiing.

Water: (Treat all water unless noted otherwise. During dry weather, water sources may not be dependable.)

There is no water at Telephone Hill or FR 205.

The only water is a wildlife tank 7 miles north of Telephone Hill and 2 miles south of FR 205. Most wildlife tanks are fenced to keep livestock out. Do not take livestock into these areas; instead, carry a collapsible water bucket to get water for your livestock.

Camping: Telephone Hill has primitive camping with shade. There is a flat area where you can pull off the road east of the trailhead, on the left. There is no water and no other amenities. If you will be driving in, bring your own water and firewood. The nearest developed campgrounds are **DeMotte Campground,** 25 miles south of Jacob Lake, or **Jacob Lake Campground,** at the junction of U.S. 89A and SR 67.

The abandoned gravel quarry offers primitive camping opportunities that are a good size for groups. The area has been closed and re-seeded. From Jacob Lake, take SR 67 approximately 9 miles south to FR 4188 near Milepost 589. Turn left.

Livestock: Telephone Hill has a flat area east of the trailhead to pull in and out with a trailer, some grass, but no water. The area is not good for large groups.

Directions to Telephone Hill: You can access the area with a passenger car. Travel south on Highway 67 from Jacob Lake, approximately 13 miles to FR 241. Turn left onto FR 241 and it is less than 0.1-mile to the point where The Kaibab Plateau Trail /Arizona Trail crosses the road.

TRAIL DESCRIPTION

The Arizona Trail follows the Kaibab Plateau Trail (KPT/AT) as it crosses FR 241 and travels north along an abandoned logging roadbed. After a gradual descent through a lovely woodland of aspen, fir, and ponderosa, the trail levels. Entering an open area, the trail disappears in the grass. Stay to the right, watching for the brown carsonite markers that mark this part of the AT.

The trail continues to follow the grassy old roadbed, crossing an unsigned junction with an abandoned road. Shortly after the junction the trail curves to the northwest, passing a marker as it begins a gentle rolling incline. The sound of vehicles on the road reminds us that although we cannot see Highway 67, our route parallels it closely at times. Topping a ridge, the route drops, rolling along below the highway. A wooden Trail #101 sign marks where the trail curves left and down.

Approximately 4.5 miles from Telephone Hill you come to the only view along this trip of the Vermilion Cliffs. Watch to the right as a vista of distant pink ramparts appears briefly, framed by aspen trees. The trail curves to the left, downhill, following just below the highway. Although they are hidden by trees, you can hear the sounds of passing vehicles. As you cross a junction with an old logging road, a blaze on a tree indicates that the trail goes left and the road continues right. The trail is faint here, and there are no other markers. When in doubt, take the route that follows closer to SR 67.

Five miles from Telephone Hill the route enters a wide-open, flat area, suitable for primitive group camping. There is plenty of room here for trucks and trailers, but no water or other amenities. This area may be accessed from SR 67 at mile post 589. If you will be driving in, bring your own water and firewood. (Those wishing to make a shorter trip can exit to the highway here.)

A wooden sign indicates that the KPT/AT continues north. Crossing a couple of abandoned logging roads, the trail joins FR 4187A, which has been closed to motor vehicles, and soon fades to a grassy roadbed. Soon after a second sign stating "No Motor Vehicles," a brown carsonite marker signals where the KPT/AT leaves the road, cutting off to the left. The trail winds through a pretty woodland of ponderosa, aspen, and juniper. CROSS-COUNTRY SKIERS AND BICYCLISTS: Approximately 1.5 miles from the gravel pit the trail drops very steeply to the bottom of a canyon. The trail follows the grassy wooded canyon bottom east, then climbs steeply, finishing with a series of switchbacks as it gains the rim of the canyon. There is a cautionary sign for cyclists and skiers on the north side.

A short distance farther the trail tops out at an abandoned dirt road and a wire-enclosed wildlife tank, the first water since Little Pleasant Valley! (If you have livestock, you may be able to climb through the fence with a collapsible bucket and retrieve water for them.) This is the only water for many miles.

The trail continues northwest, once more following the old roadbed below the highway. The route traverses a small canyon, tops out at a trail marker, and crosses an abandoned logging road. The old roadbed rolls along through a ponderosa forest, touched with fir and aspen. Following along the left side of a drainage, the route passes through dense, then open forest, punctuated by gigantic ponderosa pines. The trail climbs, topping out at a marker where the route turns left (west), crosses FR 3834, and enters the Murray Trailhead.

Trip 40-B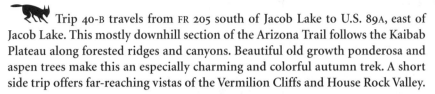

Murray Trailhead (FR 205) to Orderville Trailhead (U.S. 89A)

Trip 40-B travels from FR 205 south of Jacob Lake to U.S. 89A, east of Jacob Lake. This mostly downhill section of the Arizona Trail follows the Kaibab Plateau along forested ridges and canyons. Beautiful old growth ponderosa and aspen trees make this an especially charming and colorful autumn trek. A short side trip offers far-reaching vistas of the Vermilion Cliffs and House Rock Valley.

Wildlife Highlight: If you see an enormous bird gliding overhead, it may be a California condor! Six of the endangered birds were released in December, 1996, in the Vermilion Cliffs, just 10 miles to the east of the Orderville trailhead.

Maps:
* Kaibab National Forest Map (North).
* USGS Quads: Telephone Hill, Jacob Lake.

Difficulty: Easy to moderate.

Length: 9 miles, one way.

Elevation: 8,600–7,500 feet.

Recommended Season: May 15 to November 15, depending on the weather and road conditions. If you are skiing check with the North Kaibab Ranger District regarding vehicle access in the winter months.

Water: (Treat all water unless noted otherwise. During dry weather, water sources may not be dependable.)
* None at trailheads.
* **Ridge Tank:** Dirt tank 3 miles north of FR 205.
* **Big Ridge Tank:** Dirt tank near the gravel mine is not dependable.

Camping: Murray Trailhead has a pull-through area and a rest room. There are good primitive camping possibilities nearby, but no water and no other amenities. If you will be driving in, bring your own water and firewood.

Orderville Trailhead has a pull-through parking area for vehicles. There are flat, shady areas for primitive camping and a rest room, but no water and no other amenities. If you will be driving in, bring your own water and firewood.

The nearest developed campground is Jacob Lake Campground at the junction of U.S. 89A and SR 67.

Livestock: Murray Trailhead has a pull-through area and two hitching posts, some grass, but no water. There are some other good camping possibilities nearby.

Orderville Trailhead has a spacious pull-through with hitching posts. There is room to park several trucks and trailers. There is some grass here, but no water.

Directions to Murray Trailhead: Travel south from Jacob Lake on Highway 67 to FR 205. Turn east and travel 0.25 mile to the trailhead, marked by an aspen rail fence on the right. The junction of FR 205 and FR 3834 is just to the east of this trailhead.

Directions to Orderville (U.S. 89A) Trailhead: Orderville trailhead is on the south side of Highway 89A, 2 miles east of Jacob Lake, at the junction with FR 205.

TRAIL DESCRIPTION

The Arizona Trail follows Kaibab Plateau Trail #101 (KPT/AT) as it crosses FR 205 and enters the trees, traveling northeast. Within a short distance the trail crosses two abandoned dirt roads, the route signed with carsonite markers. The ponderosa woodland is open and airy, adorned with grand old aspens, mixed meadow grasses, and small, low-growing shrubs. The gently rolling trail ambles through the trees, to a junction with FR 205C.

Trail signs mark where the trail turns left, adjoining FR 205C heading northwest, but very shortly abandons it. The trail leaves the road cutting off to the right (north) and continues as a one-track path into a grove of aspen. The trail unexpectedly joins an abandoned dirt road coming from the left. This area is potentially confusing because the route follows the old road a short distance, then makes its unsigned exit to the left (north). For those coming from the opposite direction heading south, this junction is unsigned and easy to miss. Watch closely!

After a short distance a carsonite marker appears, guiding us north across another junction of abandoned roads. Traveling through an open forest of ponderosa, the trail makes a gentle descent into a beautiful area of mixed aspen and pine. The route continues to drop, traversing a small, aspen-shaded ravine, and tops out on a ridge. As the trail intersects another faint logging road, a trail sign indicates that the route turns left, down the ridge, adjoining the road.

In a short distance the trail abandons the old roadbed, cutting off to the right, downhill. It is not signed, so watch carefully. Carsonite markers sign where the trail crosses FR 205. After crossing the road the trail drops into a lovely sylvan setting; an enchanting canopy of large old-growth aspen, golden leaves shimmering in the Arizona sky. This is a special place, and impossible to capture in black and white.

Ascending the small drainage, the trail passes a wooden Trail #101 sign and a carsonite marker, as it continues north, meandering through charming little parks of pine and aspen. The trail encounters the first of many large ponderosa pines bearing metal tags telling us that the trees were saved as "wildlife trees." The trail becomes indistinct as it travels an open grassy area; however, the route is well signed. Old trail markings are visible on some of the large old aspen. (The ones with numbers are believed to have been left by a sheep herder in the 1930s.) The trail follows along a north-south ridgeline, below FR 225.

(As the KPT/AT crosses FR 205B, take the opportunity to follow the road to the right [east] a short distance to its junction with FR 225. There are some marvelous vistas of the Vermilion Cliffs and House Rock Valley from FR 225, which, unfortunately, are not visible from the trail.)

Continuing north from FR 205B, the trail becomes faint in spots, overgrown with grass. If you lose the trail here, angle off toward FR 225 and you will see it again as it parallels the road.

Three miles from Murray Trailhead, and shortly after crossing FR 205B the trail crosses an abandoned road to a fenced wildlife tank. This tank empties into a dirt cattle tank below. The trail skirts the wildlife tank, passing between two huge ponderosa pines, both sporting shiny tags identifying them as "wildlife trees." The trail drops down a steep bank to Ridge Tank, a muddy pond that is accessible for watering livestock. A wood #101 trail sign tells us that it is 6 miles to Highway 89A.

Ridge Tank is at the top of a very long, narrow canyon. The trail takes a sharp left down-canyon, following an abandoned road for about 3 miles. There may be cattle, especially in the upper end near the tank. The descent is moderate. As the old road travels down the long, forested defile, the evergreens give way to aspen. The drainage narrows and the sides become steeper as the elevation drops. There are occasional Carsonite markers and rock cairns, but there is no danger of losing the trail in this well-defined canyon.

The canyon ends in a clearing that has the appearance of a hobo camp, strewn with old camper shells and tents. The KPT/AT joins a gravel road, and while following the road, we can hear an incredibly loud racket that tells us the gravel mine is in operation.

Seven miles from Murray Trailhead the gravel road ends at FR 258. Watch out for huge, fast-moving gravel trucks traveling back and forth from the quarry to the left. The KPT/AT turns right, following the road north for 0.4-mile to a big wooden rail corral on the right. Inside the corral are cattle and Big Ridge Tank, a dirt tank that is seasonal, and dry the day we passed by. (The Forest Service eventually plans to move this section away from the gravel mine. Watch for signs re-routing the trail.)

At the north end of the corral the trail angles away from the road to the right and climbs a little gulch, as it ascends Big Ridge. This section is well marked. The trail levels, crosses an old logging road, and continues north following an abandoned road. Soon after, a carsonite marker indicates where the trail leaves the road on the right. A fire has gone through this area and scorched the lower branches, but the trees are still alive. We saw a flock of wild Merriam's turkey run into the forest. The trail is again an old road, well signed as it ambles through the open pine forest.

The route leaves the burned area 8.5 miles from FR 205 and, soon after, arrives at a T junction with an abandoned road. Following carsonite markers, our route takes the left fork and immediately after, the trail leaves the road to the right, going up a rocky bank. The trail ascends a hill heading north. Topping the hill, the trail levels, winding through the open forest. A few minutes later we can hear the sound of highway traffic, as the trail begins its final, easy descent to the Orderville/U.S. 89A trailhead.

41 Kaibab Plateau Trail—Northern Passage
Orderville Trailhead to Winter Road

The authors thank Susan Hittson, Kaibab National Forest, North Kaibab Ranger District, for providing this trail description.

Contact the governing agency or The Arizona Trail Association for more information on the route, signage, availability of water, and completion status of this passage.

T*HIS 14-MILE-LONG PASSAGE does not receive as much snow as the more southern passages of the Kaibab Plateau/Arizona Trail and has been described as "outstanding" for mountain bikes. The passage includes Government Reservoir, which rarely has water, and Joe's Reservoir, which may have water in the spring. From Government Reservoir to the Forest Service/BLM boundary there are many open areas to camp, off* FR *247 and 248, which are fairly close to the trail.*

PROPOSED ROUTE

From Orderville Trailhead go north across U.S. 89A toward FR 247. A wood sign directs you to the right through young pine trees to a fence and a grassy clearing. At this writing there is no gate in the fence, so you must follow the fence a couple of hundred feet to the west and go through the gate on FR 247. Return east along the fenceline until you hit the trail again. There is a small stock tank that occasionally has water in it to the left of the trail.

The trail climbs up a ridge and proceeds through large ponderosa pines on top of the plateau. With the gradual descent in elevation, you will notice a change in vegetation, as juniper and pinon trees appear, scattered among the ponderosa pines.

Two miles from the Orderville Trailhead the trail crosses FR 257 and turns to the northeast. About 1 mile from this crossing, you come to a large sinkhole to the left of the trail. This is one of the largest sinkholes in the

North Kaibab Ranger District and is an excellent example of the limestone geology of the plateau.

You will cross FR 249 in another mile. The terrain stays flat untill you reach the mouth of a beautiful little canyon. The trail travels down the canyon for a little more than a mile. When the canyon opens up at Government Reservoir, the view to the north is a breathtaking expanse of grassland ringed by large piñon and juniper trees leading deep into the far horizon. There, you see the stairsteps of the vermilion, white and pink cliffs of Utah and Bryce Canyon National Park.

Leaving Government Reservoir, travel along the east side of the grassland at the edge of the trees to Joe's Reservoir and the intersection with the Navajo Trail #19. (This historic trail traverses the north end of the Kaibab Plateau.) From Joe's Reservoir it's roughly 4 miles to the Forest Service/BLM border. The trail winds in and out of piñon and juniper trees interspersed with grassland and fabulous views to the north. This ends or begins you trip on the Kaibab Plateau portion of the Arizona Trail.

Access to the Forest Service/BLM Boundary: From the North Kaibab Visitor Center go west on U.S. 89A for two miles and turn north on FR 248. Continue on FR 248 for 11 miles to Joe's Reservoir and another 4 miles to the FS/BLM boundary fence. The beginning of the trail starts 0.5 mile down the boundary fence to the east of FR 248.

Access to the Orderville Trailhead: At the junction of U.S. 89A and FR 205, 2 miles northeast of the North Kaibab Visitor Center.

GOVERNING AGENCIES

Kaibab National Forest, North Kaibab Ranger District, Box 248, Fredonia, AZ 86022. (520) 643-7395.

BLM, Vermilion Resource Area, 345 E. Riverside Rd., St. George, Utah 84770. (801) 628-4491.

NEAREST SERVICES

Nearest services are at Jacob Lake.

42 Buckskin Mountain Passage
Winter Road to the Arizona-Utah State Line

As of this writing, sections of the Arizona Trail in this passage are not yet completed. This description outlines the *proposed route* of the Arizona Trail through this passage; it is not intended to be used as a trail guide. Much of the information included here is taken from an Arizona Trail management guide designed not for recreational use but for use in planning, developing, and managing the trail. Contact the governing agency or The Arizona Trail Association for more information on the route, signage, availability of water, and completion status of this passage.

W HEN COMPLETED, *this 12-mile passage will travel from the National Forest/BLM boundary to the Arizona– Utah state line. The passage continues along the edge of the Kaibab Plateau as it follows new trail across the Arizona Strip. The northern terminus of the Arizona Trail lies in the beautiful Coyote Valley, featuring panoramic vistas and red rock bluffs. As of 1997, 6 miles of the trail are completed and work continues.*

PROPOSED ROUTE

From the National Forest/BLM boundary of the Kaibab National Forest, which is accessed by Winter Road (high-clearance vehicles recommended), this passage will parallel the eastern edge of the Kaibab Plateau. It will eventually drop off the plateau within a few miles of the Arizona-Utah state line. The northern terminus will be just west of House Rock Valley Road at the state line, in Coyote Valley. A trailhead facility will feature an interpretive kiosk, parking, a few campsites, and a rest room. The Houserock Valley Road, which comes north from U.S. 89A links to U.S. 89 in Utah, east of Kanab, affording access to this passage either from Arizona or Utah.

GOVERNING AGENCIES

Kaibab National Forest, North Kaibab Ranger District, Box 248, Fredonia, AZ 86022. (520) 643-7395.
BLM, Vermilion Resource Area, 345 E. Riverside Rd., St. George, Utah 84770. (801) 628-4491.

FOR MORE INFORMATION

Arizona Trail Association, P.O. Box 36736, Phoenix, AZ 85067. (602) 252-4794.

NEAREST SERVICES

Nearest services are at Jacob Lake.

Appendix A
Nearest Services

Many of the communities along the Arizona Trail are separated by long distances, and are not located at intervals that will provide adequate resupply. Others are located quite far from the actual route, but will provide services if necessary. This is why caches are important. Some of these communities (listed south to north), and a number for more information, are listed in this appendix. For the communities with post offices, you should consider shipping dehydrated foods and other supplies so that they will be waiting for you when you arrive. Send the package to "Your Name", c/o General Delivery, Town, State, Zip Code, and mark the box "Hold for Arizona Trail Hiker (or Rider)." In addition, you may want to have friends and/or family meet you at predetermined dates and locations, and have them bring fresh food and other luxuries to you.

(More detailed information is given for highlighted passages.)

	Telephone	Post Office	Medical	Groceries	Lodging	Laundry	Bank	Gear	Transportation	Fuel
PASSAGE 1 **Sierra Vista or Bisbee** **Sierra Vista Services:** *Info:* (520) 458-6940	X	X	X	X	X	X	X	X	bus X	X
Bisbee Services: *Info:* (520) 432-5421	X	X	X	X	X	X	X	limited	bus X	X
PASSAGE 2 **Sierra Vista**										

	Telephone	Post Office	Medical	Groceries	Lodging	Laundry	Bank	Gear	Transportation	Fuel
PASSAGE 3 Patagonia Services: *Info:* (520) 394-0060	X	X	X	X	X	X	X	no	no	X
PASSAGE 4 Sonoita										
PASSAGE 5 Benson										
PASSAGE 6 Tucson										
PASSAGE 7 Benson										
PASSAGE 8 Benson Services: *Info:* (520) 586-2842	X	X	X	X	X	X	X	limited	bus / train X	X
PASSAGE 9 Tucson Services: *Info:* (520) 792-1212	X	X	X	X	X	X	X	X	airport, bus, train X	X
PASSAGE 10 Tucson										
PASSAGE 11 Summerhaven Services: *Info:* (520) 576-1542	X	X	Tucson	limited	X	no	no	no	no	no
PASSAGE 12 Oracle Services: *Info:* (520) 896-9322	X	X	X	X	X	X	San Manuel	San Manuel	no	X
PASSAGE 13 Oracle										

![lizard]	Telephone	Post Office	Medical	Groceries	Lodging	Laundry	Bank	Gear	Transportation	Fuel
PASSAGE 14 Kearny Services: *Info:* (520) 363-7607	X	X	X	X	X	X	X	no	no	X
PASSAGE 15 Kearny										
PASSAGE 16 Superior										
PASSAGE 17 Superior Services: *Info:* (520) 689-2441	X	X	X	X	X	X	X	no	bus X	X
PASSAGE 18 Superior										
PASSAGE 19 Roosevelt Complex Services: *Info:* (520) 467-2245	X	town of Roosevelt (520) 467-2215 no	no	X	X	X	no	X	no	no
PASSAGE 20 Roosevelt Complex										
PASSAGE 21 Roosevelt Complex										
PASSAGE 22 Payson Services: *Info:* (520) 474-4515	X	X	X	X	X	X	X	X	X	X
PASSAGE 23 Payson										
PASSAGE 24 Payson										

	Telephone	Post Office	Medical	Groceries	Lodging	Laundry	Bank	Gear	Transportation	Fuel
PASSAGE 25 Pine Services: *Info:* (520) 476-3547	X	X	X	X	no	X	no	no	no	no
PASSAGE 26 Pine										
PASSAGE 27 Clints Well Services: *Info:* (477-2211)	X	X	no	X	X	X	no	X	no	X
PASSAGE 28 Mormon Lake Village Services: *Info:* (520) 354-2227	X	X	no	X	X	no	no	no	no	no
PASSAGE 28 Mormon Lake Village										
PASSAGE 29 Flagstaff Services: *Info:* (520) 774-4505	X	X	X	X	X	X	X	X	airport, bus, train X	X
PASSAGE 30 Flagstaff										
PASSAGE 31 Flagstaff										
PASSAGE 32 Flagstaff										
PASSAGE 33 Flagstaff										
PASSAGE 34 Flagstaff										

	Telephone	Post Office	Medical	Groceries	Lodging	Laundry	Bank	Gear	Transportation	Fuel
PASSAGE 35 **Grand Canyon Village** Services: *Info:* (520) 638-2631 or (520) 638-7771	X	X	X	X	X	X	X	X	X (bus, train)	X
PASSAGE 36 **Grand Canyon Village**										
PASSAGE 37 **Phantom Ranch** Services: *Info:* (contact Grand Canyon Village)	X	no	no	no	X	no	no	no	X (mule)	X
PASSAGE 38 **North Rim Village** Services: *Info:* (520) 638-2611	X	X	X	X	X	X	no	X	no	X
PASSAGE 39 **North Rim Village**										
PASSAGE 40 **Jacob Lake** Services: *Info:* (520) 643-7232	no (Kanab, Utah)	no (Kanab, Utah)	no (Kanab, Utah)	X	X	no (Kanab, Utah)	no (Kanab, Utah)	no	no	X
PASSAGE 41 **Jacob Lake**										
PASSAGE 42 **Jacob Lake**										

Appendix B
Livestock
Outfitting, Transporting, and Overnight Boarding Services

Information for the following list was obtained by telephone. The authors did not visit any of the businesses listed below and assume no responsibility for services purchased. It is the responsibility of the reader to assess the safety and cleanliness of boarding facilities and to inquire about credentials and insurance if boarding animals or hiring guides or outfitters.

Always call in advance for reservations. If you are planning to board animals, ask what vaccination records you may need. Ask if the facility provides feed—some do not.

SOUTHERN ARIZONA
Sierra Vista
- **Frontier Outfitters**, Rt. 1, Box 26, McNeal, AZ 85617. (520) 642-3871. Outfitting and transporting. Call for information and reservations.

- **Randy and Laura Keiller**, 7683 Highway 92, Hereford, AZ 85615. (520) 378-9475. Transporting and boarding. Call for information and reservations.

- **Ken Moore,** 10955 E. Highway 92, Hereford, AZ 85615. (520) 366-5794. Transporting. Call for information and reservations.

- **E Lazy Heart Ranch,** 7290 N. Frontier Rd., McNeal, AZ 85617. (520) 364-4477. Transporting in Cochise County. Boarding. Call for information and reservations.

- **Equi Sands**, 9595 Kings Ranch Rd., Hereford, AZ 85615. (520) 378-1540. Boarding only. Call for information and reservations.

- **Scarlet Gate Llama Ranch**, 4593 Miller Canyon Rd., Hereford, AZ 85615. (520) 378-1834. Outfitting, trekking, drop camps, transporting, and boarding llamas. Call for information and reservations. November–April.

Patagonia

Arizona Trail Tours, P.O. Box 1218, Patagonia, AZ 85624. (520) 394-2701. Outfitting and boarding. Catered rides in the Sierra Vista, Sonoita, and Patagonia areas. Call for information and reservations.

Sonoita

Apache Springs Ranch, P.O. Box 230, Sonoita, AZ 85637. Camping allowed, corrals available. (520) 455-5232. Call for information and reservations.

Sonoita Fair Grounds, Highway 83, south of Highway 82, Sonoita, AZ. Overnight boarding. (520) 455-5533. Call for information and reservations.

Crown C Ranch, P.O. Box 984, Sonoita, AZ 85637. (520) 455-5739. Overnight accommodations in an historic 1930s ranch house. Corral space available. Call for information and reservations.

Benson

Redington Land and Cattle Company at Cascabel Ranch. HC 1, Box 730, Benson, AZ 85602. Fax or phone (520) 212-5555. Outfitting, catering, transporting, drop camps, equipment and horse rental, boarding, and bed-and-breakfast. Free trip planning consultations.

Rocking R Mercantile, 720 W. 4th St., Benson, AZ 85602. (520) 586-7227. Feed store. Transportation. Call for information and reservations.

Benson-Mescal: J-Six Equestrian Center offers overnight boarding for horses. (520) 586-7551. Call for information and reservations.

Tucson (southeast)

Pantano Stables, 4450 S. Houghton Road, (520) 298-1983. Boarding. Call for information and reservations. Call Nacho Molina at (520) 721-1951 for transporting livestock up the Santa Catalina (Mount Lemmon) highway.

Trails and Equestrian Center, 7601 S. Houghton Road, (520) 290-2230. Boarding. Call for information and reservations.

Rocking R Mercantile and **Redington Land & Cattle** will transport to Mount Lemmon. (See above.)

Summerhaven

Aspen Trail Bed-and-Breakfast has one corral. P.O. Box 572, Mount Lemmon, AZ 85619. (520) 576-1558. Call for information and reservations.

Tucson (north)

Catalina State Park, 9 miles north of Tucson on SR 77 (Oracle Road) offers corrals as well as a developed campground with showers. Fee area. (520) 628-5798.

Pusch Ridge Stables, 13700 N. Oracle Road, Tucson, AZ 85737. (520) 825-1664. Boarding. Outfitters. They rent mountain bikes. Call for information and reservations.

Oracle

Corrals at the American Flag Trailhead access the Arizona Trail. Water can be turned on for a small fee. Contact John Ronquillo in advance at (520) 896-2588.

Triangle Y Ranch Camp accesses the Arizona Trail and has corral space available for horses and llamas, except when camp is in session from June 1 through August 15. The camp is on FR 639, off the Old Mount Lemmon Road, 0.8-mile south of the American Flag Trailhead. Advance reservations are required. Call (620) 884-0987 or (520) 825-2209 for information.

Oracle Ridge (llama) Outfitters, P.O. Box 1243, Oracle, AZ 85623. (520) 896-2542. Custom pack trips on the Arizona Trail and surrounding areas. Overnight boarding. Tent space and showers by prior arrangement. Call for information and reservations.

CENTRAL ARIZONA

Apache Junction

OK Corral, boarding (horses only) and outfitting. (602) 982-4040. Call for information and reservations.

Phoenix

Outdoor Adventures Unlimited offers outfitting and Arizona Trail adventure horseback rides in the Superstition Wilderness and other parts of the state. Also fishing, hunting, and catering. P.O. Box 33582, Phoenix, AZ 85067. (602) 253-2789. 1-800-678-3929. Call for information and reservations.

Roosevelt Lake

Hayhook Ranch, P.O. Box 856, Roosevelt, AZ 85545. (520) 467-2354. Outfitting, boarding, and transportation across Roosevelt Bridge. Call for information and reservations.

Pine

OK Corral. Stable and outfitter. Closed during the winter months. (520) 476-4303. Call for information and reservations.

NORTHERN ARIZONA

Flagstaff

Canyon Country Outfitters, Route 4, Box 739, Flagstaff, AZ 86001. (520) 774-1676.

Hitchin' Post Stable accesses the Arizona Trail in Walnut Canyon. They board horses and llamas. Outfitters. Box 4848, Lake Mary Road, Flagstaff, AZ 86001. (520) 774-1719. Call for information and reservations.

Little Elden Springs Horse Camp accesses part of the proposed route of the Arizona Trail north of Flagstaff. There is room to park and turn trailers. Take U.S. 89 north of Flagstaff 4.5 miles to Little Elden Spring Road (FR 556). Left on FR 556 for 2 miles. Campsites, privies, BBQ grills, and hitching posts. Water is available for horses. Fee. Closed in the winter months. Call Peaks Ranger District for information and reservations.

Flying Heart Stable accesses Mount Elden. They will board horses and llamas. 8400 N. Highway 89, Flagstaff, AZ 86004. (520) 526-2788. Call for information and reservations.

MCS Stables will board horses. Borders Coconino National Forest. Highway 89A south. HC 30, Box 16, Flagstaff, AZ 86001. (520) 774-5835. Call for information and reservations.

Coconino County Fairgrounds will board horses and llamas. They are closed during the winter months. Highway 89A south. (520) 779-1762. Call for information and reservations.

Grand Canyon

There are horse camps on both the south and north rim of the Grand Canyon. Horse camps are closed during the winter. Arrangements must be made in advance to unlock gates and turn on the water. Contact the backcountry office (well in advance), Box 129, Grand Canyon, AZ 86023. (520) 638-7888, or contact Ranger Gibson at (520) 638-7875.

Canyon Country Outfitters, Route 4, Box 739, Flagstaff, AZ 86001. (520) 774-1676. Eldon Bowman offers his experience and advice, and will accompany riders, on a non-commercial basis, into the canyon.

Appendix C
Recommended Maps

The Arizona Trail appears on only a few maps as "Arizona Trail." Trail users should make themselves aware of the existing trails that make up the Arizona Trail. Many of them can be found on the maps listed below. Please remember that many of the U.S. Geological Survey maps are quite outdated and trail alignments (and the presence of springs) have changed. Prices listed are from early 1996.

U.S. Forest Service Maps
Some U.S. Forest Service maps can be ordered directly from the Southwestern Region Office of the U.S. Forest Service. A standard order form is available by contacting the office. Some specific literature is best requested from the individual national forests: USDA Forest Service, Public Affairs Office, 517 Gold Avenue, SW, Albuquerque, NM 87102. (505) 842-3292.

Coronado National Forest Maps and Literature
- Sierra Vista and Nogales Ranger Districts
- Santa Catalina Ranger District
- Pusch Ridge Wilderness—$3.00 each (postage and handling included)
- Other recreation opportunity guides may be available at no cost. Send check or money order to: Coronado National Forest, 300 W. Congress, 6th Floor, Tucson, AZ 85701.

Tonto National Forest Maps and Literature
- Tonto National Forest map—$3.00 (postage and handling included)
- Mazatzal Wilderness map—$4.00 (postage and handling included)
- Superstition Wilderness map—$4.00 (postage and handling included)
- Four Peaks Wilderness—Recreation Opportunity Guide—Free
- Superstition Wilderness—Recreation Opportunity Guide—Free
- Mazatzal Wilderness—Recreation Opportunity Guide—Free
- Highline Trails Guide—Free. Send check or money order to: Tonto National Forest, 2324 E. McDowell Road, Phoenix, AZ 85010

Coconino National Forest Maps and Literature
- Coconino National Forest map—$3.00 (postage and handling included)
- Recreation Opportunity Guide—information sheets for: Elden—Dry Lake Hills —Free; Kachina Peaks Wilderness—Free.

Send check or money order to: Coconino National Forest, 2323 E. Greenlaw Lane, Flagstaff, AZ 86004.

Kaibab National Forest Maps and Literature
- Kaibab National Forest—North Kaibab Ranger District (AZ Trail appears on map)
- Kaibab National Forest—Tusayan Ranger District

$3.00 each (postage and handling included). Send check or money order to: Kaibab National Forest, 800 S. 6th St., Williams, AZ 86046.

U.S. Geological Survey–7.5 Minute Topographic Maps (South to North)
Montezuma Pass, Miller Peak, Huachuca Peak, Canelo Pass, O'Donnell Canyon, Mt. Hughes, Mt. Wrightson, Helvetia, Empire Ranch, Spring Water Canyon, The Narrows, Rincon Peak, Galleta Flat West, Happy Valley, Mica Mountain, Piety Hill, Agua Caliente Hill, Sabino Canyon, Mt. Lemmon, Mt. Bigelow, Campo Bonito, Mammoth, North of Oracle Putnam Wash, Black Mountain, Crozier Peak, Kearny, Grayback, Hot Tamale Peak, Teapot Mountain, Mineral Mountain, Picketpost Mountain, Iron Mountain, Pinyon Mountain, Two Bar Mountain, Theodore Roosevelt Dam, Four Peaks, Boulder Mountain, Maverick Mountain, Lion Mountain, Reno Pass, Mazatzal Peak, North Peak, Cypress Butte, Cane Springs Mountain, Buckhead Mesa, Pine, Kehl Ridge, Dane Canyon, Blue Ridge Reservoir, Turkey Mountain, Happy Jack, Hutch Mountain, Mormon Lake, Elliott Canyon, Ashurst Lake, Lower Lake Mary, Flagstaff East, Flagstaff West, Winona, Sunset Crater West, Humphreys Peak, White Horse Hills, O'Leary Peak, S P Mountain, Chapel Mountain, Lockwood Canyon, Peterson Flat, Harbison Tank, Grandview Point, Tusayan East, Grand Canyon, Phantom Ranch, Bright Angel Point, Little Park Lake, Dog Point, Cane, Telephone Hill, Jacob Lake, Cooper Ridge, Buck Pasture Canyon, Coyote Buttes, Pine Hollow Canyon (Utah).

Some USGS 15.0 minute quadrangle maps, while outdated, may be helpful. Some maps may be out of print. Many university and public libraries will also have the above maps, and photocopying can save on costs. For purchasing the maps, ordering directly from U.S.G.S. is suggested. Contact U.S.G.S. for ordering information: U.S. Geological Survey, Denver, CO 80225.

You may also want to check with local map stores for availability of some of these maps.

Trail & Recreation Maps from Rainbow Expedition (3 needed)
- "Santa Rita Mountains" (being revised early 1996)
- "Rincon Mountains"
- "Santa Catalina Mountains" (being revised early 1996)

These are approximately $3.95 each (call for current prices): Rainbow Expeditions, 915 S. Sherwood Village Dr., Tucson, AZ 85710. (520) 298-2731.

Arizona Atlas & Gazetter (not essential but helpful)
Delorme Mapping, (207) 865-4171.

Other useful publications and maps can be found on the various areas through which the Arizona Trail passes. Some of these can be purchased from the various natural history associations. Future maps specifically for the Arizona Trail may become available through Trails Illustrated and other companies.

Passage Information Sheets

Passage Information Sheets for the Arizona Trail are being developed by the non-profit Arizona Trail Association. As they are developed for completed passages, they become available through the Arizona Trail Association (there may be a nominal fee). The various land-managing agencies may also have copies of the Passage Information Sheet for their respective areas (once they have been provided to them by the Arizona Trail Association). Contact the Arizona Trail Association for more information. Arizona Trail Association, P.O. Box 36736, Phoenix, AZ 85067, (602) 252-4794.

Appendix D
Where to Obtain Permits

Permits are required for some portions of the Arizona Trail that travel through national parks, preserves, or state trust lands. When permits are required it is noted within the description of the trip requiring the permit. This appendix lists the agencies and addresses for securing permits.

Grand Canyon National Park Permit(s)

Backcountry Permit: Can be secured up to four months prior to date needed. Be flexible with dates and allow yourself time to enjoy the inner canyon. Reserve early, because these permits are in great demand.

Stock Permit: For equestrians, a separate stock permit is needed in addition to the backcountry permit.

Backcountry Reservations Office: Grand Canyon National Park, P.O. Box 129, Grand Canyon, AZ 86023 • (520) 638-7888. Llamas, pets, firearms, and mountain bicycles are currently not permitted on inner canyon trails.

Saguaro National Park— Backcountry Information and Permit Application for Overnight Use

Saguaro National Park, 3693 S. Old Spanish Trail, Tucson, AZ 85730 • (520) 733-5153

Coronado National Memorial—Overnight Parking Permit (For Vehicles Parked in Memorial)

Coronado National Memorial, 4101 E. Montezuma Canyon Rd., Hereford, AZ 85615 • (520) 366-5515

Information and Application for Recreational Permit for Crossing State Trust Lands

You will need to specify the areas you will be traversing. **Arizona State Land Department,** Public Records, 1616 West Adams, Phoenix, AZ 85007 • (602) 542-2506

Recreation Permit for Cienega Creek Natural Preserve

Pima County Parks and Recreation Department, 1204 W. Silverlake, Tucson, AZ 85713-2799 • (520) 740-2690

Appendix E
Suggested Resources

The Arizona Trail Association (membership includes a newsletter). P.O. Box 36736, Phoenix, AZ 85067. (602) 252-4794. Internet: http://www.primenet.com/~aztrail. E-mail address: aztrail@primenet.com. (See membership form on last page of this book.)

Sierra Club, Grand Canyon Chapter is a nonprofit public interest organization that promotes conservation of the natural environment. The Sierra Club sponsors national service trips and volunteer work on the Arizona Trail. 516 E. Portland St., Phoenix, AZ 85004. (602) 253-8633. For national service trips: (415) 923-5629.

Pima Trails Association, a volunteer trails advocacy organization composed of hikers, equestrians, and mountain bikers (membership includes a newsletter). P.O. Box 41358, Tucson, AZ 85717. (520) 577-7919.

Huachuca Hiking Club has adopted the Arizona Trail from Mexico to Patagonia. This organization is interested in exploring and conserving our wilderness heritage through hiking, camping, and volunteer trail maintenance. The club sponsors work days on the Arizona Trail, hikes, and other activities. P.O. Box 3555, Sierra Vista, AZ 85636. Internet: http://www.primenet.com/~tomheld/hiking.htm.

Recreational Equipment Inc. sells outdoor recreational and camping gear through its catalog and retail stores. REI has provided grants to the Arizona Trail Association for building and developing the Arizona Trail. 1405 W. Southern, Tempe, AZ. (602) 967-5494 or 1-800-426-4840.

Southern Arizona Mountain Bike Association. Does volunteer work on the Arizona Trail. Contact Full Cycle, 3232 E. Speedway, Tucson, AZ 85716. (520) 327-3232.

Arizona State Horsemen's Association. Dedicated to preserving horsemen's rights and way of life in Arizona (membership includes a newsletter). P.O. Box 31758, Phoenix, AZ 85046-1758. (602) 867-6814.

County Line Riders of Catalina support responsible equestrian trail use and do volunteer work on the Arizona Trail. 4660 E. Joshua Tree Place, Tucson, AZ 85739.

Arizona Mule and Donkey Association does volunteer trail work and has adopted a segment of the Arizona Trail north of Roosevelt Lake. 5003 W. Whispering Wind Drive, Glendale, AZ 85310. (602) 581-9219.

Saddle Software Systems promotes low-impact horse camping and sells quality horse (and some mountain bike) trail packs and supplies. A percentage of the company profits are allocated to nonprofit organizations that support trails. 429 East Highway 6 & 50, Fruita, CO 81521. (970) 858-3607.

Llama and Alpaca Association of Arizona, 1107 Lockwood Street, Mesa, AZ 85203. (602) 464-8568.

The Western Music Association supports the preservation, performance, and composition of historic, traditional, and contemporary music of the American West. (Membership includes a newsletter and discount at the annual festival.) P.O. Box 35008, Tucson, AZ 85740. (520) 575-6829.

The Desert Sons ("Arizona Home" and other songs). For tapes and CDs contact: The Desert Sons, 4398 N. Via Noriega, Tucson, AZ 85749. (520) 749-0968. For bookings contact Music West Entertainment, P.O. Box 17476, Tucson, AZ 85731. (520) 290-4508.

References and Suggested Reading

Books

Armstrong, Margaret, and Kenn Schultz. *The Patagonia Adventure Guide.* Tucson, Arizona: M&K Associates, 1994.

Baker, Robert D., Robert S. Maxwell, Victor H. Treat, and Henry C. Dethloff. *Timeless Heritage: A History of the Forest Service in the Southwest.* College Station, Texas: United States Department of Agriculture, 1988.

Barr, John. *Unique Arizona.* Santa Fe, New Mexico: John Muir Publications, 1994.

Carlson, Jack, and Elizabeth Stewart. *Hikers Guide to the Superstition Wilderness.* Tempe, Arizona: Clear Creek Publishing, 1995.

Carr, John N. *Arizona Wildlife Viewing Guide.* Helena and Billings, Montana: Falcon Press, 1992.

Clark, Badger. *Sun and Saddle Leather.* Custer, South Dakota: Badger Clark Memorial Society, 1993. Badger Clark Memorial Society, Box 351, Custer SD 57730-0351. (No phone. The book is $22.45 including postage.)

Clark, Badger. *Poems of the West.* Nogales, Arizona: Greg Scott and Moco Seco Press, 1997.

De Mente, Boye. *Arizona's Indian Reservations.* Phoenix, Arizona: Phoenix Books, 1992.

Gardner, Gail I. *Orejana Bull.* Prescott, Arizona: Sharlot Hall Museum Press, 1987.

Glendening, Eber, and Pete Cowgill. *Trail Guide to the Santa Catalina Mountains.* Tucson, Arizona: Rainbow Expeditions, 1987.

Hancock, Jan. *Horse Trails in Arizona.* Phoenix, Arizona: Golden West Publishers, 1994.

Hanson, Roseann Beggy, and Jonathan Hanson. *Southern Arizona Nature Almanac: A Seasonal Guide to Pima County and Beyond.* Boulder, Colorado: Pruett Publishing Company, 1996.

Hare, Trevor. *Poisonous Dwellers of the Desert.* Tucson, Arizona: Southwest Parks and Monuments Association, 1995.

Hoffman, John F. *The Grand Canyon, National Parkways Guide.* Casper, Wyoming: World-Wide Research and Publishing Company, 1977.

Kaibab National Forest Staff. *Kaibab National Forest Visitors Guide: Williams, Chalender, and Tusayan Ranger Districts.* Stephen G. Mauer, series editor. Albuquerque, New Mexico: Southwest Natural and Cultural Heritage Association, 1990.

Leavengood, Betty. *Tucson Hiking Guide*. Second Edition. Boulder, Colorado: Pruett Publishing Company, 1997.

Leavengood, Betty, and Mike Liebert. *Hiker's Guide to the Santa Rita Mountains*. Boulder, Colorado: Pruett Publishing Company, 1994.

Maurer, Stephen G. *National Forest Visitors Guides*. Albuquerque, New Mexico: Southwest Natural and Cultural Heritage Association, various years.

Mazel, David. *Arizona Trails*. Berkeley, California: Wilderness Press, 1991.

Steele, Peter. *Far From Help! Backcountry Medical Care*. Seattle, Washington: Cloud-cap, 1991.

Taylor, Leonard. *Hiker's Guide to the Huachuca Mountains*. Sierra Vista, Arizona: Thunder Peak, 1991.

Tinsley, Jim Bob. *He Was Singin' This Song*. Orlando, Florida: University Press of Florida, 1991.

Trimble, Marshall. *Roadside History of Arizona*. Missoula, Montana: Mountain Press, 1986.

Whitney, Stephen. *Western Forests, Audubon Society Nature Guide*. New York, New York: Alfred A. Knopf, 1986.

Periodicals and Other

Arizona Africanized Bee Advisory Committee. "Africanized Honey Bee: Outdoor Recreation and Safety Tips." Arizona Department of Agriculture, Cooperative Extension, University of Arizona, Information Bulletin 11. Phoenix, Arizona.

Arizona Trail Management Guide. Arizona State Parks and Arizona Trail Partners. Phoenix, Arizona: 1995. (Available from Arizona State Parks: 602-542-7120.)

Arizona State Trails Guide (Third Edition) and historic supplements "Babe Haught Trail," "Colonel Devin Trail," and "General Cook Trail." Arizona State Parks and Arizona State Committee on Trails. Phoenix, Airzona, various years.

Arizona Trail News. Arizona Trail Association. Phoenix, Arizona, various years. A quarterly newsletter that features field reports, work projects, and Arizona Trail events. Contact the Arizona Trail Association for membership information at P.O. Box 36736, Phoenix, AZ 85067, (602) 252-4794; internet website address: http://www.primenet.com/~aztrail; email address: aztrail@primenet.com. See also membership form on page 301 of this guide.

Barstad, Jan. "Journal of a Special Place." *Arizona Highways*, September 1990.

Clemensen, Berle A. "A History of Manning Cabin," *Cattle, Copper, and Cactus: The History of Saguaro National Monument*. Denver, Colorado: National Park Service, Denver Service Center, 1987.

Dahl, Milt. *Arizona Trails*. Tempe, Arizona. A bi-monthly publication featuring hiking and backpacking trails in Arizona (P.O. Box 1653, Tempe, AZ 85280-1653, 602-786-6105; e-mail address: aztrail@primenet.com; internet web site: www.primenet.com/~aztrails/aztrails.html).

Desert Sons, The "Arizona Home" and other songs. Tucson, Arizona. For tapes and CDs contact The Desert Sons, 4398 N. Via Noriega, Tucson, AZ 85749. For bookings contact Music West entertainment, P.O. Box 57698, Tucson, AZ 85732; (520) 881-0847.

Hess, Bill. "Alchesay, Fort honors Apache Chief." *Bisbee Daily Review*, March 31, 1996.

Mckelvey, Nat. "Reckless, Romantic, Redington." *Arizona Highways*, September 1990.

National Park Service. "Coronado Hiking Trails" and "Welcome to Coronado National Memorial." History and wildlife handouts. Various years.

"Patagonia Visitors Guide." Patagonia Community Association. Patagonia, Arizona.

"Cienega Creek Natural Preserve: Management Plan Summary." Pima County Department of Transportation and Flood Control. Tucson, Arizona: McGann and Associates, 1994.

Ready, Alma. "Wild Old Days." *True West*, September 1965.

Smith, Eric. "The Arizona Trail: Essential Information for Long-Distance Trail Users." Pamphlet available from the Arizona Trail Steward, Arizona State Parks, 1300 W. Washington, Phoenix, Arizona 85007.

"A Guide to the Mount Lemmon Highway." *Sonorensis*. Tucson, Arizona: Arizona-Sonora Desert Museum, 1994.

United States Department of Health and Human Services, Centers for Disease Control. *Hantavirus Infection—Southwestern United States*. Atlanta, Georgia: 1993.

United States Department of the Interior, Bureau of Land Management. *Empire/Cienega Resource Conservation Area.*

United States Department of the Interior. Miscellaneous Forest Service pamphlets, including "On Your Own In Southwestern Mountains"; "Is The Water Safe?"; "Aspens"; "Kaibab Plateau"; "Preserving Arizona's History at Kentucky Camp"; "Highline Trails Guide." Washington, D.C.: Various years.

Index

Note: Arizona Trail Passages are listed in **boldface;** page numbers for individual trips within each Passage are in **boldface.**

Access points, 41, 43
Africanized (killer) honey bees, 35
Agua Caliente Wash, 115
Alamo Canyon Passage, 152
Alchesay, 9-10
Allen, Rex, Jr., xii (photo), 15; verse by, 114
All-Indian Pow-Wow, 216
American Flag trailhead, 140 (photo), 142
American Flag Trailhead to American Avenue, **144-46**
Anamax Mining Co., 92
Anasazi, 10, 238
Animals, precautions against, 38
Antivenin, 31
Apache Junction Chamber of Commerce, 156
Apache Lake, 163
Apache Pass, 12
Apaches, 7, 11, 48, 79, 92, 121, 143, 193, 205; arrival of, 8; Chiricahua, 9, 12; campaign against, 9, 13; Sobia-puri and, 115; White Mountain, 10
Apache Springs Ranch, 278
Apache Trail, 177
Archaeological sites, caring for, 25
Arizona, map of, ii
"Arizona" (Allen), 114
Arizona Atlas & Gazetter, 282
"Arizona August" (Gardner), 240

Arizona Boys' Ranch, 1
Arizona brown spiders, 34-35
Arizona Department of Agriculture, Africanized Honey Bee Advisory Committee of, 35
Arizona Department of Transportation, Roosevelt Bridge and, 177
Arizona Game and Fish Department, 68; licenses from, 25, 28; on water/camping, 24
Arizona Heritage Fund, 1
Arizona Historical Society Museum, 122
"Arizona Home" (Ryberg), xiv
Arizona Management Guide, trail routes from, 40
Arizona Mineral Belt Railroad Company, 193-94
"Arizona Mountain Home" (Tighe), 204, 248
Arizona Mule and Donkey Association, 285
Arizona Poison Control, information from, 28, 31, 32, 33, 34, 35
Arizona Snow Bowl, 226
Arizona-Sonoran Desert Museum, 122
Arizona State Committee on Trails (ASCOT), 2
Arizona State Horsemen's Association, 285
Arizona State Land Department, 1; permits from, 284
Arizona State Parks, xi, 1, 142, 143; IGA with, 2-3
Arizona Strip, 270

Arizona Trail: completion of, 19; history of, 7; maintaining, 3; symbols of, 20
Arizona Trail Association (ATA), xi, 3, 99, 148, 150, 187, 188, 190, 227, 228, 268, 271; formation of, 4; information from, 39, 283, 285; proposed routes and, 91, 94, 96, 98, 147, 149, 151, 152, 185, 186, 189, 212, 213, 223, 224, 225, 226, 238, 247, 270
Arizona Trail Corridor, 18
Arizona Trail Tours, 278
ASCOT. See Arizona State Committee on Trails
Ash Creek, 98
Aspen Trail Bed-and-Breakfast, 278
ATA. See Arizona Trail Association
Autry, Gene, 15, 17

Babbitt Ranches, Inc., 228
Babbitt Ranch Passage, 227-28
Babocomari River, 68
Backcountry Reservations Office, permits from, 284
Bathtub Spring, 47
Bathtub Spring to Sunnyside Canyon, 56-59
Battleground Ridge, 13
Beardsley, Kate, 2
Bears, 38
Bear Spring, 80
Bellota Ranch, 115
Benson, 115
Benson-Mescal: J-Six Equestrian Center, 278
BHP Copper, 1
Bicycles: etiquette for, 25, 26; restrictions on, 21, 26; routes for, 20
Big Dry Wash, 205
Biosphere 2, 133
Biotic communities, described, 5-7
Bisbee, 47; mining in, 14, 15
Bisbee Chamber of Commerce, 49
Bisbee Mining and Historical Museum, 15

Black Brush Ranch, 177
Black Brush Ranch, FR 83 to Roosevelt Bridge, 179-84
Black Hills, 147
Black Hills (Sonoran Desert) Passage, 147-48
Black widow spiders, 34
BLM. See Bureau of Land Management
Blue Ridge Campground, 205
Blue Ridge Passage, 203-11; log cabin on, 18, 204 (photo); map of, 203
Blue Ridge Reservoir, 205, 206
Boice, Mr. and Mrs. Frank, 92
Boot Hill, 1
"Border, The" (Clark), 10, 120
Boyce Thompson Southwestern Arboretum, 155, 156
Boyd, Skelly: verse by, 5, 154
Bright Angel Creek, 243
Bright Angel trailhead, 238, 242
Bright Angel Trailhead to Phantom Ranch, 244-46
Buckskin Mountain Passage, 270-71
Buffalo Park, 224, 225
Buffalo Soldiers, 13, 48
Buffalo Soldier Trail, 13
Bureau of Land Management (BLM), 1, 92, 269, 270; Empire-Cienega, 93; Phoenix Resource Area, 151
Burnett, Smiley, 17
Butterfield Overland Mail Line, 92
Butterfield Stage Line, 12

Cabin Loop System, 205, 206
Cactus, 6, 39, 176 (photo); precautions against, 37
Camp Crittenden, 79
Camping, 41; considerations about, 24, 43
Camp Lincoln/Camp Verde, 13
Cañada del Oro (Canyon of Gold), 133
Cañada del Oro Trail #4, 133
Canadian life zone, 1
Canelo Hills, 66 (photo), 68

Canelo Hills Passage, 67-76; map of, 67
Canelo Pass to Harshaw Road to Patagonia, **73-76**
Canyon Country Outfitters, 279, 280
Carlson, Jack, 163
Carr Canyon, 48
Carson, Kit, 9, 12-13
Catalina Camp, 132 (photo), 133
Catalina Camp Trail #401, 133
Catalina Highway, 121
Catalina Mountains, 115, 142
Catalina State Park, 278
Cavalry, 7, 9, 12-13, 48, 205
Cebadillo Pass, 115
Cebedilla Pass, 115
Cedar Ranch Camp, 226, 227
Centipedes, 33-34
Chihuahuan Desert, 5, 6
Chiricahua Cattle Company, 92
Chiricahua Mountains, 12, 47
Cienega Creek, 91, 92, 94, 95
Cienega Creek Natural Preserve, 92, 93, 94
Cienega Creek Passage, 94-95
Cienega Ranch, 92
Civilian Conservation Corps, 18, 96, 232
Clanton, Billie and Ike, 16
Clark, Badger, 16; verse by, 10, 14, 17, 46, 78, 100, 120, 132, 140, 162, 176, 214, 230, 260
Clothing, considerations about, 30, 37
Clovis people, 142
C O Bar Ranch, 227
Cochise, 1, 9
Coconino County Fairgrounds, 280
Coconino National Forest, 18, 193, 206, 212, 213, 217, 223, 224, 225, 226, 227; Maps/Literature, 281
Coconino Plateau, 231
Coconino Rim, 231
Colonel Devin Trail, 193, 194, 205
Colossal Cave, 92, 94, 96
Colossal Cave Mountain Park, 94-95, 96, 97

Conenose (kissing) bugs, 34
Copper Glance Mine, 14
Copper Queen Mine, 14
Copper Queen Hotel, 15
Coral snakes, 32
Coronado, Francisco Vásquez de, 48, 242; exploration by, 10-11, 47
Coronado Memorial Road, 49
Coronado National Forest, 18, 47, 48, 69, 80, 99, 103, 116, 122, 135, 143; ghost towns in, 14-15; Maps/Literature, 281
Coronado National Memorial, 10, 48; Huachuca Hiking Club and, 4; permits from, 284
Corrals at the American Flag Trailhead, 279
Cottonwood Canyon, 163, 177
Cottonwoods, 176 (photo)
County Line Riders of Catalina, 285
Courtesy, backcountry, 23-24, 25-28
"Cowboy, The" (poem), 15
"Cowboy and Coyote" (Clark), 214
Cowboy Gang, Earp brothers and, 16
Cowboys, 15-17; music/poetry of, 16-17
"Cowboys' Last Song, The" (Boyd), 154
Coyote Valley, 270
Crook, George, 13, 205
"Crooked Trail To Holbrook, The," 192
Crown C Ranch, 278

Defenders of Wildlife, 143
DeMotte Park, 250, 251
Desert Sons, The, 17, 286
Devin, Colonel, 13, 193
Devin's Jump Off, 193
Difficulty (trail), describing, 41
Diseases, precautions against, 36-37
Dogs, restrictions on, 27
Donnelly, Samuel, 14
Dragoon Mountains, 9, 16
"Dream of the Prairie" (Ryberg), 66
Duquesne, 69

Earp, Wyatt: O.K. Corral and, 15
Earp brothers, Cowboy Gang and, 16
East Cedar Tank, 227
East Rim View, 250
East Rim View to Telephone Hill, **254-58**
East Verde River, 188, 189, 206
Ecosystems, desert, 6
E Lazy Heart Ranch, 277
Elden-Dry Lake Hills Passage, 225
Elevation, 41, 42
Elgin, 68-69
El Tovar Hotel, 238
Empire-Cienega Passage, 91-93
Empire-Cienega Resource Conservation Area, 91
Empire Mountains, 91, 92
Empire Ranch, 92
Empirita Ranch, 92, 94
Equestrians, etiquette for, 25, 26
Equi Sands, 277
Etiquette, backcountry, 23-24, 25-28

Fire, considerations about, 24
Fischer, Luis: General Springs Cabin and, 205
Fisher Point, 214 (photo)
Fishing licenses, 28
Flagstaff, 216, 224, 231
Flagstaff-Grand Canyon Stagecoach, 230 (photo)
Flagstaff Passage, 224
Flagstaff Visitor Center, 217
Flash floods, precautions against, 30
Flowers, described, 5-7
Flying Heart Stable, 280
Forage, 26
Ford, John, 12
"Forest Ranger, The" (Clark), 17
Forest Road 303 to Interstate 40 (Cosnino), **221-22**
Forest Service. *See* U.S. Forest Service
Fort Apache, 13, 205
Fort Bowie, 12
Fort Defiance, 12

Fort Huachuca, 9, 13, 48
Fort Huachuca Museum, 13, 47, 49
Fort Lowell, 13, 115, 121
Fort Lowell Museum, 13
Fort Whipple, 13, 205
Four Peaks Wilderness, 42, 163, 177, 185, 186
Four Peaks Wilderness Passage, 185
Freeman Road, 147, 149
Frontier Days Celebration and Rodeo, 16
Frontier Outfitters, 277

Gadsden Purchase, 9, 12, 79, 103
Galiuro Mountains, 133, 142
Galiuro Wilderness, 147
Gardner, Gail I.: verse by, 240
Gardner Canyon, 79
Gardner Canyon Trailhead to Kentucky Camp, **86-87**
General Crook Trail, 13, 205
General Hitchcock Highway, 121
General Springs Cabin, 193, 204 (photo), 205
General Springs Cabin to Rock Crossing Campground, **206-9**
Geronimo, 1, 13; quote of, 8; raids by, 9
Geronimo Camp, 193
Geronimo Camp to Washington Park, **198-200**
Ghost towns, 14-15, 69
Giardia, 36
Gila monsters, 32-33
Gila River, 151
Global Positioning System (GPS), 21
Globe Ranger District, 156
Glory Hole Mine, 14
"God's Reserves" (Clark), 14
Government Reservoir, 268
Grand Canyon, xi, 11, 18, 42, 231, 240 (photo), 242, 247
Grand Canyon Chamber of Commerce, 239, 243
Grand Canyon Chapter (Sierra Club), 285

Grand Canyon Game Preserve, 251, 261

Grand Canyon National Park, 27, 41, 42, 232, 238, 239, 243, 247, 250, 251; permits from, 284

Grand Canyon National Park Boundary to East Rim View, **252-54**

Grand Canyon National Park—Inner Gorge Passage, 241-46; map of, 241

Grand Canyon National Park—North Rim Passage, 247-48

Grand Canyon National Park—South Rim Passage, 238-40

Grand Canyon Railway, 239

Grand Canyon Stageline, 227

Grandview Hotel, 231

Grandview Lookout Tower, 18, 231, 232, 238

Greaterville mining district, 80

Greenway, Jack, 92

"Greer County," 28

Grey, Zane, 15, 193, 194, 206

Gulf American Corporation, 92

Half Way Trick Tank, 238

Hamburg, 48

Hanta virus, 36-37

Happy Valley, 102

Happy Valley Passage, 98-100

Hardscrabble Mesa, 189

Harshaw, 69

Hart, Pearl, 142

Hathaway, Jim, 68

Haught, "Babe," 206

Haught, Fred, 206

Havasupai, 243

Havasupai Canyon, 243

Hayes, Ira, 10

Hayhook Ranch, 279

Hazards, considerations about, 28-39

Heat, planning for, 29

Highline Passage, 191-202; map of, 191

Highline Trail, 193

Highline Trails Guide, The, 194

Hiker's Guide to the Huachuca Mountains (Taylor), 42, 49

Hiker's Guide to the Santa Rita Mountains, A (Leavengood and Liebert), 80

Hiker's Guide to the Superstition Wilderness (Carlson and Stewart), 163, 164

Historical sites, caring for, 25

Hitchin' Post Stable, 279

Hohokam, 8, 121, 142

Homestead sites, respecting, 28

Horses, considerations about, 26

House Rock Valley, 250, 261

House Rock Valley Ranch, 261

Huachuca Hiking Club, 80, 285; work of, 3-4

Huachuca Mountain Passage, 45-66; map of, 45

Huachuca Mountains, 7, 11, 13, 14, 41, 42, 46 (photo), 47, 48, 68, 91

Hualapais, 9

"Hug a tree" strategy, 39

Hull Cabin Historic District, 231

Humphreys Peak, 226

Hunters: etiquette for, 27-28; licenses for, 28

Hutch's Pool, 121

Hutch's Pool to Summerhaven, **126-29**

Hydration, planning for, 29

Hypothermia, dealing with, 29-30

Indian War Soldiers' Song, 12

Intergovernmental agreement (IGA), 2-3

"Islands in the Sky" (Boyd), 5

Jack's Canyon, 212

Jacob Lake, 1, 261

Joe's Reservoir, 268

Jones, Charles C., 261

Kaibab Forest Products, xi, 1, 2, 261

Kaibab Lodge, 250, 251

Kaibab National Forest, 18, 227, 228, 232, 238, 239, 243, 247, 251, 261, 262, 269, 270; Maps/Literature, 282; Shewalter and, 2

Kaibab Plateau, 6, 42, 248 (photo), 250, 261, 262, 270; farming experiments on, 251

Kaibab Plateau Southern Passage, 18

Kaibab Plateau Trail, 2, 261

Kaibab Plateau Trail—Central Passage, 259-67

Kaibab Plateau Trail—Northern Passage, 268-69

Kaibab Plateau Trail—Southern Passage, 249-58

Kaibab Plateau Visitor Center, 251

Kannally, Lucille, 143

Kannally, Neil, 143

Kannally Ranch House, 142

Keiller, Randy and Laura, 277

Kelvin-Riverside Bridge, 149

Kentucky Camp, 15, 78 (photo), 79, 80

Kentucky Camp to Oak Tree Canyon/Empire-Cienega, **88-90**

Kino, Eusebio Francisco, 11, 79, 115, 121

La Fiesta de la Vaqueros Rodeo, 16

Leave no trace, 23-24

Lehner Kill Site, 8

Lemmon, John, 121

Length, describing, 41-42

Let Her Rip Mine, 14

Licenses, hunting/fishing, 28. *See also* Permits

Life zones, 6

Lightning, 30

Little Elden Springs Horse Camp, 279

Livestock, 41; damage caused by, 26-27; outfitting/transporting/boarding, 277-80; restrictions on, 21-22, 43

Llama and Alpaca Association of Arizona, 69, 286

Llamas, considerations about, 26

Lone Pine Saddle trailhead, 185, 186

Lost Dutchman Days, 155

Lost Dutchman Mine, 14, 155

Lower Sonoran Desert, 121

Lucky Cuss Mine, 14

McAneny, George, 80

McLaury brothers, 16

Madera Canyon, 79

Manning, Levi Howell, 103

Manning Camp, 102

Manning Camp to Redington Pass Road, **107-10**

Maps, 21, 29, 39, 44; describing, 41; recommended, 281-83

Marble Canyon, 250

Marshall Lake, 213, 216, 224

Marshall Lake to FR 303, **217-20**

Mazatzal Mountains, xi, 186, 187

Mazatzal Wilderness, 42, 177

Mazatzal Wilderness Passage, 188-89

MCS Stables, 280

Meadow Valley, 68

Merriam, C. H.: life zones and, 6

Mesa Ranger District, 156, 164

Meteor Crater, 18

Mexican-American War, 11, 103

Mexican Revolution, 11

Miami, mining in, 14

Miles, General: Geronimo and, 9

Miller Creek, 98, 102

Miller Peak Wilderness, 47; bicycle route around, **60-61**

Mines, 14; abandoned, 37-38

Mining, 14-15, 69, 80, 133

Mogollon, Juan Ignacio Flores, 193

Mogollon Rim, xi, 8, 13, 42, 192 (photo), 193, 194, 205; log cabins on, 18

Molino Basin, 115, 121

Molino Basin Campground to Hutch's Pool, **122-26**

Molino Basin to Summerhaven, bicycle route around, **129-30**

Montezuma Pass, 47

Montezuma Pass to Bathtub Spring, **54-56**

Montezuma Pass to Sunnyside Canyon, bicycle route around, **60-61**

Montezuma Pass to the U.S.-Mexico Border, livestock/bicycle route from, **52-53**

Moore, Ken, 277

Moqui Stage/Coconino Rim Passage, 229-37; map of, 229

Moqui Stage Station, 231

Moqui Stage Station to Russell Tank, **232-34**

Mormon Grove trailhead, 187

Mount Agassiz, 226

Mountain View Hotel, 142

Mount Elden, 216

Mount Elden Trail System, 223

Mount Lemmon, 15, 121

Mount Lemmon/Oracle Ridge Passage, 131-40; map of, 131

Mount Lemmon Ski Valley, 121, 133

Mount Lemmon Trail #5, 133

Mount Peeley, 187, 188

Mount Wrightson Wilderness, 79; bicycle route around, **85-86**

Mowry, 69

Murray Trailhead (FR 205) to Orderville Trailhead (U.S. 89A), **265-67**

Museum of the Forest, 194

Music, cowboy, 16-17

Mustang Mountains, 91

Naco Mammoth Kill Site, 8

National Leave No Trace Program, 25

National Park Service, 1, 103

Native Americans, 8-10

Native American Tourism Center, 10

Nature Conservancy, 69, 70

Nature highlights, describing, 41

Navajo, 9, 10; arrival of, 8; fair/rodeo by, 16; hanta virus and, 36

Navajo Code Talkers, 10

Nogales Ranger District (Coronado National Forest), 15

Nolan, Bob: songs by, 17

North Kaibab Ranger District, 261

North Kaibab Trail, 242

North Kaibab trailhead, 242, 247

North Kaibab Visitor Center, 262

North Rim, 42, 247-48

Oak Creek Canyon, 17

Oak Tree Canyon, 91

O.K. Corral, 1, 15

OK Corral (Apache Junction), 279

OK Corral (Pine), 279

Old Bisbee, 1

Oldham Trail, 225

Old Mount Lemmon Road, 121

"Old Prospector, The" (Clark), 46, 230

"Old Trailer, The" (Clark), 260

Old Tucson Studios, 12

Oracle, 115, 142

Oracle, The (mine claim), 142

Oracle Chamber of Commerce, 135, 143

Oracle Historical Society, 135

Oracle Passage, 141-46; map of, 141

Oracle Ridge (Llama) Outfitters, 279

Oracle State Park, 142, 143

Orderville United Order, 251

Outdoor Adventures Unlimited, 279

Outfitters, pack animals and, 22

Pack animals, considerations about, 21, 22, 26

Painted Desert, 231

Pantano Stables, 278

Pantano Wash, 91

Parker, John, 68

Parker Canyon Lake, 47, 68

Parker Canyon Lake to Canelo Pass, **70-73**

Passage Information Sheets, 283

Passages, described, 19-20, 39, 40

Patagonia, 1, 68, 79; festival in, 69, 80

Patagonia-Sonoita Creek Sanctuary, 69

Patagonia to Gardner Canyon Road, bicycle route around, **85-86**
Patagonia Tourist Information Office, 70, 80
Pat Scott Peak, 48
Payson Chamber of Commerce, 194
Pellets, packing, 26
Permits, 21, 284. *See also* Licenses
Pershing, John: Punitive Expedition by, 13
Pets, restrictions on, 27
Phantom Ranch, 242, 243
Phelps Dodge Corporation, 206
Picacho Peak, 133
Picketpost Mountain, 152, 154 (photo), 155, 156
Picketpost Mountain/Reavis Trail Canyon Passage, 153-60; map of, 153
Picketpost Mountain Trailhead to Rogers Trough, **157-60**
Picketpost Trailhead to Theodore Roosevelt Bridge, bicycle route around, **171-74**
Pima County Department of Transportation and Flood Control, 94
Pima County Flood Control District, 92
Pima County Parks and Recreation Department, 95, 97; permits from, 284
Pima County Sheriff's Posse, 1
Pimas, 8
Pima Trails Association, 285
Pinal County Department of Civil Works, 148, 150
Pinalenos, 47
Pinal Mountains, 149
Pine Mountain/Boulder Creek Passage, 186
Pine-Strawberry Chamber of Commerce, 194
Pine Trailhead to Geronimo Camp, **195-98**
Plague, 37

Planning, 22
Poetry, cowboy, 16-17
Powell, John Wesley: Grand Canyon and, 242-43
Precautions, considerations about, 28-39
Primitive roads, 19, 20
Prospectors, 14-15
Punitive Expedition, 13
Pusch Ridge Stables, 278
Pusch Ridge Wilderness, 121; bicycle route around, **129-30**

Rabies, 36
Rainbow Expedition, trail/recreation maps from, 282
"Rains, The" (Clark), 176
Ramsey Canyon Preserve, 7, 47, 48
Ranchers, etiquette towards, 27-28
"Ranger, A" (Clark), 140
Rangers, talents of, 17-18
Rattlesnakes, 31-32
Reavis, Elisha: Superstitions and, 163
Reavis Ranch to FR 83 Junction with Cottonwood Canyon Trail #120, **167-71**
Recommended season, 41, 42
Recreational Equipment Inc., 285
Redfield, Lem, 115
Redington, disasters at, 115
Redington Land and Cattle Company, 278
Redington Pass, 114 (photo), 115
Redington Pass Passage, 113-18; map of, 113
Redington Pass Road, 102, 115
Redington Pass Road to Molino Basin, **116-18**
Red Ridge Trail #2, 133
Reef Townsite, 48
Remington, Frederic, 15
Resupply opportunities, 22-23
Riders in the Sky, 17
"Ridin'" (Clark), 100
Right-of-way, rules of, 25-26

Rincon Mountains, xi, 41, 42, 47, 91, 94, 96, 98, 100 (photo), 114 (photo), 115
Rincon Mountains Passage, 101-12; map of, 101
Rincon Mountain Wilderness, 79, 98, 102; bicycle route around, 110-12
Rincon Valley Passage, 96-97
Rock Crossing Campground, 205
Rock Crossing Campground to Blue Ridge Campground, 209-11
Rocking R Mercantile, 278
Rogers, Roy, 15
Rogers Trough to Reavis Ranch, 164-67
Rogers Trough trailhead, 155, 163
Roosevelt (town), settlement of, 178
Roosevelt, Theodore, 177, 243; Grand Canyon and, 242, 251
Roosevelt Lake, 186
Roosevelt Lake Bridge, 185
Roosevelt Passage, 175-84; map of, 175
Roosevelt's Camp, 243
Routes. See Trails
Russell, Charles, 15
Russell Tank, 231
Russell Tank to Grandview Lookout, 234-37
Rust's Camp, 243
Ryberg, John A., II: verse by, xiv, 66

Saddle Mountain Passage, 187
Saddle Mountain Wilderness, 250
Saddle Software Systems, 286
Saguaro National Monument, 96, 97
Saguaro National Park, 27, 96, 102, 103; permits from, 284
Saguaros, 6, 176 (photo)
Salado, 8, 177
Salt River, 177, 178, 206
Samaniego Ridge Trail #7, 133
SAMBA. See Southern Arizona Mountain Bike Association
San Carlos Apache Reservation, 9, 205
San Francisco Peaks, 17, 18, 42, 216, 226, 231

San Francisco Peaks Passage, 226
Sanitation, considerations about, 24
San Manuel, copper smelter at, 133
San Pedro River Valley, 11, 115, 133, 147; Clovis people in, 142
San Rafael Valley, 68
Santa Catalina Mountains, 41, 42, 47, 115, 142; Hohokam in, 121
Santa Catalina Mountains Passage, 119-30
Santa Rita Mountain Passage, 77-90; map of, 77
Santa Rita Mountain Passage to the Redington Passage, bicycle route around, 110-12
Santa Rita Mountains, xi, 2, 15, 47, 68, 79, 80, 91
San Xavier Mission, Kino and, 11
Scarlet Gate Llama Ranch, 277
Schmid, Jim, 3, 3 (photo)
Schultz Pass, 225, 226
Scorpions, 28, 33
"Self-Guided Auto Tour of Scenic Southern Arizona, The Patagoni Adventure, A," 70
Services, finding, 272-76
"Sharing the Trail," 25
Shewalter, Dale, 2, 3
Sierra Ancha Mountains, 186
Sierra Ancha Wilderness, 177
Sierra Club, 1, 285; Kaibab Forest Products and, 2, 261
Sierra Madre Mountains, 47
Sierra Vista Chamber of Commerce, 49
Signage, 20-21, 38
Sinagua, 8, 216
Smith, Eric, 3, 3 (photo)
Smoking, restrictions on, 24
Snakes, precautions against, 28, 31-32
Sobiapuri, Apaches and, 115
Soldier Camp, 121
Sonoita Creek, 69, 79
Sonoita Fair Grounds, 278
Sonoran Desert, 1, 5, 6, 96, 102, 103, 147, 151, 152, 177; Clark on, 16-17

Sons of the San Joaquin, The, 17
Southern Arizona Mountain Bike
    Association (SAMBA), 80, 285
Southern Pacific Railroad, 79-80, 92
South Rim, 238-40, 240 (photo)
"Southwestern June" (Clark), 78, 162
Spanish, exploration by, 10-12
Springs, General, 205
Stetson, James, 80
Stewards, 3, 4
Stewart, Elizabeth, 163
Stopover opportunities, 22
Stoves, using, 24
Summerhaven, 121, 133
Summerhaven to Catalina Camp to
    American Flag, **135-40**
Sunflower Trail, 186
Sunnyside, 14, 69
Sunnyside Canyon, 47
Sunnyside Canyon to Parker Canyon
    Lake (Overlook) Trailhead, **62-65**
Sunset Crater Volcano, 18, 216, 226
Superior, mining in, 14
Superior Chamber of Commerce, 156
Superstition Mountains, xi, 14, 41, 149,
    162 (photo), 177
Superstition Mountains/Lost Dutch-
    man Museum, 155, 156
Superstition Wilderness, 42, 155, 163;
    bicycle route around, **171-74**
Superstition Wilderness Passage, 161-
    74; map of, 161
Supplies, finding, 22-23
Sutherland Trail #6, 133

Tarantulas, 34
Tater Canyon, 251
Taylor, Kiyo, 2
Taylor, Leonard, 42
Telegraph Canyon Road, 151, 152
Telephone Hill, 250, 260 (photo), 261
Telephone Hill (FR 241) to Murray
    Trailhead (FR 205), **262-64**
Temporal Gulch Trailhead to Gardner
    Canyon Road Trailhead, **81-84**

Theodore Roosevelt Bridge, 177, 185
Theodore Roosevelt Dam/Lake, 163,
    177-78
Thompson, William Boyce, 156
Three Bar Wildlife Area, 185
Tighe, Earl T. "Slim": verse by, 204,
    248
Tohono O'odham, 11, 103, 121
Tombstone, 1, 16
Tonto Basin, 177, 193
Tonto Basin Ranger District, 164
Tonto National Forest, 18, 151, 152,
    155, 178, 185, 186, 187, 189, 190,
    193, 194; Maps/Literature, 281
Tonto National Monument, 177, 178
Tonto Natural Bridge State Park, 189
Tortilla Mountains, 147, 149
**Tortilla Mountains (Sonoran Desert)
    Passage**, 149-50
Total Wreck Silver Mine, 14, 92
Toughnut Mine, 14
*Trail Guide to the Santa Catalina
    Mountains* (Glendening and
    Cowgill), 122
Trailheads, 19; directions to, 41, 43
Trails: conditions of, 39; descriptions
    of, 44; etiquette on, 25-28;
    future/interim, 22; other, 41, 44;
    signs/markers for, 38; staying on,
    24, 26
Trails and Equestrian Center, 278
Transition zone, 5
Trash, packing out, 23
Treaty of Guadalupe Hidalgo, 11-12,
    103
Trees, described, 5-7
Triangle Y Ranch Camp, 279
Trips, descriptions of, 40-44
Tubac, 11
Tucson Hiking Guide (Leavengood),
    103, 122
Tucson Valley, 115
Turkey Creek, 98, 102
Turkey Creek Trailhead to Manning
    Camp, **104-7**

Turkey Hills (Equestrian Bypass) Passage, 223

Tusayan (Anasazi) Ruins and Museum, 238

U.S. Forest Service, xi, 1, 2, 7, 18, 20, 38, 68; establishment of, 17; Huachuca Hiking Club and, 4; Hull Cabin and, 231; maps from, 21, 44, 281

U.S. Geological Survey, maps from, 21, 44, 282

U.S.-Mexico Border to Montezuma Pass, 49-52

U.S. Soil Conservation Service, 156

Unnamed Passage (No. 27), 212

Unnamed Passage (No. 28), 213-14

Vail, Walter L., 92

Venomous creatures, precautions against, 31-36

Vermilion Cliffs, 250, 261, 262

Villa, Pancho, 1, 13

Volunteers, 3-5, 4 (photo)

Walnut Canyon (Equestrian Bypass) Passage, 215-22

Walnut Canyon National Monument, 216, 217

Waltz, Jacob, 155; Lost Dutchman Mine and, 14

Washington Park to General Springs Cabin, 200-202

Water, 42-43; availability of, 41; camping near, 24

Wayne, John, 12, 15

Weather, planning for, 29-30

Weavers Needle, 14, 155

Western Music Association, 17, 286

Whetstone Mountains, 91, 98

White Canyon Passage, 151

White Canyon Wilderness, 151

Whiterock Mesa, 189

Whiterock Mesa/Hardscrabble Mesa Passage, 189-90

Wilderness Act (1984), 155, 164

Wilderness of Rocks Trail, 121

Wildlife, 5-7, 25

Yavapais, 9, 188

"Yellow Stuff, The" (Clark), 132

Yucca plant, 120 (photo)

Zane Grey Museum, 194

Become an Arizona Trail Member

The Arizona Trail needs the active support of outdoor enthusiasts. Help build this resource for today and legacy for future generations by joining *The Arizona Trail Association* and becoming a volunteer today!

Would you like to volunteer in any of the following ways? (check all that apply)

○ Donate materials or professional services.
  Specify: _____
○ Help raise funds for the Arizona Trail
○ Help build and maintain the Arizona Trail
○ Become a Segment Steward
○ Recruit additional volunteers
○ Membership services and development
  Other: _____

What are your primary non-motorized trail activities? (check all that apply)

○ Hiking
○ Horseback Riding
○ Bicycling
○ Cross-Country Skiing
○ Other _____

What general area along the Arizona Trail is of interest to you? (check all that apply)

○ Northern (Mogollon Rim to Utah)
○ Central (Gila River to Mogollon Rim)
○ Southern (Mexico to the Gila River)

Types of Membership (check one)

○ Individual ○ Family:......................... $25/year
○ Student ○ Senior:............................. $15/year
○ Organizations with budgets *less* than $25,000: $50/year
○ Organizations with budgets *greater* than $25,000: $100/year
○ Trailblazer Member: $100/year
○ Lifetime Member: $500
○ Trail Patron:.................................... $1000/year or more

○ New Member ○ Renewal Membership

I am sending an additional contribution of $_____ for Trail Development.

All donations are tax deductible.   **Arizona Trails Association**
P.O. Box 36736 • Phoenix, AZ 85067
(602) 252-4794 • FAX: (602) 952-1447

_____
NAME

_____
ORGANIZATION OR BUSINESS

_____
ADDRESS

_____
CITY   STATE   ZIP

_____
PHONE